Strategic Cyber Deterrence

Strategic Cyber Deterrence

The Active Cyber Defense Option

Scott Jasper

ROWMAN & LITTLEFIELD
Lanham • Boulder • New York • London

Published by Rowman & Littlefield
A wholly owned subsidiary of The Rowman & Littlefield Publishing Group, Inc.
4501 Forbes Boulevard, Suite 200, Lanham, Maryland 20706
www.rowman.com

Unit A, Whitacre Mews, 26-34 Stannary Street, London SE11 4AB

British Library Cataloguing in Publication Information Available

Library of Congress Cataloging-in-Publication Data

Names: Jasper, Scott, author.
Title: Strategic cyber deterrence : the active cyber defense option / Scott Jasper.
Description: Lanham : Rowman & Littlefield, [2017] | Includes bibliographical references and index.
Identifiers: LCCN 2017008263 (print) | LCCN 2017019453 (ebook) | ISBN 9781538104903 (Electronic) | ISBN 9781538104880 (cloth : alk. paper) | ISBN 9781538104897 (pbk. : alk. paper)
Subjects: LCSH: Computer networks—Security measures. | Computer crimes—Prevention. | Cyberspace operations (Military science)—United States. | Strategy.
Classification: LCC TK5105.59 (ebook) | LCC TK5105.59 .J375 2017 (print) | DDC 005.8/2--dc23
LC record available at https://lccn.loc.gov/2017008263

Printed in the United States of America

To Annie, Christopher, Kevin, and Brian

Contents

Acknowledgments

In writing this book, I owe much to professors Colin Gray, Beatrice Heuser, Chris Demchak, and Tom Bruneau for their insights on theoretical and conceptual issues. I also want to thank Dorothy Denning and Pablo Breuer for technical verification, Michael Schmitt and Anthony Glosson for legal validation, and also Richard Hoffman and John Feeley for historical perspective. My sincere appreciation goes to John Zerr, Shannen Parker, and Paul Adamsen at the US Cyber Command, Michael Herring at the National Security Agency, Antonio Scurlock, Laura Carlson and Preston Werntz at the US Department of Homeland Security, and Tim Walton and Gregg Tally at the Johns Hopkins University Applied Physics Lab for sharing their viewpoints on challenges and information on initiatives. In addition, I want to thank numerous cyber security industry professionals for discussing and demonstrating their security products. I want also to acknowledge the useful guidance from Marie-Claire Antoine and Mary Malley in the production of this book. In addition, I want to acknowledge the efforts of both Will True, who saw the manuscript through to publication, and Bob Silano, who prepared the index. Finally, I want to thank my wife, Annie, who gave me her steadfast support during years of research and writing. I dedicate this book to her and our three sons, Christopher, Kevin, and Brian.

Abbreviations and Acronyms

A2/AD	Anti-Access/Area Denial
ACD	Active Cyber Defense
AIS	automated indicator sharing
APT	Advanced Persistent Threat
BPHS	bulletproof hosting services
CBM	confidence-building measure
CFAA	Computer Fraud and Abuse Act
CIS	Center for Internet Security
CSIP	Cybersecurity Strategy and Implementation Plan
CMF	Cyber Mission Force
CSC	Critical Security Controls
DCO	defensive cyberspace operations
DDoS	Distributed Denial of Service
DHS	Department of Homeland Security
DISA	Defense Information Systems Agency
DIUx	Defense Innovation Unit Experimental
DNC	Democratic National Committee
DNS	domain name system
DOD	Department of Defense
EU	European Union

FBI	Federal Bureau of Investigation
FS	Financial Services
FTP	File Transfer Protocol
GDP	Gross Domestic Product
GLACY	Global Action on Cybercrime
GOP	Guardians of Peace
G-20	Group of Twenty
GPS	global positioning system
HTTP(S)	Hypertext Transfer Protocol (Secure)
IACD	Integrated Adaptive Cyber Defense
IAEA	International Atomic Energy Agency
ICANN	Internet Corporation for Assigned Names and Numbers
ICMP	Internet Control Message Protocol
ICS–CERT	Industrial Control System–Computer Emergency Response Team
ICT	Information and Communication Technology
IDM	internal defensive measures
IP	Internet protocol
IP Commission	Commission on the Theft of American Intellectual Property
ISAC	Information Sharing and Analysis Center
ISIS	Islamic State of Iraq and Syria
NSA	National Security Agency
NATO	North Atlantic Treaty Organization
NCCIC	National Cybersecurity and Communications Integration Center
NIST	National Institute of Standards and Technology
NTP	network time protocol
OPM	Office of Personnel Management
OSCE	Organization for Security and Co-operation in Europe
PII	personally identifiable information
PIN	personal identification number
POS	point-of-sale

PPD	Presidential Policy Directive
PLA	People's Liberation Army
RA	response actions
RAM	Remote Access Memory
RAT	Remote Access Trojan
SEA	Syrian Electronic Army
SIEM	security information and event management
SSL	secure sockets layer
STIX	Structured Threat Information eXpression
SQL	structured query language
TAXII	Trusted Automated eXchange of Indicator Information
TTP	tactics, techniques, and procedures
UK	United Kingdom
UN	United Nations
URL	uniform resource locator
XML	Extensible Markup Language

Part I

Thinking about Deterrence

Chapter One

Strategic Landscape

All sectors of the economy rely on the networks, systems, and services that form the integrated and interconnected global domain known as cyberspace. Information and communication technologies (ICTs) are, accordingly, essential to the defense sector, especially during the conduct of military operations. Yet protecting the cyber domain is challenging because it is currently boundary-free, subject to dynamic change, and open to all comers. Cyberspace is probed and penetrated by nation-states, hacker groups, criminal organizations, and terrorist groups. These entities, called malicious or threat actors, can be partially or wholly responsible for a cyber incident that impacts an organization's security.[1] Many of these malicious actors seek state secrets, trade secrets, technology, and ideas, or they develop the ability to strike critical infrastructure and harm advanced economies.[2] Hacker groups and criminal gangs often work in concert with state actors, under some form of control, direction, incitement, or nebulous arrangement. That intertwined relationship allows foreign governments to hide their malicious activity and claim innocence if confronted.[3] In addition, malicious actors use common tools, techniques, and talent available for purchase at very low prices on illicit websites on the underground market.[4] This convergence of actor relationships, motivations, tactics, and capabilities that complicate attribution of an attack[5] makes a singular approach to change behavior of a singular actor, such as just the nation-state, impossible and impractical.[6]

Deterrence is "the prevention of an adversary's undesired action."[7] Deterrence seeks to influence the decision-making calculus of an actor by threatening to impose costs, or denying benefits, while encouraging restraint.[8] Malicious actors conduct attacks, via cyberspace, that target "an enterprise's use of cyberspace for the purpose of disrupting, disabling, destroying, or maliciously controlling a computing environment/infrastructure; or destroying the integrity of the data or stealing controlled information."[9] Recent incidents show cyber attacks are employed and honed in a systematic, coordinated fashion to achieve actor objectives. Criminal exploitation, military or industrial espionage, nationalist hacker protests, and infrastructure infiltration or sabotage are prominent in their operations. The motivations to conduct malicious activity vary, from criminals looking for financial gain, hacktivists promoting a cause, and state actors engaging in espionage (military or economic) or infiltrating critical infrastructure.[10] In many cases the actors conducting crime, espionage, or disruption are the same. Even more so, all malicious actors in cyberspace have one thing in common: an expanding choice of attack methods. In deciding to attack, each actor will weigh the effort against the expected benefit under their own criteria or rationality. Deterrence seeks to change their perceptions of costs, benefits and restraint.[11] A daunting and critical question is whether traditional deterrence strategies are sufficient to deter malicious actors in cyberspace, or if an alternative strategy be more effective. This book will examine the sufficiency of strategic options for the wide array of malicious actors, their methods of cyber attack in actual incidents, and their motivations in campaigns of malicious cyber activity, starting with an initial look at the alleged "Russian efforts to influence the 2016 US Presidential Election."[12]

INCREASINGLY VULNERABLE SYSTEMS

Cyberspace is defined by the military as "a global domain within the information environment consisting of the interdependent network of information technology infrastructures and resident data, including the Internet, telecommunications networks, computer systems, and embedded processors and controllers."[13] For social, technical, and economic purposes, cyberspace can be considered as more than a domain but as a substrate. In this usage, a "substrate" is an underlying physical layer on which modern society is built.[14] Cyberspace uniquely underpins every facet of social, technical, and economic systems. This substrate has a topology·that is largely territorial, built by mankind unlike other traditional domains of warfare. The services relied upon in daily life, such as water distribution, health care, electricity generation, transportation, and financial transactions, depend on this underlying information technology infrastructure.[15] Systems or assets supporting these services are designated as critical infrastructure, deemed so because their incapacity or destruction would have a debilitating impact on national or economic security, public health, or safety.[16] Because most critical infrastructure supports military operations, any significant disruption to the integrity of their networks could compromise the military's abilities to protect the nation.[17] In talking about the hypothetical dangers of a "Cyber Pearl Harbor," Representative Mike Rogers stated "the threat of a catastrophic and damaging cyberattack in the United States critical infrastructure like our power or financial networks is actually becoming less hypothetical every day." [18]

Not only has the volume of malicious code, known as malware, that threatens the functioning of critical infrastructure, increased to over 390,000 new programs each day, [19] but also the means of malware delivery have expanded to take advantage of human or technological vulnerabilities. A specific method used to access equipment, computers or systems to deliver malware or other hostile outcomes is called a "cyber-attack vector" by security professionals. [20] Vast arrays of vectors threaten industrial, commercial, governmental, and military systems and devices. These attack methods have grown in complexity and sophistication, ranging from emails specifically tailored by attackers, using information found in social sites, to spark interest of individuals to click on links or open attachments loaded with malware in "spear phishing" attacks, or the planting of malicious code on legitimate sites visited by targeted individuals in what is called a "watering hole" attack. [21] Auxiliary means for malware delivery include compromises of physical devices, like when an infected flash drive inserted into a US military laptop spreads code onto network systems, [22] or compromises third-party vendors of services and supplies that have trusted access to corporate networks. [23] The most sensational and publicized methods are intrusions by groups of attackers categorized as an Advanced Persistent Threat (APT) and assaults using distributed denial of service (DDoS) methods. The APT group's form of hacking is designed to covertly penetrate networks and systems to steal or alter information, manipulate data, or cause damage. DDoS assaults disrupt website availability by overwhelming network equipment with high-volume requests by compromised computers or by consuming application processing resources. [24]

EMERGING FORMS OF CONFLICT

As a result of "cyber-attack vector" proliferation, highly motivated threat actors at any level now have myriad methods to conduct malicious activity in cyberspace. Primary areas of malicious activity are the theft or exploitation of data; disruption or denial of access or service; and destructive action comprising corruption, manipulation, and damage or the alteration of data. The buying or renting of malicious code viruses, exploits of code vulnerabilities (software and computer configuration flaws), botnets (collections of compromised computers), and command and control servers provides these actors with a ready array of tools and services. Some actors use these tools and services in cyber warfare which is defined in US military joint terminology as "an armed conflict conducted in whole or part by cyber means."[25] Here an attacker could launch a military confrontation during a period of tension by attacking civilian infrastructure, a cyberattack just prior to or simultaneously with a surprise military attack, or wait until war starts to activate implanted exploits.[26] In addition to "military operations to deny an opposing force the effective use of cyberspace systems and weapons in a conflict,"[27] state cyber campaign doctrine appears to include disruption of governmental services, financial enterprises, and media outlets. For example, in August 2008, when Russian troops engaged Georgian forces during their ground invasion, six command and control servers, managed by a cybercrime group, issued DDoS attack commands on select Georgian government, news and banking sites.[28] This instance and many others since indicate that disruptive and destructive cyber attacks on critical infrastructure are becoming a part of modern conflict.

Although "cyber warfare" as defined earlier has entered into the common lexicon, the term "cybered conflict" characterizes more appropriately the essential nature of modern military operations. Cybered conflict frames the complexity and ambiguity of struggle involving cyberspace, including hybrid warfare and insurgent campaigns that exploit the domain or use attack methods in the form discussed previously.[29] Cybered conflict symbolizes "old and new forms of conflict born of, enabled through, or dramatically altered by cyberspace."[30] For instance, malicious activity occurred in cyberspace during Russian military operations in Crimea. Operations started with the seizure of *Ukrtelecom* offices and the physical cutting of telephone and internet cables.[31] Groups like OpRussia and Russian Cyber Command that opposed annexation conducted DDoS attacks against Russian sites,[32] while pro-Russian CyberBerkut was active against NATO, in particular targeting their main public website before Crimea's vote in March 2014 to secede from Ukraine and join Russia.[33] Berkut is a reference to the feared riot squads of ousted pro-Russian President Victor Yanukovich. CyberBerkut also compromised the Central Election Commission during Ukraine's presidential election in May 2014, disabling real-time display updates in the vote count and posting false results.[34] Political conflicts between nations have also spawned cyber attacks against Western news organizations.[35] The Syrian Electronic Army, a group of pro-regime hackers, has compromised external-facing websites and social media accounts of the *New York Times*, the Associated Press, CNN, the *Huffington Post*, and *Forbes*, to promote the embattled Syrian regime.[36]

RISING SECURITY CONCERNS

The former US Secretary of Defense warned that the attacks on energy companies in the Arabian Gulf and on banks in the United States mark a significant escalation of the cyber threat and renewed concerns over still more destructive scenarios.[37] *Shamoon* malware, which is intended to destroy data, infected some thirty thousand workstations at Saudi Aramco Oil Company in August 2012, rendering them unusable.[38] A partial photo showing the burning of an American flag was used to overwrite the content of the files. Weeks later, Qatar's RasGas suffered a major malware attack that shut down its website and email servers but not production systems.[39] In September 2012, six major American banks were hit in a wave of DDoS attacks that caused Internet blackouts and delays in online banking. Even though the attackers announced the time and targets in advance, the financial institutions were unable to prevent their websites from being disrupted.[40] In Ukraine in December 2015, three different regional electricity distribution companies were attacked by malware infections that caused outages to approximately 225,000 customers. A third party entered into company computer and control systems to remote control distribution management systems and shut off substation breakers.[41] The delineations between the various phases of the operation suggest different levels of actors worked on different parts and possible collaboration between cyber criminals and state actors.[42] While most attacks to date have not spilled far beyond the digital world, security experts seem to agree that the threat to critical infrastructure is real. For example, Meredith Patterson, an information security expert says, "It is remarkably easy to just mess with the temperature someplace in a natural gas plant and catch the entire plant on fire."[43] Just because attacks on critical infrastructure don't happen very often doesn't mean they are not possible.

As of today, preparations for cybered conflict are already in the Phase Zero ("Shape") of warfare campaigns as found in the notional six-phase model of joint and multinational operations described in US joint doctrine. This doctrine presents military operations leading to "war" as a natural progression of activities, from shaping, deterring, seizing initiative, dominating, stabilizing to enabling civil authority.[44] Certainly two major adversaries are attempting to shape the world's and each other's perceptions of threat and response. The commander of US Cyber Command stated in his 2012 Congressional testimony that China was responsible for the APT intrusion into the security firm RSA–patented SecurID systems for multifactor authentication.[45] Duplicate "SecurID" electronic keys made with extracted information were used to penetrate the networks of Lockheed Martin and several other US defense contractors in May 2011.[46] The Pentagon made further allegations against China in its 2013 annual report, alluding to the use of "computer network exploitation capability to support intelligence collection against the

US diplomatic, economic, and defense industrial base sectors."[47] Exposure by an American company of a hacking campaign based in Shanghai focused on drone technology[48] confirmed the *Washington Post* published list of two dozen military systems compromised by cyber espionage emanating from China.[49]

At the Shangri-La Dialogue in Singapore in June 2013, Defense Secretary Chuck Hagel voiced this concern about "the growing threat of cyber intrusions, some of which appear to be tied to the Chinese government and military."[50] In May 2014 the Justice Department indicted five members of the Chinese Military on charges of computer fraud, damaging a computer, aggravated identify theft, and economic espionage.[51] Officials noted that the difference in US cyber activity is that economic advantage is obtained if China or others provide state-owned enterprises with extracted information to improve their competitive edge and reduce cost.[52] The cost to the United States in intellectual property (product plans, research results, and customer lists) and confidential business information (trade secrets, exploration data, and negotiating strategies) theft amounts annually to billions of dollars.[53] While most of the intrusions seen to date originating from China appear oriented toward collecting intelligence rather than launching attacks, each objective requires access and a compromise for espionage could become disruptive or destructive with little notice by the same actor.

China has in return made much of what it calls the United States' "global" cyber activity, evidenced by the discovery in June 2010 of the Stuxnet virus infecting nuclear facilities in Iran.[54] More recent revelations prominently disparaged by Chinese statements include the United States penetrating of the servers of the telecommunications firm Huawei to learn how to conduct surveillance or offensive cyber operations against countries that buy the Chinese-made equipment.[55] After Washington filed criminal charges against the Chinese military officers in 2014, an editorial in the *Global Times*, a subsidiary of the *People's Daily*, the official journal of China's Communist Party, said, "Regarding the issue of network security, the US is such a mincing rascal that we must stop developing any illusions about it." The *Global Times* asserted that the United States "spies both home and abroad with the PRISM program of the National Security Agency (NSA)" and "still owes an apology to Beijing" over the NSA hacking of its network.[56] The challenge for national security is that, while the accusations are flying around, the deceiving, penetrating, exploiting, and extracting continues to increase. The current responses are clearly insufficient and moving out of cybered conflict Phase Zero is highly undesirable.

In China, the state–criminal nexus is evident as cyber intruders who commit crimes and espionage use similar methods—for instance by employing the same Remote Access Trojan tools (that capture and extract information) to include Poison Ivy, Ghost, and PlugX.[57] Some state actors also "moonlight" for financial gain, further complicating attribution. China also uses professional hackers for hire, like the Hidden Lynx group, located in China. Hidden Lynx hackers obtain very specific information that could be used to gain competitive advantages at both a corporate and nation state level. [58] They have been involved in several high-profile campaigns, to include Operation Aurora, the intrusions on Google and more than thirty other companies disclosed in 2010 that revealed the complexity and obscurity of APT. [59] Part of China and Iran's Anti-Access and Area Denial (A2/AD) strategies to blunt outside interference is the condoning or outsourcing of cyber power to proxy groups. An activist group known as the Cutting Sword of Justice took responsibility for the cyber destruction at Saudi Aramco. A hacker group called Izz ad-Din al-Qassam Cyber Fighters took credit in online posts for the US bank assault, supposedly in retaliation for an anti-Islam video that mocks the Prophet Muhammad. Investigators eventually traced attack signatures in both cases to Iranian hackers with government ties. [60] This multiplicity of instances by a nexus of nation-states, hacker groups, and criminal organizations that are now in the public domain is presumably matched by many more not publicly known. Governments have every reason to search for responses to such challenges and deterrence is a key response.

DETERRENCE STRATEGIES

Traditional deterrence stems from an adversary's belief that a threat of retaliation exists, the intended action cannot succeed, or the costs outweigh the benefits of acting. [61] Therefore deterrence centers on ways to impose costs, deny benefit, or encourage restraint. The strategic debate during the Cold War over how best to deter nuclear attack normally was divided into "deterrence by punishment" (threat of retaliation that imposes costs) and "deterrence by denial" (limitation of damage by denial of success). [62] Since US policy would not condone today the punishment of another country, a more appropriate view of this form of deterrence would simply be retaliation. With the strategic interdependence that has resulted from contemporary globalization, one might also add deterrence by entanglement (presumably cooperation on mutual interests encourages restraint to avoid unintended consequences and antagonizing third parties). [63] These three traditional strategic deterrence options could conceivably apply in some fashion for cyberspace.

The number of actors to be deterred is the first of many challenges in applying the traditional deterrence approach. For a deterrence strategy to be effective, it must be based on capability (possessing the means to influence behavior), credibility (instilling believability that counter actions may actually be deployed), and communication (sending the right message to the desired audience). [64] The achievement of these conditions for effective deterrence is extremely difficult in cybered conflict. State capabilities to influence the behavior of malicious actors in cyberspace are constrained by their ability to operate with anonymity, impunity and deniability; even if actors are convinced that counter actions may be deployed, their rationality cannot be assumed; and the audience of actors conducting cyber attacks is vast and varied in motivations and intentions. The point of deterrence is to add another consideration to the attacker's decision-making calculus.[65] Yet affecting the wide array of actors in cyberspace is a problem since deterrence has to work in the mind of each attacker under different circumstances. Even if the attacker is rational, their motivations to achieve political objectives, national pride, personal satisfaction, or monetary gain are not easily deterrable. Chris Demchak has offered an alternative "theory of action" in which a malicious actor or group's decision is a function of legitimacy, need, and confidence related to the act itself, the latter primarily through transforming the ease of action, irrespective of actor culture.[66] The more each of those elements is pushed below a threshold, the malicious act is "disrupted," but pushing the elements for a wide range of actors simultaneously is difficult.

Hence a new means of deterrence is required for a cybered world. Identifying the need to "integrate newer behavioral approaches outside a rational state-based actor construct," the Assistant Chief of Staff for US Strategic Deterrence and Nuclear Integration recommended moving beyond reliance solely on "imposition of costs to integrate denial of benefits and other methods for encouraging restraint."[67] To make this move beyond Cold War vestiges, the focus must be on closer linking deterrence to the desired effect of altering behavior, regardless of the actor being deterred.[68] For rational state actors, the strategy of deterrence by entanglement can encourage responsible behavior (to not conduct, endorse, or allow malicious cyber activity in their territory) through cooperation based on economic and political relationships between governments. However, for the wider array of malicious actors, a different strategy has to be considered to achieve the central premise of deterrence—altering an adversary's behavior.

An updated strategic option designed for this new form of continuous cybered conflict is titled "active cyber defense." The strategy reinforces both deterrence by denial and deterrence by retaliation. It combines internal systemic resilience to halt malicious cyber activity after an intrusion with tailored disruption capacities to thwart malicious actor objectives.[69] Hence active cyber defense supports denial by making it harder to carry out a cyber attack and supports retaliation by providing more options to inflict punishment. This new means to achieve deterrence also encourages adversary restraint in peacetime cybered conflict, by shaping perceptions of costs and benefits of a cyber attack irrespective of the character or number of actors to be deterred.[70] Active cyber defense involves the synchronized detection, analysis and mitigation of network security breaches in cyber relevant time combined with the aggressive use of legal countermeasures deployed outside the victim's network.[71] Inside the defender's network, active cyber defense stops or limits damage through detective controls and remediation actions, seamlessly automated in a common framework of integration. The promise of active cyber defense is in internal countermeasures that act without regard to the identity or type of malicious actor or their motivations, only to detect, isolate or eradicate their malware. Outside the victim's network, active cyber defense offers a range of countermeasures for use by the state or private organization depending on technical feasibility and legal authorities. The selection of countermeasures will vary for the type of malicious actor based on circumstances and risk.

The main issue today was summed up well by Senator Inhope, during the Senate hearing to consider the nomination for the new commander of US Cyber Command, in stating, "the lack of a cyber-deterrence policy . . . [has] left us more vulnerable to continued cyber aggression." When the nominee was asked "how do we prevent that," Vice Admiral Rogers responded "We're generating capability, we're generating capacity. . . . But in the end I believe we've got to get some idea of deterrence within the cyber arena."[72] The concept of traditional deterrence is still hotly debated in the cyber community, because, for instance, traditional nuclear deterrence relies on an adversary having knowledge of the destruction that will result from transgressions but that clarity is not possible in cyber since the secrecy about cyber weapons is necessary to preserve their effectiveness.[73] The strategy of active cyber defense, however, does not intrinsically require clear adversary knowledge of the mechanisms that defeat attacks. It also appears less likely to escalate conflict by requiring the deterring state to make demands or posture in a threatening manner either. The promise of active cyber defense warrants examination of evidence to determine if it is more likely to alter an adversary's behavior than current methods attempted for traditional deterrence strategies in the emerging forum of peacetime conflict.

Given the breadth, speed, and volume of cyberspace's predators, active cyber defense technologies will be automated and have the ability to interdict, isolate, or remove threats. As a means to strengthen deterrence, the intent is to deny benefits to adversaries by ensuring systemic resilience, by engaging, deceiving, or stopping adversaries, and by imposing costs through disruption capacities, regardless of the source. The concept of "systemic resilience" means a defender's state or network has the capacity of combined social and technical systems to proactively recognize, adapt to, absorb, and innovate around disturbances or disruptions.[74] Given how the nature of cyber attacks has changed, it would be ideal to develop overarching internal systemic resilience and tailored disruption capacities to meet the failings of traditional deterrence strategies.[75] Yet, the implementation of this form of robust cyber power would require unprecedented cooperation among all stakeholders in industry, government, and defense spheres due to the inherent complexity in socio-economic-technical systems. However, the necessary obtainment of spontaneous self-organizing order in interactions between these complex adaptive systems with so many interconnected parts will take a long time and an alternative is needed now.

COMPREHENSIVE APPROACHES

In the interim, the nation's national security community needs to consider less all-inclusive strategies for deterrence that center on collaborative efforts to achieve some aspects of *emergence* in complex systems. The property of *emergence* is roughly described by the common phrase "the action of the whole is more than the sum of the actions of the parts."[76] As an initial point, the 2009 US Cyberspace Policy Review delineated the need for a comprehensive framework to facilitate coordinated responses by government, the private sector, and allies to a significant cyber threat or incident. The report recognizes that "addressing network security issues requires a public-private partnership as well as international cooperation and norms."[77] Likewise, the 2014 US Joint Staff Unity of Effort Framework Solution Guide recognizes that the government and the private sector have to coordinate their activities to prepare for cyber threats. The Joint Staff realizes that achieving unity of effort to meet national security goals is problematic due to challenges in information sharing, competing priorities, and uncoordinated activities.[78] PPD-41 issued by the White House in 2016 codifies that "significant cyber incidents demand unity of effort within the Federal Government and especially close coordination between the public and private sectors."[79]

NATO experiences offer a starting point to design a comprehensive approach for operations in a domain of interest (like cyber deterrence). The former director of the National Security Agency (NSA) argued "government, industry and our allies have to work together" to prepare for catastrophic cyber attacks in our future.[80] The North Atlantic Treaty Organization (NATO) has aligned parties in various operations through a comprehensive approach based on shared "principles and collaborative processes that enhance the likelihood of favorable and enduring outcomes within a particular situation."[81] NATO proclaimed "the need to promote a comprehensive approach applies not only to operations, but more broadly to many of NATO's efforts to deal with 21st century security challenges, such as . . . protecting against cyber attacks."[82] To be effective in continuous cybered conflict, the NATO methodology has to be modified and translated for different operational conditions, structural characteristics, and prominent partners, to include commercial actors. The White House provided a laudable example of embracing a comprehensive approach for cyber deterrence by suggesting public and private sector partnerships for cyber defense of critical infrastructure sectors. [83] Within this context, a partnership would be defined as close cooperation between parties having common interests in achieving a shared vision. The 2010 Comprehensive National Cybersecurity Initiative aimed to build out such an approach to cyber defense strategy that deters "interference" and attack in cyberspace. The challenge is to align the efforts of all involved parties for a common purpose in all forms of deterrence. However, if traditional deterrence does not work, and this partnership lags in its unity of effort, then active cyber defense could nonetheless offer a means to strengthen deterrence by combining systemic resilience and disruption capacities. [84]

STRATEGIC OPTIONS DEFINED

The term strategy is described as the direction and use made of means by chosen ways in order to achieve the desired ends of national policy. [85] An analysis of the sufficiency of strategic cyber deterrence options (retaliation, denial, entanglement or active cyber defense) to alter malicious actor behavior in cyberspace requires answers to the following questions:

1. To what extent will the threat of the use of all necessary means, often in kind, in response to hostile acts in cyberspace achieve deterrence by retaliation?
2. By what degree do protective measures improve the security of networks and systems to deny adversaries the benefit of attack?
3. To what level will cooperative measures for entanglement based on mutual interests restrain behavior in conducting, endorsing or allowing malicious cyber activity?
4. By what extent does evidence show that active cyber defense is technically capable and legally viable as a means for dissuading and deterring malicious actors?

Initial answers to the four questions are found in the following summaries of initiatives, issues, and constraints in the strategic options and applied in an illustrative case below:

Deterrence by Retaliation is defined by the effort to directly impose costs for hostile acts in cyberspace. Retaliation is based on the right to use all necessary means to defend the Nation, Allies, partners and interests in cyberspace. Means for a proportional and justified response include diplomatic, informational, military, and economic, as appropriate for the malicious actor and consistent with applicable international law. [86] Military response options may include using cyber and kinetic capabilities. Under some circumstances, hostile acts in cyberspace could constitute an armed attack within the meaning of Article 51 of the UN Charter. Established principles would apply in the context of an armed attack (*Jus ad bellum*). First, the right of self-defense applies against an imminent or actual armed attack whether the attacker is a state or nonstate actor. Second, the use of force in self-defense must be limited to what is necessary and proportionate to address an imminent or actual use of force. Third, states are required to take measures to ensure their territories are not used for purposes of armed activities against other states. The use of cyber tools in the context of armed conflict (*Jus in bello*) is addressed by existing rules and principles of the international law of armed conflict.

On whether or not a cyber operation constitutes an armed attack, according to the Tallinn Manual 2.0 on the International Law Applicable to Cyber Operations Rule 71, "depends on the scale and effects."[87] Cyber operations that result in death or injury of individuals or destruction or damage of objects could be defined as an armed attack.[88] Although Stuxnet caused physical damage, the International Group of Experts that developed the Tallinn Manual was divided on whether the damage constituted an armed attack. Future cyber attacks could be structured to transmit data or subtly modify, degrade, or corrupt data in a malicious but not immediately apparent manner.[89] The NATO Enhanced Cyber Defense Policy affirms that cyber defense is part of NATO's core task of collective defense. Any decision as to whether a cyber attack would invoke Article 5 of the Washington Treaty is subject to political decisions by the North Atlantic Council on a case-by-case basis.[90] Although the manner in which the North Atlantic Council will assess each cyber attack remains ambiguous as no predetermined standards for assessment exist and countries hold various and differing internal criteria,[91] this ambiguity gives an adversary good reason to use cyber as a method of attack against critical infrastructure.[92]

The imposition of costs in deterrence by retaliation is intended to reduce any threat actor's willingness or ability to initiate or continue an offensive operation. While some argue the fundamental interconnectedness of networks means the effects of responsive cyber operations cannot be limited, others claim that contained operations are possible even within broadly connected systems.[93] However, deliberate, inadvertent or accidental escalation could trigger a chain reaction that raises the level of conflict beyond any contemplated by any party to the conflict.[94] In the United States only the president can approve a cyber operation likely to result in significant consequences, a tough decision due to inability to predict collateral damage and uncertainty over political effect.[95] Equally, the threat of massive cyber retribution would probably encourage actors to seek low levels of cyber attacks that fall below the threshold that would trigger such retaliation in kind.[96] In many cases, victim countries may be constrained to seek justice rather than retribution. In court, victim states can press for access to individuals or information and use refusal to cooperate as a justification for retaliation. However, until retaliation by any means does ensue, there is no punishment and hence, no deterrence.[97]

Deterrence by Denial is defined by the effort to withhold any benefit from malicious activity in cyberspace and thereby over time encourage perceptions of cyber attacks as pointless endeavors. Denial of any malicious actor's objectives occurs by increasing the security of networks and systems. In this context, security is "a condition that results from the establishment and maintenance of protective measures that enable an enterprise to perform its mission or critical functions despite risks posed by threats to its use of information systems."[98] In this context protective measures limit damage by reducing risk, and specific actions for risk reduction can include the promulgation of security strategies or policies to avoid or accept risk; the implementation of security controls to mitigate or diminish risk; and organizational arrangements to share or transfer risk.[99] A variety of protective measures are contained and endorsed in best practice guidelines for businesses, organizations, and consumers. An example of a best practice for security strategies is the employment of a defense-in-depth approach that emphasizes "multiple, overlapping, and mutually supportive defensive systems to guard against single-point failures in any specific technology or protection method."[100] Examples of best practices regarding security policies include the use of encryption to protect sensitive data, the restriction of removable media, and the enforcement of effective passwords.

While best practice guidelines help reduce risk from cyber threats, more methodical approaches for the identification and application of other protective measures, like specific safeguards, are contained in a variety of frameworks. Safeguards are prescribed to protect the confidentiality, integrity, and availability of an information system. Safeguards may include security features, management constraints, personnel security, and security of physical structures, areas, and devices. Safeguards are synonymous with security controls.[101] The Center for Internet Security (CIS) produced Critical Security Controls for Effective Cyber Defense that offers a set of actions based on the combined knowledge of actual attacks and effective defenses.[102] The controls deny benefit of attack by monitoring networks and systems, detecting attack attempts, identifying compromised machines, and interrupting infiltration. The top three drivers for adopting the controls are increasing visibility of attacks, improving response and reducing risk.[103] When the US Congress failed to enact necessary legislation, President Obama signed an Executive Order for the development of a cybersecurity framework that incorporates voluntary consensus standards and industry best practices. The inaugural cybersecurity framework is built around the core functions of identify, protect, detect, respond, and recover.[104] The Critical Security Controls are part of the framework's informative references that illustrate methods to accomplish core functions.

Cyber intelligence on threats and vulnerabilities leads to better risk-informed decision making on investments in relevant security controls. Organizational arrangements for the sharing of cyber intelligence are another form of protective measures to reduce risk. As called for in the aforementioned Executive Order, the National Cybersecurity and Communications Integration Center (NCCIC) coordinates with the private sector, and also government and international partners. The NCCIC integrates analysis and data into a comprehensive series of actionable and shareable information products. In addition, the NCCIC engages with information sharing and analysis centers (ISACs) to protect portions of critical information technology that they interact with, operate, manage, or own. For example, the NCCIC collaborated with the Financial Services ISAC during the 2012 series of DDoS assaults on US major banks to provide technical data and assistance to financial institutions. Data included DDoS–related IP addresses and supporting contextual information, which was also provided to over 120 international partners.[105] The NCCIC has been designated by PPD-41 as the lead coordinator for asset response.[106]

Agencies and companies acknowledge the need to share more data about threats across enterprise boundaries but are worried about liability and risk. Commercial offerings to share data, like the Internet Identity's Active Trust platform, let contributors retain ownership of data and control dissemination.[107] Yet in reality, only cybersecurity legislation can enable the private sector to share real-time cyber threat activity detected on its networks without fear of violating civil liberties and rights to privacy of citizens.[108] In December 2015, President Obama signed the Cybersecurity Act of 2015 as part of an emergency budget omnibus bill. The legislation gives liability protection to companies that share information with the government but requires them to strip away personal data first.[109] Even with passage of this legislation, participation in sharing arrangements, and also adoption of industry best practices, for securing cyberspace remains voluntary for the private sector that largely owns the nation's critical infrastructure.[110] This is the same private sector that finds out about 85 percent of cyber breeches from an external party usually months after an intrusion.[111] For in reality today, it is not a matter of if a company will be breached, but when.[112]

Deterrence by entanglement is defined by the effort to encourage responsible state behavior (and thus restrain malicious behavior) by raising the perceived value of maintaining and not endangering the returns from government to government cooperation on mutual interests. To some extent, nations share political, economic, commercial, and strategic interdependence in cyberspace and so all to some degree share vulnerability. The United Nations Secretary-General has stated, "While all Nations appreciate the enormous benefits of ICTs, there is also broad recognition that misuse poses risks to international peace and security."[113] The 2013 report by the Group of Governmental Experts emphasized this shared vulnerability by observing that the development and spread of sophisticated tools and techniques for cyber attack increases the risk of mistaken attribution and unintended escalation. The report also notes that states have affirmed the need for cooperative action against threats resulting from misuse of ICTs. While states have to lead these efforts, effective cooperation would benefit from participation by the private sector and civil society (in a comprehensive approach). The 2013 report, and an updated version in 2015, specifies an array of actions, to include norms, rules and principles of responsible state behavior in cyberspace, such as prohibiting harm to critical infrastructure and emergency response systems, and confidence-building measures, which aid deterrence through risk reduction.[114]

One action to strengthen deterrence by entanglement is the implementation of formal binding agreements between states. Arms control aims to establish legal regimes that make conflict less likely. Their objective is to reduce the existence of, or restrict the use of certain weapons. However, imposing limitations on the development and proliferation of cyber-weapons is difficult because their properties are incompatible with rationale for arms control treaties.[115] The lack of universal consensus on what even constitutes a cyber weapon complicates verification of compliance. Most of the technology relied on in an offensive capacity is inherently dual-use, like vulnerability assessment tools that scan an organization's systems and data for security gaps that an attacker could leverage to gain access,[116] and software that can be minimally repurposed for malicious action.[117] Another hindrance for arms control enforcement is that the creator or source of the weapon is not often the user, for example, in state-sponsored hacktivist campaigns where cyber tools with instructions are provided to patriotic hackers supporting a cause.

Absent useful formal treaties, a broad assortment of cooperative measures has been promoted to restrain state activity, or state-sponsored or endorsed activity, of a malicious manner in cyberspace. Internationally acceptable norms, rules and principles of responsible behavior by states could encourage order in cyber activity if fully implemented and enforced. They start with the premise that International law, and in particular the Charter of the United Nations is applicable to cyberspace. The Seoul Conference on Cyberspace in 2013 resulted in a "Framework for and Commitment to Open and Secure Cyberspace" that offers guidelines for governments and organizations on coping with cybercrime and cyberwar.[118] These guidelines include verbatim norms of behavior proposed in 2013 by the UN Group of Government Experts for States to meet their international obligations regarding wrongful acts attributed to them, not use proxies to commit wrongful acts, and ensure their territories are not used by nonstate actors for unlawful acts.[119] The fourth Global Conference on Cyberspace in The Hague in 2015 gathered representatives from governments, private sector and civil society to promote practical cooperation in cyberspace, to enhance cyber capacity building, and to discuss norms for responsible behavior in cyberspace.[120]

Regional or bilateral dialogue can establish voluntary confidence-building measures to promote trust and assurance, such as those agreed upon by the United States and Russia for sharing of threat indicators.[121] Other practical measures to increase predictability and reduce misperception include exchange of views on national policies, like an informative briefing by the Obama administration in 2014 to Chinese officials on Pentagon doctrine for defending against and conducting cyber attacks.[122] Finally, capacity-building assistance might be necessary for states to fulfill their responsibilities in securing cyberspace. Efforts for assistance range from developing technical skill and sharing best practices, to strengthening national legal frameworks. Overall, cooperative measures have potential to address cyber related threats, vulnerabilities, and risks, but they require extensive cooperation that is often thwarted by a clash of competing state interests. For example, Beijing suspended a Sino–US working group on cyber issues after the indictment of the Unit 61398 members, citing "we should encourage organizations and individuals whose rights have been infringed to stand up and sue Washington."[123] Ostensibly China "has been a "rule-taker," but is becoming a "rule-maker" who is promoting new norms and rules of the game that fit its national interests."[124]

Active cyber defense is defined as the real-time detection, analysis and mitigation of network security breaches combined with the aggressive use of legal countermeasures beyond network and state territorial boundaries. Scholars have described active cyber defense as a range of actions that engage the adversary before and during a cyber incident. Their listings of the broad spectrum of applicable activities include the use of honeypots, beaconing, sinkholing, and deception, which raise adversary costs through interference, delay, obstruction, or trickery.[125] Typical examples of these techniques would be use of a honeypot to see which documents the adversary chooses to exfiltrate, remotely tracking stolen documents by passive watermarks on files, redirecting the malware on an infected computer to communicate not with an attacker but with a safe server, or allowing the attacker to steal documents that contain false or misleading information, respectively.[126] More aggressive countermeasures outside of the victim's network include taking control of remote computers to stop attacks or launching denial of service attacks against attacking machines.

Today, the cyber security industry is shifting to more reactive forms of active cyber defense, predicated on automated and integrated technologies that have the ability to identify, interdict, isolate, or remove threats inside the network.[127] An early pioneer in the field was Hexis Cyber Solutions, which created and fielded HawkEye G as an automated threat removal platform.[128] This next generation cyber security platform, now acquired by WatchGuard Technologies,[129] provides endpoint and network sensing, threat detection analytics, and automated countermeasures that remove advanced threats at machine speed inside the network before adversaries can steal data, compromise intellectual property or cause process disruption. Once HawkEye G detects and investigates a cyber threat, it deploys network-based countermeasures (like blocking traffic or redirecting it to a Bot Trap) and host-based countermeasures (such as killing the malware process or quarantining malicious files) to remediate and remove the threat.[130] In respect for corporate reluctance to adopt machine-enabled defensives for fear of algorithmic misfires with unexpected results, Hexis provided choices for HawkEye G settings, either to use corporate policies to control automatic countermeasure execution or to allow machine-guided execution to optimize human-in-the-loop threat response and removal. HawkEye G was selected by the US intelligence community as part of an integrated active cyber defense solution named SHORTSTOP for protecting federal agencies' networks against advanced adversaries.[131]

For outside the network, Rule 20 of the Tallinn Manual 2.0 says "A State may be entitled to take countermeasures, whether cyber in nature or not, in response to a breach of an international legal obligation that it is owed by another State."[132] Furthermore the Manual states there is "no prohibition against injured States turning to a private firm, including foreign companies, to conduct cyber countermeasures on their behalf against responsible States."[133] Hack back is when the victim acts on its own initiative with a counterstrike to stop an ongoing attack, or even hack into their network to delete or alter stolen information.[134] Although "an increasing number of U.S. companies are taking retaliatory action,"[135] for private sector actors to act on their own using hack back, existing legal constraints would have to be adapted to allow use of these tactics.[136] The primary law in the United States that applies to more aggressive techniques is the Computer Fraud and Abuse Act (CFAA), codified as Title 18, Section 1030. A defendant can violate the CFAA by accessing a "protected computer" without authorization or by exceeding authorized access.[137] So today "it's illegal to chase bad guys up the wire, even if you have the capability to do so—it's illegal to shoot back."[138] However, one could argue US common law admits certain rights of self-defense and of defense of property in preventing the commission of a crime against an individual or a corporation. Applying the latter for hostile cyber attacks, the range of permitted actions is roughly comparable to the range for *nonlethal* self-defense. While individuals are not permitted to engage in re-venge or retaliation for a crime, they are—in some instances—entitled to take otherwise-prohibited actions for the purpose of preventing or averting an imminent crime or one that is in progress. Yet in most cases, challenges in quickly obtaining definitive attribution preclude exercising this right.[139] Therefore today a private sector actor may realistically only respond to hos-tile attacks within its network while the state can legally act outside the network.

Finally, any strategy of deterrence based on active cyber defense has to consider the defense department component that defines the concept as the "synchronized, real-time capability to discover, detect, analyze, and mitigate threats and vulnerabilities."[140] For the military, these tasks are very similar to defensive cyberspace operations described by the Director of Operations at US Cyber Command as "passive and active cyberspace defense activities that allow us to outmaneuver an adversary."[141] Defensive cyberspace operations (DCO) provide the ability to discover, detect, analyze, and mitigate threats with malicious capability and intent to affect key cyber terrain. Subcategories of these operations are internal defensive measures (IDM), actions taken internally, and response actions (RA) taken outside the information environ-ment. Tasks for IDM are hunting on friendly terrain for threats and directing internal appropriate responses, whereas RA is about going after the shooter outside friendly network space to stop the attack. The commander, Fleet Cyber Command, readily admits "we have people that hunt bad actors."[142]

ILLUSTRATIVE CASE

The US Chairman of the Joint Chiefs of Staff has said "cyber attacks are incredibly disruptive and could disable this country's critical infrastruc-ture."[143] While tangible evidence readily supports that assertion, not all cyber attacks rise to that level of harm against key resources, but they can have a significant economic or political effect. Take for instance, the 2016 hack into the Democratic National Committee (DNC) network that created political fallout through what could be considered a coercive campaign. The breach offers an illustrative case for an initial look at the sufficiency of traditional cyber deterrence strategies or an alternative strategy. The *Washington Post* reported in June that "Russian government hackers penetrated the computer network of the Democratic National Committee and gained access to the entire database of opposition research on GOP presidential candidate Donald Trump."[144] Committee officials said the intruders also were able to read all email and chat traffic. After discovering the intrusion in late April, the com-mittee reached out immediately to the cyber firm CrowdStrike to investigate. In May, CrowdStrike identified two separate Russian intelligence-affiliated hacker groups present in the network. One group named Cozy Bear (APT29) had gained access the prior summer and the other named Fancy Bear (APT28) in April.[145] A comparative analysis of malware samples for coding structures and obfuscation techniques by Fidelis Cybersecurity supported the CrowdStrike findings.[146]

Dmitry Peskov, a spokesman for President Vladimir Putin, immediately told foreign journalists in Moscow that "I absolutely rule out the possibility that the government or government agencies were involved in this."[147] Although Russia denied the DNC hack, both groups in question have been accused of hacking on their behalf. FireEye has documented a series of cyber espionage campaigns by APT28 in Eastern Europe and European security organizations that would likely benefit the Russian government.[148] Likewise, CrowdStrike claims that APT29 hacked the White House, State Department, and US Joint Chiefs of Staff.[149] Although the target of the DNC hacks appeared to be presidential candidate Donald Trump, the true purpose seemed to emerge in late July when WikiLeaks dumped nearly twenty thousand emails from top DNC officials. Several of the released emails revealed that officials floated ideas about ways to undermine the candidacy of former presidential candidate Bernie Sanders,[150] contrary to party leader aims to appear unified behind presumptive presidential nominee Hillary Clinton.[151] The immediate fallout for the DNC was severe as just one day before the Democratic convention was ready to begin, the DNC chairwoman announced her resignation, while enraged Sanders supporters protested and disrupted the convention.[152] Multiple Democrats alleged "the Russian government stole the emails and provided them to WikiLeaks in an effort to help Republican presidential nominee Donald Trump win the November election."[153] The leaks of damaging emails related to the Clinton campaign continued all the way up to the election.[154]

Since no financial information was reported to be accessed by the Russian hacker groups, only personal details of wealthy donors including celebrities,[155] it appears their motivations or those of their state sponsor were not for profit but political in nature, apparently to understand and influence political decisions in the United States. After all, Russia had set precedent for this sort of coercive activity by interfering through proxy hacker groups in the presidential elections in Ukraine in 2014.[156] Finally on October 7, 2016, the US Director of National Intelligence stated with confidence "that the Russian Government directed the recent compromises of e-mails from U.S. persons and institutions, including U.S. political organizations. . . . We believe based on the scope and sensitivity of these efforts, that only Russia's senior-most officials could have authorized these activities."[157] Although counter to that statement and detrimental to attribution, WikiLeaks founder Julian Assange adamantly claimed that the source for the hacked emails "is not the Russian government and it is not a state party."[158]

In regard to what deterrence strategy might be effective in a proportional and justified response to the DNC incident, for starters, deterrence by retaliation by military means falters, since according to Tallinn Manual general editor Michael Schmitt, "it's not a situation that would allow the U.S. to respond in self-defense militarily."[159] The effectiveness of other means to impose costs such as diplomatic overtures and legal indictments would be doubtful, since the Kremlin called the US allegations "nonsense" and they would not likely cooperate.[160] For deterrence by denial, any layered protective measures in place on the DNC network obviously failed and significant investment would be necessary to counter the advanced techniques of this type of sophisticated actor. For deterrence by entanglement, the United States does a cooperation pact but not a formal binding agreement with Russia for protection of the information resources of their states. Although Russia has tacitly agreed to international norms through participation in the UN Group of Government Experts findings, the direct attribution to the act or the proxies would be difficult to hold them legally accountable. Security expert James Lewis sums up the situation well in stating, "If we couldn't deter Moscow from going into the Ukraine, we're not going to deter them from hacking us."[161] His statement gives credence to the use of active cyber defense. While the initial entry in the network would still not have been blocked, the breach could have been detected and mitigated earlier by automated capabilities that discover and interpret subtle behaviors in enterprise activity. Subsequent verifiable alerts would have initiated external disruptive countermeasure considerations, for which Schmitt said unlawful intervention gave the United States grounds to undertake.[162] A detailed analysis of strategic options and the actual US response will be presented in the final chapter.

EXPECTED OUTCOMES

In the illustrative case of alleged state-sponsored espionage, and in other disruptive or destructive cyber attacks, each traditional deterrence strategy has limits in effectiveness in preventing malicious activity. Deterrence is intended to convince adversaries not to take malicious actions by means of decisive influence over their decision making.[163] There are ways to enhance the sufficiency of traditional deterrence strategies including: impose real consequences (retaliation), employ proactive defenses (denial), and pursue diplomatic concessions (entanglement). Incidents like the DNC hack can be good because they force states to take a stance and perhaps pursue laws and norms they otherwise would not have endorsed.[164] Deterrence options are not mutually exclusive and US doctrine, for instance, uses a mixed approach, especially across diplomatic, legal, economic, and military dimensions. Whether these options can achieve decisive influence or whether the strategy of active cyber defense is necessary is a key question of this book. The data shows these traditional methods don't work as planned or needed in cybered conflict. *Active cyber defense* actually strengthens deterrence by denial and retaliation, through systemic resilience and disruption capacities that both frustrate and punish the wide range of malicious actors regardless of origin or intentions.

The chapter analysis will address the evidence of limits to or constraints on the effectiveness of strategic cyber deterrence options as stated in the four questions. Measures will be used to provide a basis for describing fluctuating levels of effectiveness. Specific measures of attacks, time, and costs will be used where applicable to evaluate option utility and sufficiency. For example, at the tactical level, the chapter analysis will consider the impact of the options on attacks (number of attempted or successful penetrations), time (of threat detection, response and mitigation), and costs (for the malicious actor or the victim). Then at the strategic level, the final analysis will consider impact of the options on attacks (volume of noise across social, technical, and economic systems), time (in mitigation of systemic security losses), and costs (in the order of magnitude of gross domestic products). If deemed necessary, the alternative strategy of active cyber defense will be constructed from the findings to the extent merited in the analysis.

The use of a comprehensive approach in application of the deterrence options will be explored in the analysis throughout the chapters, in accordance with the 2014 US Quadrennial Defense Review mandate that deterrence of cyber threats requires a multi-stakeholder coalition that enables "the lawful application of the authorities, responsibilities, and capabilities resident across the U.S. Government, industry, and international allies and partners."[165] Also relative aspects of the theories of strategy and deterrence will be applied in the analysis based on usage in historical and modern periods. The challenge in determining sufficiency of the strategic cyber deterrence options resides in the number and type of malicious actors, with various motivations, and an assortment of common or overlapping attack vectors at their easy disposal. Therefore the analysis will determine whether each option meets the conditions of capability, credibility, and communication to be considered as a sufficient strategy for the deterrence of cyber attacks.

The book will make every effort to correlate actual threat incident details to public assertions of effectiveness in order to make a fair assessment. While many other works only describe the conditions and effects of attacks, this examination highlights attack methods for the purpose of relating threat and vulnerability evidence to strategy options and decisions. Although conceptual literature[166] and workshop proceedings[167] exist on cyber deterrence theory, there is little empirical work of this nature attempting to compare traditional strategies across complex social and technical issues equally. For application of a more comprehensive approach, conferences[168] and speeches[169] have addressed the subject but lack a unified framework. In response to the void, this book produces an empirically grounded alternative strategy of active cyber defense for consideration for selection. As stated earlier by Admiral Michael Rogers, the proliferation of malicious actors and cyber-attack vectors does not allow time to "get some idea of deterrence within the cyber arena."

NOTES

1. Ivy Wigmore, "Threat Actor Definition," Security Threats and Countermeasures Glossary, January 2016.

2. Robert Anderson Jr. "Cybersecurity, Terrorism, and Beyond: Addressing Evolving Threats to the Homeland," testimony before the Committee on Homeland Security and Government Affairs, US Senate, September 10, 2014.

3. Ian Duncan, "Cyber Command Chief: Foreign Governments Use Criminals to Hack U.S. Systems," *Baltimore Sun*, March 16, 2016.

4. Dell Secure Works, "Underground Hacker Markets," Annual Report, April 2016, 1–22.

5. Mandiant, "M Trends 2015, A View from the Front Lines," Alexandria, Virginia, June 2015: 20–22.

6. The basis of this introduction first appeared in *Strategic Studies Quarterly* 9, no. 1 (Spring 2015).

7. US Department of Defense, *Joint Operation Planning,* Joint Publication 5-0 (Washington, DC: Office of the Chairman, Joint Chiefs of Staff, August 11, 2011): E-2.

8. US Department of Defense, *Deterrence Operations Joint Operating Concept*, Version 2.0, (Washington, DC: US Strategic Command, December 2006), 5.

9. National Institute of Standards and Technology, "Glossary of Key Information Security Terms," NISTIR 7298 Revision 2 (May 2013): 57.

10. Adam Bromwich, Symantec, "Emerging Cyber Threats to the United States," Testimony before House Committee on Homeland Security, February 25, 2016.

11. U.S. Department of Defense, *The DOD Cyber Strategy*, April 2015: 11.

12. Office of the Director of National Intelligence, "Assessing Russian Activities and Intentions in Recent US Elections," Intelligence Community Assessment (January 6, 2017): ii.

13. See *DOD Dictionary of Military and Associated Terms* (Washington, DC: The Joint Staff, As Amended through 15 October 2016), 60 .

14. David J. Betz and Tim Stevens, *Cyberspace and the State: Toward a Strategy for Cyber-Power* (New York: Routledge, 2011), 37.

15. Sean P. McGurk, National Cybersecurity and Communications Integration Center Director, "The DHS Cybersecurity Mission: Promoting Innovation and Securing Critical Infrastructure," Testimony before the US House Committee on Homeland Security, April 15, 2011.

16. Executive Office of the President, "Executive Order—Improving Critical Infrastructure Cybersecurity," Washington, DC: The White House, February 12, 2013.

17. William J. Lynn III, Deputy Secretary of Defense, "Remarks on the Department of Defense Cyber Strategy," Delivered at National Defense University, Washington, DC, July 14, 2011.

18. Mike Rogers, "Cybersecurity Threats: The Way Forward," Hearing of the House (Select) Intelligence Committee, Washington, DC, November 20, 2014.

19. AV Test, The Independent IT-Security Institute, *Malware Statistics*, August 9, 2016, https://www.av-test.org/en/statistics/malware/.

20. Kevin G. Coleman, "The Cyber Commander's eHandbook: The Strategies and Tactics of Digital Conflict," version 4, Technolytics, 2013, 52–80.

21. Symantec, "Internet Security Threat Report," vol. 19 (April 2014): 26, 34.

22. William J. Lynn III, Deputy Secretary of Defense, "Defending a New Domain: The Pentagon's Cyberstrategy," *Foreign Affairs*, September/October 2010.

23. Chris Strohm, "U.S. Intelligence to Help Companies Avert Supply-Chain Hacking," *Bloomberg News*, August 10, 2016.

24. Securosis, "Defending against Denial of Service Attacks," White Paper, Version 1.3, October 31, 2012, 1–24.

25. James E. Cartwright, "Joint Terminology for Cyberspace Operations" (Washington, DC: Office of the Vice Chairman of the Joint Chiefs of Staff, November 2010), 8.

26. Martin C. Libicki, *Cyberdeterrence and Cyberwar* (Santa Monica, CA: RAND Corporation, 2009): 143–49.

27. Joint Terminology for Cyberspace Operations, 8.

28. Jeff Carr, "Russia/Georgia Cyber War—Findings and Analysis," Project Grey Goose: Phase I Report, October 17, 2008.

29. Chris Demchak, "Cybered Conflict, Cyber Power, and Security Resilience as Strategy," *Cyberspace and National Security* (Washington, DC: Georgetown University Press, 2012), 121–36.

30. Peter Dombrowski and Chris Demchak, "Cyber War, Cybered Conflict, and the Maritime Domain," *Naval War College Review* (April 1, 2014): 3.

31. John Leyden, "Battle Apparently Underway in Russia-Ukraine Conflict, *The Register*, March 4, 2014.

32. Mark Clayton, "Massive Cyberattacks Slam Official Sites in Russia, Ukraine," *Christian Science Monitor*, March 18, 2014.

33. Adrian Croft and Peter Apps, "NATO Websites Hit in Cyber Attack Linked to Crimea Tension," *Reuters*, March 16, 2014.

34. Nikolay Koval, "Revolution Hacking," in *Cyber War in Perspective: Russian Aggression against Ukraine*, chap. 6 (Tallinn, Estonia: NATO Cooperative Cyber Defense Center of Excellence Publications, 2015), 55–58.

35. Mandiant, "M Trends: Beyond the Breach," Alexandria, Virginia (April 2014): 1–7.

36. Patrick Tucker, "Syrian Electronic Army Threatens to Hack CENTCOM," *Defense One*, March 3, 2014.

37. Leon E. Panetta, "Defending the Nation from Cyber Attack," Business Executives for National Security, New York, October 11, 2012.

38. Kelly Jackson Higgins, "Shamoon Code 'Amateur' but Effective," *Dark Reading*, September 11, 2012.

39. Danielle Walker, "Natural Gas Giant RasGas Targeted in Cyber Attack," *SC Magazine*, August 31, 2012.

40. Nicole Perlroth, "Attacks on 6 Banks Frustrate Customers," *New York Times*, September 30, 2012.

41. Electrical Information Sharing and Analysis Center, "Analysis of the Cyber Attack on the Ukrainian Power Grid," March 18, 2016, 1–25.

42. Kim Zetter, "Inside the Cunning, Unprecedented Hack of Ukraine's Power Grid," *Wired*, March 3, 2016.

43. Lorenzo Franceschi-Bicchierai, "How Cyberattacks on Critical Infrastructure Could Cause Real-Life Disasters," *Motherboard*, August 16, 2016.

44. US Department of Defense, *Joint Operation Planning*, Joint Publication 5-0 (Washington, DC: Office of the Chairman, Joint Chiefs of Staff, August 11, 2011), III-38 to III-44.

45. Kelly Jackson Higgins, "China Hacked RSA, U.S. Official Says," *Dark Reading*, March 29, 2012.

46. Jim Finkle and Andrea Shalal-Esa, "Hackers Breached U.S. Defense Contractors," *Reuters*, May 27, 2011.

47. US Secretary of Defense, "Annual Report to Congress: Military and Security Developments Involving the People's Republic of China," May 2013, 36.

48. Edward Wong, "China's Push for Drones Fueled by U.S. Secrets," *International Herald Tribune*," September 23, 2013, 1.

49. Oliver Knox, "Chinese Hackers Breach Key US Weapons Designs," *Yahoo News*, May 28, 2013, and later further confirmation by Agence France-Presse, "Report: Chinese Soldiers Linked to US Military Hacking Case," *Defense News*, January 20, 2016.

50. Reuben F. Johnson and James Hardy, "Hagel Reiterates Cyber Charges against China," *Jane's Defense Weekly*, June 12, 2013.

51. US District Court, Indictment, Criminal No. 14-118, Filed May 1, 2014, 1–48.

52. Scott Jasper, "Are US and Chinese Cyber Intrusions So Different?" *The Diplomat*, September 9, 2013.

53. McAfee, "Net Losses: Estimating the Global Cost of Cybercrime," with Center for Strategic and International Studies, June 2014, 1–23.

54. David E. Sanger, "Obama Order Sped up Wave of Cyberattacks against Iran," *New York Times*, June 1, 2012.

55. David E. Sanger, "N.S.A. Breached Chinese Servers Seen as Security Threat," *New York Times*, March 22, 2014.

56. "High-Level Hooligan: Chinese Media Vents Spleen over US Cybercrime Charges," *RT News*, May 21, 2014.

57. Kelly Jackson Higgins, "Chinese Cyberespionage Tool Updated for Traditional Cybercrime," *Dark Reading*, November 27, 2012.

58. Stephen Doherty, Jozsef Gegeny, Branko Spasojevic, and Jonell Baltazar, "Hidden Lynx—Professional Hackers for Hire," Version 1.0, Symantec, September 17, 2013.

59. William Jackson, "How Google Attacks Changed the Security Game," *Government Computer News*, September 1, 2010.

60. Siobhan Gorman and Julian E. Barnes, "U.S. Says Iranian Hackers Are behind Electronic Assaults on U.S. Banks, Foreign Energy," *Wall Street Journal*, October 12, 2012.

61. U.S. Department of Defense, *Joint Operations,* Joint Publication 3-0 (Washington, DC: Office of the Chairman, Joint Chiefs of Staff, 17 January 2017): IV-4.

62. Schuyler Forester, "Theoretical Foundations: Deterrence in the Nuclear Age," in *American Defense Policy*, Schuyler Foerster and Edward Wright, eds., 6th ed. (Baltimore: Johns Hopkins University Press, 1990), 47–51.

63. Roger Harrison et al., "Space Deterrence: The Delicate Balance of Risk," *Space and Defense* 3 (Summer 2009).

64. Department of Defense, *Joint Operations,* Joint Publication 3-0 (Washington, DC: Office of the Chairman, Joint Chiefs of Staff, 17 January 2017): xxii.

65. Martin C. Libicki, *Cyberdeterrence and Cyberwar* (Santa Monica, CA: RAND Corporation, 2009), 6–37.

66. Chris Demchak, *Wars of Disruption and Resilience: Cybered Conflict, Power, and National Security* (Athens: University of Georgia Press, September 2011).

67. William A. Chambers, "Foreword," in *Thinking about Deterrence*, Adam Lowther, ed., xii (Maxwell Air Force Base, AL: Air University Press, 2014).

68. Adam Lowther, "The Evolution of Deterrence," in *Thinking about Deterrence*, Adam Lowther, ed., 3–4 (Maxwell Air Force Base, Alabama: Air University Press, 2014).

69. Chris C. Demchak, "Economic and Political Coercion and a Rising Cyber Westphalia," *Peacetime Regime for State Activities in Cyberspace* (Tallinn, Estonia: NATO Cooperative Cyber Defence Centre of Excellence, 2013), 595–620.

70. Schulyer Forester, "Strategies of Deterrence," *Conflict and Cooperation in the Global Commons* (Washington, DC: Georgetown University Press, September 2012): 55–67.

71. Robert S. Dewar, "The Triptych of Cyber Security: A Classification of Active Cyber Defense," in *Proceedings 6th International Conference on Cyber Conflict* (Tallinn, Estonia: Cooperative Cyber Defence Centre of Excellence, June 2014), 7–21.

72. "Hearing to consider the Nominations of . . . VADM Michael S. Rogers, USN to be Admiral and Director, National Security Agency/ Chief, Central Security Services/ Commander, U.S. Cyber Command," Statements Before the Senate Committee on Armed Services," March 11, 2014.

73. Zachary Fryer-Biggs, "US Cyber Moves beyond Protection," *Defense News*, March 16, 2014.

74. Louise K. Comfort, Arjen Boin, and Chris C. Demchak, *Designing Resilience: Preparing for Extreme Events* (University of Pittsburgh, September 2010): 1–12.

75. Chris C. Demchak, "Economic and Political Coercion and a Rising Cyber Westphalia," *Peacetime Regime for State Activities in Cyberspace* (Tallinn, Estonia: NATO Cooperative Cyber Defence Centre of Excellence, 2013), 595–620.

76. John H. Holland, *Complexity: A Very Short Introduction* (New York: Oxford University Press, 2014).

77. US Executive Office of the President, "Cyberspace Policy Review, Assuring a Trusted and Resilient Information and Communication Infrastructure" (Washington, DC: The White House, May 2009), i.

78. US Department of Defense, *Unity of Effort Framework Solution Guide* (Suffolk, VA: US Joint Staff J-7, August 31, 2014), foreword.

79. Executive Office of the President, *Presidential Policy Directive—United States Cyber Incident Coordination*, PPD-41 (Washington, DC: The White House, July 26, 2016).

80. Cheryl Pellerin, "Alexander: Defending against Cyberattacks Requires Collaboration," News Article, Defense.gov, October 30, 2013.

81. United Kingdom, Ministry of Defence, "The Comprehensive Approach," Joint Discussion Note 4/05, Shrivenham: Joint Doctrine and Concepts Centre, 2006, 1-4 to 1-5.

82. North Atlantic Treaty Organization, "A Comprehensive Approach," October 27, 2010.

83. US Executive Office of the President, *The Comprehensive National Cybersecurity Initiative*, Initiative #10 and 12, March 2010, 5.

84. Chris C. Demchak, "Economic and Political Coercion and a Rising Cyber Westphalia," *Peacetime Regime for State Activities in Cyberspace* (Tallinn, Estonia: NATO Cooperative Cyber Defence Centre of Excellence, 2013), 595–620. This work introduces the concepts of *systemic resilience* and *disruption capacities* in socio-technical-economic systems as key components of relative national power in a cybered world. My book expands the concepts and repurposes them for a different intent in arguing for new means for deterrence.

85. Arthur F. Lykke Jr., "Toward an Understanding of Military Strategy," *Guide to Strategy*, (Carlisle, PA: US Army War College, 1983), February 2001, 179–85.

86. Executive Office of the President, *International Strategy for Cyberspace: Prosperity, Security, and Openness in a Networked World* (Washington, DC: The White House, May 2011), 13–14.

87. Michael Schmitt, *Tallinn Manual 2.0 on the International Law Applicable to Cyber Operations* Second Edition, (Cambridge: Cambridge University Press, 2017), 339.

88. Michael N. Schmitt, "Attack as a Term of Art in International Law: The Cyber Operations Context," *Proceedings 4th International Conference on Cyber Conflict*" (Tallinn, Estonia: Cooperative Cyber Defence Centre of Excellence, 2012), 283–93.

89. Martin R. Stytz and Sheila B. Banks, "Toward Attaining Cyber Dominance," *Strategic Studies Quarterly* (Spring 2014): 60.

90. North Atlantic Treaty Organization, "Wales Summit Declaration," Paragraph 72, September 5, 2014.

91. Stephen Jackson, "NATO Article 5 and Cyber Warfare: NATO's Ambiguous and Outdated Procedure for Determining When Cyber Aggression Qualifies as an Armed Attack," Center for Infrastructure Protection and Homeland Security, George Mason University, August 16, 2016.

92. V. Joubert, "Five Years after Estonia's Cyber Attacks: Lessons Learned for NATO?" *Research Paper* 76, Rome: NATO Defense College (2012): 5.

93. Maren Leed, "Offensive Cyber Capabilities at the Operational Level," *Center for Strategic and International Studies* (September 2013): 2–3.

94. Herbert Lin, "Escalation Dynamics and Conflict Termination in Cyberspace," *Strategic Studies Quarterly* (Fall 2012): 52–55.

95. James Lewis, "Low-Level Cyberattacks Are Common but Truly Damaging Ones Are Rare," *Washington Post*, October 9, 2013.

96. Sean Lawson, "Putting the War in Cyberwar: Metaphor, Analogy, and Cybersecurity Discourse in the United States," *First Monday* 17, no. 7 (July 2, 2012).

97. Martin Libicki, "Pulling Punches in Cyberspace," *Proceedings of a Workshop on Deterring Cyberattacks* (Washington, DC: National Academies Press, 2010), 123–47.

98. Computer Security Division, Information Technology Laboratory, National Institute of Standards and Technology (NIST), "Glossary of Key Information Security Terms," NISTIR 7298, Revision 2 (May 2013): 173.

99. Computer Security Division, Information Technology Laboratory, National Institute of Standards and Technology (NIST), "Managing Information Security Risk," NIST Special Publication 800-39 (March 2011): 41.

100. Symantec Corporation, "Internet Security Threat Report," 19 (April 2014): 87–89.

101. Computer Security Division, Information Technology Laboratory, National Institute of Standards and Technology (NIST), "Security and Privacy Controls for Federal Information Systems and Organizations," NIST Special Publication 800-53, Revision 4, Appendix B (April 2013): B-20.

102. The Center for Internet Security, "The CIS Critical Security Controls for Effective Cyber Defense," Version 6.0 (October 15, 2015): 1–89.

103. John Pescatore and Tony Sager, "Critical Security Controls Survey: Moving from Awareness to Action," A SANS Whitepaper, June 2013.

104. National Institute of Standards and Technology, "Framework for Improving Critical Infrastructure Cybersecurity," Version 1.0, February 12, 2014.

105. Roberta Stempfley and Lawrence Zelvin, "Statement before the House Committee on Homeland Security," May 16, 2013.

106. DHS Press Office, "Statement by Secretary Jeh C. Johnson Regarding PPD-41, Cyber Incident Coordination," July 26, 2016.

107. William Jackson, "Social Platform for Sharing Cyber Threat Intel Opens Up," *Government Computer News* (March 2014): 6.

108. Keith B. Alexander, "Statement before the House Committee on Armed Services," March 12, 2014.

109. U.S. Congress, "Consolidated Appropriations Act, 2016," Division N—Cybersecurity Act of 2015, December 15, 2015, 1728–70.

110. Department of Homeland Security, "NIPP 2013: Partnering for Critical Infrastructure Security and Resilience," March 2013, 1–14.

111. Verizon, "2014 Data Breach Investigations Report," June 2014, 41.

112. Danny Palmer, "It is not about if you will be penetrated, but when, warns NSA Chief," *Computing News*, July 16, 2015.

113. United Nations General Assembly, "Group of Governmental Experts on Developments in the Field of Information and Telecommunications in the Context of International Security," A/68/98, June 24, 2013, 4.

114. United Nations General Assembly, "Group of Governmental Experts on Developments in the Field of Information and Telecommunications in the Context of International Security," A/70/174, July 22, 2015, 8–9.

115. Louise Arimatsu, "A Treaty for Governing Cyber-Weapons," *Proceedings 4th International Conference on Cyber Conflict* (Tallinn, Estonia: Cooperative Cyber Defence Centre of Excellence, 2012): 91–109.

116. Brad Causey, "Finding Vulnerabilities by Attacking Your Own Environment," *Information Week Reports*, November 2012.

117. US Department of Defense, *Cyberspace Policy Report*, November 2011, 8.

118. H. E. Yun Byung-se, Minister of Foreign Affairs, "Seoul Conference on Cyberspace," Seoul, South Korea, October 17–18, 2013.

119. United Nations General Assembly, "Group of Governmental Experts on Developments in the Field of Information and Telecommunications in the Context of International Security," A/68/98, June 24, 2013, 8.

120. "About the Global Conference on CyberSpace." The Hague, April 16–17, 2015.

121. Executive Office of the President, "Fact Sheet: US–Russian Cooperation on Information and Communications Technology Security" (Washington, DC: The White House, June 17, 2013).

122. David E. Sanger, "U.S. Tries Candor to Assure China on Cyberattacks," *New York Times*, April 6, 2014.

123. "High-Level Hooligan: Chinese Media Vents Spleen over US Cybercrime Charges," *RT News*, May 21, 2014.

124. Scott Kennedy, "China in Global Governance: What Kind of Status Quo Power?" Chapter One, *From Rule Takers to Rule Makers: the Growing Role of Chinese in Global Governance*, Co-published by the Research Center for Chinese Politics and Business and the International Centre for Trade and Sustainable Development, September 2012: 9.

125. Franklin D. Kramer and Melanie J. Teplinsky, "Cybersecurity and Tailored Deterrence," Atlantic Council, December 2013, 6.

126. Irving Lachow, "Active Cyber Defense: A Framework for Policy Makers," Center for a New American Security, February 2013, 1–10.

127. James P. Farwell and Rafal Rohozinski, "The New Reality of Cyber War," *Survival: Global Politics and Strategy*, August 1, 2012, 110.

128. Hexis Cyber Solutions, "HawkEye G," Data Sheet, 2015, 1–2.

129. Chris Warfield, "WatchGuard Acquires Hexis HawkEye G to Deliver Holistic Network Security from the Network to the Endpoint," WatchGuard Technologies, Press Release, June 7, 2016.

130. Hexis Cyber Solutions, "How to Automate Cyber Threat Removal," A HawkEye G Technical White Paper, Release 3.1, October 2015, 9.

131. Hexis Cyber Solutions, "HawkEye G Selected as Part of an Active Cyber Defense System to Protect Federal Networks from Advanced Cyber Attacks," Press Release, March 12, 2015.

132. Michael Schmitt, *Tallinn Manual 2.0 on the International Law Applicable to Cyber Operations,* Second Edition (Cambridge University Press, 2017): 111.

133. Ibid, 131.

134. Scott Cohn, "Companies Battle Cyberattacks Using 'Hack Back,'" *CNBC News*, June 4, 2013.

135. Joseph Menn, "Hacked Companies Fight Back with Controversial steps," *Reuters*, June 18, 2012.

136. Jeffery Carr, "Cyber Laws May Need Tweaking," *SC Magazine*, December 2012: 50.

137. 18 U.S. Code § 1030 Fraud and related activity in connection with computers.

138. Patience Wait, "Cyberthreats Grow More Ominous: Former NSA Chief," *Information Week*, October 11, 2013.

139. William A. Owens, Kenneth W. Dam, and Herbert S. Lin, *Technology, Policy, Law, and Ethics Regarding U.S. Acquisition and Use of Cyberattack Capabilities* (Washington, DC: National Academies Press, 2009), 204–5.

140. US Department of Defense, *Strategy for Operating in Cyberspace*, July 2011, 13.

141. Brett T. Williams, "The Joint Force Commander's Guide to Cyberspace Operations," *Joint Force Quarterly* no. 73, 2nd Quarter (2014): 12–19.

142. Richard R. Burgass, "Fleet Cyber Commander: "We Have People That Hunt Bad Actors," Seapower Magazine Online, December 2, 2014.

143. Martin E. Dempsey, "Cyber Attacks Could Disable Critical US Infrastructure," Interview, Press TV, January 12, 2015.

144. Ellen Nakashima, "Russian Government Hackers Penetrated DNC, Stole Opposition Research on Trump," *Washington Post*, June 14, 2016.

145. Dmitri Alperovitch, "Bears in the Midst: Intrusion into the Democratic National Committee," *CrowdStrike Blog*, June 15, 2016.

146. Teri Robinson, "Guccifer 2.0 Out—Cozy Bear, Fancy Bear Hacked DNC, Fidelis Analysis Shows," *SC Magazine*, June 21, 2016.

147. Andrew Roth, "Russia Denies DNC Hack and Says Maybe Someone Forgot the Password," *Washington Post*, June 15, 2016.

148. FireEye, "APT28: A Window into Russia's Cyber Espionage Operations," Special Report, 2014, 1–28.

149. Dmitri Alperovitch, "Bears in the Midst: Intrusion into the Democratic National Committee," *CrowdStrike Blog*, June 15, 2016.

150. Alana Abramson and Shushannah Walshe, "The 4 Most Damaging Emails from the DNC WikiLeaks dump," *ABC News*, July 25, 2016, http://abcnews.go.com/Politics/damaging-emails-dnc-wikileaks-dump/story?id=40852448.

151. Julian Routh, "Emails Show DNC Taking Aim at Sanders," *Wall Street Journal*, July 26, 2016.

152. Jeff Zeleny, M. J. Lee and Eric Bradner, "Dems Open Convention without Wasserman Schultz," *CNN Politics*, July 25, 2016.

153. Damian Paletta and Devlin Barrett, "Russians Accused of Hacking DNC," *Wall Street Journal*, July 26, 2016.

154. Dave Boyer, "Obama Briefed On Intel Report Of Russian Hacking In Election," *Washington Times*, January 5, 2017; and David Sherfinski, "State Department: 'Pretty Obvious' Russia Was Trying to Hurt Hillary Clinton," *Washington Times*, January 6, 2017.

155. Greg Masters, "Fallout from DNC Hack Broadens to Donors, Including Celebrities," *SC Magazine*, August 12, 2016.

156. Nikolay Koval, "Revolution Hacking," *Cyber War in Perspective: Russian Aggression against Ukraine*, chap. 6 (Tallinn, Estonia: NATO Cooperative Cyber Defense Center of Excellence Publications, 2015), 55–58.

157. Director of National Intelligence, "Joint DHS and ODNI Election Security Statement," Press Release, October 7, 2016, 1.

158. Sean Hannity, "Assange: Russian Government Not the Source of WikiLeaks Emails, *Fox News*, January 3, 2017.

159. Ellen Nakashima, "Russia's apparent meddling in U.S. election is not an act of war, cyber expert says," *The Washington Post*, February 7, 2017.

160. Dmitry Solovyov, "Moscow Says U.S. Cyber Attack Claims Fan 'Anti-Russian Hysteria,'" *Reuters*, October 8, 2016.

161. David E. Sanger and Nicole Perlroth, "What Options Does the U.S. Have after Accusing Russia of Hacks?" *New York Times*, October 8, 2016.

162. Ellen Nakashima, "Russia's apparent meddling in U.S. election is not an act of war, cyber expert says," *The Washington Post*, February 7, 2017.

163. US Department of Defense, *Deterrence Operations Joint Operating Concept*, Version 2.0, (Washington, DC: US Strategic Command, December 2006), 7–27.

164. Mark Pomerleau, "Hope for Global Cyber Norms Struggles following Russian Hacking Allegations," *C4ISRNET*, January 5, 2017.

165. U.S. Department of Defense, *Quadrennial Defense Review 2014*, May: 15.

166. Will Goodman, "Cyber Deterrence: Tougher in Theory Than in Practice?" *Strategic Studies Quarterly* (Fall 2010): 102–35.

167. National Research Council, *Proceedings of a Workshop on Deterring Cyber Attacks*, National Academies Press, 2012.

168. Organization for Security and Co-operation in Europe (2011), "A Comprehensive Approach to Cyber Security: Exploring the Future OSCE Role," Conference, Hofburg, Vienna, May 9–10.

169. James Lewis, "Rethinking Cyber Security—A Comprehensive Approach," Sasakawa Peace Foundation, Tokyo, September 12, 2011.

Chapter Two

Cyber Attacks

An attack in cyberspace is defined as "any kind of malicious activity that attempts to collect, disrupt, deny, degrade, or destroy information system resources or the information itself."[1] Malicious activity includes the theft or exploitation of data; disruption or denial of access or service; and destructive action including corruption, manipulation, alteration of data, and damage to systems. The array of actors conducting malicious activity is vast and varied in their motivations. They usually desire to achieve some form of reputation, satisfaction, monetary gain, national pride, or advantage. Their actual decision to act is based on meeting the actor's sense of legitimacy, need, and confidence related to the act itself.[2] Actors use malicious code to steal data, tarnish reputations, disrupt services, or sabotage systems. They operate with no discernible legal or ethical restraints.[3] The targets for their attacks are not just private companies, but also military installations, government offices, energy supply and transportation control facilities, financial and telecommunications systems, and other critical infrastructure nodes.

Cyber attacks are increasing in scale and severity of impact, while the cyber networks, systems and services that support military, commercial and social activities remain vulnerable to theft, espionage, disruption and destruction. The Director of National Intelligence foresees an ongoing series of cyber attacks from a variety of sources "will impose cumulative costs on US economic competitiveness and national security."[4] An institute survey found in 2014 that the most costly attacks for large organizations in all industry sectors were by web-based attacks, denial of services, malicious insiders, and malicious code, to include Structured Query Language (SQL) injection. The average time to contain a cyber attack was thirty-one days, during which business disruption accounted for 38 percent of total external costs.[5] Another Industry survey of over eight hundred IT security decision makers and practitioners across North America and Europe revealed 71 percent of their networks were breached in 2014, again a nearly 10 percent increase from the previous year. Phishing/spear-phishing, malware, and zero-day attacks were perceived as the greatest risk for responding organizations.[6]

The commander, US Cyber Command, has admitted "despite your best efforts, you must prepare and assume that you will be penetrated."[7] This undeniable truth is a direct result of the gap between an organization's ability to defend itself and the adversaries' ability to circumvent those defenses.[8] The adversary has considerable resources and expertise at their disposal to conduct attacks, while victim organizations often have limited resources and budgets to launch an adequate defense. It is an unfair and asymmetric fight because offense is easier and cheaper.[9] This tactical imbalance of power impedes the fundamental premise of traditional deterrence strategies, which is convincing the attacker that costs outweigh benefits. This chapter will examine the relative ease by which all levels of malicious actor access information systems through various types of attack methods. These actors operate from distant locations without any real risks or repercussions. They can with impunity freely choose the scale, proximity, and precision of their attacks.[10] Using examples of actual cyber incidents, the chapter will delineate the wide range of malicious actors, and their methods and motivations in their campaigns of malicious activity. It will finish on the need to deter malicious actors from causing significant consequences through cyber attacks on complex socio-technical-economic systems.

ATTACK METHODS

The asymmetric nature of the cyber threat that undermines traditional deterrence strategies demands an understanding of how exactly and easily a malicious actor can access equipment, computers or systems. Malicious actors use various methods, termed "cyber-attack vectors" to access microprocessor controlled equipment, computers or systems to deliver a hostile payload or a malicious outcome.[11] The attack vector creates a path to exploit a software or code vulnerability that compromises the equipment, computer, or system for the installation of malicious code, also known as malware. Malicious code is software or firmware intended to perform an unauthorized process that will have adverse impact on the confidentiality, integrity, or availability of an information system. Common forms of malware include worms (that spread freely), viruses (that activate upon execution), and Trojans (that allow remote control of the infected system). Ransomware is a type of malware that infects computers and restricts user access to systems or data unless a ransom is paid.[12] Most malicious code attempts to evade detection by various means such as the use of polymorphism to automatically change its code whenever it is downloaded, allowing the malware to escape signature-based antivirus sensors.

The term vulnerability implies a weakness in a system or in a piece of software, commonly called a "bug." Software exploits are used to take advantage of these flaws or misconfigurations in operating systems and applications. They can be found in exploit kits available for purchase on hacking forums; the most active in 2015 is titled Angler. The average price for exploit kits is $800–$1500 a month.[13] The kits include software exploits for known vulnerabilities in end-user technologies such as Internet Explorer, Adobe Flash, and Oracle Java. Over 80 percent of the vulnerabilities in exploit kits were published in the past two years. The speed with which exploit kit developers deploy new exploits takes advantage of the gap in time between initial vulnerability disclosure and the implementation of software patches at an organization.[14] Yet vulnerability scanning data reveals that 21 percent of client vulnerabilities found in every industry sector are more than three years old, meaning the organization does not patch it and it is open for exploitation.[15] The exploit kit scans victim systems to find those open or zero-day vulnerabilities, identifies effective exploits for those vulnerabilities, exploits the target system vulnerability, and drops into the system the attacker's payload of malware.[16] Exploit kits continue to evolve at a much faster pace than the people defending and using the systems can respond.[17]

The most common attack vectors to exploit vulnerabilities and spread malicious code are "spear phishing" by sending an email to a specific person in the hope they will run a malicious attachment or click a malicious link, or by "drive by download" which occurs when visiting a compromised webpage.[18] These personalized attacks are difficult to prevent because they capitalize on human behaviors[19] such as trust, compassion, or curiosity.[20] More so, human behavioral trends and advanced technique trends are the reason that if targeted by an advanced attacker, a breach is inevitable. The following sections will examine the most successful attack methods by which malicious actors deliver a hostile payload or harmful outcome.

Spear Phishing

Social Engineering

It is almost certain that in a "spear phishing" campaign, some member of an organization will click upon a malicious attachment or link. The security firm Mandiant analyzed over eight million results of sanctioned phishing tests in 2015 to find that 30 percent of phishing messages were opened by the target and about 12 percent went on to click on the attachment or link.[21] The reason is because phishing attacks have evolved from mass emails with blatantly phony messages to lower volume and highly targeted emails that appear more legitimate. The spear phishing attack process usually starts by hackers gathering intelligence on targets from social networking websites; then they compromise a legitimate domain familiar to the target to gain access to a reputable email address, from which they send a socially engineered email to the target recipient. A large percentage of recipients act on the email by clicking on a malicious attachment or an embedded URL (web address) that links to a legitimate but compromised website that downloads exploits and malware.[22] Cyber criminals send messages to customers that appear to come from a company's domain. For the health-care, banking, and payments industry, malicious emails trick people into sharing sensitive information with hackers, leading to identity theft, while eroding customer trust.[23]

Spear phishing lures unsuspecting people to act or provide information via seemingly trustworthy electronic communications. In some cases victims are asked to input their login credentials and they comply on what are fake sites. Arguably one of the most notable examples of phishing success is seen in the Operation Aurora attacks in 2010 on Google, Adobe, and over thirty other US corporations. Hackers used a high level of target profiling and social engineering to employ fake but personalized emails to trick employees and ultimately download malware which exploited a zero-day vulnerability (also not yet patched) in Internet Explorer.[24] Today's spear phishing attacks are more sophisticated in content, and even more effective. For instance, the technique was used to penetrate the unclassified networks of both the White House in 2014[25] and the US Joint Staff in 2015.[26] Also today, the volume of attack attempts are astonishingly high and nefarious, as the number of phishing emails reached 6.3 million in the first quarter of 2016, with 93 percent containing ransomware.[27]

Watering Hole

Web-Based Attack

Watering hole attacks have advantages over spear phishing, such as the ability to bypass email filtering security technologies.[28] These web-based attacks, sometimes referred to as "strategic web compromise," occur when malicious actors infect a legitimate website with malware by SQL injection attack or some other means for the purpose of targeting visitors of that site. In a watering hole attack, the individual target does not need to be socially engineered into acting; instead all that is required is for a website of interest to a target group to be compromised and the attacker to wait like a predatory tiger for its prey. State-sponsored hackers use watering hole attacks to compromise large groups within the same industry, like an attack on the IHS.com website, that is the parent of Jane's Information Group and other sources of military, intelligence, or political analysis, by the Chinese state-sponsored group known as "FlowerLady." When users visited the compromised site, a PlugX file was downloaded onto the victim's machine and within ten seconds this Remote Access Trojan received commands and sent data to an attacker-controlled domain. Although users can be trained to detect spear phishing, there is no way for the user to recognize a compromised and legitimate popular website. [29]

Exploits of zero-day vulnerabilities are occasionally deployed in watering hole attacks, such as the incident of a newly uncovered flaw in Internet Explorer served up through the US Veterans of Foreign War's website. [30] In a similar incident, two zero-day vulnerabilities, this time in Adobe Flash and Internet Explorer, were leveraged in a watering hole attack on the Forbes website. The Chinese hacking group Codoso infected the "Thought of the Day" widget with the intent to perform "drive by download" attacks. [31] For days only certain visitors who clicked on the widget were redirected to another site where their computers could be infected with malware. The attack targeted only companies within the defense industry and financial services industries despite the broad audience of the Forbes site. [32] Although attackers must compromise a legitimate website in this attack vector, surprisingly scans of public websites have found that 16 percent are vulnerable enough to allow attackers to access and alter website content, signifying watering hole attacks are not going away. [33]

Point-of-Sale

RAM Scraping

Headlines of breaches at several large retailers through point-of-sale (POS) intrusions highlight the use of low-cost malware available on criminal forums to achieve disproportionate financial gains without any substantial risk of real-time activity detection. This vector begins with the compromise of a POS device (terminals where customers swipe a payment card at a checkout counter) that is open to the Internet and protected with weak or default passwords, by issuing likely credentials (called Brute force) to access the device. [34] Or the vendor using the POS is compromised by an email or web attack lure. Then RAM (Remote Access Memory) scrapper malware is installed which captures payment card data while processed in memory before it is encrypted for storage or transmission. The data is written to a text file which is later sent to an offsite server. [35] This credit or debit card data is usually offered for sale on the Dark Web. [36] Often discovery of the payment card breach does not occur until the criminals are noticed to be using the data for fraud and other illicit purposes by law enforcement or fraud detection entities. Payment card track data is more valued in the criminal marketplace than just names, numbers, dates, and codes because it can be used to manufacture counterfeit credit cards.[37]

In the point-of-sale breach at US–based retailer Target in late 2013, actors were able to steal data for as many as seventy million credit card and debit card accounts.[38] Within weeks of the breach, underground markets were flooded with stolen account information, selling in batches of one million cards and going from $20 to more than $100 per card.[39] The malware that infected POS devices was a hybrid of Kaptoxa and Reedum, both derived from the BlackPOS code sold on cybercrime forums. The BlackPOS malware is small in size, is designed to bypass firewall software, and costs only $2,300.[40] The malware continuously scanned the memory of infected devices for patterns that looked like payment card numbers and logged them to a file that was transferred to an internal server at regular intervals until exfiltrated to external servers. Target confirmed the encrypted PINs (personal identification numbers) of payment cards were stolen in the breach; however, they felt confident they were secure because the PIN cannot be decrypted without the right key, at least until attempts were noticed on underground hacking forums to decrypt a large batch of PIN numbers belonging to the Target breach.[41] In 2015, headline-making remote payment card breaches shifted from large retailers to hotel chains.[42] Twenty hotels in the HEI Hotels and Resorts group, including Marriott, Hyatt, Le Meridien, Sheraton, Westin and the Intercontinental chains, reported payment card data hacks by POS malware from December 2015 to June 2016.[43]

Web Application

SQL Injection

Web application attacks are typically against an organization's internet facing applications. In 2014, 26 percent of observed web application attacks were injection style, such as SQL injection. This vector allows attackers to exploit a web application vulnerability to access or change data. This means they type computer code in the fields of a web form input box, instead of something like a last name or credit card number. The technique takes advantage of applications that don't correctly validate requests before passing them to back-end databases.[44] The SQL commands can dupe the database system into running code that outputs sensitive information, like intellectual property or customer accounts. The SQL code can also allow the attacker to steal the site's administrator password, manipulate data enabling for example the defacement of the website, or compromise the site to host malware for "drive by download" by visitors. The risk of SQL injection is compounded by automated tools that detect and exploit web application vulnerabilities, such as the open source tool Sqlmap or the Iranian built tool Havij.[45] Comprehensive features make Havij stand out from other tools, such as capabilities to bypass security products, like web application firewalls or intrusion detection systems. [46]

An institute study in 2014 of the SQL injection threat revealed that 65 percent of the organizations surveyed experienced an SQL injection attack that successfully evaded their perimeter defenses in the last twelve months. [47] Famous breaches by SQL injection include at Heartland Payment Systems, Sony, Nokia, and Adobe where an attacker dumped a database of 150,000 emails and passwords of Adobe customers and partners. [48] The Navy Marine Corps Intranet network, consisting of 800,000 users at 2,500 locations, was also deeply penetrated by SQL injection in 2013. Hackers entered through a Navy website available to the public and found their way to unprotected databases. [49] Even the NASDAQ Stock Exchange fell victim to an SQL injection in a global hacking operation. One hacker identified a vulnerability in a password-reminder page of the NASDAQ website, crafted a text string that injected SQL programming code and obtained encrypted login credentials. [50] While never penetrating the main servers supporting trading operations, the hacking ring eventually had enough information to perform network or systems administrator functions on the servers. [51]

Distributed Denial of Service

DDoS Methods

Distributed Denial of Service (DDoS) attacks are popular because of access to high performance virtual machines, massive botnets, and service offerings. Assailants can perform the attacks with a high probability of success and a low probability of getting caught. DDoS attacks typically flood a target server with thousands of communication requests originating from multiple compromised machines known as a botnet. DDoS assaults serve a variety of purposes, such as to make social or political statements or take down or interrupt government or commercial sites in cybered conflict. DDoS attacks are also used as a part of multivector blended attacks or as a distraction mechanism. For example, during a large barrage on a victim's server, an attacker can conduct an SQL injection, hoping the noise covers the hack attempt. [52] Or in a hack on financial services institution accounts, a DDoS attack can flood the bank's network and keep the IT department busy while criminals transfer funds and cover their tracks. [53] For instance, in the Dyre Wolf malware campaign, a cybercrime gang based in Eastern Europe distracted banks with DDoS attacks that shut down websites to draw attention away from wire transfers to their offshore accounts. [54]

There are two types of DDoS attacks, either a network centric attack that uses up bandwidth or application layer attack which overloads a service. [55] In a volumetric attack targeting the network and transport layers,[56] large amounts of data packets and other traffic consume all of the network and server's available resources. These attacks cause traffic congestion and service disruption for legitimate users trying to gain access. Volumetric attacks are getting larger, more sophisticated and lasting for longer durations. Many of the large-scale DDoS attacks, of nearly 400 Gbps, use reflection and amplification techniques through the network time protocol (NTP) or domain name system (DNS).[57] Another example of an attack at the network layer is "Slowloris" that slowly delivers request headers, forcing the web server to keep connections open, without ever completing the requests, whereas in an application layer attack, a web application vulnerability or feature is exploited when attacks that mimic legitimate user traffic overwhelm a server or database powering the application.[58] An illustration of an application database attack is "Abuse of Functions" where blasting bad password requests locks out legitimate users because of a restricted number of failed logins.[59]

MALICIOUS ACTORS AND MOTIVATIONS

A complex audience exists that needs to be deterred, ranging from non-state actors, such as Anonymous, to rising, increasingly aggressive large-scale state actors. As of late 2016, more than 30 nation-states, many hostile to Western values, are developing offensive cyber attack capabilities. The rampant proliferation of cyber capabilities will allow standoff and remote operations, especially in the initial phases of military operations in conflict. Cyber attacks against information networks and critical infrastructure can bypass traditional defenses, disrupt command and control, and undermine political will. Most concerning are state adversaries with sophisticated capabilities that could be prone to conduct preemptive attack and rapid escalation.[60] Non-state actors will exploit advanced technologies for nefarious purposes. For example, hacker groups will use cyber operations to advance their political or social cause while criminal organizations will use persistent capabilities for theft or extortion. Furthermore, terrorist groups will use Internet-based technology to incite fear and facilitate operations.

A plethora of cyber incidents reveal that malicious actors employ attack vectors in a systematic, coordinated fashion in an attempt to achieve their objectives. Criminal organizations and terrorist groups are mostly *bad actors* with average to good skills, while nation-states and hacker groups, are considered to be *wicked actors* that have exquisite skills, high threat-enduring motivations, and the ability to organize to create deep harm. The globally unfettered structure of the cyber substrate offers asymmetric advantages in the scale, proximity, and precision of actor attacks. Actors can scale their attack organization from five to five thousand other internet users, can operate at any proximity to their targets from five to five thousand miles away, and can target with any level of precision from one entity, five individuals, or entire systems.[61] A clandestine black market provides malicious actors with powerful and easy-to-use sets of tools and services for all manner of theft, exploitation, disruption and destruction, in some cases with little or no technical skills required.[62]

Malicious actors have in-house attack capabilities or can contract with hackers for hire. Professional hackers have access to illicit websites that traffic tools and talent, such as Darkode, a sophisticated English language Internet forum. Darkode offers exploit kits, botnets, ransomware programs and zero-day attack tools.[63] Even though Darkode was shut down by the FBI, in less than two weeks the forum was rebuilt with new security measures.[64] Bulletproof hosting services (BPHS) shield these sorts of malicious sites that sell or trade malware, security exploits, and also stolen personal and financial data. BPHS protects malicious sites by appearing as a legitimate service provider to avoid suspicion and by residing in countries with lax law enforcement jurisdiction if exposed.[65] These illicit, inherent, and intrinsic advantages allow actors to operate with little risk of repercussion. To better understand the challenges in influencing malicious actor decisions to benefit from these advantages, the following section will investigate their motivations for employing doctrine and capabilities in actual cyber incidents.

Nation-States

North Korea

According to a report by HP Security Research, Leader Kim Jong-un has referred to cyber warfare capabilities as "a magic weapon" in conjunction with nuclear weapons and missiles.[66] He has poured resources into the next generation of the weapons of warfare—skills in hacking and computer science.[67] Consequently the South Korean Defense Ministry has reported that North Korea has a six-thousand member Cyber Army.[68] Several of the Cyber Army divisions have been ordered to secure critical data on weapons development from nuclear armed states, particularly in nuclear warhead miniaturization and ballistic missile technology.[69] One of the units, 121, of the General Bureau of Reconnaissance is suspected in particular by US investigators of being behind the attack on Sony Pictures and by South Korea for staging a series of disruptive attacks in Seoul.[70] For North Korea, cyber warfare is considered to be the modern chapter of asymmetrical warfare, intended to offset aging and declining conventional capabilities.[71] For instance in June 2016, North Korean hackers stole wing designs for the F-15, a US fighter jet, from a South Korean company, in a campaign that exfiltrated more than forty thousand documents related to the defense industry.[72] Cyber warfare capabilities are an important asset for North Korea in the face of its perceived enemies, the United States and South Korea, who are both heavily dependent upon technological infrastructure for social, economic, and political stability.

North Korea's cyber activity appears to follow a distinct pattern, either around the time of US–South Korean joint military exercises, correlated with a significant date, or in response to political events. For instance, following the UN emergency meeting condemning the North Korean underground nuclear test in May 2009 and subsequent South Korean joining of the Proliferation Security Initiative, called an act of war by the North, a wave of attacks struck South Korean and US government entities, coinciding with the Fourth of July, the US Independence Day. The DDoS attacks saturated target websites, like the White House, Defense Department, and New York Stock Exchange in the United States and the presidential Blue House, Defense Ministry and National Assembly in South Korea, with access requests for several hours.[73] In March 2011, after US testimony on undeclared North Korean uranium enrichment facilities, almost thirty South Korean media, financial, and critical infrastructure targets suffered a DDoS and disk-wiping malware attack.[74] Next, the third example of this pattern occurred in March 2013, after the United States and South Korea began their annual joint military exercise near the North Korean Peninsula, with cyber attacks upon the South Korean Shinhan Bank and NongHyup Bank, and television media outlets, YTN, MBC, and KBS. The organizations were crippled as data was lost and machines were unable to reboot.[75] The pattern continued at the start of similar military drills in March 2016, when South Korea's National Intelligence Service accused Pyongyang of attempting hacks into government websites and smartphones.[76]

The North Korean pattern of behavior indicates state-sponsored cyber actors launch attacks in response to a political trigger perceived to be a threat to the regime. The nation's official political ideology of *juche*, which emphasizes maintaining self-reliance and displaying one's strength, provides context for the regime's motivations. *Juche* places the survival of the regime as its primary goal and therefore any perceived threat to the regime may be targeted.[77] The regime fears losing control of the populace to outside cultural and political influence, as shown in its reaction to the film *The Interview* that portrayed their leader as sadistic. A statement by a spokesman for the Ministry of Foreign Affairs called the comedy film "an act of war that we will never tolerate" and vowed "a decisive and merciless countermeasure" if "the United States administration tacitly approves or supports the release of this film."[78] Obviously the attack upon Sony Pictures five months later should not have come as a surprise. The leaders of the North Korean regime appear committed to demonstrate the illusion of a powerful entity through destructive and coercive cyber attacks at no matter what cost of irresponsible behavior.[79]

Iran

Similar to North Korea, cyber doctrine in Iran relies heavily on asymmetrical warfare tactics. However, in contrast to the use of military units by North Korea, Iran leverages hacker crews as a force multiplier to make up for the lack of military capability.[80] Given Iran's long history of employing proxies for terrorist acts, there is little reason to think Iran would hesitate to engage proxy groups for cyber attacks against perceived adversaries.[81] Several pro-Iran hacker groups share common traits in they view Western entities and Israel as enemies, are heavily influenced by Islamic principles, make their exploits public, and associate with one another. The most renowned vigilante groups are the Iranian Cyber Army, the Islamic Cyber Resistance Group, and the Ashiyane Digital Security Team who has apparent ties to Iran's premier Sharif University.

Iranian hacker crews are used in reaction to political events. For example in August 2012, when the European Union decided to boycott Iranian oil exports, the Iranian activist group Cutting Sword of Justice took credit for attacking Saudi Aramco Oil Company with the Shamoon malware. Analysts suspect Iran may have commissioned the attack to exert influence after the Kingdom's oil minister pledged to boost production to compensate for the sanctions.[82] Then in September, a hacker group called Izz ad-Din al-Qassam Cyber Fighters took credit for denial of service attacks on six major American banks. Al-Qassam announced the attacks on Pastebin, criticizing Israel and the United States and citing the film *Innocence of Muslims* that mocks the Prophet Muhammad as motivation for the attacks. The group's Operation Ababil caused Internet blackouts and delays in online banking.[83] Three months later, the group Parastoo, linked to an Iranian Special Forces unit, hacked the computer servers of the International Atomic Energy Agency (IAEA) involved in the contentious inspections of Iranian facilities. Parastoo published sensitive diagrams, satellite photos, and other documents pilfered from IAEA servers.[84]

Similar to North Korea's cyber strategy but different again from their use of military units, Iranian hacker crews are also being used to position the nation to impact critical infrastructure on a global scale. An advanced malware campaign named Operation Cleaver waged against an array of targets indicates Iranian motivations to extract sensitive materials and establish beachheads for sabotage. The name Cleaver is a string of code found several times in custom software used in the attacks. An Iranian team dubbed Tarh Andishan has compromised more than fifty victims in sixteen countries in the operation. Networks and systems have been targeted in critical industries, like energy, utilities, airlines and transportation, and companies such as aerospace and telecommunications. For attribution, an IP (Internet protocol) address in Iran was found to be used by one of the primary attackers to conduct

SQL injections, control backdoors, and exflitrate information. Also, domains used in the campaign were registered in Iran and the infrastructure was hosted by an Iranian provider.[85] The state-sponsored campaign's objectives may be to use sensitive data taken from critical infrastructure companies to damage control systems. As the only nation to actually suffer a catastrophic cyber attack, namely Stuxnet blamed on the United States and Israel, Iran may have the will to intentionally conduct this sort of cyber mayhem, or the capability to inadvertently do so as well.[86]

China

The Chinese government's engagement in cyber espionage for commercial advantage was exposed in May 2014, when the US Justice Department charged five People's Liberation Army (PLA) officers with hacking into five US companies to steal trade secrets.[87] This type of espionage under dispute threatens business interests in key industries, especially if the Chinese government provides state-owned enterprises with extracted information to improve their competitive edge, cut research and development timetables, and reduce cost.[88] The PLA officers in the indictment work for Unit 61398, also known as APT1 (an APT group), which has penetrated the networks of at least 141 organizations in 15 countries.[89] Another global campaign run by another APT group from China that appears to steal information beneficial to Chinese companies is named NetTraveler.[90] This group doesn't use zero-day attacks but instead exploits two well-known vulnerabilities in Microsoft Office. Their attacks start with spear phishing emails using attachments rigged with the Office exploits. Their malware infected more than 350 victims in 40 countries, allowing theft of more than 22 gigabytes of data.[91] The domains of interest the group sought were space exploration, nanotechnology, energy production, nuclear power, lasers, medicine, and communications.[92] These sorts of attacks lead the director of the US Defense Intelligence Agency to warn that America's technological edge over China is at risk.[93]

Compared to espionage in peacetime, Chinese military doctrine in wartime calls for computer network operations to disrupt and damage the networks of an adversary's infrastructure facilities, such as power and telecommunications systems.[94] The finding of an intrusion in a honeypot resembling the industrial control system of a water plant in the United States, attributed to Unit 61398 in July 2013, indicates ongoing intelligence collection on critical infrastructure.[95] Chinese military analysts have also concluded that logistics and power projection are potential vulnerabilities in modern warfare.[96] The cases described by US Senate investigators of China breaking into computer networks of private transportation companies working for the US military appear to be an attempt to prepare the digital battlefield for a potential conflict.[97] Chinese intrusions into the networks of US defense contractors and industries threaten military operations, equipment and readiness. In May 2013, the *Washington Post* described a classified report by the Defense Science Board, which lists more than twenty-four US weapon systems accessed by Chinese intruders, to include the Aegis ballistic missile defense system, the F/A-18 tactical fighter jet, the V-22 Osprey vertical takeoff aircraft, and the multi-mission Littoral Combat Ship.[98] After Chinese hackers infiltrated Lockheed Martin's network, it is no wonder the new Chinese J-31 jet aircraft strikingly resembles the low observable features of the F-35 Joint Strike Fighter under production by the United States and its allies.[99]

Ongoing cyber operations by China mirror "its leadership's priorities of economic growth, domestic political stability and military preparedness" according to the US Director of National Intelligence.[100] Ensuring the obtainment of these priorities through cyber activity supports the expansion of comprehensive national power which perpetuates Chinese Communist Party rule.[101] Maintaining economic growth involves industrial cyber espionage of US and other foreign targets; domestic stability occurs through information control and propaganda; and preparing for military scenarios consists of military modernization and computer network operations. The actions of Chinese hackers appear consistent with these efforts to increase national power and prestige.[102] Likewise, foreign policy and military developments over the past several years indicate that cyber operations are a high priority for the Chinese government. China's most recent Defense White Paper noted that cyberspace is a "new domain of national security and area of strategic competition."[103] Therefore in the foreseeable future, Chinese behavior in cyberspace may not change in intentions unless major shifts occur in regional politics or incentives change the calculus of risk.[104]

Russia

Although China is the object of US allegations of cyber spying, the US Director of National Intelligence said, "I worry a lot more about the Russians."[105] This avowal is partly because of the Russian government's ability to covertly team with business and criminal entities to generate cyber capabilities that threaten perceived opponents. Clues of this nexus emerged in April 2007 in the DDoS attack on Estonia during riots over the movement of a Soviet World War II memorial from the city center and in Georgia in August 2008 during armed conflict with the Russian Federation over South Ossetia. The assault against the webpages of Estonian government ministries, financial institutions, and media outlets came from a botnet associated with a Russian cybercrime group operating from St. Petersburg, with links to the Russian Business Network.[106] The command and control servers used to issue attack commands on Georgian websites, after Russian ground troops engaged Georgian forces, were registered through a BPHS provider in Russia and the domains were hosted by a business front for cybercrime activities. [107] In both of these incidents, Russian-language Internet forums posted instructions, malware, and targets for patriotic hackers to participate in the campaign, [108] although in the 2014 Crimea incursion, Russian did not use the same playbook. First, the Nashi youth organization that participated in attacks in both Estonia and Georgia is no more, and second, regarding forums recruiting volunteers, many Russian hackers support an independent Ukraine. [109] Instead, Russia relied on the nationalist hacking group CyberBerkut to run a disinformation campaign to stir unrest. [110] Throughout 2015, in the continued state conflict, CyberBerkut conducted DDoS attacks against multiple German and Ukrainian government websites and nationalist Ukrainian rivals. [111]

Russian actors have engaged in challenging international norms in cyberspace. [112] In the area of intelligence collection, the government has benefited from a campaign by a group known as APT28, or Fancy Bear. [113] This group, unlike Chinese actors, does not appear to conduct intellectual property theft for economic gain, but collects information on defense and geopolitical issues. APT28 has been engaged in espionage against targets in the Caucasus, Eastern Europe, and European security organizations. It uses spear phishing to target its victims with emails that mention specific topics or lures relevant to recipients, written in local languages. The group also registers domains that mimic those of legitimate news, politics, or other websites of topics relevant to particular targets, from which to download malware and gain backdoor system access for reconnaissance, monitoring, and theft. APT28 attempts to obfuscate code, [114] implement counter-analysis techniques and encrypt stolen information during exfiltration. [115] Researchers made a connection to the Russian government because the malware was written during working hours in Russia's major cities, on computers with Russian language settings, and for targets aligned with Russian interests. [116] Apparently Fancy Bear continues to seek information on political matters for Russian intelligence, since the malware obfuscation techniques discovered in the DNC hack in April 2016 have been attributed to the group. [117] The APT28 exposure of Russia's cyber espionage operations is not the first, as another spear phishing campaign known as Red October was unveiled in 2012 targeting diplomatic entities mainly in Eastern Europe and Central Asia. [118]

Although discovery of cyber espionage is disturbing enough, Russia appears to be preparing for computer network attacks against Western critical infrastructure. At least one government-sponsored APT group, named Energetic Bear, alternatively known as Dragonfly, has infected industrial control systems of energy-related companies. [119] Dragonfly began targeting US and European energy grid operators, electricity generation firms, and petroleum pipeline operators in early 2013 with three infection tactics. The earliest method was by spear phishing emails to selected executives containing a malicious PDF attachment, then the watering hole compromise of energy industry and control system–related websites, and finally the infection of legitimate software packages available for download by three different industrial control system equipment providers. Dragonfly uses both custom-built and underground market–available malware to access and control compromised computers.[120] The group has not only provided its state sponsor with persistent access for spying, but also with sabotage capabilities that could cause disruption to energy supplies in the event of cybered conflict.

United States

After revelation that the United States pierced the networks of the Chinese telecommunications company Huawei to conduct surveillance,[121] a Huawei senior executive in the United States said, "The irony is that exactly what they are doing to us is what they have always charged that the Chinese are doing through us."[122] This assertion prompted President Obama to tell Chinese President Xi at a meeting in The Hague that the United States, unlike China, does not use its technological powers to steal corporate data and give the data to its own companies; instead, its spying is solely for national security priorities.[123] Three other discoveries support this spying contention based on the alleged implication of the United States to the Stuxnet intrusion upon Iranian nuclear enrichment facilities.[124] The first is the data-mining *Flame* virus that shares portions of its code with the Stuxnet malware, for instance, exploiting vulnerabilities in the same printing routine. Flame was found to have infiltrated thousands of computers in Iran and the adjacent areas in 2012. The virus copied keyboard entries, sifted through emails and text messages, captured screen shots, and recorded microphone sounds.[125] Although Iranian leaders claimed the massive data loss caused by Flame to be tantamount to an attack, in defense of the US position on allowable surveillance, if guilty, Flame should only be considered an act of digital espionage, not defined or prohibited in international law.[126]

Circumstantial evidence also associates the United States with the Gauss virus found in 2012 on some 2,500 computers, largely in Lebanon.[127] A notable security firm said they were confident the Gauss virus was written by the same programmers who created Flame, by extension linked to Stuxnet, because of significant similarities in code and architecture, to include C++ computer language and encryption methods.[128] The Gauss virus, so-called because of this name in its code, acquired logins for email as well as instant messaging, social accounts, and financial transactions. In this case the targeting of banking customers was likely American cyber espionage against the Syrian regime and the Hezbollah organization.[129] The last revelation is the Duqu virus infiltration, which is named for files used by its key logger to store collected data such as DQx.tmp.[130] Duqu was detected in 2011 to be mining data from Hungarian and Iranian computers. Commonalities in the drivers suggest the Duqu and Stuxnet programs were created by the same platform and that early versions of Duqu gathered intelligence for the Stuxnet operation.[131]

Although deductive reasoning suggests that the four computer viruses which surfaced in the Middle East in three years were state-sponsored because they share a common architectural platform, it is possible the code was made available underground and repurposed or reused by other actors. That possibility is refuted by Kaspersky researchers in an analysis and comparison of code for advanced hacking tools stolen from the National Security Agency in August 2016,[132] to malware code used by the Equation Group that Ars Technica has attributed to both Stuxnet and Flame. The fact the code is functionally identical and shares specific traits demonstrates that Equation Group had clear connections to the National Security Agency.[133] The hard reality that the four cyber incidents are affiliated with the United States actually lends credence to the White House press secretary's declaration that US "intelligence programs serve a specific national security mission."[134]

Hacker Groups

The Syrian Electronic Army (SEA) supports the state government in a nebulous arrangement. Based in Syria since 2011, with accomplices in Germany,[135] the SEA has hacked and defaced over forty sites to voice political sentiments in support of the Assad regime. They gain access to blog or social media accounts and use that medium to spread propaganda. SEA tactics include setting up fake Facebook and YouTube sites to collect login credentials and compromising websites with the automated SQL injection exploit tool Havij.[136] In one defacement, SEA sent phishing emails to employees containing a link to a website that mimicked a news agency's external email login page. After gaining compromised accounts, the SEA targeted email distribution lists to obtain credentials of users with access to the company's content management system, from which SEA could deface news articles. The SEA also gained access to a marketing email account to reset the agency's Twitter password and send unauthorized tweets.[137] One of their most famous attacks was the takeover of the Associated Press Twitter account via phishing in April 2013 and subsequent tweeting a message that a bomb exploded in the White House injuring President Obama, which temporarily plunged the Dow.[138] One Syrian hacker claims the state pays the SEA to work for them.[139]

A clearer example of a hacker group for hire, but in this case for the theft of research information and military secrets, is the Appin Security Group in India. This group of talented hackers is suspected of targeting organizations in Pakistan, China, Norway, and the United States.[140] The attackers leveraged already-patched vulnerabilities in products like Microsoft Word and Oracle's Java and did not use malware that employs techniques to evade detection, such as obfuscation or encryption, indicating they saw no need to implement advanced techniques because simple ways worked.[141] On the other hand, the APT group named Hidden Lynx is a professional team with more advanced capabilities that appears to offer the Chinese government a "hackers for hire" operation, since much of their attack infrastructure and tools originate in China. Since 2011, this APT has used primarily watering hole and spear phishing attacks to target hundreds of commercial and government organizations worldwide in concurrent campaigns. The most heavily sought industry has been financial services, particularly investment banks and asset management agencies to gain competitive information, and also the defense industry in pursuit of confidential information.[142]

The hacker group *Anonymous* is a self-proclaimed Internet movement with a decentralized structure that "operates on ideas rather than directives."[143] Their collective motivation to express dissent over perceived injustices was first revealed in Operation Payback in 2010. When PayPal, Visa and MasterCard stopped processing payments to WikiLeaks, which publishes leaked documents on its website, Anonymous called the actions an affront to Internet freedom and retaliated with DDoS attacks.[144] Average citizens, mostly from the United States, participated in a campaign to disable corporate websites, after downloading over 40,000 copies of software designed to flood websites.[145] However, Anonymous organizers realized the volunteer pool was insufficient and engaged two botnet masters to use their private collections of 75,000 and 50,000 compromised computers to create more damaging effects.[146] The subsequent arrest of fourteen individuals alleged to have participated in the attacks on PayPal's website brought a stern warning from FBI director Steve Chabinsky that "we want to send a message that chaos on the Internet is unacceptable."[147] In response, the global hacking collective stated, "Your threats to arrest us are meaningless to us as you cannot arrest an idea."[148]

In a further affirmation of how hard it is to deter all actors and activities in cyberspace, Anonymous has claimed to have "NO leader" and that "nothing is official," but to be everywhere "helping to give voices to the voiceless."[149] Anonymous has issued two "declarations of war." The first occurred in November 2015 when the hacktivist collective declared total war against the Islamic State after the terror attacks in Paris that killed over 130 people. In a video message posted in French, Anonymous announced the beginning of #OpParis, a campaign to find ISIS's social media channels and supporters online.[150] For starters, the group claimed to take down 20,000 ISIS-affiliated Twitter accounts to take revenge for the Paris attacks.[151] Twitter said the claim is inaccurate, as they do not review anonymous lists posted online.[152]

The second declaration of 'total war' was made in March 2016 on presidential candidate Donald Trump. A YouTube video accused the candidate of shocking "the entire planet with your appalling actions and ideas."[153] Anonymous urged the hacker community to take down Donald Trump's websites and expose damaging secrets. They even provided a list of applicable sites and personal information.

Criminal Organizations

The merge in criminal tactics and tools with state-sponsored or state-hired APT groups complicates analysis of actor objectives when interpreting technical behavior. For instance, according to one US official, differentiating between Russian criminal hackers and government hackers is difficult because they use cyber surveillance tools created by each other. The United States still has not figured out whether criminals or government hackers infiltrated a classified military system in 2008 because both employ the same cyber tool used in the incident.[154] Tactical overlap between malicious actor types exists in the use of spear phishing and interactive social engineering, the contacting of victims through popular social network data, in addition to the use of publicly available toolkits and the creation of custom-built malware.[155] Also, both actor types have found the attacking of a primary target through a secondary or tertiary service provider is one of the easiest avenues of compromise[156] For example, Eastern European hackers that stole forty million credit card numbers from the retail giant Target creatively used a third party to get into the Target Corporation network to install their malware. The breach began with an email phishing attack sent to employees at a heating, ventilation, and air conditioning firm that did business with the nationwide retailer. The criminals broke in and stole credentials Target had issued to the firm for electronic billing, contract submission, and project management to eventually access the corporate network that housed the card payment system.[157]

Whether based in Russia, China, Africa, the United States, or anywhere else on the globe, organized criminal syndicates, armed with innovative technologies and techniques, outwit stalwart cyber defenses. Criminals move fast to exploit flaws as evidenced in a data breach at Home Depot. Senior executives at the Hardware giant assembled a task force in the weeks after the data theft at Target Corporation to draw up a plan to avoid becoming a victim of a similar attack, although by the time Home Depot signed a contract to install new technology to fully encrypt payment card data, hackers had already cracked their payment system.[158] In September 2014, the company announced that criminals had used custom-built malware to put payment card information at risk for approximately fifty-six million payment cards. The company also released estimates for the cost of the breach in staffing and services at $62 million.[159] Similar to the Target breach, the hackers used a vendor's stolen log-on credentials to penetrate Home Depot's computer network and install malware on self-checkout registers. The use of stolen credentials from third parties is a continuing trend that has expanded to use of credentials from compromised outsourced IT service providers. Criminals can leverage the elevated privileges of the IT administrators to move throughout the victim's networks undetected.[160] By starting an attack inside the network, criminals bypass perimeter cyber defenses. The financial barrier for criminals to conduct cyber attacks continues to drop as underground forums offer sophisticated hacking and malware packages, including security software checking services for malware detection, at low costs.[161]

Terrorist Groups

Only one terrorist organization, namely the Islamic State in Syria and Iraq, or ISIS, has exploited the internet for campaign gains and conducted low-level cyber attacks. The Islamic State initially established a "Cyber Caliphate," with the aim of using jihadist developed encryption software to mount catastrophic hacking attacks on America and the West.[162] In January 2015, sympathizers of the Islamic State took control of the US Central Command Twitter accounts, changing the profile photo to a black-and-white image of a fighter wearing a Keffiyeh, or scarf, and posting at the top of the page "CyberCaliphate" and "i love you isis."[163] The hackers also posted tweets with phone numbers of officers, unclassified military scenarios, and threats against military members. Using the Command YouTube account, hackers also posted two videos, of attacks on US troops and of fighters wielding weapons. Although the Pentagon labeled this incident as little more "than a cyberprank," a senior congressman called the intrusion a cyberattack and "severely disturbing."[164]

Not unexpectedly, the terrorist group ISIS is trying to develop cyber capabilities "to carry out digital attacks on critical systems, like hospitals, air traffic controls and power plants."[165] Yet a threat report by the cyber security firm CrowdStrike assesses that the terrorist group most likely possesses only rudimentary intrusion capabilities to include keyloggers and network surveillance software for use in finding dissidents and spies. There is at least one attributable report of ISIS using primitive malware to locate dissident operatives in Syria. Overall because of published online content, CrowdStrike believes the terrorist group likely has "an adequate level of technical ability to successfully carry out offensive operations against targeted individuals.[166] That level could increase through the creation in April 2016 of a mega hacking unit called the United Cyber Caliphate, which combines the Cyber Caliphate Army, an ISIS hacking unit, with other pro-ISIS groups. The United Cyber Caliphate immediately stole and posted the names and addresses of over three thousand of the "most important citizens of #NewYork and #Brooklyn," asking sympathizers of the terror group to use the information to carry out lone-wolf attacks.[167] Likewise in June 2016, the United Cyber Caliphate released a "kill list" of around eight thousand individuals on the encrypted messaging app Telegram, with a message to "kill them strongly to take revenge for Muslims."[168]

SYSTEMIC CONSEQUENCES

Admiral Michael Rogers, the commander of U.S. Cyber Command, stated, "we expect state and unaffiliated cyber actors to become bolder and seek more capable means to affect us and our allies."[169] The *Islamic State* terrorist organization aims to affirm that statement with video threats of an all-out cyber crusade against the United States and Europe. Rogers worries that cyber means could give the terrorist group offensive capabilities to wage attacks, by using the Internet as "a vehicle to inflict pain against the United States and others."[170] Likewise, Rogers believes China, along with one or two other countries, already has cyber capabilities that could shut down the electric grid in parts of the United States.[171] These statements of potential malevolent cyber activity point to increasing risk to socio-technical-economic systems, making deterrence both more crucial and harder than ever.

Leadership at the US National Protection and Programs Directorate assert that "malicious actors, including those at nation-state level, are motivated by a variety of reasons that include espionage, political and ideological beliefs, and financial gain."[172] For APT28, exposed in the *Russia* section, their motivations appear to be expanding from just espionage, pertaining to defense and geopolitical issues that would be useful to a government, to financial gain, according to an industry report that uncovered plans by the threat group to attack international financial institutions. Most likely APT28 would use a spear-phishing campaign, their attack vector of choice, with well-crafted emails containing either a malicious file or web hyperlink to what recipients believe is an actual, but compromised, website.[173]

The seriousness of cyber attacks is rising, causing significant harm to security and damage to the economies of major Western nations. No one, it seems is immune, from health-care companies to the tech industry, critical infrastructure, and entertainment sector. Official government assessments parallel industry threat predictions about the looming security concerns. Small nation-states, like North Korea or Iran, are conducting cybered conflict by launching crippling distributed denial of service attacks or using malware to wipe computer master boot records. Long-term players, like China or Russia, are already using better methods to remain hidden on victims' networks. Similarly, sophisticated cyber criminals, like those from Eastern Europe, are adopting an APT approach to collect personal intelligence, looking and acting more like nation-state cyber espionage actors.[174] Even more troubling, renowned security expert Eugene Kaspersky has stated he is "really afraid some terrorist group will pay cyber criminals to develop and deploy [devastating] weapons on their behalf."[175] Finally, politically or socially motivated attacks will continue as hacker groups like Anonymous take advantage of showcase events on the world stage to promote their malevolent ideas.[176] The collective judgement is that attacks and campaigns will only grow in frequency and sophistication, as malicious actors develop and use new "cyber-attack vectors" in multiple-stage attacks[177] to exploit vulnerabilities all across the socio-technical-economic systems of defending nations to illegally or coercively obtain political, economic or military advantages. Deterrence is preferable to kinetic war as the losses through cyberspace grow. The difficulty is that current theories and tools of deterrence are overchallenged by the magnitude of the near term.

NOTES

1. National Institute of Standards and Technology, "Glossary of Key Information Security Terms," NISTIR 7298 Revision 2, May 2013, 11.

2. Chris Demchak, *Wars of Disruption and Resilience: Cybered Conflict, Power, and National Security* (Athens: University of Georgia Press, September 2011).

3. Michael S. Rogers, Statement before the House Committee on Armed Services, March 4, 2015.

4. James R. Clapper, "Worldwide Threat Assessment of the US Intelligence Community," Statement for the Record for the Senate Armed Services Committee, February 26, 2015, 1–3.

5. Ponemon Institute, "2014 Global Report on the Cost of Cyber Crime," Research Report, October 2014, 1–29.

6. CyberEdge Group, "2015 Cyberthreat Defense Report: North America and Europe," March 2015, 1–18.

7. Robert Wall and Alexis Flynn, "NSA Chief Expects More Cyberattacks Like OPM Hack," *Wall Street Journal*, July 15, 2015.

8. Kevin Mandia, "Advanced Cyber Threats Facing Our Nation," Written Testimony before the Permanent Select Committee on Intelligence, U.S. House of Representatives, February 14, 2013, 1–3.

9. Nick Woltman, "Cyber-Security Expert Kevin Mandia Addresses Local Business Leaders," Live Events, twincities.com, February 20, 2014.

10. Peter Dombrowski and Chris Demchak, "Cyber War, Cybered Conflict, and the Maritime Domain," *Naval War College Review* (April 1, 2014): 83.

11. Kevin G. Coleman, "The Cyber Commander's eHandbook: The Strategies and Tactics of Digital Conflict," version 4, Technolytics (2013): 55–81.

12. United States Computer Emergency Readiness Team, "TA16-091A: Ransomware and Recent Variants," National Cyber Awareness System, March 31, 2016, 1–4.

13. Websense, "2015 Threat Report," White Paper, Websense Security Labs, 2015, 5.

14. Solutionary, "Global Threat Intelligence Report," 2015 NTT Group, 15–27.

15. Solutionary, "Global Threat Intelligence Report," 2016 NTT Group, 13–14.

16. Websense, "The Seven Stages of Advanced Threats," White Paper, Websense Security Labs, 2013, 2.

17. Nick Lewis, "Exploit Kits Evolved: How to Defend against the Latest Attack Toolkits," Tech Target, August 31, 2015.

18. David Emm, "The Threat Landscape," Kaspersky Lab, 2013.

19. Symantec, "Fraud Alert: Phishing— The Latest Tactics and Potential Business Impacts," White Paper, 2014, 1–8.

20. Greg Otto, "Research Looks at Why Phishing Attacks Are So Hard to Avoid," *FedScoop*, August 4, 2016, http://fedscoop.com/phishing-attacks-email-facebook-black-hat-2016.

21. Verizon, "2016 Data Breach Investigations Report," May 2016, 18.

22. Websense, "Defending against Today's Targeted Phishing Attacks," White Paper, 2012, 1–5.

23. Agari, "The State of Email Trust 2014," White Paper, 2014, 1–8.

24. Mathew J. Schwartz, "Leaked Cables Indicate Chinese Military Hackers Attacked U.S." *Information Week*, April 19, 2011.

25. Evan Perez and Shimon Prokupecz, "How the U.S. Thinks Russians Hacked the White House, *CNN.com*, April 8, 2015.

26. David Martin, "Russian Hack Almost Brought the U.S. Military to Its Knees," *CBS News*, December 15, 2016, with initial report by Craig Whitlock and Missy Ryan, "U.S. suspects Russia in Hack of Pentagon Computer Network," *The Washington Post*, August 6, 2015.

27. Chloe Green, "93% of Phishing Emails Now Contain Ransomware," *Information Age*, security blog post, June 6, 2016.

28. Brandan Blevins, "Spear Phishing Still Popular, but More Watering Hole Attacks Coming," *Tech Target*, January 24, 2014.

29. News, "Water Hole Replacing Spear-Phishing as State-Sponsored Weapon of Choice," infosecurity-magazine.com, July 17, 2013.

30. Brandan Blevins, "FireEye Finds Active Watering Hole Attack Using IE Zero-Day Exploit," *Tech Target*, February 14, 2014.

31. Ericka Chickowski, "Chinese Hacking Group Codoso Team Uses Forbes.com as Watering Hole," *Dark Reading*, February 10, 2015.

32. Andrea Peterson, "Forbes Web Site Was Compromised by Chinese Cyberespionage Group, Researchers Say," *Washington Post*, February 10, 2015.

33. Symantec, "Internet Security Threat Report," vol. 19, April 2014, 34.

34. Verizon, "2014 Data Breach Investigations Report," June 2014, 16–18.

35. Websense, "Point-of-Sale Malware and the Seven Stages Attack Model," White Paper, Websense Security Labs, 2014, 1.

36. SurfWatch Labs, "Dark Web Situational Awareness Report," White Paper, 2015, 3.

37. CrowdStrike, "Global Threat Intel Report," 2014, 15.

38. Maggie McGrath, "Target Data Breach Spilled Info on as Many as 70 Million Customers," *Forbes*, January 10, 2014.

39. Brian Krebs, "Cards Stolen in Target Breach Flood Underground Markets," krebsonsecurity.com, December 20, 2013.

40. Brian Krebs, "A First Look at the Target Intrusion, Malware," krebsonsecurity.com, January 15, 2014.

41. Swati Khandelwal, "Hackers behind TARGET Data Breach Looking for Pro-cracker to Decrypt Credit Card PINs," thehackernews.com, January 10, 2014.

42. 2016 Data Breach Investigations Report, 31.

43. Warwick Ashford, "POS Malware Attacks Highlight Need for Security Standards in Hotel Industry," *Computer Weekly*, August 16, 2016.

44. Michael Cobb, "How to Prevent SQL Injection Attacks by Validating User Input," *Tech Target*, March 31, 2015.

45. Imperva, "An Anatomy of a SQL Injection Attack," Hacker Intelligence Summary Report, Monthly Trend Report #4, September 2011, 1–4.

46. Nick Lewis, "Defend against the SQL Injection Tool Havij, Other SQL Injection Tools," *Tech Target*, March 31, 2015.

47. Ponemon Institute, "The SQL Injection Threat Study," Research Report, April 2014.

48. Kelley Jackson Higgins, "Adobe Hacker Says He Used SQL Injection to Grab Database of 150,000 User Accounts," *Dark Reading*, November 14, 2012.

49. Siobhan Gorman, "Navy Hacking Blamed on Iran Tied to H-P Contract," *Wall Street Journal*, March 6, 2014.

50. Dan Goodwin, "NASDAQ Is Owned," Risk Assessment/Security and Hacktivism Blog, arstechnica.com, July 25, 2013.

51. Nathaniel Popper, "Wall Street's Exposure to Hacking Laid Bare," *New York Times*, July 25, 2013.

52. Stephen Lawton, "DDoS: Back in Vogue," ebook: An SC Magazine publication, Sponsored by f5, 2015, 1–9.

53. Rik Turner, "Tackling the DDoS Threat to Banking in 2014," Ovum, White Paper, January 27, 2014, 1–10.

54. Maxim Tamarov, "Dyre Malware Returns to Rob Banks of Millions," *Tech Target*, April 8, 2015.

55. Margaret Rouse, "Distributed Denial-of-Service Attack (DDoS)," *Tech Target*, March 31, 2015.

56. The Open Systems Interconnection model defines seven conceptual layers in a communications network.

57. Brandan Blevins, "Vendor Reports Largest-Ever NTP Reflection-Driven DDoS Attack," *Tech Target*, May 13, 2015.

58. Imperva, "The Top 10 DDoS Attack Trends," White Paper, 2015, 1–13.

59. Securosis, "Defending against Application Denial of Service Attacks," White Paper, Version 1.6, December 20, 2013, 1–12.

60. The Honorable James R. Clapper, et al., "Foreign Cyber Threats to the United States," Joint Statement for the Record to the Senate Armed Services Committee, 5 January 2017: 4.

61. Chris C. Demchak, "Resilience and Cyberspace: Recognizing the Challenges of a Global Socio-Cyber Infrastructure (GSCI)," *Journal of Comparative Policy Analysis: Research and Practice* (July 12, 2012): 263–65.

62. Cyveillance, "Intelligence for Security," White Paper, January 2015, 4.

63. Ellen Nakashima, "Major Computer Hacking Forum Shut Down by 20 Countries, U.S. Announces," *Washington Post*, July 15, 2015.

64. Michael Heller, "Darkode Criminal Forum Reborn Less Than Two Weeks after DOJ Shutdown," *Tech Target*, July 31, 2015.

65. Olivia Eckerson, "New Report Sheds Light on the Growing Threat of Bulletproof Hosting Services," *Tech Target*, August 5, 2015.

66. Brian Krebs, "FBI: North Korea to Blame for Sony Hack," krebsonsecurity.com, December 19, 2014.

67. Charlie Osborne, "A Glimpse into the World of North Korea's Hacking Elite," zdnet.com, December 5, 2014.

68. Associated Press, "South Korea: North Korea Has 6,000 Member Cyber Army," *ABC News*, January 6, 2015.

69. Jenny Jun, Scott LaFoy, and Ethan Sohn, "What Do We Know about Past North Korean Cyber Attacks and Their Capabilities?" Korea Chair Platform, Center for Strategic and International Studies, December 12, 2014, 1.

70. Jeyup S. Kwaak, "Sony Hack Shines Light on North Korea's Cyber Attackers," *Wall Street Journal*, December 17, 2014.

71. HP Security Research, "Profiling an Enigma: The Mystery of North Korea's Cyber Threat Landscape," HP Security Briefing Episode 16, August 2014.

72. Jack Kim, "North Korea Mounts Long-Running Hack of South Korean Computers, Says Seoul," *Reuters*, June 13, 2016, plus Alastair Gale and Kwanwoo Jun, "North Korean Hackers Stole F-15 Wing Designs, Seoul Says," *Wall Street Journal*, June 13, 2016.

73. "Governments Hit by Cyber Attack," *BBC News*, July 8, 2009.

74. "South Korea Hit by Cyber Attacks," *BBC News*, March 4, 2011.

75. Kelley Jackson Higgins, "Loud Data-Annihilation Cyberattacks Hit South Korean Banks, Media Outlets," *Dark Reading*, March 20, 2013.

76. Alastair Gale, "South Korea Accuses North of Hacking as Tensions Escalate," *Wall Street Journal*, March 7, 2016.

77. HP Security Research, "Profiling an Enigma."

78. Choe Sang-Hun, "North Korea Warns U.S. Over Film Mocking Its Leader: Kim Jong-un Declares 'War' on 'The Interview,'" *New York Times*, June 25, 2014.

79. Sung Kim, "The North Korean Threat: Nuclear, Missiles and Cyber," Testimony before the House Foreign Affairs Committee, Washington, DC, January 13, 2015.

80. HP Security Research, "Islamic Republic of Iran," HP Security Briefing Episode 11, February 2014.

81. Frank J. Cilluffo, "The Iranian Cyber Threat to the United States," Statement before the House of Representatives Committee on Homeland Security, April 26, 2012, 4.

82. Kelly Jackson Higgins, "Shamoon, Saudi Aramco, and Targeted Destruction," *Dark Reading*, August 22, 2012.

83. Nicole Perlroth, "Attacks on 6 Banks Frustrate Customers," *New York Times*, September 30, 2012.

84. Eli Lake, "Did Iran's Cyber-Army Hack into the IAEA's computers?" *The Daily Beast*, December 5, 2012.

85. Stuart McClure, Operation Cleaver, Cylance Report, December 2014.

86. Patrick Tucker, "Can Iran Turn off Your Lights?" *Defense One*, December 9, 2014.

87. US District Court, Indictment, Criminal No. 14-118, Filed May 1, 2014, 1–48.

88. Larry M. Wortzel, "Cyber Espionage and the Theft of U.S. Intellectual Property and Technology," Testimony before the House of Representatives, July 9, 2013, 7.

89. Mandiant, "APT1: Exposing One of China's Cyber Espionage Units," February 27, 2013.

90. Kaspersky Global Research and Analysis Team, "The NetTraveler (aka Travnet)," 2013, 1–25.

91. Kelly Jackson Higgins, "NetTraveler Cyberespionage Campaign Uncovered," *Dark Reading*, June 4, 2013.

92. GReAT, Kaspersky Lab Expert, "NetTraveler Is Running! Red Star APT Attacks Compromise High-Profile Victims," Securelist, June 4, 2013.

93. Associated Press, "Intel Chief Warns US Tech Threatened by China Cybertheft," *New York Times*, February 3, 2015.

94. Larry M. Wortzel, "Cyber Espionage and the Theft of U.S. Intellectual Property and Technology," Testimony before the House of Representatives, July 9, 2013, 4.

95. Larry M. Wortzel, "China's Military Modernization and Cyber Activities," *Strategic Studies Quarterly* (Spring 2014): 12.

96. US Secretary of Defense, "Annual Report to Congress: Military and Security Developments Involving the People's Republic of China," May 2013, 33.

97. Danny Yadron, "Chinese Hacked U.S. Military Contractors, Senate Panel Says Hackers Broke into Computer Networks 20 Times in a Year," *Wall Street Journal*, September 18, 2014.

98. Ellen Nakashima, "Confidential Report Lists U.S. Weapons System Designs Compromised by Chinese Companies," *Washington Post*, May 27, 2013.

99. Paul McLeary and David Francis, "Pentagon Says It Is Moving to Protect Its Cyber Flanks," Foreign Policy, The Cable Blog, April 9, 2015.

100. James R. Clapper, "Worldwide Threat Assessment of the US Intelligence Community," Statement for the Record, House Permanent Select Committee on Intelligence, February 4, 2014, 2.

101. US Secretary of Defense, "Annual Report to Congress: Military and Security Developments Involving the People's Republic of China," April 2015, 21.

102. James A. Lewis, "Economic Warfare and Cyberspace," *China's Cyberpower: International and Domestic Priorities*, Austrian Strategic Policy Institute, November 2014, 3–5.

103. US Secretary of Defense, "Annual Report to Congress: Military and Security Developments Involving the People's Republic of China," April 2016, 64.

104. Amy Chang, "Warring State: China's Cybersecurity Strategy," Center for a New American Security, December 2014, 7–8.

105. Danny Yadron and Siobhan Gorman, "Hacking Trail Leads to Russia, Experts Say," *Wall Street Journal*, October 28, 2014.

106. Binoy Kampmark, "Cyber Warfare Between Estonia and Russia," *Contemporary Review* (Autumn 2007): 288–93; and Iftach Ian Amit, "Cyber [Crime/War]: Linking State Governed Cyber Warfare with Online Criminal Groups," *Security and Innovation* (2010): 4.

107. Jeff Carr, "Russia/Georgia Cyber War—Findings and Analysis," Project Grey Goose: Phase I Report, October 17, 2008; and Iftach Ian Amit, "Cyber [Crime/War]: Linking State Governed Cyber Warfare with Online Criminal Groups," *Security and Innovation* (2010): 5.

108. Eneken Tikk, Kadri Kaska, and Liis Vihul, "International Cyber Incidents: Legal Considerations" (Tallinn, Estonia: NATO Cooperative Cyber Defence Centre of Excellence, 2009), 14–32, 66–76.

109. Jeffrey Carr, "Rival Hackers Fighting Proxy War over Crimea," *CNN Special*, March 25, 2104.

110. CrowdStrike, "Global Threat Intel Report," 2014, 25–27, John Bumgarner, "A Cyber History of the Ukraine Conflict," *Dark Reading*, March 27, 2014, and, Doug Bernard, "Russia-Ukraine Crisis Could Trigger Cyber War," *Voice of America*, April 20, 2014.

111. CrowdStrike, "Global Threat Intel Report," 2015, 24–29.

112. Ash Carter, Secretary of Defense, "2017 Defense Posture Statement: Taking the Long View, Investing for the Future," February 2016, 17.

113. CrowdStrike, "Global Threat Intel Report," 2014, 58–59.

114. Reza Hedayat and Lorenzo Cavallaro, "The Devil's Right Hand: An Investigation on Malware-Oriented Obfuscation Techniques," Royal Holloway, August 2016, 1–10.

115. FireEye, "APT28: A Window into Russia's Cyber Espionage Operations," Special Report, 2014, 1–28.

116. Nicole Perlroth, "Online Security Experts Link More Breaches to Russian Government," *New York Times*, October 29, 2014, B3.

117. Teri Robinson, "Guccifer 2.0 Out—Cozy Bear, Fancy Bear Hacked DNC, Fidelis Analysis Shows," SC Magazine, June 21, 2016, http://www.scmagazine.com/guccifer-20-out---cozy-bear-fancy-bear-hacked-dnc-fidelis-analysis-shows/printarticle/504441/.

118. Kelly Jackson Higgins, "Red October Attacks: The New Face of Cyberespionage," *Dark Reading*, January 14, 2013.

119. Khatuna Mshvidobadze, "Creeping Bear: The Growing Cyber Threat from Russia," *Jane's Defense Weekly*, December 17, 2014, 20.

120. Symantec, "Dragonfly: Cyberespionage Attacks against Energy Suppliers," Security Response, July 7, 2014.

121. "Targeting Huawei: NSA Spied on Chinese Government and Networking Firm," *Spiegel Online*, March 22, 2014.

122. David E. Sanger, "N.S.A. Breached Chinese Servers Seen as Security Threat," *New York Times*, March 22, 2014.

123. David E. Sanger, "U.S. Tries Candor to Assure China on Cyberattacks," *New York Times*, April 7, 2014.

124. David E. Sanger, "Obama Order Sped Up Wave of Cyberattacks against Iran," *New York Times*, June 1, 2012.

125. Jared Newman, "The Flame Virus: Your FAQs Answered," *PC World*, May 30, 2012.

126. Jason Koebler, "World Powers Play Blame Game with Flame Virus," *US News and World Report*, May 30, 2012.

127. Mathew J. Schwartz, "Gauss Espionage Malware: 7 Key Facts," *Information Week*, August 10, 2012.

128. Kaspersky Lab Global Research and Analysis Team, "Gauss: Abnormal Distribution," 2012, 1–10.

129. Nichole Perlroth, "Virus Seeking Bank Data Is Tied to Attack on Iran," *New York Times*, August 9, 2012.

130. Kenneth Rapoza, "Duqu Virus Likely Handiwork of Sophisticated Government, Kaspersky Lab Says," *Forbes*, October 21, 2011.

131. Robert Lemos, "Four Takeaways from the Stuxnet-Duqu Connection," *Information Week Reports*, February 2012, 7.

132. Ellen Nakashima, "Powerful NSA Hacking Tools Have Been Revealed Online," *Washington Post*, August 16, 2016.

133. Dan Goodwin, "Confirmed: Hacking Tool Leak Came from "Omnipotent" NSA-tied Group," Ars Technica, Risk Assessment, Blog Post, August 16, 2016.

134. Ashley Frantz and Paul Armstrong, "Beijing Denounces U.S. Hacking Charges against Chinese Army Officers," *CNN News*, May 20, 2014.

135. Graham Cluley, "Syrian Electronic Army Hacker Pleads Guilty after Sending Victim Scan of His Passport," Tripwire, The State of Security Blog, September 29, 2016.

136. HP Security Research, "Syrian Electronic Army," HPSR Threat Intelligence Briefing Episode 3, April 2013, 1–29.

137. Mandiant, "M Trends: Beyond the Breach," Alexandria, Virginia, April 2014, 5–6.

138. Max Fisher, "Syrian Hackers Claim AP Hack That Tipped Stock Market by $136 billion. Is It Terrorism?" *Washington Post*, April 23, 2013.

139. Seamus Mirodan, "Online Pirate Army Fights for Downfall of Assad," *The Irish Times*, December 19, 2012.

140. Ali Raza, "Espionage-for-Hire Operation Hangover Unveils New Indian Cyber Threats," Posted at hacksurfer.com on August 7, 2013.

141. Dan Kaplan, "Espionage Hacking Campaign 'Operation Hangover' Originates in India," *SC Magazine*, News Section, May 20, 2013.

142. Stephen Doherty, Jozsef Gegeny, Branko Spasojevic, and Jonell Baltazar, "Hidden Lynx—Professional Hackers for Hire," Version 1.0, Symantec, September 17, 2013.

143. "ANON OPS: A Press Release," Blog Posting, Wired.com, December 10, 2010.

144. Charlie Savage, "F.B.I. Warrants Into Service Attacks by WikiLeaks Supporters," *New York Times*, January 27, 2011.

145. Oren Dorell, "Hackers multiply attacks on popular websites," *USA Today*, December 10, 2010.

146. Parmy Olson, *We are anonymous: Inside the hacker world of LulzSec, Anonymous, and the global cyber insurgency*, (New York: Back Bay Books, 2013).

147. Tom Gjelten, "FBI Tries To Send Message With Hacker Arrests," NPR, National Security Section, July 20, 2011.

148. Zach Epstein, "Anonymous hackers to FBI: There is nothing you can do to stop us," *BGR*, July 21, 2011.

149. "AnonNews – Everything Anonymous," IRC Radio, Blog Posting, Creative Commons, February 26, 2011.

150. Swati Khandelwal, "#ParisAttacks – Anonymous declares War on ISIS: We will hunt you down!" *The Hacker News*, November 16, 2015.

151. Swati Khandelwal, "Anonymous Hacking Group Takes Down 20,000 ISIS Twitter accounts," *The Hacker News*, November 21, 2015.

152. Abhishek Awasthi, "Twitter says Anonymous' list of alleged ISIS accounts is highly inaccurate," *TechWorm*, November 21, 2015.

153. Bradley Barth, "Anonymous escalates offensive against Trump, declares 'total war,' *SC Magazine*, March 15, 2016.

154. Danny Yadron and Siobhan Gorman, "Hacking Trail Leads to Russia, Experts Say," *Wall Street Journal*, October 28, 2014.

155. Mandiant, "M Trends 2015: A View from the Front Lines," Alexandria, Virginia, June 2015, 20–22.

156. Institute for Critical Infrastructure Technology, "Handing Over the Keys to the Castle," July 2015, 19.

157. Brian Krebs, "Email Attack on Vendor Set up Breach at Target," krebsonsecurity.com, February 12, 2014.

158. Danny Yadron and Shelly Banjo, "Home Depot Upped Defenses, But Hacker Moved Faster," *Wall Street Journal*, September 12, 2014.

159. Stephen Holmes and Diane Dayhoff, "The Home Depot Completes Malware Elimination and Enhanced Encryption of Payment Data in All U.S. Stores," The Home Depot, Atlanta, September 18, 2014.

160. Mandiant, "M-Trends 2016," Special Report, February 2016, 24–27.

161. Michael Winter, "Home Depot Hackers Used Vendor Log-on to Steal Data, e-Mails," *USA Today*, November 7, 2014.

162. Jamie Dettmer, "Digital Jihad: ISIS, Al Qaeda Seek a cyber Caliphate to Launch Attacks on US," *Fox News*, September 14, 2014.

163. Jose Pagliery, Jamie Crawford, and Ashley Killough, "CENTCOM Twitter Account Hacked, Suspended," *CNN News*, January 12, 2015.

164. Julian E. Barnes and Danny Yadron, "U.S. Probes Hacking of Military Twitter Accounts by Pro-Islamic State Group," *Wall Street Journal*, January 12, 2015.

165. Nicole Perlroth, "Security Experts and Officials Diverge on ISIS as Hacking Threat," *New York Times*, December 24, 2015.

166. CrowdStrike, "2015 Global Threat Report," February 3, 2016: 63.

167. Catalin Cimpanu, "ISIS Hackers Join Forces to Create Mega Hacking Unit," SoftPedia, April 25, 2016.

168. India Ashok, "Longest-ever Isis 'kill list' including over 8,000 people released by United Cyber Caliphate," International Business Times, June 9, 2016.

169. Michael S. Rogers, Statement before the House Committee on Armed Services, March 4, 2015.

170. Cory Bennett and Elise Viebeck, "ISIS preps for cyber war," *The Hill*, May 17, 2015 and Billy Mitchell, Senators consider splitting NSA/CyberCom director position," *Fedscoop*, April 5, 2016.

171. Catherine Herridge, "NSA Director: China can damage US power grid," *Fox News*, November 20, 2014.

172. Suzanne Spaulding and Phyllis Schneck, Written testimony for a House Security Hearing, February 25, 2015.

173. Eduard Kovacs, "Russian Cyber Espionage Group Planning to Hit Banks: Report," *Tech Target*, May 13, 2015.

174. Ryan Sherstobitoff, "Cyber Espionage," McAfee Labs Threats Report, November 2014, 6.

175. Warwick Ashford, "Terror Groups Likely to Be First to Unleash Cyber Weapons, Says Eugene Kaspersky," *Computer Weekly*, October 6, 2016.

176. Mandiant, "M Trends: Beyond the Breach," Alexandria, Virginia, April 2014, 1–7.

177. James Andrew Lewis, "Cyber Threat and Response: Combating Advanced Attacks and Cyber Espionage," Center for Strategic and International Studies, March 2014, 1–8.

Chapter Three

Theoretical Foundations

The Prussian philosopher-general Carl von Clausewitz wrote that "the primary purpose of any theory is to clarify concepts and ideas that have become, as it were, confused and entangled."[1] The use of theory as a foundation for analysis of strategic cyber deterrence options requires a thorough understanding of applicable concepts and ideas. This chapter explores how the theories of *strategy* and *deterrence* underpin the creation of traditional strategic deterrence options or an alternative strategy most likely to influence the behavior of malicious actors in cyberspace. It reviews national strategic choices made in three historical periods to illustrate the role deterrence plays with respect to strategies, as a subset, a backup, an element of one or another choice. Specifically, the chapter examines the use of coercive diplomacy and preemption before World War II, escalation dominance and countervailing strategy during the Cold War, and superiority in cyberspace and other domains or functional models in an era of Rising Cyber Power. In each of the three historical periods, the chapter explores how theories of deterrence found in these periods apply or not in the formulation and implementation of strategic cyber deterrence options. Finally, in recognition of the intrinsic complexity found in various socio-economic-technical systems, the chapter concludes with an explanation of why a comprehensive approach enhances organizational interaction for the deterrence of malicious actors in cyberspace.

THEORIES OF STRATEGY AND DETERRENCE

The general theory of strategy can be plainly defined as the "direction and use made of means by chosen ways in order to achieve desired ends."[2] Strategy is subordinate to the more inclusive subject of security and in turn security is regarded as a field of politics. Thus at the level of national strategy, the functional means consist of any and all among the vital assets of a designated security community used for the purposes of policy as decided by politics. Another more specific view of national strategy is the use of "political, economic, and psychological powers of a nation, together with its armed forces, during peace and war, to secure a nation's objectives."[3] Here the distinction between the theory and practice of strategy is both objective and subjective. In practice the strategist must always balance political ends with available means, orchestrated in appropriate ways. However, strategy is complicated in its many working parts, and causes and effects are inherently problematic. Ends, ways, and means have to be unarguably different in meaning from each other as they are interdependent. Yet in principle, the simple relationship of ends, ways, and means in a Trinitarian formula serves as an organizing concept for managing the complexity, confusion, and chaos of disordered behaviors and events.[4]

Strategy can also be thought of as the link between political aims and the use of force, or its threat. Therefore, another suitable version of strategy is the pursuit of political aims by the use or possession of military means. This link between policy at the highest level and the use of military force as its tools is postulated by Clausewitz in his narrow definition of strategy merely as "the use of engagements for the object of war," where war is "an act of force to compel our enemy to do our will." His seminal writings reason that the aim in war is the imposition of one's will upon the enemy, and to see all strategy as the pursuit of that aim, while taking into consideration the interaction of one's own side with the enemy.[5] According to this reasoning, a succinct and normative application of the Trinitarian formula for describing strategy would be "the art of the dialectics of wills that use force to resolve their conflict."[6] For in various forms of conflict, the use or threat of force for the purposes of policy has to overcome, or at least diminish, resistance manifested by human will.[7] Political will is usually based on the advancement and survival of national interests. As a manifestation of political will, strategic deterrence options convince adversaries not to take actions that threaten national interests.

The general theory of deterrence is defined as the use of means of decisive influence over adversary decision making. Decisive influence is achieved by threatening to impose costs, or by denying benefits, while ensuring restraint by persuading an actor that restraint will result in an acceptable outcome.[8] For deterrence to alter behavior, it must instill a belief in an adversary that a threat of retaliation actually exists, the intended action cannot succeed, or the costs outweigh the benefits of acting. Therefore effective deterrence requires capability (possess the means to influence behavior), credibility (that proposed actions may actually be employed), and communication (sending the intended message to the desired audience).[9] Prevailing capability must be coupled with appropriate credibility and communication.

If a state has all the capability required to respond, but lacks the will to launch a credible reprisal or the reputation that it would, deterrence fails. Even if a state has the capability and credibility (will and reputation) to respond effectively, it must communicate its position. For unless others receive the message clearly, they will not fully understand the probable repercussions of potential actions and deterrence will break down. Finally, if credible capability is obtained, but credibility erodes, a greater response may be required to reintroduce the belief in an adversary that malicious actions will not be tolerated by the state. [10]

The US Department of Defense (DOD) Cyber Strategy contends that because of the variety and number of malicious actors in cyberspace and the relative availability of attack tools, an effective deterrence strategy requires a range of policies and capabilities to affect a state or non-state actor's behavior. [11] In light of the escalating cyber threat, the US military declares it will contribute to a comprehensive cyber deterrence strategy to deter malicious actors that seek to harm national interests during times of peace, crisis, or conflict. While military deterrence is considered most often, there are other useful instruments of power available to states, to include diplomatic, economic, and law enforcement levers. The concept of deterrence is often the cornerstone of national security strategy in dealing with powerful and emerging threats. The national security strategy itself can signal resolve and readiness to deter potential adversaries. [12] That includes the deterrence of adversaries as a way to secure national interests. [13] To illustrate the role deterrence plays with respect to strategies, as a subset, a backup, an element of one or another choice, examples of national strategic choices will be examined in the three historical periods of pre–World War II, during the Cold War, and in an era of Rising Cyber Power.

PRE–WORLD WAR II PREDICAMENTS

The political uses of force are varied and pervasive in the relations of states. Any instrument of military power that can inflict damage upon an adversary may also affect his conduct, even if force is never used. The necessary condition for this effect is that the parties concerned perceive that the capabilities will be or are actually deployed, thus allowing those capabilities to affect their decisions. In peacetime the most versatile and extensive means for political influence is by sea power. Inherent mobility, tactical flexibility, and wide geographic reach render sea power particularly useful as an instrument of foreign policy. Land-based forces, either ground or air, can be used to encourage friends or coerce enemies, but with more constraints and risks. Naval forces, by virtue of their perceived capabilities, their role as a symbol of national power, and their manifestation of political will represent a foreclosure of military options.[14] In the absence of hostilities, such as before World War II in Europe and Latin America, the indirect threat or use of limited naval force by the United Kingdom, Italy, Germany, and the United States served as a form of coercive diplomacy. At the onset of hostilities, such as before World War II in the Pacific, the use of naval forces by Japan served as a means of preemption.

Coercive Diplomacy

The strategy of coercive diplomacy combines techniques of deterrence and compellence to elicit desired actions. The component of deterrence prevents undesirable actions by instilling a fear of consequences into a targeted actor. Yet the deterrent threat only changes the consequences if the act in question is taken. Whereas the element of compellence offers the actor positive reinforcement for taking actions he otherwise would not. Compellence usually involves initiating an action that can cease but only if the opponent responds.[15] Coercive deterrence in the form of gunboat diplomacy dates back over a century. Gunboat diplomacy is the threat of or use of limited naval force, other than in an act of war, in order to secure advantage or avert loss, in the furtherance of an international dispute. Gunboat diplomacy can be by definitive, purposeful, or expressive force.[16] A classic example of definitive force occurred in February 1940 when the German naval auxiliary *Altmark*, suspected of carrying British prisoners, gained shelter in the territorial waters of neutral Norway. The *HMS Cossack* with four other destroyers and a cruiser intercepted the auxiliary under escort by Norwegian torpedo boats. Captain Vian of the *Cossack* was under direct orders from Winston Churchill to liberate the prisoners and if fired upon, to defend himself using no more force than is necessary. He was also told to suggest to the Norwegians "that honor is served by submitting to superior force."[17] After informing the torpedo boat commander of his intent to proceed with or without consent, Captain Vian boarded the *Altmark* and steamed out of the fjord with 299 British subjects.

Limited naval force is used purposefully in order to change the policy or character of a foreign government. The landing of Italian troops on the Greek island of Corfu in August 1923 illustrates the principles involved. Italy had demanded financial and symbolic reparations for the massacre of their Military Mission in Greek territory. After a month long occupation of Corfu, the Greek government complied with every demand.[18] Like in the *Altmark* incident, the Corfu objective was defined and communicated to the victim to avoid further unrelated violence. Other purposeful instances in Latin America demonstrate British policy advances through the use of gunboat diplomacy. After the shipwrecked *Prince of Wales* was plundered on the Brazilian coast in April 1862 and naval officers on leave from the *HMS Forte* manhandled in June 1862, Britain dispatched two men-of-war to capture six Brazilian vessels in demand for compensation for the plunder and apologies for the arrest. In Argentina in 1875, when the British government was under pressure from bankers, railway and ship owners to safeguard property during civil unrest, the British sailed a gunboat up the River Parana to threaten the port of Rosario to force a reverse liquidation of a British bank. Then in December 1902, when Venezuela failed to make payments on debts, British sailors boarded and sunk the *General Crespo* and the *Totumo*. A subsequent blockade by British, German, and Italian ships compelled the Venezuelan government to pay. [19]

The United States also used gunboat diplomacy by purposeful force in Latin America in the years before World War II. Instances include the Destroyer *USS Thornton* arrived at the town of Manzanillo in Mexico in 1920 to liberate it from bandits;[20] the presence of four hundred US Marines embarked on the *USS Pennsylvania* to persuade Panama in 1921 to conform to a US decision regarding her border dispute with Costa Rica;[21] US Marines landed at Puerta Ceiba in Honduras in 1924 to protect US interests during civil disturbances;[22] and Marines landed at Bluefields in Nicaragua in 1926 to protect US nationals and property from civil war. [23] The United States likewise employed warships for expressive force in Latin America to further objectives of her foreign policy. Expressive force uses limited naval force to emphasize attitudes or to lend credibility to otherwise unconvincing statements. For example, in 1936 President Roosevelt arrived at Buenos Aires in Argentina in the Cruiser *Indianapolis* escorted by the *USS Chester* to attend the first session of the Inter-American Conference for the Maintenance of Peace amidst US reluctance to accept Argentinian doctrine prohibiting interference in other countries. [24] Expressive force can be a key to diplomatic success. As American Diplomat George Kennan, who formulated the policy of "containment" for fighting the Cold War, once remarked, "you have no idea how much it contributes to the general politeness and pleasantness of diplomacy when you have a quiet little force in the background." [25]

Preemption

The strategy of preemption contains an element of deterrence. Preemption is defined as the anticipatory use of force in the face of an imminent attack. [26] Here deterrence is a factor since preemption is designed to dissuade an aggressor from doing what he originally would do. The proven potential for further harm by the preemptor is intended to influence decisions of the aggressor. For centuries international law has recognized that nations need not suffer an attack before they can lawfully take action to defend themselves against forces that present an imminent danger of attack, [27] provided the action taken, at a point in time when the opportunity arises to eliminate the threat, is in proportion to the threat, and avoids excessive force. [28] Usually at this point a decision for war has been taken by the aggressor. The preemptor can try to disrupt the unfolding assault instead of electing to receive the attack before reacting. The strategy of prevention differs both in its timing and motivation. While the preemptor has no choice than to conduct a first strike in a rapid manner, the preventer chooses to launch military action because of fears for the future should it fail to act now. Preventive action, for choice, should take the form of a raid, not an invasion and occupation. Both strategies are about self-defense. The main difference is that in prevention, the proposition exists that the preventer is able to detect and to anticipate a deadly menace, or at least predict an intolerable major negative power shift. To preempt is to act on the basis of certain contemporary knowledge, while in contrast, to prevent is to launch action deprived of temporal discipline.[29] The Japanese in the first half of the twentieth century enacted both precepts, first at Port Arthur and second at Pearl Harbor.

The Japanese strike on the Russian Pacific fleet stationed at Port Arthur on the Chinese coast on February 8, 1904, initiated the two-year Russo-Japanese War. Japanese destroyers launched their torpedoes to achieve hits on three ships. Japanese leaders deliberately acted to secure a military advantage before a declaration of war. The cause of war on the Asian mainland was a matter of prevention of an emerging threat to national security. Russian aggression to challenge Japan's vital interests in Korea and home islands threatened its national existence. The answer on how to engage this formidable foe was the strategy of preemption. Japan needed to preclude the Russian naval forces from interfering with the transfer of its army to the Korean Peninsula. Russia was confident that its great prestige would deter Japan from going to war. It built up naval forces at Port Arthur and land forces in Manchuria, but the Japanese decided on war and severed diplomatic relations days before the preemptive strike. Although the damaged Russian ships were repaired and returned to action, the fleet would never emerge successfully from Port Arthur.[30] Nevertheless, the war continued as the Russians committed additional resources to the fight. Russia's Second Fleet passed through the straits of Korea to engage the Japanese Navy near the island of Tsushima in May 1905. After two days of battle, the Japanese warships captured or destroyed thirty-one Russian ships.[31] Preemption at Port Arthur had contributed to success at Tsushima by ensuring a clash of equal numbers, and to the peace that followed, which gave Japan control over Korea and thereby security from invasion.

The Japanese attack on the American fleet at Pearl Harbor on December 7, 1941, resulted in destruction or damage to eight battleships and three hundred aircraft, and US declaration of war against Japan.[32] The cause of the preemptive raid was primarily the threatened economic destruction of Japan by the United States. The American attempts to deter Japanese expansion into the Southwestern Pacific through deployment of the US Fleet to Pearl

Harbor, economic sanctions that deprived Japan of 80 percent of its oil requirements, and dispatch of B-17 bombers to the Philippines had failed due to Japanese pride. America insisted that Japan leave both conquered Indochina and China as a condition for restoration of trade, essentially abandoning its empire and submitting to the economic domination of the hostile United States.[33] Given the scope of Japan's imperial ambitions and alliance with Nazi Germany, Japanese leaders in September 1941 believed that war was inevitable, and prepared to attack in advance.[34] The longer Japan took to start a preventive war with the United States, the less its chance of success, given the oil embargo and declining military power. Japan needed to seize the Dutch East Indies to obtain a substitute for American oil. The naval strike on Pearl Harbor was to be just a flanking raid, not an occupation, in support of the conquest of Malaya, Singapore, the Indies, and the Philippines. However, two months before Pearl Harbor, Admiral Yamamoto predicted, "It is obvious that a Japanese-American war will become a protracted one."[35] Tokyo's grand strategy was to fight the United States to a stalemate in a brutal, island-by-island battle and extract some kind of political settlement that would preserve imperial interests. The strategy of preemption was meant to buy time to construct a defense zone for negotiations.[36]

Cyber Deterrence Implications

The strategy of coercive diplomacy employed in Europe and Latin America in the examples above depended on the threat of or use of limited force. Coercive diplomacy shows determination so an adversary under pressure concludes it must make concessions. The key contrast with classical diplomacy is that coercion, although limited, is not merely a remote contingency. The prospects for successful coercive diplomacy depend on the costs of noncompliance that can be imposed on the target state. Costs can be imposed by economic sanctions as well as by military force.[37] Economic sanctions are an increasingly prominent tool of statecraft. They are the threat by a government to disrupt economic exchange with the target state, unless the target acquiesces to an articulated demand. If the target complies, the sanctions are not imposed.[38] Although emerging, cyber power has yet to exert anywhere near the same level of political influence of sea power. For unlike naval forces, cyber capabilities do yet not reflect a symbol of national power and the manifestation of political will. To both deter and coerce an adversary in the absence of hostilities, an additional instrument of power besides cyber, like economic sanctions, should be considered in any strategy of coercive diplomacy.

The strategy of preemption, for preventative reasons, as seen in the Japanese attacks on Port Arthur and on Pearl Harbor, is difficult to implement in the cyber realm. The use of preemption depends on detecting moves early and forestalling attacks by moving first, the equivalent of a first strike. The challenge of situational awareness in cyberspace hinders the understanding of adversary origins and intentions. Therefore a preemption strategy in cyberspace is prone to misattribution and overreactions or miscalculations.[39] However, international law does allow any nation to defend itself from threats, and the United States has perhaps applied that concept to conduct preventive, and prepare for preemptive, cyber-related actions, to control dangers in its external security environment. The Stuxnet worm attack on Iranian nuclear facilities to destroy uranium enrichment centrifuges, although never acknowledged by the United States, could be considered a preventive cyber attack to forestall a nuclear attack. Furthermore, the United States developed an elaborate plan for a cyber attack on Iran in case diplomatic efforts to limit its nuclear program failed and Iran lashed out at the United States and allies in the region. American personnel placed electronic implants in Iranian computer networks to "prepare the battlefield" for preemptive strikes on Iranian air defenses, communications systems and power grid.[40] A secret legal review of America's use of cyber weapons has concluded that the president has "the broad power to order a preemptive strike if the United States detects credible evidence of a major digital attack looming from abroad."[41] The preemptive strike would attack adversary computer networks by injecting them with destructive code. Yet officials have kept secret what that threshold would be to maintain ambiguity in an adversary's mind, inducing an element of deterrence, the threat of retaliation.

COLD WAR CHOICES

In January 1954, Secretary of State Dulles announced that the United States intended in the future to deter aggression by depending "primarily upon a capacity to retaliate, instantly, by means and at places of our choosing."[42] The policy became known as massive retaliation and was interpreted as a threat to devastate Soviet economic and political centers in response to any aggression, no matter how limited. Meanwhile the Soviet Union was mounting a substantial threat against America's Allies, and it was not to be long before the continental United States was at risk from Soviet aircraft. Thus the adoption of this concept made the United States more reliant on the deterrent effect of nuclear weapons, and ultimately its credibility would depend on taking nuclear risks on its allies' behalf. With the Soviet Union in the lead on the development of intercontinental ballistic missiles, US analysts introduced the concepts of first and second strike, the ability to absorb a first strike and inflict a devastating retaliation. The requirement for the second strike force was to be survivable. The placement of intercontinental missile forces in reinforced-concrete underground silos and also on nuclear-powered submarines by both sides eventually resulted in a condition of stability based on invulnerable retaliatory forces.[43] Although a global stalemate for nuclear war was attained, a pressing problem the United States still faced was how to extend nuclear deterrence over faraway allies in a technically credible manner.

Ultimately for the United States, national strategy is about the expansion of American interests and the security of the American people. Yet in the Cold War, the perceived need to protect the European periphery against the Soviet Union drove the design and execution of an American strategy of onshore containment. For this strategy the United States had ample geopolitical and economic resources to extend protection over allies and friends confronting Soviet land power. However, since both the Soviet and NATO governments regarded nuclear weapons as useable weapons of war, the United States was left with no choice but to assume nuclear weapons were instruments of policy capable of functioning as means in the Trinitarian formula. Therefore the United States elevated nuclear weapons to a dominant position in national strategy. This decision was consistent with the American way of war that called for maximum violence for quick results.[44] The American policy to use nuclear weapons in a strategy of Soviet containment remained firm throughout the nearly thirty years of the Cold War; however, the strategic concepts or ways for their use changed as advances were made and realized in the destructive potential of the weapons or means of the policy.

Escalation Dominance

The strategy of escalation outlines promised responses to deter adversaries. During the Cold War, escalation was the basic concept around which attempts to develop a credible nuclear strategy evolved. A ladder of escalation conceptualizes how activities in a given scenario maintain dominance at any particular level of escalation. Clearly set guidelines at ladder rungs integrate reactions and deterrence with policy decisions. Since crossing of the nuclear threshold would produce unpredictable results, the most useful escalation dominance would start at the conventional level in a concept of flexible response. In 1961, the American government began to posit that a major nuclear war might not, and need not, be a simple contest in destructive fury. Secretary of Defense McNamara gave a speech in June 1962 on the idea that deterrence might operate even in wartime, where belligerents might out of self-interest limit the destructive nature of nuclear war. Each might feel that the destruction of enemy people and cities, as called for in massive retaliation, would serve no decisive military purpose, but that a continued threat to destroy them might serve a purpose. McNamara said the United States has come to the conclusion that in general war "the destruction of the enemy's military forces, not of his civilian population" would give the opponent the "strongest imaginable incentive to refrain from striking our own cities."[45]

Less than six months after McNamara's expression of this conclusion, President Kennedy solemnly stated that any nuclear missile launched from Cuba on the United States would require a full retaliatory response upon the Soviet Union.[46] Leading up to that point in time, the Soviet Union had faced a widening window of vulnerability with the buildup of American strategic nuclear forces. For the Soviets, reducing the threat of a US first strike would take several years. However, the Soviets did possess a surplus of shorter range missiles that could not reach the United States from Soviet bases but could if based in Cuba. Faced with few options, the Soviets decided to move existing weapons to Cuba from which they could reach American targets. The US discovery of Soviet ballistic weapons in Cuba in October 1962 instigated the thirteen-day Cuban missile crisis. After previous deterrent threats to the Soviet government that offensive weapons in Cuba would not be tolerated, the United States made the choice to respond with a compellant threat, specifically a naval blockade, called quarantine, coupled with a demand for withdrawal of the missiles. This form of value-maximizing escalation ended the crisis, with the Soviet removal of the missiles.[47] Fortunately the crisis did not escalate across a threshold that had been previously accepted by both sides.

With an acceptance of the growing American position to not use an automatic nuclear response to conventional Soviet aggression, NATO adopted in 1967 the concept of flexible response. In this strategic concept, attempts would be made to respond to conventional aggression by the Soviets with conventional means. If that failed, NATO would move to tactical nuclear weapons, and if necessary, the final recourse would be the US strategic nuclear arsenal. This progression effectively adhered to use of an escalation ladder.[48] NATO appeared to be aiming for escalation dominance by deliberate progression. In 1974, the concept of escalation dominance emerged again in an announcement by Secretary of Defense Schlesinger that a range of nuclear options would reduce dependence on threats of assured destruction. Schlesinger made clear it was neither feasible nor desirable to develop a true first strike capability but in major conflict nuclear weapons would impede enemy advance and warn against continued aggression.[49] In a scenario of assured destruction a condition of stability is balanced if neither opponent in striking first gains the advantage of destroying the other's ability to strike back. This stalemate guarantees deterrence since no rational actor could dare to choose a course of action equivalent to national suicide. This deduction assumes rational behavior motivated by a conscious calculation of advantages based on an explicit value system.[50]

Countervailing Strategy

The danger in a strategy of escalation lies in its predictability. If an aggressor knows the steps of the ladder, then they can test the rules and assess resolve to climb the ladder. In 1980, US President Carter unveiled a countervailing strategy by signing Presidential Directive 59 that brought it into force. The strategy implied should the Soviet Union move up the escalation ladder, the United States would be able to respond effectively to exchanges at each level. PD-59 sought a nuclear force posture that guaranteed a "high degree of flexibility, enduring survivability, and adequate performance in the face of enemy actions." The strategy emphasized that "if deterrence fails initially, we must be capable of fighting successfully so that the adversary would not achieve his war aims and would suffer costs that are unacceptable, or in any event greater than his gains, from having initiated an attack."[51] To make this feasible, PD-59 described targeting categories appropriate to implement a countervailing strategy that put the weight of the initial response on military and control targets. Rapid planning targets covered nuclear forces, command and control, stationary and mobile forces, and industrial facilities that support the military, while preplanned strike options remained for attacks on the political control system or general industrial capacity.

A key component of PD-59 was to use high-tech intelligence to find nuclear weapons targets on the battlefield, strike those targets, and then assess the damage. A "look-shoot-look" capability would allow the president and his advisers to improvise targeting during the war. This flexible targeting system was supposed to provide an adequate deterrent, along with rigid preplanned strategic options.[52] Drafters of PD-59 believed they could control escalation during a nuclear war, but gave up "victory" as an aim. Likewise, Soviet leadership did not think either side could win a nuclear war.[53] PD-59 sought to create the forces and codify the will to retaliate, but to actually deter, the Soviet leadership had to be convinced the Americans would do so. US Defense Secretary Brown publicly discussed the major precepts of the countervailing strategy during the SALT arms control hearings in 1970 and at a NATO Nuclear planning group in early 1980. The policy of PD-59 was dubbed the countervailing strategy because its fundamental feature is the proposition that deterrence over the full range of nuclear contingencies requires the United States to have forces and plans for their use that convince the Soviets that no plausible outcome of aggression would represent victory.[54]

Nonetheless, by 1985 Soviet debate reached a consensus that nuclear war is so farfetched and dangerous that it has become an instrument of policy only in theory, and thus an instrument of policy that cannot be used. That year Marshal Ogarkov, the Soviet Chief of the General Staff, published a revised description of the modern theater operation, in which military action is conducted without resorting to nuclear weapons. In his book, Ogarkov wrote of a new US capability to wage a protracted conventional war through the concept of Air-Land Battle. This development inspired a new revolution in Soviet military affairs that involved changes in Soviet doctrine generated by emerging technologies. The Soviets saw the need for precision conventional means with the same ranges as those of nuclear weapons. By 1986 they were fielding long-range cruise missiles such as the SS-NX-24 to pose a nonnuclear threat to US and Eurasian airfields and nuclear weapons.[55] Meanwhile the United States pursued their so-called revolution in military affairs, developing the communications, precision weapons, and intelligence system to provide reach and awareness for deep air-land battle engagements.[56] These revolutions persisted on both sides through the end of the Cold War in 1991.

Cyber Deterrence Implications

Theories of deterrence provided the basis for the American strategy of containment of the Soviet Union in the Cold War. The United States extended deterrence through the threat of nuclear use on behalf of its allies, in insisting that an attack on the territory of NATO may invoke a US nuclear retaliatory strike. The United States eventually developed an invulnerable retaliatory capability in its strategic triad of intercontinental ballistic missiles in hardened silos, submarine launched ballistic missiles, and dispersed strategic bombers. There was really no defense against nuclear weapons delivery by these platforms, either by ballistic missile defense or by air defense. And even if defenses were available and robust, the damage that could be inflicted by surviving missiles or bombers would be viewed as an unacceptable cost. Therefore the Cold War deterrence framework relied heavily on the threat of punishment by punitive destruction.[57] Here offensive retaliation is not only costly to the aggressor, but also makes a first strike unsuccessful in its objective. This results in a denial of victory, or more precisely the denial of success by the attacker in achievement of military and political objectives. Therefore, deterrence by denial, in contrast to deterrence by punishment, stresses the role of defense to limit the damage the defender will suffer. Damage limitation enables survival, denies attacker success, and enables retaliatory strikes to terminate the conflict on the defender's terms.

After the Cold War ended, US government officials exhibited continued confidence in the nuclear deterrence framework based on the assumption that unified national actors would make decisions regarding the use of nuclear weapons in a reasonable and predictable fashion. However, for a wider variety of malicious actors, confident predictions about deterrence should be viewed with skepticism because of the human element in deterrence, where a leader must agree to be deterred. Desperate or determined leaders that are intent on their chosen course can be inattentive or impervious to the commitments or threats of their foes. Even the rationality of an opponent's decision making does not guarantee they will be receptive to strategies of deterrence, including very severe threats. As noted earlier, the rational decision maker chooses a course of action that is calculated to be most suitable for achieving their preferred goal based on available information. Rationality does not imply that the decision maker's prioritization of goals and values will be considered to be reasonable to outside observers. Therefore, rational decision making can underpin behavior judged by observers to be insensible, shocking or even criminal. For example, rational leaders with extreme ideological views may pursue goals that are sensible to them, but through behavior that appears unreasonable to observers based on their own moral set of values and standards. [58]

The Cold War deterrence framework was discovered and practiced based on a particular context, not only a limited number of rational national actors, but also their capacity to deliver nuclear weapons. To assume that nuclear deterrence must fit well enough the circumstances for other attempts to deter in the twenty-first century would be a gross and avoidable error. [59] Nuclear deterrence is about one specific and highly lethal type of physical weapon. The capability of the weapon to produce destructive effects is clear and demonstrated. Yet the success of nuclear deterrence relies on the nature of the weapon, which inherently limits casual development and deployment. [60] The use of the weapon would be a rare occurrence and attribution for any attack, at least by ballistic missile or strategic bomber, is most certainly assured. Therefore the theory of nuclear deterrence relies primarily on retaliation or punishment for use of this particular type of weapon, in the form of nuclear counterstrikes. All other efforts today to produce a deterrent effect center on the weapon itself, through denial of access, by restricting the spread of knowledge and materials to develop the weapons, by norms, in the form of international agreements that limit the acquisition and use of nuclear technologies, or by active defense, entitled more succinctly as ballistic missile defense.

Prominent defense officials have summed up the prevailing view that "traditional Cold War deterrence models of assured retaliation do not apply to cyberspace." [61] Their reasoning stems primarily from the difficulty in obtaining timely and accurate attribution of actions in cyberspace. Especially since the complexities associated with cyber attacks are compounded by the use of compromised servers and uncooperative countries. [62] Without attribution that connects the action to an individual or state actor with confidence and verifiability, policy makers are constrained in making decisions on offensive retaliation. [63] Also, unlike nuclear attacks that produce only destructive effect, cyber attacks can be used for disruptions or espionage, which causes challenges for policy makers in determining whether the action rises to the level of an armed attack that justifies retaliation. In the Cold War, the possession of nuclear weapons meant it was possible to deter by threatening horrific retaliation without maintaining any serious defenses. In the cyber era, threatening harm on the attacker can also be inflicted by a stout defense, frustrating the attack or making it too costly to overcome. This form of denial of benefit convinces the opponent to reject undertaking even a seriously prepared attack.[64] Therefore, for cyberspace, effective deterrence rests not only upon ensuring the capability to respond to hostile acts, but also upon the security of networks and systems.[65]

RISING CYBER POWER

Over the past four decades, through the development of information and communication technology, the World Wide Web and the Internet have evolved into a global medium for collaboration and interaction between computers and individuals. Through the physical and digital manifestation of this medium, cyberspace has become a primary conduit for transactions vital to every facet of modern life and security. While society has benefited from connectivity and interoperability, developments in cyberspace have provided means for the US military, its allies, and partner nations to maintain strategic, continuing advantage, although unfettered access to cyberspace also provides malicious actors the avenue to compromise the integrity of critical infrastructure in direct or indirect ways. Most critical infrastructure that empowers national economies, like financial systems, the power grid, and health systems, runs on networks connected to the Internet. Concern entails what a set of systematic cyber attacks might do: for example, in thinking of real-life examples, such as an air traffic control system going down and disrupting flights, or blackouts that plunge cities into darkness.[66] Therefore a paradox exists within cyberspace, as while technological developments have enhanced the prosperity and security of nations, the same developments have led to increased vulnerabilities and critical dependence on cyberspace, for both society and the military.

This paradox has contributed to the rise of cyber power, broadly defined as the ability to "exploit cyberspace to create advantages and influence events."[67] As applied for these outcomes, many definitions of cyber power "emphasize how cyberspace can be used to fulfil the ends of strategy."[68] Accordingly cyber power can be considered as the "process of converting information into strategic effect."[69] This view considers the instrumentality of cyber power but neglects to discuss the process of using that power in the face of a willful and determined adversary. A more explicit definition of cyber power is "the national ability to disrupt [the] obscured bad actor somewhere in the digital globe, whether nonstate or state, in proportion to its motivations/capabilities to attack with violent effects and yet be resilient against exposed or enhanced nasty surprises across all critical nationally sustaining systems."[70] This definition recognizes that cyber power is employed as a strategic instrument against a malicious actor that is attempting to use cyberspace for their own ends. The obtainment of stated effects, through systemic resilience and disruption capacities, can be part of an overall national strategy. The attraction of cyber power as a strategic instrument lies in the ability for global reach with a certain degree of desired anonymity. This characteristic can be useful in peace, conflict, or war.

Just as a state actor can create strategic effects against globally distributed targets through cyber power, so can malicious actors outside a state's immediate jurisdiction "exercise power against the wishes of a state with little or no chance of being traced or interdicted by the state."[71] The reduction in time and space through instantaneous interactions increases the number of malicious actors that were previously constrained by temporal or physical separations.[72] Thus the domain is "marked by power diffusion,"[73] where large countries will share the domain with new actors and have trouble controlling their borders in the domain. Those new actors are vast, diverse, sometimes anonymous, and operate with an advantage in the offense over the defense. States and other actors will attempt to exercise cyber power to obtain preferred outcomes either within cyberspace or in other domains outside cyberspace. Both will use hard power through coercion and payment or use soft power through agenda framing, attraction, or persuasion.[74] Forms of hard power can include denial of service attacks and insertion of malware to steal data within cyberspace or cyber attacks on industrial control systems that physically reside outside cyberspace. Examples of soft power would be setting standards for the security of software used in cyberspace or an online propaganda campaign to influence citizens outside of cyberspace. The diffusion of power complicates the development of state strategy to counter nonstate actors with newfound capacity to exercise both hard and soft power in cyberspace.

Strategy brings together lines of effort to manage challenges in the strategic environment. A pervasive property of the environment is complexity, which rises when a state faces a greater number of threats, a more diverse set of security actors, and a more interdependent and networked environment.[75] Decision makers face uncertainty in the identity and capabilities of the threats and actors operating in the environment. A number of strategic choices exist to respond to uncertainty, a byproduct of complexity. One of these choices is the proactive strategy of shaping, where the "expectations and behaviors of others can be shaped through the power of ideas or superior capabilities."[76] Shaping embraces a wide range of options, to include the use of cyber power, to alter the strategic environment so that serious challenges do not emerge. The concept of "shape" is referred to as Phase Zero of the notional six-phase model of joint and multinational operations described in

US joint doctrine. This doctrine presents military operations leading to "war" as a natural progression of activities, from shaping to deterring, seizing initiative, dominating, stabilizing, and enabling civil authority. The intent of "deter" in Phase One is to deter undesirable actor activities by demonstrating capabilities and resolve.[77]

In the military context, cyber power "is equivalent to military power in the physical domains,"[78] which are air, land, maritime, and outer space. Cyber power is enacted through cyberspace operations, which employ cyberspace capabilities to achieve objectives in or through cyberspace. A cyberspace capability is "a device, computer program, or technique designed to create an effect in or through cyberspace."[79] Cyberspace operations are conducted and synchronized across the range of military operations. The concept of cyberspace superiority is achieved when the degree of dominance in cyberspace by one force "permits the secure, reliable conduct of operations by that force, and its related land, air, maritime, and space forces at a given time and place without prohibitive interference by an adversary."[80] As seen in recent incidents, cyberspace operations serve as a component of warfare. Militaries can use cyber operations to disrupt command and control, sever logistic pipelines, degrade weapons performance and produce political or psychological effects. Most cyber attacks will not produce destructive effects similar to kinetic weapons, but can disrupt data and services, damage networks and computers, and maybe destroy machinery.[81]

Other Domain or Functional Models

Cyberspace is often described as a global common. Likeminded nations have labeled the global commons as shared spaces—cyber, space, air, and oceans—which exist outside exclusive sovereign jurisdictions.[82] Access to these shared spaces is at risk due to increased competition and provocative behaviors. Therefore, the United States and its allies are promoting rules for responsible behavior in shared spaces while creating capabilities to assure access.[83] While the US military has removed cyberspace as one of the global commons in their concepts of operation,[84] the analogy at the strategic level has proven useful for resolving issues nations face in regard to domain security, and for guiding regulatory frameworks, such as those envisioned in the theory of entanglement.[85] Deterrence by entanglement is a way to entrench potential adversaries in a shared network they would not attack because of mutual interests and unintended consequences.[86] For example, an attack on the commercial satellite infrastructure in outer space that facilitates military communications would have huge consequences on the wealth of globalized economies. Besides economic entanglement, nations also share a degree of technological entanglement (and potential economic loss) in space, like in applications of Global Positioning Systems data.[87] Mechanisms to promote responsible behavior in space, like confidence-building measures, can be adapted for cyberspace, due to similarities in the unique characteristics of the domains, such as the difficulty in attribution of attacks.[88]

Warfighting concepts found in other domains suggest a new strategy for securing cyberspace resides in technical combinations of offensive and defensive operations occurring simultaneously and in concert.[89] An operational perspective for countering air and missile threats indicates the relationship between offensive and defensive systems.[90] To confront the tyranny of the offense-dominated environment of air and missile threats, offensive counter-air operations prevent the launch of threats, while defensive counterair operations use active and passive measures to defeat threats attempting to penetrate through friendly airspace. Active measures include defensive weapons in an integrated defense-in-depth system. Passive measures include deception, dispersion, reconstitution, detection, and warning systems, and protective construction.[91] An example of an active air and missile defense system is the Patriot surface-to-air missile system, which uses an aerial interceptor missile and advanced radar system to detect and shoot down hostile aircraft and missiles. The concept definition can be adapted to the cyber domain, where active cyber defense is taken to be direct defensive action taken to destroy, nullify, or reduce the effectiveness of cyber threats, while passive cyber defense is about all other measures to minimize their effectiveness.[92] These definitions allow the examination of various active and passive measures to see how they act or interact, simultaneously or in concert, against hostile cyber threats.

Cyber Deterrence Implications

In an era of Rising Cyber Power, a tailored deterrence approach can serve as a vital part of a cyber security strategy designed to prevent and reduce adversarial intrusions. One such approach recommended by notable academics emphasizes raising costs of, and reducing benefits from, cyber attacks, to include use of economic sanctions, mandatory standards for protection and resilience, international agreements, and active defense.[93] The US government's approach on its cyber security strategy focuses on four key elements: (1) to improve defenses to manage risk more effectively; (2) to improve the ability to disrupt, respond to, and recover from cyber attacks; (3) to enhance international cooperation to hold bad actors accountable; and (4) to make cyberspace intrinsically more secure by building more resilient networks.[94] Effective resilience measures can convince malicious actors of the futility of commencing cyber attacks on networks. Therefore, the Defense Department has incorporated the necessity to strengthen the overall resilience of US systems in its new cyber strategy.

The US defense strategy adds resilience as a factor in effective deterrence. Resilience is deemed necessary to withstand a potential attack if it penetrates defenses. The Defense Department intends to invest in resilient systems so they may continue operations in the face of disruptive or destructive cyber attacks. The department realizes it cannot foster resilience in organizations that fall outside its authority. Therefore for resilience measures to succeed as a factor in deterrence, other agencies must work with critical infrastructure and key resource owners to develop resilient systems.[95] The vast majority of large-scale socio-economic-technical systems from electrical grids to manufacturing supply chains have become vulnerable to nasty surprises in cyberspace. The increasing complexity of these systems challenges efforts to increase resilience. Complexity rises as the number, differentiation, and interdependence of elements and nodes rises. If a surprise can cascade over enough nodes, it becomes a systemic event.[96] The challenge in accommodating surprise is to gain sufficient knowledge of threats and vulnerabilities. A proven mechanism is necessary to self-organize disparate organizations in their efforts to generate resilience.

COMPREHENSIVE APPROACH APPLICATIONS

The comprehensive approach is a proven mechanism for coordinating efforts to respond to security challenges. Absent a precise definition, the phrase "mobilizing the resources of an entire society to succeed in modern missions" encapsulates the meaning.[97] The model builds on a whole-of-government approach, to include the additional capabilities of allies and partners, nongovernmental and private voluntary organizations, international organizations, and the private sector.[98] Intended to enhance organizational interaction, the comprehensive approach is a way of thinking or a method, instead of a mechanical process.[99] Although reaching consensus on the objectives of the approach can be elusive, any discussion requires identifying the underlying apparatus of this approach, which is cooperation among actors when feasible, and integration of capabilities when possible. Although acknowledging the complexities and challenges, employing a comprehensive approach may lessen distrust and hesitancy among the participants, boosting the number of organizations willing to accept responsibilities in modern missions.

The fundamentals of a comprehensive approach include interdependence in political, security, economic, and social systems; cooperation by constant communication, dialogue and negotiation; prioritization of multiple competing demands; nesting of short-term objectives into longer-term goals; flexibility in sequenced or phased actions; and measurements of progress in translating goals into outcomes.[100] Just as important as understanding the fundamentals are the unified principles for planning and conducting operations with all relevant actors in an increasingly complex environment.[101] The four unified principles of the approach identified by the United Nations are: first, a shared vision of strategic objectives; second, congruence of purpose, through unity of effort by all parties, not of command by a single governing body[102] (in this context, congruence is defined as agreeing or coinciding as a state of compatibility); third, some level of coordination with all relevant actors that enhance effectiveness; and fourth, successful use of the comprehensive approach requires mutual awareness and deliberate consideration of the charters, interests, limitations, and perspectives of stakeholders. With a comprehensive approach, organizations are tasked to do things they do best. Proper application could yield efficiencies in allocating resources and reducing duplication of effort. The principles are not a panacea for all problems seen in a multidimensional environment, but even modest gains in facilitating cooperative interaction justify the effort.

The comprehensive approach uses cooperative interaction to advance the common interests of organizations. To be useful in deterring cyber attacks, the approach needs to overcome a clash of self-interests that prevent cooperation, where one party strives to maintain economic or military advantage. For instance, the private sector is reluctant to share cyber threat data with the government because it does not believe the latter can protect the confidentiality of an attacked company, which may devalue stocks or compromise proprietary information to the advantage of competitors, and protect personally identifiable information (PII) which might be in stolen data.[103] A state might not agree to cooperative action if binding rules constrain their preferred method of competition in cyberspace. Critical to gaining consensus for the comprehensive approach is the multilateral characteristic of diffuse reciprocity, whereby parties recognize their self-interests will be satisfied over the long term. Examination of models and precedents in other domains could identify principles and mechanisms that foster greater cooperation and transparency. Winston Beauchamp, the deputy undersecretary of the Air Force for space touts how space operators have the "equivalent of maritime rules of the sea about encounters and how to deal with them."[104] Many of the provisions of the emerging International Code of Conduct for Outer Space Activities can be translated for cyberspace, such as to avoid harmful interference with outer space activities, to prevent outer space from becoming an arena of conflict, and to reinforce international norms for responsible behavior in outer space.[105]

The comprehensive approach does not apply only to operations by friendly entities; for example, hybrid threats can "avail themselves of a comprehensive range of methods and weapons to accomplish their objectives—a comprehensive approach to goal obtainment."[106] Therefore, to rapidly adapt to new threats, the chairman of the US Joint Chiefs of Staff states that "success will increasingly depend on how well our military instrument can support the other instruments of power and enable our network of allies and partners."[107] His comment openly acknowledges the role of the military in a contribution to a comprehensive approach for security. The term for the military component is "full spectrum operations," explained in doctrine as the "range of operations forces conduct in war and military operations other than war."[108] For preparation and response to cyber attacks, the Joint Staff proclaims success is dependent upon unity of effort enabled by collaboration among partners, to include the private sector.[109] This claim is consistent with an affirmation by the NATO Enhanced Cyber Defense Policy that "strong partnerships play a key role in addressing cyber threats and risks."[110] NATO consequently intends to engage actively on cyber issues with relevant partner nations and international organizations plus intensify cooperation with industry. Private sector expertise and innovations are seen as crucial by NATO to achieve the objectives of the Enhanced Cyber Defense Policy. One of these is the strategic deterrence of cyber attacks.

NOTES

1. Carl von Clausewitz, *On War*, trans, Michael Howard and Peter Paret (Princeton, NJ: Princeton University Press, 1976), 132.

2. Colin S. Gray, *The Strategy Bridge: Theory for Practice* (New York: Oxford University Press, 2010), 18.

3. Arthur F. Lykke Jr. "Toward an Understanding of Military Strategy," *Guide to Strategy* (Carlisle, PA: US Army War College, February 2001), 179–85.

4. Colin S. Gray, "The Whole House of Strategy," *Joint Force Quarterly* no. 71, 4th Quarter (2013), 58–62.

5. Beatrice Heuser, *The Evolution of Strategy: Thinking War from Antiquity to the Present* (Cambridge: Cambridge University Press, 2010), 1–17.

6. Edward N. Luttwak, *Strategy: The Logic of War and Peace* (Cambridge, MA: Belknap Press of Harvard University Press, 1987), 241.

7. B. H. Liddell Hart, "The Theory of Strategy," *Military Strategy: Theory and Application* (Carlisle Barracks: US Army War College, 1983), 3-22 to 3-23.

8. Kevin Chilton and Greg Weaver, "Waging Deterrence in the Twenty-first Century," *Strategic Studies Quarterly* (Spring 2009): 31–42.

9. US Department of Defense, *Joint Operations,* Joint Publication 3-0 (Washington, DC: Office of the Chairman, Joint Chiefs of Staff, August 11, 2011), xx.

10. Peter Roberts and Andrew Hardie, "The Validity of Deterrence in the Twenty-first Century," Royal United Services Institute, Occasional Paper, August 2015, 5–9.

11. Ash Carter, Secretary of Defense, *The DoD Cyber Strategy*, April 17, 2015, 10–26.

12. Executive Office of the President, *National Security Strategy* (Washington, DC: The White House, February 2015), 1.

13. US Department of Defense, *The National Military Strategy* (Washington, DC: Office of the Chairman, Joint Chiefs of Staff, June 2015), 5–7.

14. Edward N. Luttwark, *The Political Uses of Sea Power* (Baltimore: Johns Hopkins University Press, 1974), v–34.

15. Thomas Schelling, *Arms and Influence* (New Haven, CT: Yale University Press, 1966), 69–78.

16. James Cable, *Gunboat Diplomacy 1919–1991* (London: Palgrave Macmillan, 1994), 1–64.

17. Sir P. Vian, *Action This Day* (London: Fredrick Muller, 1960), passim.

18. J. Barros, *The Corfu Incident of 1923* (Princeton, NJ: Princeton University Press, 1965).

19. Andrew Graham-Yooll, *Imperial Skirmishes: War and Gunboat Diplomacy in Latin America* (Brooklyn, NY: Olive Branch Press, 2002), 90–157.

20. *Papers relating to the Foreign Relations of the United States*, vol. 3 (Washington, DC: US Government Printing Office, 1936), 153.

21. Council on Foreign Relations, *American Relations in the Caribbean* (New Haven, CT: Yale University Press, 1929), chap. 5.

22. *Papers relating to the Foreign Relations of the United States*, vol. 2 (Washington, DC: US Government Printing Office, 1924), 300–324.

23. W. Kamman, *A Search for Stability* (Notre Dame, IN: University of Notre Dame Press, 1968), 58.

24. *Franklin D. Roosevelt and Foreign Affairs*, vol. 3 (Cambridge, MA: Harvard University Press, 1969).

25. Stephan M. Walt, "Which Works Best: Force or Diplomacy?" *Foreign Policy*, August 21, 2013.

26. James B. Steinberg, Michael E. O'Hanlon, and Susan E. Rice, "The New National Security Strategy and Preemption," Policy Brief #113, Brookings Institution, December 2002, 1–6.

27. President George W. Bush, "The National Security Strategy of the United States of America," The White House, September 2002, 15.

28. Harry S. Laver, "Preemption and the Evolution of America's Strategic Defense," *Parameters* (Summer 2005): 107–20.

29. Colin S. Gray, "The Implications of Preemptive and Preventive War Doctrines: A Reconsideration," *A Strategic Studies Institute Publication* (July 2007): 1–60.

30. Matthew J. Flynn, *First Strike: Preemptive War in Modern History* (New York: Routledge, 2008), 55–66.

31. Ronald H. Spector, *At War, At Sea: Sailors and Naval Combat in the Twentieth Century* (New York: Viking Penguin Publishers, 2001), 1–21.

32. Ronald H. Spector, *Eagle against the Sun: The American War with Japan* (New York: Free Press, 1985), 1–8.

33. Jeffrey Record, "Japan's Decision for War in 1941: Some Enduring Lessons," A Strategic Studies Institute Publication, February 2009: 1–70.

34. Louis Morton, *The War in the Pacific*, United States Army in World War II Series (Washington, DC: US Government Printing Office, 1978), 92–93.

35. Sadao Asada, *From Mahan to Pearl Harbor: The Imperial Japanese Navy and the United States* (Annapolis, MD: Naval Institute Press, 2006), 277.

36. Tomoyuki Ishizu and Raymond Callahan, "The Rising Sun Strikes: The Japanese Invasions," in *The Pacific War*, chap. 3 (Oxford: Osprey Publishing, 2010), 47–61.

37. Bruce Jentleson, "Coercive Diplomacy: Scope and Limits in the Contemporary World," Policy Analysis Brief, The Stanley Foundation, December 2006, 1–3.

38. Daniel W. Drezner, "The Hidden Hand of Economic Coercion," *International Organization* 57, no. 3 (2003): 643–59.

39. Robert A. Miller, Daniel T. Kuehl, and Irving Lachow, "Cyber War: Issues in Attack and Defense," *Joint Force Quarterly* no. 61, 2nd Quarter (2011): 18–23.

40. David E. Sanger and Mark Mazzetti, "U.S. Had Cyberattack Plan If Iran Nuclear Dispute Led to Conflict," *New York Times*, February 16, 2016.

41. David E. Sanger and Thom Shanker, "Broad Powers Seen for Obama in Cyberstrikes," *New York Times*, February 3, 2013.

42. John Foster Dulles, "The Evolution of Foreign Policy," Department of State Bulletin, vol. 30, January 25, 1954.

43. Lawrence Freedman, "The First Two Generations of Nuclear Strategists," *Makers of Modern Strategy* (Princeton, NJ: Princeton University Press, 1986), 735–78.

44. Colin S. Gray, "Strategy in the Nuclear Age: The United States, 1945–1991," in *The Making of Strategy* (New York: Cambridge University Press, 1994), 579–613.

45. Secretary of Defense Robert McNamara, Commencement Address, University of Michigan, June 16, 1962.

46. Albert and Roberta Wohlstetter, "Controlling the Risks in Cuba, Adelphi Papers, 17 (London: Institute for Strategic Studies, 1965).

47. Graham Allison and Philip Zelikow, *Essence of Decision: Explaining the Cuban Missile Crisis*, 2nd ed. (New York: Addison Wesley Longman, 1999), 1–142.

48. Roger L. L. Facer, "Conventional Forces and the NATO Strategy of Flexible Response," R-3209-FF (Santa Monica, CA: Rand Corporation, January 1985), 1–18.

49. Lawrence Freedman, "The First Two Generations of Nuclear Strategists," *Makers of Modern Strategy* (Princeton, NJ: Princeton University Press, 1986), 766–75.

50. Thomas Schelling, *The Strategy of Conflict* (Cambridge, MA: Harvard University Press, 1960), 4, 232.

51. President Jimmy Carter, "Nuclear Weapons Employment Policy," Presidential Directive/NSC-59 (Declassified), July 25, 1980.

52. William Burr, "Jimmy Carter's Controversial Nuclear Targeting Directive PD-59 Declassified," National Security Archive, September 14, 2012.

53. William Burr, "How to Fight a Nuclear War," *Foreign Policy*, September 14, 2012.

54. Walter Slocombe, "The Countervailing Strategy," *International Security* 5, no. 4 (Spring 1981): 21–22.

55. Mary C. FitzGerald, "Marshal Ogarkov and the New Revolution in Soviet Military Affairs," Research Memorandum, Center for Naval Analyses, January 1987, 1–25.

56. William A. Owens, "The Once and Future Revolution in Military Affairs," *Joint Force Quarterly* (Summer 2002): 55–61.

57. Schuyler Forester, "Theoretical Foundations: Deterrence in the Nuclear Age," in *American Defense Policy*, Schuyler Forester and Edward Wright, eds., 6th ed. (Baltimore: Johns Hopkins University Press, 1990), 42–51.

58. Keith B. Payne and C. Dale Walton, "Deterrence in the Post-Cold War World," *Strategy in the Contemporary World* (New York: Oxford University Press, 2002), 170–73.

59. Colin S. Gray, *Perspectives on Strategy* (New York: Oxford University Press, 2013), 116–52.

60. Dorothy E. Denning, "Rethinking the Cyber Domain and Deterrence," *Joint Force Quarterly* no. 77, 2nd Quarter (2015): 8–12.

61. William J. Lynn III, "Defending a New Domain," *Foreign Affairs* (September–October 2010): 97–108.

62. Kevin G. Coleman, "US Cyber Defenses Outmatched by Hackers," *Defense Systems*, August 2011, 2.

63. Major General Maurice H. Forsyth, USAF, "Cyberspace Operations," Air Force Doctrine Document 3-12, July 15, 2010, 10.

64. Patrick M. Morgan, "Applicability of Traditional Deterrence Concepts and Theory to the Cyber Realm," *Proceedings of a Workshop on Deterring Cyberattacks* (Washington, DC: National Academies Press, 2010), 55–56.

65. US Department of Defense, *Cyberspace Policy Report*, November 2011, 7.

66. President Barack Obama, "Remarks at the Cybersecurity and Consumer Protection Summit," Stanford University, Palo Alto, California, February 13, 2015.

67. E. Lincoln Bonner III, "Cyber Power for 21st-Century Joint Warfare," *Joint Force Quarterly* no. 74, 3rd Quarter (2014): 102–9.

68. John B. Sheldon, "The Rise of Cyberpower," in *Strategy in the Contemporary World*, John Baylis, James J. Wirtz, and Colin S. Gray, eds., 5th ed. (New York: Oxford University Press, 2016), 285.

69. Sheldon, "The Rise of Cyberpower," 285.

70. Chris Demchak, *Wars of Disruption and Resilience: Cybered Conflict, Power, and National Security* (Athens: University of Georgia Press, September 2011), x.

71. David J. Betz and Tim Stevens, *Cyberspace and the State: Toward a Strategy for Cyber-Power* (New York: Routledge, 2011), 39.

72. Betz and Stevens, *Cyberspace and the State*, 39.

73. Joseph S. Nye Jr., "Cyber Power," Belfer Center for Science and International Affairs, Harvard Kennedy School, May 2010, 3.

74. Nye, "Cyber Power," 4–7.

75. Chris Demchak, *Complex Machines: Modernization in the U.S. Armed Services* (Ithaca, NY: Cornell University Press, 1991).

76. Emily O. Goldman, *Power in Uncertain Times* (Stanford, CA: Stanford University Press, 2011), 1–21.

77. US Department of Defense, *Joint Operation Planning,* US Joint Publication 5-0 (Washington, DC: The Joint Staff, August 11, 2011), III-38 to III-44.

78. Ragnhild Siedler, "Hard Power in Cyberspace: CNA as a Political Means," in *Proceedings 8th International Conference on Cyber Conflict* (Tallinn, Estonia: CCD COE, June 2016), 24.

79. US Department of Defense, *Cyberspace Operations,* Joint Publication 3-12 (R) (Washington, DC: The Joint Staff, February 5, 2013), I-6.

80. US Department of Defense, *DOD Dictionary of Military and Associated Terms* (Washington, DC: The Joint Staff, As Amended through October 15, 2016), 60.

81. James A. Lewis, "Cyber War: Definitions, Deterrence and Foreign Policy," Statement before the House Committee on Foreign Affairs, September 30, 2015.

82. Major General Mark A. Barret, USAF et al., "Assured Access to the Global Commons," (Norfolk, VA: Supreme Allied Command Transformation, April 3, 2011), 5.

83. Executive Office of the President, *The National Security Strategy* (Washington, DC: The White House, February 2015), 12.

84. Dan Shinego, "Defining the Term: Global Commons," News and Notes on Multi-Service Collaboration to Address A2/AD, vol. 2, no. 1 (October 2015): 1.

85. Julie J. C. H. Ryan, Daniel J. Ryan, and Eneken Tikk, "Cybersecurity Regulation: Using Analogies to Develop Frameworks for Regulation," in *International Cyber Security Legal and Policy Proceedings* (Tallinn, Estonia: CCD COE, 2010), 76–99.

86. Schulyer Forester, "Strategies of Deterrence," in *Conflict and Cooperation in the Global Commons*, Scott Jasper, ed., 55–67 (Washington, DC: Georgetown University Press, 2012).

87. Roger Harrison, Collins G. Shackelford, and Deron R. Jackson, "Space Deterrence: The Delicate Balance of Risk," *Space and Defense*, Eisenhower Center for Space and Defense Studies, 3, no. 1 (Summer 2009): 1–22.

88. Marc J. Berkowitz, "Shaping the Outer Space and Cyberspace Environments," in *Conflict and Cooperation in the Global Commons*, Scott Jasper, ed., 190–213 (Washington, DC: Georgetown University Press, 2012).

89. Kamal T. Jabbour and E. Paul Ratazzi, "Deterrence in Cyberspace," *Thinking About Deterrence* (Maxwell Air Force Base, Alabama: Air University Press, December 2013), 37–50.

90. Leon Sloss, "The Strategist's Perspective," in *Ballistic Missile Defense*, Ashton B. Carter and David N. Schwartz, editors (Washington, DC: The Brookings Institute, 1984), 24–48.

91. US Department of Defense, Countering Air and Missile Threats, Joint Publication 3-01 (Washington, DC: The Joint Staff, March 23, 2012), I-2 to I-5.

92. Dorothy E. Denning and Bradley J. Strawser, "Active Cyber Defense: Applying Air Defense to the Cyber Domain," *Cyber Analogies*, Technical Report, Naval Postgraduate School (2014): 64–75.

93. Franklin D. Kramer and Melanie J. Teplinsky, "Cybersecurity and Tailored Deterrence," Atlantic Council, December 2013, 1–10.

94. Lisa O. Monaco, "Strengthening Our Nation's Cyber Defenses," Remarks as Prepared for Delivery, The Wilson Center, Washington, DC, February 10, 2015.

95. US Department of Defense, *The DoD Cyber Strategy*, April 17, 2015, 10–11.

96. Chris C. Demchak, "Resilience and Cyberspace: Recognizing the Challenges of a Global Socio-Cyber Infrastructure (GSCI)," *Journal of Comparative Policy Analysis: Research and Practice* (July 12, 2012): 254–58.

97. James G. Stavridis, "The Comprehensive Approach in Afghanistan," *PRISM* 2 no. 2 (March, 2011): 65–76.

98. Stephan J. Hadley and William J. Perry, *The QDR in Perspective: Meeting America's National Security Needs in the 21st Century* (Washington, DC: US Institute of Peace, July 29, 2010), 31–32.

99. Kristina Rintakoski and Mikko Autti, *Trends, Challenges and Possibilities for Cooperation in Crisis Prevention and Management* (Helsinki, Finland: Crisis Management Initiative, June 17, 2008), 1–34.

100. United States Institute of Peace, "Fundamentals of a Comprehensive Approach," in *Guiding Principles for Stabilization and Reconstruction*, 5-30 to 5-32 (Washington, DC: United States Institute of Peace Press, 2009).

101. Scott Jasper and Scott Moreland, "A Comprehensive Approach to Multidimensional Operations," *Journal of International Peacekeeping* 19 (2015): 191–210.

102. Michael Hallet and Oke Thorngren, "Attempting a Comprehensive Approach Definition and Its Implications for Reconceptualizing Capability Development," chap. 3, *Capability Development in Support of Comprehensive Approaches* (National Defense University, December 2011), 35–50.

103. Larry Clinton, "Cyber Security Social Contract," in *Conflict and Cooperation in the Global Commons*, Scott Jasper, ed., 185–98 (Washington, DC: Georgetown University Press, 2012).

104. Amber Corrin, "How DoD Is Re-Writing the Rules of Space," *C4ISR&Networks*, April 28, 2016.

105. European Union, "International Code of Conduct for Outer Space Activities," Version 31, March 2014, 1–13.

106. Michael Aaronson et al., "NATO Countering the Hybrid Threat," *PRISM* 2, no. 4, (September 2011): 111–24.

107. Marcus Weisgerber, "Dempsey's Final Instruction to the Pentagon: Prepare for a Long War," *Defense One*, July 1, 2015.

108. Russell W. Glenn, "Thoughts on Hybrid Conflict," *Small Wars Journal*, March 2, 2009, 1–8.

109. US Department of Defense, *Unity of Effort Framework Solution Guide* (Suffolk, VA: US Joint Staff J-7, August 31, 2014), foreword.

110. North Atlantic Treaty Organization, "Wales Summit Declaration," Paragraph 72, September 5, 2014.

Part II

Traditional Deterrence Strategies

Chapter Four

Deterrence by Retaliation

The strategy of deterrence by retaliation is based upon the threat to impose costs for hostile acts in cyberspace. Nations reserve the right to respond by all necessary means, often in kind, to an attack on their interests. Since deterrence is partially a function of perception, the strategic option of retaliation works by convincing a potential adversary that it will suffer unacceptable costs if it acts in an undesirable manner. Deterrence by retaliation seeks to change the cost-benefit calculations of a malicious actor by proving that a response by the victim to an attack will occur at or in a chosen time, manner, and place. This influence occurs through not only the clear articulation of declaratory policy to use all necessary means in response, but also the overt display of effective response capabilities. The threat of or use of all necessary means and the potential for harm deters an actor from carrying out a course of action to attack, but only if the costs are viewed to outweigh the benefits. Thus successful deterrence requires not only the capabilities to harm the malicious actor, but also the communication of will to launch a reprisal coupled with the credible reputation to actually do so. Furthermore, the initiator of retaliation must have the resolve to accept any harm or pain that may be caused by a reprisal act in response to the original deterrent act. [1]

Yet in today's threat environment, cyber attacks seriously challenge the strategic option of deterrence by retaliation. Senator John McCain stoutly claimed that "our adversaries view our response to malicious cyber activity as timid and ineffectual," since we have not proven that the "consequences of continued cyberattacks against us outweigh the benefit." [2] Not only has retaliation failed because of choices to apply it poorly, it is not suited for cyberspace and cannot be effective. To date few malicious actors responsible for significant cyber attacks on critical infrastructure have faced criminal justice. The five members of the Chinese Military indicted in May 2014 on charges of computer fraud, damaging a computer, and aggravated identify theft are no closer to seeing the inside of a federal courtroom while China's campaign of economic espionage against US firms continues.[3] US authorities did file charges ranging from securities fraud to money laundering on criminals in cases bearing some link to the massive cyber attack on JP Morgan Chase Bank in 2014.[4] Yet it took eighteen months before prosecutors publicly and directly linked the suspects to the hack.[5] When asked do we need to go on the offensive in ways that we have not before, Admiral Michael Rogers, the head of the NSA, responded "I think clearly we have got to change the current dynamic. To date, most nation-states, most groups, most individuals, have come to the conclusion that there is little price to pay for the actions they're taken."[6] Uttering that the United States is at a tipping point, Admiral Rogers openly inquires, "how can we increase our capacity on the offensive side here to get to that point of deterrence."

Lawmakers in the United States have voiced frustration with the lack of an effective deterrent strategy for cyber attacks.[7] US Deputy Secretary of Defense Robert Work told a congressional committee that a key objective of his department's cyber strategy "is to develop cyber options to hold an aggressor at risk in cyberspace if required," although Secretary Work admitted that "in many instances non-cyber capabilities may provide a more appropriate or effective response."[8] Therefore the range of means to directly impose costs for hostile acts in cyberspace span military cyber operations, diplomatic engagements, law enforcement measures, economic sanctions, and even the use of kinetic capabilities. These means are reviewed for what is necessary to change an actor's perception or simply which means will work best to convince a malicious actor, whether from a nation-state, hacker group, criminal organization, or terrorist group, that the costs of conducting an attack outweigh any potential benefits. This chapter starts with an illustrative case that depicts an example of a justified and proportionate response by the US government to a destructive and vindictive cyber attack by a nation-state. It then examines the circumstances and concerns for employing the range of necessary means and to what extent will the threat of or use of them, often in kind, achieve deterrence by retaliation in response to hostile acts in cyberspace.

ILLUSTRATIVE CASE

An increasing frequency of cyber attacks was seen in the 2014 threat landscape, underscored by theft of data at retailers such as Target, hardware store Home Depot, luxury goods Neiman Marcus, craft chain Michaels, and grocer Supervalu,[9] and at banks like JP Morgan Chase. However, the most sensational act was the destructive and coercive cyber attack on Sony Pictures

Entertainment. The attack was a game-changer because it wasn't about profit, but a dictator trying to impose censorship and prevent free expression. On November 24, 2014, images of a neon red skull appeared on computer screens at the entertainment giant Sony. An accompanying message by a group called "#GOP," standing for Guardians of Peace, threatened to release data secrets if undisclosed demands were not met. Sony initially downplayed the intimidating promise, still bruised from an attack months prior that forced their PlayStation network offline.[10] However, along with the vivid warning expressed to Sony Pictures employees, hackers launched a so-called wiper attack deleting files and disabling computers. They used malicious software similar to the virus seen in attacks on South Korean banks and media outlets the previous year in a campaign dubbed Dark Seoul.[11] Soon after, sensitive personal information regarding thousands of employees of Sony Pictures and confidential emails by executives were leaked online, along with five new or unreleased films.

On December 16, 2014, Guardians of Peace posted on the Pastebin website another threat that people who see Sony's movie *The Interview* would suffer a "bitter fate."[12] The comedy portrays the leader of North Korea as a sadistically irrational tyrant. This menacing promise prompted Sony Pictures to cancel the Christmas release of the movie at the largest multiplex theater chains in North America.[13] President Obama criticized the decision by Sony to cancel the release of *The Interview* as a bad precedent and stated "we will respond proportionately and we will respond in a place and time and manner we choose."[14] The FBI concluded the North Korean government is responsible for the incident at Sony Pictures based in part on analysis of data deletion malware similarities in lines of code and encryption algorithms previously developed by North Korean actors and the discovery that several IP addresses used were associated with known North Korea infrastructure.[15] Although the evidence appeared circumstantial, technical malware analysis confirms the attack was not the work of suspected insiders or hacktivists.[16]

The FBI observed "the destructive nature of this attack, coupled with its coercive nature, sets it apart," as North Korea's actions were intended "to inflict significant harm on a U.S. business and suppress the right of American citizens to express themselves."[17] Yet even with confidence in attribution, US policy makers did not have "an established menu of proportionate response options" for this low-intensity cyber attack.[18] Any military retaliation would be out of proportion and would risk escalation, no trade exists for sanctions, and any legal action in indictments would be pointless. Nevertheless the United States did respond in a limited way, potentially covertly and definitely overtly. Perhaps a coincidence, soon after the president's pronouncement, the Internet in North Korea, available only to the elite, the military and the propaganda apparatus, went dark for nearly ten hours.[19] Days later, under an Executive Order signed by President Obama, the Treasury Department imposed financial measures on three North Korean organizations and ten officials. The legislative basis for the sanctions for "destructive, coercive cyber-related actions" was violation of four United Nations Security Council Resolutions and commission of serious human rights abuses.[20] The targets of the sanctions were the Reconnaissance General Bureau, which probably orchestrated the cyber operation, the Korea Mining Development Trading Corporation, their main arms dealer, and the Korean Tangun Trading Corporation, responsible for defense research and development, plus individuals operating out of Russia, Iran, Syria, China, and Namibia with suspected connections to the North Korean government.[21]

The Sony attack was sophisticated enough that a prominent security company felt Sony could not have been fully prepared.[22] North Korea used "spear phishing" attacks in early September to steal "credentials" of a Sony systems administrator, which allowed the hackers to roam freely inside Sony's systems.[23] Hackers spent two months collecting passwords and mapping the network before activating a virus named Destover that wiped data and crashed the system in a ten-minute time bomb. Available on the black market, Destover also functions as a backdoor to an affected network, allowing remote access without detection of intruders.[24] Destover contains configuration files created on systems using Korean language. Not only did analysis of Destover used by #GOP and the virus used in the Dark Seoul attack by the Whois Team reveal similarities in techniques and code, but also comparisons exist in the computer screen images used by the claimed perpetrators in warnings, threats, and original skeletal artwork.[25] The cyber defenses at Sony had failed and the US government resorted to retaliation against a nation-state through an instrument of power, namely economic sanctions intended to inflict some new financial pain, particularly in exports of military goods and services.

MILITARY RESPONSE OPTIONS

The United States chose not to use a military response, at least an overt one, to impose costs on North Korea in the Sony incident despite attribution by the FBI. The options for a military response include using cyber or kinetic capabilities. The attack on Sony, although cited by Admiral Rogers as an attack on critical infrastructure in US territory,[26] did not cross the threshold for the use of forceful military means in retaliation. According to Michael Schmitt, "Pursuant to Article 51 of the United Nations Charter and customary international law, if the malicious cyber operation against Sony had constituted a "use of force" rising to a level of an "armed attack," the United States would have been entitled to respond forcefully, whether by kinetic or cyber means."[27] The attack against Sony involved the release of sensitive information and the destruction of data. Although disruptive and costly, the effects were not at the level of an armed attack. Likewise the attack, although severe, would probably not be characterized as a use of force by the international community. However, the cyber attack against Sony, since attributed to the State of North Korea, was a violation of US sovereignty. As such, under the law of state responsibility, the attack amounted to an "internationally wrongful act." The commission of an internationally wrongful act entitles an injured state to engage in countermeasures in order to persuade the responsible state to return to a state of lawfulness,[28] for which the United States might have done covertly by crippling the Internet in North Korea for a brief period of time.

In the Sony case, the United States did make a determination on attribution one month after the attack. Attribution plays a key role in signaling, or proving, that a response by the victim to an attack will occur. Yet tracing cyber attacks back to their origin is difficult. Attackers evade detection by using hijacked systems as proxies or by changing (spoofing) the source field of IP data packets.[29] Attackers can also modify (spoof) the media access control address of network devices to mask identify or poison a DNS server to redirect users to a malicious website.[30] Technical attribution seeks to identify IP ownership or domain registration, but other indicators can help to attribute attacks, such as tradecraft tools, code styles, resource language, and time zone information such as malware build time or command and control check in times.[31] "Attribution is not impossible, it's just hard," according to General Michael Hayden, former director of the Central Intelligence Agency, and "good attribution does not include up to the point of beyond all reasonable doubt," rather "this is about enabling governments to act in the face of continued doubt."[32] That entails acting without meeting some sort of judicial standard to protect national interest, and if necessary by military means. If a decision to maintain credibility by military means is made, then a plethora of considerations follow for use of cyber or kinetic weapons in a proportional and justified response.

Response Thresholds

The threshold for use of military means in response to a cyber attack by a nation-state is imprecise. Difficulties in reaching international consensus on what qualifies as the "use of force" rising to a level of an "an armed attack" in cyberspace impedes the application of international law to cyber operations, which are defined as "the employment of cyber capabilities where the primary purpose is to achieve objectives in or through cyberspace."[33] The lack of a common understanding on these terms and conditions also restricts the ability to deter cyber attacks. In the Charter of the United Nations, Article 2 calls on all members to "refrain in their international relations from the threat or use of force against the territorial integrity or political independence of any state."[34] The most serious and dangerous form of the use of force is aggression. Acts that qualify as aggression include invasion, blockade, bombardment, and other attacks by armed forces of a state on the land, sea or air forces of another state.[35] The Russian occupation of Crimea qualified as aggression, since Russia exercised territorial control without the consent of the Ukrainian Government. However, an act qualifying as a use of force need not be undertaken by a state's armed forces. For example, an act would qualify if undertaken by a state's intelligence agencies or by a private contractor whose conduct is attributable to the state. Cyber operations may in certain circumstances constitute a use of force within the meaning of Article 2, if they cause effects that, if caused by traditional physical means, would be clearly regarded as a use of force. For example, the United States would categorize cyber operations as a use of force if they: (1) "trigger a nuclear plant meltdown"; (2) "open a dam above a populated area, causing destruction"; or (3) "disable air traffic control services resulting in airplane crashes."[36]

The term "use of force" is not to be equated with the term "armed attack." Not every use of force rises to the level of an armed attack. Likewise the choice of means of attack is immaterial to the determination. For example, it is universally accepted that chemical, biological, and radiological attacks of the requisite scale and effects constitute armed attacks. Under identical reasoning, Rule 71 of the Tallinn Manual 2.0 states that "whether a cyber operation constitutes an armed attack depends on its scale and effects." The parameters for scale and effects are "unsettled beyond the criteria they need to be grave." The International Group of Experts that wrote the Tallinn Manual 2.0 agreed that "a cyber operation that seriously injures or kills a number of persons or that causes significant damage to, or destruction of, property would satisfy the scale and effects requirement." They also agreed that "acts of cyber intelligence gathering or cyber theft, as well as cyber operations that involve brief or periodic interruption of nonessential cyber services do not qualify as armed attacks.[37] The US view is similar on cyber operations that resemble traditional signal intelligence activities, in considering cyber intrusions to collect data for national security purposes as within the realm of international law.[38]

Resort to Force

The body of international law titled *jus ad bellum* governs a state's resort to military force, including through cyber operations, as an instrument of its national policy. Certain criteria for *jus ad bellum* have been drawn from principles as part of Just War Tradition.[39] The principles start with a competent authority to order war for a just cause, such as self-defense. Article 51 of the Charter of the United Nations demarcates "the inherent right of individu-al or collective self-defense if an armed attack occurs against a Member of the United Nations."[40] Traditionally, Article 51 has been characterized as applicable to armed attacks undertaken by one nation-state against another, but recent practice establishes a right of self-defense in the face of armed attacks by nonstate actors, such as terrorist or rebel groups. Not all states accept the United Nations strict criteria on armed attack. For instance, "the United States has long taken the position that the inherent right of self-defense potentially applies against any illegal use of force."[41] Regardless of viewpoint, to constitute legitimate self-defense, the defending state's use of force must be necessary and proportionate, which limits the application of retaliation in cyber conflict because of constraints on the use of overwhelm-ing force.

Necessity requires that "a use of force, including cyber operations that amount to a use of force, be needed to successfully repel an imminent armed attack or defeat one that is underway."[42] For example, if passive cyber de-fenses like firewalls are "adequate to reliably and completely thwart a cyber armed attack, other measures, whether cyber or kinetic, at the level of a use of force are impermissible."[43] Likewise, other nonforceful measures, such as diplomacy, economic sanctions or law enforcement must be insufficient to address the situation. Proportionality addresses how much force, including through cyber operations, is permissible once force is deemed necessary. The measures taken in self-defense must be proportionate "in scale, scope, dura-tion, and intensity" to the nature of the threat being addressed.[44] There is no requirement for the measures taken to be of that which constituted an armed attack—for instance, "a cyber use of force may be resorted to in response to a kinetic armed attack, and vice versa."[45] For illustration the insertion of a logic bomb would qualify as an imminent armed attack if specified condi-tions for activation are likely to occur. In the case of an ongoing pattern or campaign of cyber operations, proportionality can be assessed by what force is reasonably necessary to discourage future armed attacks or the threat there-of.

Justification for a resort to force for the North Atlantic Treaty Organiza-tion resides in Article 5 of the North Atlantic Treaty, where "the Parties agree that an armed attack against one of more of them in Europe or North America shall be considered an attack against them all."[46] Consequently "they agree that, if such an armed attack occurs, each of them, in exercise of the right of individual or collective self-defense . . . will assist the Party or Parties so attacked."[47] This principle named collective defense binds members togeth-er, committing them to protect each other. Article 5 was invoked for the first time in its history after the 9/11 terrorist attacks against the United States. The NATO Summit in Wales in 2014 affirmed "that cyber defense is part of the NATO's core task of collective defense."[48] Rule 74 of the Tallinn Manual 2.0 reiterates that "collective defense against a cyber operation amounting to an armed attack may only be exercised at the request of the victim state and within the scope of the request."[49] The victim state may, for instance, limit assistance to nonkinetic measures, consistent with NATO's emphasis on defense.

At the 2016 NATO Summit in Warsaw, the Heads of State and Government reaffirmed "NATO's defensive mandate," and recognized "cyberspace as a domain of operations in which NATO must defend itself as effectively as it does in the air, on land, and at sea."[50] This declaration is intended to maintain freedom of action and support broader deterrence and defense, through integration of cyber defense into operations and missions. Even more so in following the principle of restraint, the Heads affirmed their "commitment to act in accordance with international law, including the UN Charter, international humanitarian law, and human rights law, as applicable."[51] The strengthening of cyber defensive capabilities will include the latest cutting edge technologies. Overall the communique stays in line with NATO's Enhanced Policy on Cyber Defense, but any follow-up discussions or decisions on offensive capabilities will be important, since the lack of a well-articulated offensive cyber capability does affect NATO's ability to deter or defend against cyber attacks.[52] To that extent, the Polish think tank Kosciuszko Institute is already calling for NATO development of offensive cyber capabilities.[53]

In Armed Conflict

The body of international law titled *jus in bello* regulates how hostilities may be conducted in cases of declared war or any armed conflict and protects those affected by them. Practically the term armed conflict has replaced the notion of war as an international legal concept. Rule 80 of the Tallinn Manual 2.0 states that "cyber operations executed in the context of an armed conflict are subject to the law of armed conflict."[54] This rule applies in both international (between two or more states or countries) and noninternational (between a state and an organized armed group) situations of armed conflict. For the first situation, the law of armed conflict did govern cyber operations that occurred during the armed conflict between Russia and Georgia in 2008 because they were undertaken in furtherance of that conflict. For the latter situation, the International Committee of the Red Cross has characterized the protracted hostilities in eastern Ukraine as a noninternational armed conflict between the government of Ukraine and separatists from the cities of Donetsk and Luhansk. Although there is widespread belief that Moscow supports the separatists, Russia would have to actively participate or exercise overall control for the situation to be considered an international armed conflict.[55] By contrast, even though Estonia in 2007 was the target of persistent cyber operations targeting civilian infrastructure, the law of armed conflict did not apply because the situation did not rise to the level of armed conflict.

Regardless of the situation, it is the policy of the US DOD that members will comply with the law of war during all armed conflicts, however such conflicts are characterized, and in all other military operations.[56] Under *jus in bello* the law of war is also known as the law of armed conflict and international humanitarian law. According to the International Committee of the Red Cross, the means and methods of warfare which resort to cyber technology are subject to international humanitarian law.[57] Therefore the customary and fundamental principles of the law of war, specifically military necessity, distinction, proportionality, and humanity apply to the conduct of cyber operations.[58] The aforementioned law of war principles aptly "work as interdependent and reinforcing parts of a coherent system."[59] Military necessity justifies the use of all measures needed to defeat the enemy as quickly and efficiently as possible. Distinction requires parties to the conflict at all times to distinguish between the civilian population and combatants and between civilian objects and military objectives, and accordingly direct operations only against military objectives. Humanity, the prohibition of the causing of unnecessary suffering, forbids actions unnecessary to accomplish a legitimate military objective. Proportionality requires that justified actions not be unreasonable or excessive. This principle obliges persons to refrain from attacking where the expected harm incidental to attacks outweighs the military advantage anticipated to be gained.[60]

Cyber Capability Employment

Any examination of targeting for the employment of cyber capabilities starts with the principle of distinction which restricts operations against civilians and civilian objects that do not qualify as military objectives. Usually military attacks will only be directed at military targets. By their nature, location, purpose, or use, military targets are those objects whose total or partial destruction, capture, or neutralization offers a direct and concrete military advantage. For example, a command and control facility and cyber infrastructure for military tasks would qualify. Aside from military equipment, objects can qualify by the use criterion, like air traffic control or global positioning systems (GPS) that serve both civilian and military systems, irrespective of the extent of civilian reliance on them.[61] Persons directly participating in hostilities qualify, such as those conducting a denial of service operation or building a botnet for enemy use. Otherwise it is only legal to conduct cyber operations against civilians and civilian objects so long as they are not harmed or injured. In this case, relevant factors that suggest a cyber operation is allowed are whether it causes only reversible or temporary effects, such as defacing a government webpage, a minor disruption of Internet services, brief interference with communications, and dissemination of propaganda. [62]

The principle of distinction also prohibits use of indiscriminate means. Cyber weapons are indiscriminate if incapable of distinguishing between combatants and civilians or civilian objects and military objectives. A destructive computer virus that spreads and destroys uncontrollably within civilian Internet systems would be prohibited as an inherently indiscriminate weapon. Consider, for example, malware introduced into a military system that spreads randomly into civilian networks, or malware placed on a website open to civilians and combatants, or innocuous email attachments sent to combatant's private account that could be forwarded to civilians. [63] Even for legal weapons, the risk of cascading and collateral effects is a pervasive feature of weaponry. Due to policy concerns, rules of engagement may limit cyber operations to those that result in no or low levels of collateral effects. Even if a proposed cyber operation is permissible after a collateral effects analysis, it must also be permissible under a law of war proportionality analysis. [64] The principle of proportionality prohibits a cyber operation which may be expected to cause incidental loss of civilian life, injury to civilians, damage to civilian objects, or any combination thereof, that would be excessive in relation to the anticipated concrete and direct military advantage. An example would be a cyber attack on the dual-use GPS, which, although a lawful target, would most likely cause harm, for instance, to merchant vessels and civil aircraft, potentially excessive to military advantage. [65]

To avoid law of war prohibitions, expect advanced cyber weapons used by states in armed conflict to exploit particular vulnerabilities in specific, closed systems. Take, for instance, the Stuxnet operation found in June 2010 to be infecting the Bushehr and Natanz nuclear facilities in Iran. [66] In light of the damage caused to nearly one thousand Iranian centrifuges, [67] some of the International Group of Experts that wrote the Tallinn Manual held the view that the Stuxnet operations reached the armed attack threshold. [68] Stuxnet "has been called a cyber weapon," according to the senior vice president of Integrity Global Security, because "the intent was to cause physical damage and maybe to kill people." [69] The malware was most likely delivered into the closed nuclear systems by an infected USB drive. [70] It exploited a total of four unpatched Microsoft vulnerabilities, of which two had yet to be disclosed. [71] Stuxnet was written to target specific frequency converter drives used to control the speed of a device. The malware doesn't sabotage any frequency converter, just drives made by particular companies that run at high speeds, between 807Hz and 1210Hz like those used for uranium enrichment. [72] Accordingly, the malicious code adhered to the principles of distinction and proportionality because it attacked specific gas centrifuges operating at a speed unique to the machines. Although the facilities may have been used for civilian purposes, they were reasonably assumed to have a military role and not merely a remote possibility, and therefore legitimate targets.[73] The Stuxnet malware did demonstrate the risk of unintentional or unanticipated migration into civilian systems by escaping the Iranian nuclear enrichment plants. The malware was found on one hundred thousand infected hosts in more than twenty-five countries.[74]

Kinetic Capability Choices

As evidenced through alleged involvement in the Stuxnet operation, US policy is to conduct offensive cyber operations in a manner consistent with the policy principles and legal regimes for kinetic capabilities, including the law of armed conflict.[75] In some cases, the use of kinetic options in other domains strengthens legitimacy and credibility to respond to malicious cyber activity. For example, when overmatched online by the Islamic State propaganda machine, the United States turned to lethal force against this terrorist group in an attempt to stop an avalanche of videos and statements. US airstrikes in military operations against the Islamic State have terminated several high-level media division operatives, including Junaid Hussain, a British-born computer expert.[76] Hussain was killed by a drone strike while he was in a car in Raqqa, Syria. Hussain was viewed by US officials as a top terrorist threat because he would post names, addresses, and photos of US troops on his Twitter feed and suggest followers find and kill the person. He also developed a Remote Access Trojan to hack into computers and was training other Islamic State members in how to use hacker techniques.[77] In the case of Hussain, his affiliation with the terrorist group Islamic State made him a member of an organized armed group, which made him a legitimate target in an armed conflict.[78]

OTHER RESPONSE OPTIONS

Lisa Monaco, the assistant to the US President for Homeland Security and Counterterrorism, contended that "meeting cyber threats requires a whole-of-government approach that uses all the appropriate tools available."[79] The approach relies on unity of effort within the federal government and close coordination between public and private sectors to achieve optimal results based on shared interests.[80] Appropriate tools include global diplomacy, law enforcement expertise, economic clout, and when necessary military capability. Monaco stressed that those who would harm the United States should know that they can be found and will be held to account. A RAND Corporation study agrees with the intrinsic value of the first tool of global diplomacy in reaching the conclusion that the best means for deterring, for instance, Chinese behavior is by diplomatic action.[81] However, holding a pragmatic nation-state actor like China to account for activity it conducts or allows

inside its borders requires not just global diplomacy, but also coercive diplomacy, which combines techniques of deterrence and compellence to elicit
desired actions.[82] The law enforcement component of deterrence by retaliation attempts to prevent undesirable actions by instilling a fear of punishment
into a targeted actor. Yet for actors outside state borders, the deterrent threat
only works if there is interstate cooperation. For an uncooperative state, the
element of compellence offers positive reinforcement for taking actions it
otherwise would not take. To compel responsible state behavior, economic
sanctions initiate harmful actions that can cease, but only if the uncooperative state responds favorably by ceasing its malicious activity or by cooperat-
ing in the punishment of malicious actors inside its territory.

Law Enforcement

State cooperation between law enforcement agencies is essential to hold
malicious actors accountable for their crimes in cyberspace. The Budapest
Convention on Cybercrime, the first such international treaty, outlines the
widest possible means of cooperation to investigate crimes involving "computer systems and data, or for the collection of evidence in electronic form of
a criminal offence."[83] Over thirty-five nations, largely in Europe, in addition
to Canada, Japan, South Africa, and the United States have acceded to the
treaty, and many others are in various stages of ratifying it. The convention
provides arrangements to stem cross-border crimes while recognizing diver-
gent interpretations of national sovereignty. At the tenth-anniversary meeting
of the Council of Europe on adoption of the convention, the Secretary General declared that "the treaty still represents the only accepted international text
on how to protect against and control online crime while at the same time
respecting human rights."[84] Since then the European Union and the Council
of Europe initiated a three-year joint project titled Global Action on Cybercrime (GLACY) aimed at supporting countries worldwide in the implementation of the Budapest Convention on Cybercrime. GLACY held international conferences, courses, and workshops "to enable criminal justice authorities
to engage in international cooperation on cybercrime and electronic evidence
on the basis of the Budapest Convention on Cybercrime." Results of the
events were expected to garner progress in the areas of harmonization of
legislation, judicial training, law enforcement capacities, international cooperation, and information sharing.[85]

Cooperation between state law enforcement agencies has resulted in arrest or extradition of criminals, terrorists and hackers operating in cyberspace. For example, in New York in July 2015, three Estonian men were
sentenced to over three years in prison for their involvement in an Internet
scheme that infected more than four million computers in over one hundred
countries. The US District Judge said he wanted it to be known that those

who breach the security of computers on a large scale will "face very substantial risks." The men were arrested in Estonia and served time in Estonia prisons before extraditions to the United States.[86] In another case in October 2015, Malaysian police detained Ardit Ferizi, a citizen of Kosovo, on a US provisional arrest warrant. The US Justice Department accused him of stealing the personal data of US service members and passing it to Islamic State member Junaid Hussain. Ferizi had hacked into a server used by a US online retail company and obtained data on about one hundred thousand people, from which he sent details of 1,351 military and government personnel to the Islamic State.[87] Ferizi was extradited to the United States and charged with computer hacking, identify theft, and providing material support to a terrorist organization.[88] In June 2015, Ferizi pleaded guilty.[89] In March 2016, the US Justice Department charged three alleged members of the SEA with computer hacking conspiracies targeting government agencies and media companies. Dmitri Alperovitch, cofounder of CrowdStrike, astutely observed, "This is yet another law enforcement win that [shows] no one is above the law, but these are not major criminals that were posing a threat to the United States."[90]

Economic Sanctions

A successful example of sanctions changing the behavior of an uncooperative nation-state was those imposed by the UN Security Council on Iran during 2010–2013 for lack of compliance with resolutions to ensure the peaceful nature of its nuclear program. The sanctions contributed to the acceptance by Iran in July 2015 of a comprehensive accord that exchanges constraints on its nuclear program for broad sanctions relief. The UN sanctions had caused Iran's crude oil exports to fall by over a million barrels per day and its economy to shrink by about 10 percent.[91] In January 2016, the IAEA verified that Iran had met its commitments as set out in Annex V of the accord, and the United States initiated steps to meet its obligations to lift sanctions.[92] Not all nations agreed with the accord, in particular Israeli Prime Minister Netanyahu told the US Congress before acceptance that the deal would not block Iran's way to a bomb "but paves its way to a bomb."[93] Israel vowed to act alone if necessary to prevent Iran from obtaining a nuclear weapon, and could decide the deal is so bad that force is necessary. After all, the Israeli Air Force has already taken out nuclear reactors in Iraq and Syria.[94] Pro-Israel Lobbies also expressed concern that once the deal is done, and Iran becomes a nuclear threshold state, there would be no peaceful way to stop Iran from building a nuclear weapon, except to resort to force.[95] When asked whether the United States failed to use all of its leverage, including a credible threat of force, President Obama said "I think that criticism is misguided . . . we have cut off every pathway for Iran to develop a nuclear weapon" and "if we can in fact resolve some of these differences, without resort to force, that will be a lot better for us and the people of that region."[96]

The accord reached in Vienna to limit the Iranian nuclear program is the most detailed nonproliferation agreement ever devised, but only in years will the world know if it was a reasonable bet.[97] The White House obviously recognizes the value of combining diplomacy with sanctions, and the prospect of both for changing malicious cyber behavior. In April 2015, President Obama signed an Executive Order to deal with the threat of malicious cyber-enabled activities originating from or directed by persons located outside the United States. The Order blocks the property and interests of persons found to be harming or compromising the provision of services by a computer or network that support one or more entities in a critical infrastructure sector; causing a significant disruption to the availability of a computer or networks, including through a distributed denial of service attack; and causing a significant misappropriation of funds or economic resources, trade secrets, personal identifiers, or financial information for commercial or competitive advantage or private financial gain.[98] It authorizes the Secretary of the Treasury to impose sanctions on those individuals and entities that are responsible for cyber-enabled activities that threaten the national security, foreign policy, economic health, or financial stability of the United States.[99] By sanctioning these actors, their access to American financial systems, companies, and territory is restricted, which basically harms their ability to commit malicious acts and to profit from them.[100] Michael Daniel, former assistant to President Obama, said the order will "enable us to have a new way of both deterring and imposing costs on malicious cyber actors, wherever they may be and across a range of threats."[101] Although in heeding the warning by former Secretary of the Treasury Jack Lew on the risk of overreliance on sanctions, "in the absence of satisfying policy options, we risk deploying sanctions that . . . disadvantage U.S. companies . . . and expose our economy to retribution."[102]

NECESSARY MEANS UTILITY

US Secretary of Defense Ashton Carter has stated, "Adversaries should know that our preference for deterrence and our defensive posture don't diminish our willingness to use cyber options if necessary."[103] His communication of a willingness to take cyber-enabled action in a deterrent posture is apparently backed by capability to do so, although the credibility to evoke military retaliation is suspect given few publicly known examples to date. Doing nothing signals to other nation-states, other groups, and other actors that malicious behavior is okay and will not generate a response. Congressman Mac Thornberry, chairman of the House Armed Services Committee, adamantly stated "We have to figure out how to retaliate against an attack."[104] The problem starts with identifying the attacker and ends with the uncertain consequences of deploying a cyber weapon if necessary. Attributing malicious activity in cyberspace to actors with sufficient confidence and verifiability to hold them accountable is difficult. If attribution is certain enough to respond, the effects from escalation in counterattacks could reverberate across the Internet. A stockpile of cyber weapons is simply not good enough to deter malicious actors if the threat to use them is not credible enough to act when necessary.

The challenge is when to decisively act, especially if the circumstances of a cyber attack fall close to the threshold for military response. When does a cyber attack upon critical infrastructure, such as civilian financial systems, public utility sectors like power grids, or critical defense industries, justify a military counter strike? The Tallinn Manual says it depends on the scale and effects of the attack, yet the precise point at which the extent of death, injury, damage, destruction, or suffering qualifies as an armed attack is unclear. In the United States, the basic framework for the military to intervene in protecting nonmilitary networks and take retaliatory action would be in the event of significant consequence typically reflecting loss of life. As to whether there is a clear threshold that would trigger military intervention, the Deputy Commander of US Cyber Command, Lieutenant General James McLaughlin has said, "to be honest, it will never be black and white."[105] There is a structure in the government for a request to come forward for Cyber Command to take action. However, given the range of domestic and international actors from the civilian, commercial, and governmental sectors involved in cyberspace, any cyber operation will have to consider complicated issues such as fratricide avoidance, role of noncombatants, proportional use of force, and rules of engagement.[106]

Even still an argument exists that the need for an appropriate response in real time to a cyber attack on critical infrastructure requires explicit policies to be in place.[107] Therefore, Senator Mike Rounds has introduced legislation that would "require the executive branch to define which of these actions constitute a cyber act of war, which would allow our military to be better able to respond to cyber-attacks."[108] Although with the threshold defined to reach a decision for the military to return fire, can collateral damage be avoided if the intrusions were launched through thousands of hijacked computers in third-country or target nation sites? The containment of effects to the intended target set within a highly networked, potentially globally interconnected system is more difficult than against closed systems that may be only accessed locally. If effects cannot be meaningfully limited, controlled, or known, any cyber attack in retaliation, no matter how discretely intended, could have massive unintended consequences and pose significant political risk.[109] The inability to predict collateral damage and uncertainty over political effect requires caution,[110] especially since unintentional results could lead to escalation, which is an unplanned rise in the scope or intensity of a conflict. Escalation is an interactive concept in which action by one party triggers a response. Inadvertent escalation occurs when one party takes actions that it does not believe are escalatory, but cross a threshold of the other party. Accidental escalation occurs when an operational action has direct effects that are unintended. Of concern is a chain reaction, in which actions feed off each other to raise the conflict to a level not initially contemplated by any party.[111]

Once a conflict evolves, termination of cyber activity is not trivial. With detection and attribution so difficult, will it be clear when one side has stopped attacking another? One should consider three termination paths: negotiation, tacit deescalation, and petering out.[112] A cease-fire agreement in cyberspace presumes assurance that all parties will understand, monitor, and adhere to the terms of the agreement. These conditions are strained by conceptual differences in terminology and technical limitations in verification. Each side could cheat by shifting from visible disruption to more subtle corruption attacks. Or they could use third parties, like hacker crews or patriotic hackers, outside the agreement to reap unilateral advantages from attacks. In mutual deescalation, formal adjudication of the original issues is not necessary; both sides just need to believe that neither would make much headway through further cyber attacks. Unfortunately, in tacit deescalation the same validation problems exist, except are worst since there would only be a rough consensus on what was and was not considered a violation. In the third path, hope exists that attacks peter out, if each side concludes that attacks are growing difficult to conduct and pointless for the retaliation effort, but hope is never a strategy to follow.

The use of means for retaliation other than cyber operations alleviates many intrinsic concerns. A prime example of the utility of a law enforcement attempt to impose cost is the indictment of three men that allegedly hacked JP Morgan in 2014. The indictment reveals a broad network of criminal activity with computer hacking at its center.[113] JP Morgan is actually listed as Victim 1 of 12. The range of illicit activities run by the conspirators included securities market manipulation, unlawful Internet gambling, illicit payment processing, and an unlawful bitcoin exchange. In the list of Statutory Allegations, the conspirators were charged with twenty-three criminal counts, including computer hacking, wire fraud, and securities fraud, all under violations of Title 18, United States Code.[114] The indictment indicates existing laws are sufficient to cover a gambit of malicious cyber activities. The larger hurdle is finding the attribution to bring the criminals to justice in a timely manner to impose costs for their malicious behavior. The time from JP Morgan reporting the hack in the media to the indictments was about fifteen months. Maybe that time line is enough to communicate resolve to prosecute, but the charges need to hold in a conviction to produce credibility in legal action. However, even filing the charges does signal the threat of retaliation through employment disqualifications and travel restrictions. A high-profile Russian hacker found out justice is patient, for after being tracked for a decade by the US Secret Service, he was apprehended on vacation in the Maldives, extradited, and convicted in a federal court in 2016.[115]

As for the use of economic sanctions, the Executive Order imposing such on North Korea for the Sony attack was the first time the United States cited cyberattacks in sanctioning another nation-state.[116] Yet the sanctions could be of dubious value since they have not worked in changing the isolated regime's behavior. Following a nuclear test by Pyongyang in 2013, the UN Security Council adopted sanctions to tighten financial restrictions on North Korea. Despite any pain imposed by these sanctions, North Korea successfully detonated a hydrogen bomb in January 2016.[117] Concern resides in the international community that North Korea will succeed in mating a nuclear weapon to an accurate missile.[118] The Chinese resisted broad new sanctions against Pyongyang following the nuclear test,[119] but did finally agree after North Korea launched a long-range rocket in February 2016.[120] Still undeterred by sanctions, Pyongyang kept on launching missiles shortly after, starting with a submarine-launched ballistic missile in April 2016,[121] and two Musudan intermediate-range road-mobile missiles in June 2016.[122] After the Security Council threatened "further significant measures,"[123] North Korea promptly responded with its fifth underground nuclear test that produced a more powerful explosive yield.[124] Despite calls for new punitive action, years of sanctions show the approach is ineffective.[125] For instance, a loophole in the sanctions allows North Korea to sell coal if the proceeds are used for humanitarian purposes[126] and shipments of coal to China have far exceeded the UN Security Council ceiling on such shipments that China helped pass.[127]

The Chinese Foreign Minister had adamantly stated "sanctions are not an end in themselves," in promoting the need to bring the nuclear issue on the Korean Peninsula back to the track of negotiation.[128] In this regard sanctions provide pressure for negotiations, such as in the historic Iran nuclear deal, but the pressure of sanctions cannot be relieved or forgone if other violations of international order occur. For example, Iran could have violated a United Nations Security Council resolution with its ballistic missile test in October 2015 during fulfillment of the nuclear accord.[129] Iran tested a long-range missile called the Emad which according to their Defense Minister was capable of precise control.[130] In response, regardless of the perceived good will garnered in the nuclear agreement, the US Treasury Department sanctioned nearly a dozen Iranian-linked entities for their alleged role in Iran's ballistic missile program.[131] Likewise the sanctions relief from the nuclear deal has not relieved tensions in the maritime domain, where boats from the Islamic Revolutionary Guard Corps have increasingly harassed US military vessels transiting the Straits of Hormuz through dangerous close-in maneuvers.[132] Finally in the cyber domain, Iran is only looking to enhance cyber capabilities for use as a tolerated form of behavior,[133] just like a high-speed boat approaches foreign military ships.

AN INSUFFICIENT DETERRENCE OPTION

The US military is working to become more transparent about offensive planning in cyberspace, hoping that communication of such information will deter cyberattacks. For example, public media releases indicate contractors have been asked to compete for a nearly half-billion dollar military contract to develop and if necessary deploy lethal cyber weapons.[134] The use of these weapons as an instrument of deterrence also requires transparency in direct attribution, so an actor knows any threat of retaliation is credible.[135] The executive director of US Cyber Command has said they are looking for loud offensive cyber "tools that can be definitely traced back to the United States military," to possibly deter future intrusions.[136] At the classified level, massive cyber weapon capability could exist to hold an adversary at significant risk. Powerful and authentic espionage tools created by hackers at the NSA, to include several exploits and a number of implants, have been mysteriously leaked online. The software would be used to take over firewalls that are used "in the largest and most critical commercial, educational and government agencies around the world."[137] Therefore, malicious actors should not take the lack of a cyber response as a lack of capability or an unwillingness to use it if deemed necessary.

The United States has used cyber operations against the terrorist group Islamic State, breaking into computers of fighters to implant malware that mines for intelligence and blocking their use of encrypted communications.[138] Yet, despite an ongoing process to build and demonstrate a cyber deterrent, according to Admiral Rogers, foreign countries and criminal hackers still believe there is "little price to pay" for breaching the US government or US companies.[139] Therefore, without risk of punishment, cyberattacks continue unabated against federal agencies[140] and civilian companies.[141] Malicious actors appear to have developed a greater tolerance for risk and plan their attacks to avoid triggering credible military deterrent responses, staying below the implicit thresholds of "use of force" or "armed attack." Nevertheless the experience of sanctions and indictments do show there are viable alternatives to the threat and use of military force, especially for cyber espionage and crime.[142]

Despite the dropping of "cyber bombs" on the Islamic State, according to Deputy Secretary Work,[143] loose groups of supportive hackers have joined forces to create a mega hacking unit named the United Cyber Caliphate to run defacement and doxing campaigns.[144] Contrary to this development, it turns out that legal action to indict five PLA officers in May 2014 did have an effect in China. In the months that followed the indictment, the Chinese military quietly begin to dismantle their economic espionage campaign apparatus. It initially appeared legal measures by the United States had altered the behavior of portions of the Chinese government, but in reality, the mission was just shifted to the Ministry of State Security. This ministry is better suited anyway for economic espionage, with elite contract hackers that can better hide telltale digital trails, and with direct channels to state-owned enterprises.[145] Already active and productive, the Ministry is most likely behind the intrusions into Anthem Health Service in 2014[146] and the US Office of Personnel Management in 2015.[147] If law enforcement is not sufficient, that leaves economic sanctions, which require a threshold of attribution lower than beyond reasonable doubt for legal action. Yet not just the threat of them is enough; actual imposition in a demonstration of credibility, to create a real effect on nation-state sponsored cyber activity, may be necessary. The United States did not hesitate to impose sanctions on North Korea for the Sony attack. However, the Executive Order, while expansive in legal breadth, was weak in implementation, targeting three organizations already on the US sanctions list and ten individuals not directly involved in cyber warfare.[148]

Overall, today malicious actors are left guessing if costs can or will be imposed upon them for malicious cyber activities. The possession of capabilities and communication of consequences is not quite consistent. President-elect Donald Trump told a veterans group in October 2016, "As a deterrent against attacks on our critical resources, the United States must possess—and has to—the unquestioned capacity to launch crippling cyber counterattacks." Furthermore, "America's dominance in the arena must be unquestioned. Today, it's totally questioned. People don't even know if we have the capability that we are supposed to have,"[149] although for retaliation by military means, maybe it is alright to keep adversaries like nation-states and terrorist groups guessing on capability. For under the "idea of a threat that leaves something to chance,"[150] they will be kept guessing on what the punishment will be, not whether there will be punishment. In talking about advanced technologies, Deputy Secretary Work stated, "We will reveal to deter and conceal for warfighting advantage. I want our competitors to wonder what's behind the black curtain."[151]

Well-respected reporter David Sanger countered Secretary Work in saying "we are facing a shroud of secrecy, which is undermining the deterrent effect."[152] America could have a secret arsenal of the most powerful cyber weapons on Earth. Their development would be for use as a component of any future military campaign. How and when these capabilities will be used outside armed conflict is uncertain. Congressman Jim Himes, ranking member of the House Intelligence subcommittee on Cybersecurity, asked, "What is the legitimate retaliation for an act of war?" and sums up the current predicament well in stating, "In place of norms and definitions you've just got a series of endless question marks. That's a dangerous world because uncertainty in this world equals risk."[153] So it appears today, for at least the United States, in accordance with the principle of necessity, all peaceful alternatives must be exhausted before a resort to force.[154] This staunch policy most likely means attackers will continue to believe there is "little price to pay" for their malicious activity, and the strategy of deterrence by retaliation will remain an insufficient strategic cyber deterrence option.

NOTES

1. Peter Roberts and Andrew Hardie, "The Validity of Deterrence in the Twenty-first Century," Royal United Services Institute, Occasional Paper, August 2015, 5–9.

2. Greg Otto, "Clapper Not Optimistic on China Cyber Deal," *Fedscoop*, September 29, 2015.

3. Elias Groll, "The U.S. Hoped Indicting 5 Chinese Hackers Would Deter Beijing's Cyberwarriors. It Hasn't Worked," *Foreign Policy*, September 2, 2015, 1–12.

4. Joab Jackson, "5 Arrested in JP Morgan Hacking Case," *Computer World*, July 22, 2015.

5. Nicole Hong, "Charges Announced in J.P. Morgan Hacking Case," *Morningstar*, November 10, 2015.

6. Dennis K. Berman, "Adm. Michael Rogers on the Prospect of a Digital Pearl Harbor," *Wall Street Journal*, October 26, 2015.

7. Joe Gould, "Constructing a Cyber Superpower," Focus US Cyber Command, *Defense News*, June 29, 2015.

8. Robert O. Work, Deputy Secretary of Defense, "Cybersecurity Risks to DoD Networks and Infrastructure," Statement before the Senate Armed Services Committee, September 29, 2015.

9. Rachel Feintzeig, Clint Boulton, and Joann S. Lublin, "Fears Spread of Sony-Style Hack," *Wall Street Journal*, December 7, 2014.

10. Richard Taylor, "Sony Pictures Computer System Hacked in Online Attack," *BBC News*, Technology Section, November 25, 2014.

11. Ellen Nakashima, Craig Timberg, and Andrea Peterson, "Sony Pictures Hack Appears to Be Linked to North Korea, Investigators Say," *Washington Post*, December 5, 2014.

12. David Goldman and Jose Pagliery, "Sony Hackers Threaten Moviegoers with Terrorist Acts," *CNN News*, Money Section, December 15, 2014.

13. Drew Harwell and Ellen Nakashima, "Hackers' Threats Prompt Sony Pictures to Shelve Christmas Release of *The Interview*," *Washington Post*, Economy Section, December 18, 2014.

14. Devlin Barrett and Bryon Tau, "Obama Says Sony 'Made a Mistake' Canceling Film," *Wall Street Journal*, Politics and Policy Section, December 19, 2014.

15. FBI National Press Office, "Update on Sony Investigation," The Federal Bureau of Investigation, Washington, DC, December 19, 2014.

16. Noveta, "Operation Blockbuster: Unraveling the Long Threat of the Sony Attack," February 2016, 12–13.

17. FBI National Press Office, "Update on Sony Investigation," The Federal Bureau of Investigation, Washington, DC, December 19, 2014.

18. Jenny Kim, Scott LaFoy, and Ethan Sohn, "North Korea's Cyber Operations: Strategy and Responses," Center for Strategic and International Studies, December 2015, 7.

19. Nichole Perlroth and David E. Sanger, "North Korea Loses Its Link to the Internet," *New York Times*, December 22, 2014.

20. President Barack Obama, "Imposing Additional Sanctions with Respect to North Korea," Executive Order, The White House, January 2, 2015.

21. Carol Morello and Greg Miller, "U.S. Imposes Sanction on N. Korea Following Attack on Sony," *Washington Post*, January 2, 2015.

22. Danny Yadron, "Cyberattack on Sony Is Called Sophisticated," *Wall Street Journal*, December 7, 2014.

23. David E. Sanger and Martin Fackler , "U.S. Hacked North Korean before Attack on Sony," *International New York Times*, January 18, 2015, 1 and 3.

24. Pavel Alpeyev and Grace Huang, "Sony Hacker Snooped for Months, Then Planted 10-Minute Time Bomb," *Bloomberg News*, December 22, 2014.

25. Kurt Baumgartner, "Sony/Destover: Mystery North Korean Actor's Destructive and Past Network Activity," *Securelist Blog Research*, December 4, 2014.

26. Ian Kelly, "Cyber Attacks on Critical Infrastructure on the Rise," ID Experts Blog, August 24, 2016, https://www2.idexpertscorp.com/blog/single/cyber-attacks-on-critical-infra-structure-on-the-rise.

27. Michael Schmitt, "International Law and Cyber Attacks: Sony v. North Korea," *Just Security*, December 17, 2014, 1.

28. Michael Schmitt, "International Law and Cyber Attacks: Sony v. North Korea," *Just Security*, December 17, 2014, 2.

29. Larry Greenemeier, "Seeking Address: Why Cyber Attacks Are So Difficult to Trace Back to Hackers," *Scientific American*, June 11, 2011.

30. Mauno Pihelgas, "Back-Tracing and Anonymity in Cyberspace," *Peacetime Regime for State Activities in Cyberspace* (Tallinn, Estonia: NATO Cooperative Cyber Defence Centre of Excellence, 2013), 31–60.

31. Dmitri Alperovitch, "The Art of Attribution: Identifying and Pursuing Your Cyber Adversaries," RSA Conference, February 24–28, 2014, 13.

32. General Michael V. Hayden, "HBO What to Do about Cyberattacks," Council on Foreign Relations Event Transcript, October 6, 2015, 28.

33. U.S. Department of Defense, *Cyberspace Operations,* US Joint Publication 3-12 (R), (Washington, DC: The Joint Staff, February 5, 2013): v.

34. United Nations, Charter of the United Nations, Chapter VII, Article 2, San Francisco, CA, October 24, 1945.

35. United Nations, General Assembly, Resolution 3314 (XXIX), December 14, 1974.

36. Harold Hongkin Koh, Legal Advisor, Department of State, "International Law in Cyberspace," Remarks at USCYBERCOM Inter-Agency Legal Conference, Ft. Meade, Maryland, September 18, 2012.

37. Michael N. Schmitt, *Tallinn Manual 2.0 on the International Law Applicable to Cyber Operations*, Second Edition (Cambridge University Press, 2017), 339-341.

38. Executive Office of the President, *Presidential Policy Directive on Signals Intelligence Activities*, PPD-28 (Washington, DC: The White House, January 17, 2014).

39. Office of General Counsel, *Department of Defense Law of War Manual*, June 2015 (Updated December 2016), 38–42.

40. United Nations, Charter of the United Nations, Chapter VII, Article 51, San Francisco, CA, October 24, 1945.

41. Office of General Counsel, *Department of Defense Law of War Manual*, June 2015 (Updated December 2016), 47.

42. Michael N. Schmitt, *Tallinn Manual 2.0 on the International Law applicable to Cyber Operations*, (Cambridge University Press, 2017): 348.

43. Schmitt, *Tallinn Manual on the International Law Applicable to Cyber Operations*, 349.

44. Schmitt, *Tallinn Manual on the International Law Applicable to Cyber Warfare*, 349.

45. Schmitt, *Tallinn Manual on the International Law Applicable to Cyber Warfare*, 349.

46. North Atlantic Treaty Organization, "The North Atlantic Treaty," Article 5, Washington, D.C., April 4, 1949.

47. North Atlantic Treaty Organization, "The North Atlantic Treaty," Article 5, Washington, DC, April 4, 1949.

48. North Atlantic Treaty Organization, "Wales Summit Declaration," Paragraph 72, September 5, 2014.

49. Michael N. Schmitt, *Tallinn Manual 2.0 on the International Law applicable to Cyber Operations*, Second Edition (Cambridge University Press, 2017): 354.

50. North Atlantic Treaty Organization, "Warsaw Summit Communique," Paragraph 70, July 9, 2016.

51. North Atlantic Treaty Organization, "Warsaw Summit Communique."

52. James A. Lewis, "The Role of Offensive Cyber Operations in NATO's Collective Defense," A NATO CCD COE Publication on Strategic Cyber Security, Tallinn Paper No. 8, 2015, 2–10.

53. Wieslaw Gozdziewicz et al., "NATO Road to Cybersecurity," The Kosciuszko Institute, August 25, 2016, 1–77.

54. Schmitt, *Tallinn Manual 2.0 on the International Law Applicable to Cyber Operations*, 375.

55. Jan Stinissen, "A Legal Framework for Cyber Operations in Ukraine," in *Cyber War in Perspective: Russian Aggression against Ukraine*, chap. 14 (Tallinn, Estonia: NATO Cooperative Cyber Defense Center of Excellence Publications, 2015), 123–34.

56. US Department of Defense, *Cyberspace Operations*, US Joint Publication 3-12 (R) (Washington, DC: The Joint Staff, February 5, 2013), III-10.

57. Catherine Lotrionte, "Cyber War: Definitions, Deterrence and Foreign Policy," Statement before the House Committee on Foreign Affairs, September 30, 2015.

58. Office of General Counsel, *Department of Defense Law of War Manual*, June 2015 (Updated December 2016), 1013.

59. Office of General Counsel, *Department of Defense Law of War Manual*, 50–51.

60. Office of General Counsel, *Department of Defense Law of War Manual*, 51–65.

61. Michael Peck, "The Pentagon Is Worried about Hacked GPS," *The National Interest*, January 14, 2016.

62. Office of General Counsel, *Department of Defense Law of War Manual*, 1022.

63. Michael N. Schmitt, "The Law of Cyber Targeting," A NATO CCD COE Publication on Strategic Cyber Security, Tallinn Paper No. 7 (2015): 7–19.

64. US Department of Defense, *Cyberspace Operations*, US Joint Publication 3-12 (R) (Washington, DC: The Joint Staff, February 5, 2013), IV-4.

65. Schmitt, *Tallinn Manual on the International Law Applicable to Cyber Operations*, 470-472.

66. "Iran: Stuxnet Worm, Computer Terrorism," Press TV, October 13, 2010.

67. IISS Strategic Comments, "Stuxnet: Targeting Iran's Nuclear Programme," vol. 17, Comment 6, February 2011.

68. Schmitt, *Tallinn Manual on the International Law Applicable to Cyber Operations*, 342.

69. William Jackson, "Stuxnet vulnerabilities in industrial controls," *Government Computer News*, October 1, 2010.

70. Gregg Keizer, "Is Stuxnet the Best Malware Ever?" *Computer World*, September 16, 2010.

71. Nicolas Falliere, Liam O. Murchu, and Eric Chien, "W32.Stuxnet Dossier," Symantec Security Response, Version 1.3, November 2010.

72. Kim Zetter, "Clues Suggest Stuxnet Virus Was Built for Subtle Nuclear Sabotage," *Wired*, November 15, 2010.

73. John Richardson, "Stuxnet as Cyberwarfare: Applying the Law of War to the Virtual Battlefield," *Journal of Computer and Information Law* 29 (Fall 2011): 1–37.

74. William Jackson, "Stuxnet Reveals Vulnerabilities in Industrial Controls," *Government Computer News*, October 1, 2010.

75. US Department of Defense, *Cyberspace Policy Report*, November 2011, 5.

76. Greg Miller and Souad Mekhennet, "Inside the Surreal World of the Islamic State's Propaganda Machine," *Washington Post*, November 20, 2015.

77. Margaret Coker, Danny Yadron, and Damian Paletta, "Hacker Killed by Drone Was Islamic State's Secret Weapon," *Wall Street Journal*, August 27, 2015.

78. Jeffrey Carr, "The Legal Rationale for Killing an Enemy Hacker (or Could You Be the Next Junaid Hussain)?" Blogspot, Digital Dao: Evolving Hostilities in the Global Cyber Commons, September 1, 2015.

79. Lisa O. Monaco, "Strengthening Our Nation's Cyber Defenses," Remarks as Prepared for Delivery, The Wilson Center, Washington, DC, February 10, 2015.

80. Executive Office of the President, *Presidential Policy Directive—United States Cyber Incident Coordination*, PPD-41 (Washington, DC: The White House, July 26, 2016).

81. Abram N. Shulsky, *Deterrence Theory and Chinese Behavior* (Santa Monica, CA: RAND Corporation, 2014).

82. Thomas Schelling, *Arms and Influence* (New Haven, CT: Yale University Press, 1966), 69–78.

83. Council of Europe, "Convention on Cybercrime," Budapest, Hungary, November 23, 2001: 1–24.

84. Speech by the Secretary General, "Budapest Convention on Cybercrime," 10th Anniversary meeting, Strasbourg, November 23, 2011.

85. Council of Europe, "Global Action on Cybercrime," Capacity Building, located at http://www.coe.int/en/web/cybercrime/glacy, accessed January 7, 2017.

86. Larry Neumeister, "3 Estonian Men Get over 3 Years in Prison for Cyberfraud," *Daily Herald*, July 23, 2015.

87. Ellen Nakashima, "U.S. Accuses Hacker of Stealing Military Members' Data and Giving It to ISIS," *Washington Post*, October 16, 2015.

88. Aaron Boyd, "Hacker Who Outed Feds' info Charged with Terrorism," *C4ISR &Networks*, January 28, 2016.

89. Rachel Weiner and Ellen Nakashima, "Hacker Admits He Gave Military Member's Data to the Islamic State," *Washington Post*, June 15, 2016.

90. Andrea Peterson and Ellen Nakashima, "U.S. charges three suspected Syrian Electronic Army Hackers," *The Washington Post*, March 22, 2016.

91. Kenneth Katzman, "Iran Sanctions," Congressional Research Service, CRS Report RS20871, January 21, 2016.

92. Dianne E. Rennack, "Iran: U.S. Economic Sanctions and the Authority to Lift Restrictions," Congressional Research Service, CRS Report R43311, January 22, 2016.

93. Barak Ravid, "Netanyahu Tells U.S. Congress: This Deal Paves Iran's Path to the Bomb," *Haaretz*, March 3, 2015.

94. Jeremy Diamond, "Could Military Force Still Be Used against Iran?" *CNN News*, Politics Section, April 2, 2015.

95. The American Israel Public Affairs Committee, "Analysis: The Iran Nuclear Deal," July 28, 2015, 1–10.

96. Thomas L. Friedman, "Obama Makes His Case on Iran Nuclear Deal," *New York Times*, July 14, 2015.

97. Bruno Tertrais, "Iran: An Experiment in Strategic Risk-Taking," *Survival: Global Politics and Strategy*, October–November 2015, 67–73.

98. President Barack Obama, "Blocking the Property of Certain Persons Engaging in Significant Malicious Cyber-Enabled Activities," Executive Order, The White House, April 1, 2015.

99. Michael Daniel, "Our Latest Tool to Combat Cyber Attacks: What You Need to Know," Fact Sheet, The White House, April 1, 2015.

100. Aaron Boyd, "Treasury Finalizes Rule for Imposing Cyber Sanctions," *Federal Times*, January 4, 2016.

101. Aaron Boyd, "Obama: Cyberattacks Continue to Be National Emergency," *Federal Times*, March 10, 2016.

102. William J. Burns and Jared Cohen, "The Rules of the Brave New Cyberworld," *Foreign Policy*, February 16, 2017.

103. Amber Corrin, "Cyber Goes on the Offense," *C4ISR &Networks*, June 2015, 32.

104. W. J. Hennigan and Brian Bennett, "Pentagon Seeks Cyberweapons Strong Enough to Deter Attacks," *The LA Times*, July 31, 2015.

105. Zachary Fryer-Biggs, "21st Century Spy Wars," Cyber Espionage Briefing, *Jane's Defense Weekly*, November 11, 2015, 26–30.

106. Brett T. Williams, "Ten Propositions Regarding Cyberspace Operations," *Joint Force Quarterly* no. 61, 2nd Quarter (2011): 11–16.

107. Mike Rounds, "Defining a Cyber Act of War," *Wall Street Journal*, May 8, 2016.

108. Cyber/IT Blog, "Rounds Introduces Cyber War Definition Bill," *Defense Daily*, May 10, 2016.

109. Maren Leed, "Offensive Cyber Capabilities at the Operational Level," Center for Strategic and International Studies, September 2013, 1–9.

110. James Lewis, "Low-Level Cyberattacks Are Common but Truly Damaging Ones Are Rare," *Washington Post*, October 9, 2013.

111. Herbert Lin, "Escalation Dynamics and Conflict Termination in Cyberspace," *Strategic Studies Quarterly* (Fall 2012): 52–63.

112. Martin C. Libicki, *Cyberdeterrence and Cyberwar* (Santa Monica, CA: RAND Corporation, 2009), 135–37.

113. Nicole Hong, "Charges Announced in J.P. Morgan Hacking Case," *Wall Street Journal*, November 10, 2015.

114. US District Court, Indictment, Criminal No. S1 15 Cr. 333 (LTS), Unsealed November 10, 2015, 1–68.

115. Kate O'Keeffe and Jacob Gershman, "Russian Convicted in Hacking Case," *Wall Street Journal*, August 26, 2016.

116. Michael A. Memoli and Ryan Faughnder, "U.S. Sanctions on North Korea Suggest Prospect of Further Retaliation," *Los Angeles Times*, January 2, 2015.

117. Alastair Gale and Kwanwoo Jun, "North Korea Says It Successfully Conducted Hydrogen-Bomb Test," *Wall Street Journal*, January 6, 2016.

118. Steve Almasy and Euan McKirdy, "North Korea: Our Nuclear Warheads Can Fit on Missiles," *CNN News*, March 9, 2016.

119. Jane Perlez and David E. Sanger, "John Kerry Urges China to Curb North Korea's Nuclear Pursuits," *New York Times*, January 27, 2016.

120. Farnaz Fassihi, "U.S., China Agree to Sanction North Korea on Nuclear Program," *Wall Street Journal*, February 25, 2016.

121. Don Melvin, Jim Sciutto and Will Ripley, "North Korea Launches Missile from Submarine," *CNN News*, April 24, 2016.

122. Luis Martinez, "North Korea Launches 2 Intermediate-Range Missiles," *ABC News*, June 21, 2016.

123. Edith M. Lederer, "UN Security Council Condemns North Korea Missile Tests," *Associated Press*, September 6, 2016.

124. Choe Sang-Hun and Jane Perlez, "North Korea Tests a Mightier Nuclear Bomb, Raising Tension," *New York Times*, September 8, 2016.

125. Alastair Gale, "Pyongyang Faces More-Punitive Sanctions," *Wall Street Journal*, August 25, 2016.

126. Jane Perlez, "China's Silence Reinforces Its North Korea Calculus," *New York Times*, September 12, 2016.

127. Chun Han Wong, "North Korea Coal Exports to China Breached U.N. Cap," *The Wall Street Journal*, February 23, 2017.

128. Felicia Schwartz, "China, U.S. Divided on Response to North Korea's Nuclear Blast," *Wall Street Journal*, January 28, 2016.

129. Kenneth Katzman, "Iran, Gulf Security, and U.S. Policy," Congressional Research Service, CRS Report RL32048, January 14, 2016, 25.

130. Aresu Eqbali and Asa Fitch, "Iran Test-Fires New Missile," *Wall Street Journal*, October 12, 2015.

131. Jay Solomon, "U.S. Sanctions 11 Iranian-Tied Entities for Role in Tehran's Ballistic Missile Program," *Wall Street Journal*, January 17, 2016.

132. Paul Sonne, "Iran Vessels Harassed U.S. Destroyer Near Persian Gulf, *Wall Street Journal*, August 24, 2016; and Gordon Lubold, "In Common Occurrence, Iranian Boats Veer Close to U.S. Warship," *Wall Street Journal*, July 11, 2016.

133. Michael Eisenstadt, "Iran's Lengthening Cyber Shadow," Research Notes, *The Washington Institute for Near East Policy* no. 34 (July 2016): 1–20.

134. Aliya Sternstein, "Pentagon Contractors Developing Lethal Cyber Weapons," *Nextgov*, November 4, 2015.

135. United Kingdom Ministry of Defense, "Future Operating Environment 2035," First Edition, December 2015, 20.

136. Chris Bing, "U.S. Cyber Command director: We Want 'Loud,' Offensive Cyber Tools," *Fedscoop*, August 30, 2016.

137. Ellen Nakashima, "Powerful NSA Hacking Tools Have Been Revealed Online," *Washington Post*, August 16, 2016.

138. Shane Harris, "U.S. Ratchets Up Cyber Attacks on ISIS," *The Daily Beast*, April 17, 2016.

139. Damian Paletta, "NSA Chief Says Cyberattack at Pentagon Was Sophisticated, Persistent," *Wall Street Journal*, September 8, 2015.

140. Riley Walters, "Continued Federal Cyber Breaches in 2015," *The Heritage Foundation*, Issue Brief, No. 4488, November 19, 2015.

141. Riley Walters, "Cyber Attacks on U.S. Companies in 2016," *The Heritage Foundation*, Issue Brief, No. 4636, December 2, 2016.

142. James A. Lewis, "Cyber War: Definitions, Deterrence and Foreign Policy," Statement before the House Committee on Foreign Affairs, September 30, 2015.

143. Amber Corrin, "U.S. Goes to Cyber War with ISIS," *C4ISR &Networks*, April 14, 2016.

144. Catalin Cimpanu, "ISIS Hackers Join Forces to Create Mega Hacking Unit," *Softpedia*, April 25, 2016.

145. Ellen Nakashima, "Following U.S. Indictments, China Shifts Commercial Hacking Away from Military to Civilian Agency," *Washington Post*, November 30, 2015.

146. Michael A. Riley and Jordan Robertson, "Chinese State-Sponsored Hackers Suspected in Anthem Attack," *Bloomberg News*, February 5, 2015.

147. Kirstin Finklea, "Cyber Intrusion into U.S. Office of Personnel Management: In Brief," Congressional Research Service, CRS Report R44111, July 17, 2015.

148. Bruce Klingner, "The U.S. Needs to Respond to North Korea's Latest Cyber Attack," *The Heritage Foundation*, Issue Brief #4367, March 20, 2015.

149. Aaron Boyd, "Trump Administration Promises More Aggressive, Less Political Cyber Stance," *Federal Times*, November 9, 2016.

150. Thomas Schelling, *The Strategy of Conflict* (Cambridge, MA: Harvard University Press, 1960), 187–203.

151. Aaron Mehta, "Work Outlines Key Steps in Third Offset Tech Development," *Defense News*, December 14, 2015.

152. David Sanger, Keynote Address, CyCon 2016, Tallinn, Estonia, June 3, 2016.

153. Danny Vinik, "America's Secret Arsenal," *Politico*, The Agenda: The Cyber Issue, December 9, 2015.

154. Office of General Counsel, *Department of Defense Law of War Manual*, June 2015 (Updated December 2016), 42.

Chapter Five

Deterrence by Denial

The strategy of deterrence by denial of benefit from malicious activity in cyberspace seeks to convince any malicious actor their attacks will fail to achieve their desired outcome or simpler still, seeks to deny their success. The US Defense Department Chief Information Officer tacitly endorses this strategy in stating, "one of the best ways to reduce the cyber threat is to make it harder and more costly for adversaries to initiate attacks."[1] He opines that innovative security measures along with strategic security planning and training could make launching attacks on departmental resources time-consuming and futile. Since deterrence is partially a function of perception, the strategic option of denial works in the mind of the adversary by decreasing the likelihood that an intended attack will succeed. Deterrence by denial focuses on increasing capabilities to defend networks and systems from cyber attack by any actor, no matter whether that actor is a nation-state, hacker group, criminal organization, or terrorist group. In their 2015 Cyber Strategy, the US Defense Department recognizes the importance of working with other departments, agencies, international allies, and partners, and also the private sector to strengthen deterrence by denial through improved cyber security.[2] In doing so, the development and implementation of effective protective measures deny any potential attacker the benefit of succeeding.

However, in the current threat landscape, cyber attacks seriously challenge the strategic option of deterrence by denial. The incidents seen today range from basic criminal schemes to massive denial of service attacks to sophisticated (and sometimes destructive) intrusions into critical infrastructure networks and systems. Most of the headlines focus on data breeches in government and across the spectrum of industries, and rightfully so, as the number of identities exposed through these breaches over the past three years alone surpasses one billion.[3] The economic impact can be immediate with the theft of money or long term with the loss of intellectual property. The success of malicious actors in cyberspace is partly due to the weakest link in defense, the behavior of users combined with the effectiveness of social engineering methods, such as reconnaissance-based spear phishing which can lead to exploit execution or compromised passwords. The latter can be leveraged in second generation activity, such as in recent government breaches in the United States where illegally obtained valid credentials were acquired by social engineering methods.[4] Once the actor gets inside the organization, only 31 percent of victims discover the breach by internal means and for the rest alerts can come months later after stolen property is found in the wild,[5] although encouraging news comes from a 2015 report by the Online Trust Alliance that contends 90 percent of recent breaches could have been prevented if organizations had implemented the most basic cyber security best practices.[6]

Protective measures to reduce risk and enhance security include the promulgation of security strategies, the implementation of security controls, and the sharing of cyber threat information. The strategy of deterrence by denial seeks to change the cost-benefit calculations of a malicious actor by credibly signaling, or proving, that an attack will fail.[7] Security strategies articulate proven models for the identification and deployment of defensive capabilities, such as security controls or best practices. The use of cyber security frameworks result in the selection of risk, informed investments in these security controls and associated security solution products, which are ideally enhanced by shared cyber threat information. Preferably these security controls and solutions are deployed to block, detect, and interrupt the actor at the various phases of the cyber attack process. Through risk management, the strategic selection and positioning of credible capabilities along the attack process offer the fluid form of deterrence aptly named denial of benefit. This chapter starts with an illustrative case that depicts the unfortunate failure of deterrence by denial of benefit or success. It then examines an assortment of promising protective measures and by what degree through risk management they improve the security of networks and systems to deny malicious actors the benefit of attack.

ILLUSTRATIVE CASE

In June 2015, the US Office of Personnel Management (OPM) revealed that based on incident detection and forensic investigation that a cyber intrusion affecting information technology systems and data may have compromised the personnel information of approximately four million former and current federal employees.[8] A month later, OPM reported a separate incident targeting databases housing background investigation records of 21.5 million individuals.[9] According to US-CERT, the first hack of OPM systems occurred in July 2012. The attacker stole manuals and IT architecture information. That breach was halted by OPM after almost two years and reported to Congress.[10] Then in May 2014, a second, most likely related, attacker established a foothold in the OPM network and moved to the security clearance database, which exposed Standard Form 86 data entries where applicants list contacts and relatives, mental illness, drug and alcohol abuse, past arrests, bankruptcies, and more. That security data revealed the identities of almost everyone who has gotten a US security clearance.[11] The second attacker then moved laterally to breach systems maintained at a Department of Interior–shared data center in October 2014, which resulted in the loss of files for every federal employee, every federal retiree, and up to one million former federal employees. The hackers stole military records and veterans' status information, address, birth date, pay history, insurance and pension information, and age, gender, and race data.[12] Then in March 2015, the second attacker stole the fingerprint data of 5.6 million federal employees. Collectively the personnel records provide a foreign government the ability to blackmail or impersonate or exploit federal employees to gain access to secrets or computer networks.

Finally in April 2015, OPM reported to US-CERT an unknown secure sockets layer (SSL) certificate beaconing to an unknown site and deployed first CylanceV and later Cylance Protect security solutions which identified malware used by the second attacker. A week later, a product demo by CyTech Services of a network forensics software package also found malware embedded on the network.[13] Further forensics indicated the second attacker stole access credentials from the contractor KeyPoint and used those credentials to break into OPM systems.[14] This finding makes sense for, according to an inspector general report, outsiders entering the OPM system were not subjected to multifactor authentication, where for example systems require a code that is sent to a cell phone to be entered before giving access to a user. A host of deficiencies left OPM open to attack—for instance, it did not possess an inventory of all computer servers and devices with access to its network nor did it regularly scan for vulnerabilities in the system.[15] Consequently in the first attack, it is possible that OPM was breached through an unpatched vulnerability. Overall OPM suffered from an antiquated cybersecurity infrastructure, abysmal security practices, and ill-equipped personnel. If OPM had implemented proper IT governance practices, used encryption and assigned least privilege user access, the organization could have pushed the attacker closer to a threshold where the cost of resources outweighed the benefit of the data.[16]

The director of National Intelligence said Chinese hackers are the leading suspect in the OPM intrusion, to which a spokesman for the Chinese Embassy in Washington responded, "we hope relevant parties of the US side can stop making unfounded and hypothetical accusations, and work constructively with China to address cybersecurity issues."[17] Even though forensic evidence leaves little doubt that China was responsible, the Obama administration chose not to make any official assertion about attribution due to concern over exposing details of the United States' own espionage and capabilities. Even more so, the response to penetrations targeting government-held data have been restrained, in part because such breaches are regarded as within traditional parameters of espionage. Seen as fair game, the former head of the Central Intelligence Agency said "This is espionage," and "I don't blame the Chinese for this at all. If I [as head of the National Security Agency] could have done it, I would have done it in a heartbeat."[18] Instead, President Obama vowed to bolster cyber defenses to deny benefit of attack, saying the United States has old computer systems with "significant vulnerabilities" and needs to be "much more aggressive" in stepping up defenses.[19]

Cyber warfare author Jeffrey Carr agreed that the way to fix the administration's cybersecurity problem isn't to retaliate against a foreign government since digital espionage is the new normal. Carr believes that "deterrence is possible" but "doesn't come from force or trying to instill fear," but instead from "enabling security protocols that make sensitive or valuable data so hard to steal that the effort isn't worth the reward."[20] That means a complete overhaul of how the government employs protective measures, ferreting out weaknesses in security and correcting them. No one should have been surprised by the OPM hacks. The inspector general audit in 2014 had found serious flaws in the network and the way it was managed. OPM is a monolithic agency run by politically appointed leaders who lack the expertise to make informed decisions on protective measures. Leadership needs to understand and appreciate cyber risk so they can authorize their IT security department to develop and deploy defenses against cyber threats.[21] At OPM, the director eventually resigned after political pressure from Congress during the fallout investigation.[22] In retrospect, the national security consequences of a successful hack at OPM should not have been a surprise. The signs were all there for it to happen, as it had the vulnerabilities, no security-focused leadership, and a capable and motivated malicious actor that was not convinced their attacks would fail.[23] After a House Committee investigation, Representative Jason Chaffetz noted, "with some basic hygiene, some good tools, an awareness and some talent, they [OPM] really could have prevented this."[24]

SECURITY STRATEGIES

The lessons of the OPM hack can be applied in a range of protective measures that attempt to reduce cyber risk. These start with the development of cyber security strategies for the placement of defensive capabilities. Traditionally organizations focus their defenses at the perimeter of the network in the belief that this strategy makes it difficult for an attacker to penetrate systems. Typical passive defenses at the perimeter, like Anti-Virus software, which detect known malware signatures, and Blacklists, which blocks known malicious websites, have become less effective as the volume and complexity of threats increases.[25] Once the perimeter is breached, as often occurs, the attackers have free reign within the network. In a test by the security industry firm FireEye, network and email appliances were placed among 1,216 organizations in sixty-three countries across more than twenty industries from October 2013 to March 2014. Analysis of the data generated from the trial deployments of the appliances revealed that 97 percent of the organizations had been breached and more than 75 percent of the organizations had active command-and-control communications between their internal systems and outside servers, meaning that the attackers had control of the breached systems and were possibly exfiltrating data from them.[26] To compensate for the failure of one layer of the system, like at the perimeter, organizations use a multilayer security strategy aptly named defense-in-depth.

Defense-in-depth strategies emphasize multiple, overlapping, and mutually supportive defenses, such as security controls or best practices, to guard against single-point failures in any specific technology or protection method. Security controls are synonymous with safeguards and countermeasures, which may include security features, management constraints, personnel security, and security of physical structures, areas, and devices.[27] A defense-in-depth strategy also accentuates the continual deployment of defenses to protect multiple threat points, including network, endpoint, web, and email security.[28] In designing a multilayered security infrastructure, numerous security controls and best practices can be implemented by an organization. One way to consider implementing controls is by using preventive and detective categories at the data, application, host, network, and physical layers. The security industry firm Tripwire offers here some of the main controls and where to consider for implementation:[29]

Preventive Security Controls

- Encryption (Data layer) = encrypt sensitive information whether at rest or in transit.
- User Access Control (Data, Host layers) = access rights reflect level users require.
- Software Patching (Application layer) = update with latest software patch releases.
- Malware Detection (Host layer) = install software to identify and prevent malware.

- System Hardening (Application, Host, Network layers) = remove default user accounts and passwords, remove unnecessary services, and adjust permissions.
- Network Access Control (Network layer) = isolate sensitive systems from main network into secure segments with strict access rules.
- Security Awareness Training (Physical layer) = train users to recognize threats.
- Policies/Procedures (Physical layer) = publish user roles and penalties if ignored.

Detective Security Controls

- File Integrity Monitoring (Data, Application, Host layers) = regularly monitor for replacements of or changes to critical system files.
- Vulnerability Management (Application, Host, Network layers) = regular testing to identify vulnerabilities in software, configurations or processes.
- Change Control (Application, Host, Network layers) = actively monitoring for unauthorized changes on key systems.
- Incident Alerting (Host, Network layers) = identify suspicious activity and be alerted to it by intrusion detection/prevention systems.
- Log Monitoring (Data, Application, Host, Network layers) = monitor log files for unusual entries or certain security events.
- Security Configuration Management (Network layer) = secure new systems or applications that are added to the infrastructure.

It should be obvious there is no one solution in an increasingly sophisticated and complex threat landscape. The security strategy of defense-in-depth offers a multilayered security approach in which a combination of integrated technologies attempt to provide protection and detection against known, unknown and advanced malware and threats.[30] Defense-in-depth is widely accepted by industry and the military as a way to enhance cyber defensive capabilities through layered sensors and countermeasures.[31] For example, the US Navy has released new cyber standards that specifically require a defense-in-depth approach.[32] Ideally these defenses are configured by leveraging industry security products informed by cyber threat intelligence.

Cyber Threat Intelligence

To effectively defend against cyber attacks an organization needs access to synthesized information about specific threats to specific targets. The fused product called cyber threat intelligence consists of threat information on malicious actor tactics, techniques, and procedures plus suggested actions to counter an attack and also threat indicators that an attack is imminent, is underway or that compromise may have already occurred. Cyber threat intelligence provides the ability to recognize and act upon this information or indicators, of attack and compromise, in a timely manner. Indicators of attack represent early warning signs, such as code execution, persistence, command and control, or lateral movement. Indicators of compromise show the presence of malware, signatures, exploits, vulnerabilities, or IP addresses.[33] To be effective, cyber threat intelligence exhibits the characteristics of timely— delivered rapidly to provide opportunity for the recipient to anticipate the threat and prepare a suitable response; relevant—applicable to recipient operating environment to address likely threats; and actionable—identifies actions the recipient can take to counter the threat.

For security teams trying to implement and manage security controls to thwart cyber attacks, threat intelligence can make a difference in risk management. The addition of threat intelligence in a security program can provide information and indicators to prioritize and adjust security controls to stop the latest attacks.[34] For example, a Fortune 100 financial services organization that faces 250,000 threats a day recently incorporated a threat intelligence platform to aggregate threat data and integrate existing security tools.[35] In a 2016 institute survey of IT security practitioners in the United States involved in endpoint security in a variety of organizations, 77 percent say they have added or plan to adopt a threat intelligence component.[36] However, an organization needs not only access to timely, relevant, and actionable cyber threat intelligence but also the ability to act on that intelligence. Security vendors gather information about active threats and use that information to inform their industry security products. Many security solution products have been optimized to integrate or incorporate threat intelligence data feeds. For example, the IBM X-Force research team develops threat intelligence and countermeasure technologies for IBM products.

The IBM X-Force team monitors global threats around the clock to understand the latest vulnerabilities and exploit techniques. They use fully automated web crawlers to inspect millions of websites every day to build a URL reputation database. They also leverage intelligence to categorize IP addresses into threat categories, including malware hosts, spam sources, dynamic IPs, anonymous proxies, botnet command and control servers, and scanning IPs, with reputation scores that assist in traffic blocking decisions. In addition, the team categorizes web applications by threat origination and tracks security vulnerabilities. Other organizations can leverage the latest X-Force research through the IBM X-Force Exchange, launched in 2015 to share evidence and discoveries.[37] Or organizations can view on-demand webcasts by the threat research team on topics such as trends and findings in volume of attacks, affected industries, prevalent types of attacks, and the key factors enabling them.[38] Products within the IBM Security portfolio have been optimized to integrate or incorporate X-Force capabilities, such as the

IBM Security Network Intrusion Prevention System uses X-Force feeds for URL filtering, IP source blocking, application action control, and virtual patch shielding of observed vulnerabilities.[39] It is no surprise that in a 2015 SANS institute survey of organizations, 54 percent of them use intrusion monitoring platforms to accept and consolidate cyber threat intelligence feeds.[40] The challenge for deterrence by denial is the remaining percent of organizations that don't use these feeds.

Cyber Kill Chain

Layering controls informed by cyber threat intelligence provide reinforcing protections that attempt to halt attacks in progress. Yet before an organization can hope to thwart its adversaries and convince them that their efforts are futile, the organization must understand the adversary's attack methods. One of the most popular models of the methods used in the cyber attack process is the "intrusion kill chain" first popularized in a 2010 paper by Lockheed Martin researchers.[41] A kill chain is a systematic process to target and engage an adversary to create a desired outcome. The integrated, end-to-end process is described as a "chain" because any one deficiency will break the entire process. The intrusion or simply cyber kill chain is identified in seven phases, specifically consisting of reconnaissance, weaponization, delivery, exploitation, installation, command and control, and actions on objectives. The phases describe the sequence of activities used by malicious actors, with specific tools and techniques within each phase, to obtain essential objectives required to proceed to the next phase in a cyber attack.[42] Definitions for the kill chain phases are as follows:

Cyber Kill Chain

1. Reconnaissance = harvesting email addresses, social relationships, and information on specific technologies.
2. Weaponization = coupling an exploit with a remote access Trojan into a deliverable payload.
3. Delivery = transmission of the weapon to the victim via email, web, USB, or mobile devices.
4. Exploitation = of application or operating system vulnerability or an operating system feature to execute code.
5. Installation = of malware on the asset to maintain persistence.
6. Command and Control = for remote manipulation of victim's system.
7. Action on Objectives = intruders use hands-on access inside the target environment to accomplish their goal.

The cyber kill chain becomes a model for defense when defenders align defensive capabilities, such as security controls or best practices, to the specific processes that a malicious actor undertakes to target and engage the victim's system. A defensive actions matrix can be constructed to identify and inject solutions and procedures that can impact an attacker's progress at various phases of the kill chain. For example, the use of software patching denies the exploitation phase and malware detection products stop the installation phase. Security firms will analyze real-world attacks and offer suggestions on where their industry products or practices could detect, deny, disrupt, or contain an attack at each phase of the cyber kill chain. For example, Dell SecureWorks has examined the 2013 attack on Target Corporation to provide recommendations for securing POS systems. The Dell suggestions are similar to the preventive and detective security controls listed previously, but also include an assortment of solutions and procedures at the particular kill chain phase to include: [43]

Defensive Actions Matrix (2013 Target Breach)

- Database Security (Reconnaissance) = manage and audit database accounts.
- Threat Intelligence (Weaponization) = leverage external and internal sources to gain visibility into specific types of attacks and indicators to detect these attacks.
- Application Whitelisting (Delivery) = limit sets of software that can be run on system.
- Endpoint Malware Protection (Exploitation) = antivirus and host intrusion prevention system identify and block malicious malware.
- Two-factor Authentication (Installation) = reduce effectiveness of password stealing and cracking attempts.
- Network Intrusion Detection System (Command and Control) = identify traffic patterns matching scanning, malware C2 communication and data exfiltration.
- Data Loss Prevention (Actions on Objective) = use information tagging, packet inspection, and network monitoring to identify movement of sensitive data.

However, the trouble with using a patchwork of legacy solutions, called "best of breed" from multiple vendors, is they take manual intervention once a breach occurs. The use of point products also makes it difficult to coordinate and share intelligence among various devices. For example, if a sandboxing device, which isolates and runs suspicious code, detects an unknown threat, it might not automatically share indicators with an intrusion prevention system, which detects malware. Therefore, prominent leaders in the cyber security industry recommend use of their integrated and automated products to act across the cyber kill chain. For example, Palo Alto Networks presents its Next-Generation Security Platform as a multi-layered defense solution that integrates next-generation firewalls, cloud-based threat intelligence, and advanced endpoint protection. The Next-Generation platform inspects all network traffic and offers many security features designed to prevent and detect at every phase of the cyber kill chain wherever the organization's data may reside: in the cloud, on premise, in the network and on the endpoint.[44] The WildFire intelligence cloud, a custom-built evasion-resistant virtual environment that uses hundreds of behavioral characteristics, static indicators and machine learning, inspects all files passing through the platform in order to prevent and detect known and unknown malware and exploits.[45] The Palo Alto Networks platform integrates the process of prevention and detection down the kill chain so that network defenders do not have to do it themselves. It does that by establishing a system-of-systems that communicate with each other within the platform and integrates a host of third-party tools behind the scenes in an effort to reduce the workload of all network defenders.[46]

Solutions like the Palo Alto Networks Platform offer a potent means to deny the benefit of an attack. In a cyber intrusion the real benefit to the attacker is the exfiltration of data at last stage in the kill chain. Critics of the cyber kill chain philosophy argue that too much emphasis is on the early stages which take relatively little time, whereas the final steps by the attacker can take months.[47] In support of that notion, Black Hat 2016 attendees were told the popular cyber kill chain "doesn't focus enough on what to do after adversaries break into networks successfully, which they inevitably will do."[48] Another prevalent counterpoint is the list of attack vectors is longer than those covered by the chain model, like the insider threat. Admittedly the kill chain is more suited to preventing intrusion and a highly determined and skilled attacker will find a way into the system. Therefore, focusing on detecting ongoing attacks in the final stages of Command and Control and also Actions on Objectives is imperative before the damage is done. This requires detective security controls that automatically detect and analyze subtle changes in user and computer behavior, like File Integrity Monitoring, Change Control, and Log Monitoring as listed previously.

SECURITY CONTROLS

Guidance for the identification and application of protective measures in the form of security controls are contained in a variety of security frameworks. Security controls are safeguards or countermeasures prescribed for an information system to protect the confidentiality, integrity, and availability of the system and its information. Security controls can be found in the National Institute of Standards and Technology Special Publication 800-53. In many cases the controls identify industry best practices, also informally promulgated by leading security firms in annual reports. For example, the Symantec Corporation publishes Best Practice Guidelines for Businesses and for Consumers. In the first category suggestions include use encryption to protect sensitive data, implement a removable media policy, be aggressive in updating and patching, enforce an effective password policy, and restrict email attachments. For the latter, recommendations include think before you click, guard your personal data, protect yourself and update regularly. In reviewing a number of good external best practice guidelines, Symantec specifically endorses the Critical Security Controls (CSC) maintained by the Center for Internet Security and also the Cybersecurity Framework produced by the National Institute of Standards and Technology.[49]

Critical Security Controls

The Critical Security Controls (CSC) is a framework that offers safeguards for computer security based on the combined knowledge of actual attacks and effective defenses.[50] Twenty sets of safeguards are suggested to detect, prevent, and mitigate damage from the most common attacks. The goal of the CSCs is to protect critical assets and information by strengthening an organization's defensive posture through continuous, automated protection and monitoring of information technology infrastructure. Thus the controls deny benefit of attack by monitoring networks and systems, detecting attack attempts, identifying compromised machines, and interrupting infiltration. An organization implements, automates, and measures the effectiveness of each CSC through the application of subcontrols that are categorized as either "Foundational" or "Advanced" as an aid to prioritization and planning.[51] The CSCs also identify applicable commercial tools to detect, track, control, prevent, and correct weaknesses or misuse at threat points.[52] Suggested security tools listed by control range from Network Access Control, Vulnerability Assessment, Application Whitelisting, and Intrusion Prevention Systems to Web Application Firewalls, Patch Management, Data Loss Prevention, and Encryption.[53] Many security solution firms map their products against the CSCs to illustrate how their features and capabilities meet safeguard requirements.[54]

The first four CSCs (1–4) alone are seen as especially very valuable by organizations such as the NSA that rates them "very high" in mitigation capability and "high" in technical maturity. They directly address risk management, starting with (1) Device and Software, (2) Inventory, (3) Secure Configurations, and (4) Continuous Vulnerability Assessment and Remediation, across a large number of systems in an enterprise. An organization could reduce the impact of cyber threats on the confidentiality, integrity, and availability of information through proper project planning, resource allocation and prioritization based on CSCs 1–4. This assertion can be affirmed in analyzing data breaches of four major US technology firms, namely Twitter, Facebook, Apple, and Microsoft, in February 2013 resulting from vulnerabilities in the Java application. In each situation the attacker followed the pattern of the intrusion kill chain, discovered software weakness (reconnaissance), wrote exploit code (weaponization), posted the code on a "watering hole" website (delivery), lured victims to the site (exploitation), downloaded attack code (installation), compromised the victim's computers (command and control), and got what they wanted (actions on objective). CSCs 1–4 could have prevented attack success at various points of the kill chain, through baseline device control, application version updating, forbidding code execution from untrusted websites, noting configuration changes, and scanning systems for vulnerable applications in outdated versions of Java. [55]

Application of best practices like patch management, contained in CSC 4 for Continuous Vulnerability Assessment and Remediation, can only prevent attacks if used, as evidenced in the compromise of computers in the NetTraveler cyber espionage campaign. The malware infected more than 350 victims in forty countries from 2005 through 2013. [56] NetTraveler exploits two well-known vulnerabilities in Microsoft office, a Windows Common Controls bug (CVE-2012-0158) and flaws in MS Word (CVE-2010-3333), both patched for these errors years ago. All the victims had to do was patch their systems. Instead, the APT group using NetTraveler stole more than twenty-two gigabytes of data from their victims. [57] Likewise, application of the best practice of removable media policy implementation, contained in CSC 8 for Malware Defenses, could have prevented an attack like Stuxnet, where the virus was delivered by thumb drives used by contractors working at the Iranian nuclear enrichment facility. The CSCs were crafted to answer the question: "Where should I start to improve my cyber defenses?" [58] Their implementation in order could deny attack benefit as they prioritize and focus on a small number of actionable controls with a high potential payoff. The first five alone provide effective defense against 80 percent of attacks. [59] The 2016 NTT Group provides further guidance for practical application of security controls to the cyber kill chain. [60] The challenge for deterrence by denial is the number of organizations that don't use the controls.

Cybersecurity Framework

In 2013, President Obama declared that the cyber threat to critical infrastructure represents one of the most serious challenges to national security. Therefore, to enhance the security and resilience of national infrastructure, he signed Executive Order 13636 for "Improving Critical Infrastructure Cybersecurity." The order directs the development of a "Cybersecurity Framework" to reduce cyber risks to critical infrastructure. A framework can provide direction, focus, and guidance to not just reduce risk, but also reduce downtime.[61] The order mandates that the framework shall include a set of standards and procedures that align policy, business, and technological ways to address cyber risks. To help identify, assess, and manage cyber risk, the framework is intended to provide a prioritized, performance-based, and cost-effective approach, including information security measures and controls. It will provide technology-neutral guidance so users benefit from a competitive market for products and services.[62] The inaugural Cybersecurity Framework was released one year later in February 2014 by the National Institute of Standards and Technology (NIST). It is constructed around a Framework Core containing a set of cybersecurity activities, desired outcomes, and applicable references that are common across critical infrastructure sectors. The core consists of five concurrent and continuous functions: Identify, Protect, Detect, Respond, and Recover. The framework incorporates international voluntary consensus standards and industry best practices to accomplish activities under the functions. The CSCs are part of the framework's informative references.[63]

Leading companies attest that the framework has enhanced their ability to set security priorities, develop capital and operational expenditure budgets, and deploy security solutions.[64] Their endorsement stems from use of the Framework Profile characterized as the alignment of standards and practices to the Framework Core in a particular implementation scenario. The profile enables organizations to establish a roadmap that is aligned with business objectives, regulatory requirements, and risk management priorities. An organization first creates an "as is" Current Profile by reviewing all the Categories and Subcategories in the Core, and after assessing emerging cyber threats, develops a "to be" Target Profile. The organization then compares the Current and Target Profile to determine gaps in Security Controls. Next after a cost-benefit analysis of risk tolerance and available resources, they develop and implement an Action Plan to fix gaps. The risk tolerance is based on an acceptable level of risk for acquisition of products and delivery of services. The Deputy Homeland Security Secretary, Alejandro Mayorkas, has touted the framework as a document that has lifted cyber security awareness in private companies. In remarks at the Billington International Cybersecurity Summit, he implored a roomful of global experts to use it as a model for their home governments.[65]

INFORMATION SHARING

Organizations in the same critical infrastructure or industry sector often face malicious actors that use common tactics, techniques and procedures that target the same types of systems and information. One organization's detection of a cyber attack can become another's prevention. When cyber threat information and indicators are exchanged within sharing communities, recipient organizations are able to deploy effective countermeasures that block or detect similar intrusions. For example, an organization can use shared knowledge of indicators to disrupt the cyber kill chain. Through identifying indicators and determining where in the chain these indicators occur, defensive strategies and techniques can be applied precisely within the kill chain process. For instance, security controls or solutions can be deployed to disrupt a malicious actor before achieving exploit phase execution. If the actor has already reached the installation phase, then the organization's defensive strategy shifts to detect actor presence on the network or system and craft an effective response. At each phase of the kill chain, shared threat information or indicators help to anticipate actor behavior and deploy defenses. Thus, by the sharing of cyber threat information and indicators, an organization benefits from the collective experience, resources, and capabilities of its peers. [66]

Threat Intelligence Sources

Information alone does not equal intelligence. Intelligence is gained when context is applied to information—giving it meaning and operational significance. [67] In a survey of over 378 organizations, 57 percent of respondents say the cyber intelligence currently available to their organization is often too stale to enable them to grasp the strategies, motivations, tactics, and location of attackers. [68] Many lack current intelligence in the form of reports on latest hacker techniques or indicators of compromise that can spot and mitigate threats. So where does current threat intelligence come from? Sources of threat intelligence are found in a variety of places both internal and external to an organization. Internally an organization can create a threat intelligence program using their IDS/IPS, SIEM, and AV products and investing in a team of researchers and analysts to process and correlate collected data. This team can review local data logs for malware, incident data, or IP addresses; perform forensic analysis on infected hard drives looking for attack patterns; and analyze login attempts or swipe access into server rooms. [69] Since internally performing analysis on this magnitude of data is no small task, organizations can subscribe to external threat intelligence services provided by security vendors. [70] An organization can also take a third option to participate in a sector or an industry-specific sharing community.

In the threat intelligence service option, some commercial providers provide data feeds in standard file formats that can be used in a variety of security platforms from different manufacturers. Other vendors offer levels of service that build upon one another, with the base service being a data feed subscription that requires the use of proprietary security appliances, such as FireEye Threat Intelligence. The basic option enhances the value of FireEye Threat Prevention platforms by providing ongoing updates of technical indicators. The most advanced FireEye Intelligence capability provides dossiers on advanced threat groups as well as profiles of targeted industries.[71] In some cases, a third-party security provider will use external feeds to support automated actions, like Hexis Cyber Solutions did in their HawkEye G integrated active cyber defense platform. Key criteria exist for evaluating which threat intelligence service providers are the best fit for an organization's needs. Evaluation points to use in research and comparison include for data feeds—what is the number, focus, format, and source; for equipment—what type, existing or proprietary, can accept the feeds; for alerts/reports—are there real-time alerts and industry-specific reports; for price—are subscriptions tiered based on number of users; and for service support—is it timely 24/7/365 telephone access to engineers? The cost of data feed subscriptions is in the range of $1,500 to $10,000 per month depending on number of feeds.[72]

Sharing Arrangements

Threat information and indicator sharing can and should be an important element in efforts to ensure defenders stay ahead of the threat. In a sharing community arrangement, an enterprise can join, for instance, an ISAC to improve the quantity and quality of available threat information. The concept of the ISAC was introduced and promulgated pursuant to Presidential Decision Directive, PDD-63, signed on May 22, 1998. In PDD-63 the federal government asked each critical infrastructure sector to establish sector specific information-sharing organizations to share information about threats and vulnerabilities within each sector.[73] For example, the Financial Services (FS) ISAC is a 501(c)6 nonprofit self-funded organization which has grown to more than five thousand members from various commercial banks, credit unions, brokerage firms, insurance companies, payment centers, and trade associations. FS-ISAC sharing activities include the delivery of timely, relevant and actionable cyber and physical email alerts, and also an anonymous online submission capability to facilitate member sharing of threat, vulnerability and incident information.[74] The NCCIC coordinates with the ISACs for the federal government on the sharing of information related to cybersecurity risks and incidents.

Substantial barriers to optimal sharing of cyber threat information by private sector entities exist. Their concerns reside in legal liability, antitrust violations, potential misuse, and risks of disclosure, especially of trade secrets and other proprietary information. They often complain that the federal government does not share its information, in particular classified information, and there is little reciprocity or other incentives for them to share with government.[75] Legislative proposals try to address these common concerns. In 2015 a total of six bills were introduced and reviewed in the US Congress with varying provisions aimed at facilitating sharing of information among private-sector entities and providing protections from liability that might arise from sharing.[76] Finally on December 18, 2015, President Obama signed the Cybersecurity Act of 2015 over the objections of civil liberties groups.[77] Title 1 of the Act gives antitrust exemptions and liability immunity to companies that send the government cyber threat indicators or defensive measures. The act states that data will be gathered in a manner that removes personal information of a specific individual or information that identifies a specific individual not directly related to a cybersecurity threat.[78] Still industry concerns linger over the bill, mostly on trusting the government on the use or security of the data.[79] For the government to truly facilitate private sector sharing, it must not just implement privacy safeguards, but also establish viable controls on use, define limitations on liability, and create a value proposition, in regard to cost and risk, or fail to address industry interests and needs.[80]

RISK MANAGEMENT

Despite ever-improving defenses, the vast array of attack methods will hold networks and systems at risk for years to come. According to the Director of National Intelligence, "the cyber threat cannot be eliminated; rather, cyber risk must be managed."[81] The director is concerned that some private sector entities do not account for foreign cyber threats or the systemic interdependencies between critical infrastructure sectors in their risk calculus. Through the process of risk management, leaders consider risk to national interests from malicious actors using cyberspace to their advantage. Risk is defined as a measure of the extent to which an entity is threatened by a potential circumstance or event, and typically a function of adverse impacts and likelihood of occurrence. Risk management is a comprehensive process that requires organizations to frame risk, assess risk, respond to risk, and monitor risk.[82] The first component of framing risk or establishing a risk context requires an organization to identify assumptions, constraints, tolerance, and priorities or tradeoffs. The purpose of the assess risk component is to identify threats to the organization, internal and external vulnerabilities, the harm that may occur from threats and vulnerabilities in the form of consequences or impacts, and the likelihood that harm will occur.[83] The purpose of the third component of risk response is to develop, evaluate, determine, and implement courses of action for responding to risk. The fourth component addresses how organizations monitor risk over time.

An important factor in deterrence by denial is the determination of risk tolerance in the risk frame component. Risk tolerance is the level of risk or degree of uncertainty that is acceptable to the organization. Risk tolerant organizations may be concerned with only those threats experienced by peer organizations and not try to defeat all actors and attack vectors, whereas less tolerant organizations will be concerned about all threats that are theoretically possible across their attack surface. In regard to risk response, less tolerant organizations are likely to prefer mature safeguards and countermeasures that have a proven track record. Such organizations may decide to employ multiple safeguards and countermeasures from multiple sources or vendors in a "best of breed" defensive actions matrix. Hence risk tolerance plays a significant role in security solution investment strategies. The strategic investments required to address the risk from high volume bad actors, like volunteer hacktivists or less skilled nation-states, are different than the investments needed to address the risk from wicked actors, like APT groups. To address less sophisticated threats, organizations can invest in proven security controls to address known vulnerabilities, whereas for advanced persistent threats, organizations will have to invest in cutting edge technologies over the course of several years.

Risk-based decisions manage potential threat impact on the confidentiality, integrity, or availability of information being processed, stored, or transmitted by information systems. More risk tolerant organizations may focus on investments that provide mission or business gains at the expense of malicious actors gaining benefit from compromising information systems. The massive breaches at Yahoo in 2013 and 2014 affecting 1.5 billion user accounts are an example of "a consistent lack of interest in security"[84] because of "a low priority to defense against hacker threat."[85] On the contrary, less tolerant organizations will attempt to deny all benefit of cyber attack, even at the expense of achieving some mission or business goals. For organizations that handle critical or sensitive information the emphasis is on preventing unauthorized disclosure or the loss of confidentiality. In contrast, for organizations where the nature of operations or business depends on their functionality, the emphasis will be on maintaining the availability of information while protecting its integrity. Risk response identifies, evaluates, decides on, and implements appropriate courses of action to accept, avoid, mitigate, share or transfer risk. Courses of action for risk response are evaluated in terms of impact on organization mission or business needs and functions. To avoid risk, an organization might eliminate networked connections and employ an "air gap" between two domains. Risk mitigation can include use of security controls informed by threat intelligence, and of organizational policies, like restricting mobile device or removable media usage.

Risk sharing or transfer is the shifting of risk liability and responsibility to another organization.[86] An example of risk sharing would be the purchasing of commercial vendor services to protect against volumetric DDoS attacks. In this arrangement, inbound malicious traffic is shifted to commercial servers that can accommodate high bandwidth packet requests. For example, the Akamai network defeats attacks measured in tens, or even hundreds, of Gbps. The Akamai Kona Site Defender deflects DDoS traffic targeted at the network layer, such as SYN or UDP packets. It defines and enforces IP whitelists and blacklists to protect the website. Defender also incorporates a highly scalable Web Application Firewall to absorb DDoS traffic target at the application layer, such as HTTP floods that issue erroneous requests. Over 210,000 edge servers distributed around the world are used to compare application requests to known attack profiles.[87] The Kona Rule set protects against recent threats, such by Low Orbit Ion Cannon, used by Anonymous, or the Havij SQL injection tool, used by Iranian hacker groups.[88] The Akamai cloud-based network, used on any given day for 80 percent of US government web traffic, provides another layer of defense-in-depth protection.[89]

An example of risk transfer is the purchase of cyber security insurance. Brokers and underwriters generally consider how companies manage cyber risk when assessing qualifications for coverage. They pay particular attention to company adoption, implementation, and enforcement of cyber security practices and procedures.[90] If qualified, the various elements of a protection policy can include "liability for a security or privacy breach . . . costs of notifying customers of a breach . . . losses from business interruption . . . costs for restoring or replacing lost or damaged data . . . liability for directors or officers of a company targeted by an attack . . . and costs associated with settling cyber extortion threats."[91] Given an ongoing lack of actuarial data, this wide range of factors in writing policies can result in insurance coverage that does not adequately address actual risk, particularly for reputation damage and security remediation associated with large breaches experienced today. For instance, the cost related to the theft of fifty-six million sets of credit and debit card data at Home Depot in 2014 is expected to reach into the billions, with only $100 million covered by insurance.[92]

PROTECTIVE MEASURE UTILITY

Organizational risk tolerance dictates the selection of risk response courses of action. Protective measures to reduce risk, which include the promulgation of security strategies, the implementation of security controls, and the sharing of cyber threat information, deny to some extent the benefit of attack. However, organizations need to have resources and processes in place to implement these protective measures if they are to improve the security of their networks and systems. The data breaches at the OPM illustrate the result of blatant neglect of security strategies. Subsequent recognition of systemic failures at other US government agencies spurred White House declaration of a "30-day Cybersecurity Sprint" to shore up protective measures. As part of the effort, the Federal Chief Information Officer instructed federal agencies to patch critical vulnerabilities without delay, accelerate implementation of multifactor authentication, tighten policies for privileged users, and immediately deploy indicators provided by the Department of Homeland Security (DHS) regarding malicious actor techniques, tactics, and procedures.[93] The last mandate reiterates that organizations need to know their attackers and the techniques they use to exfiltrate valuable data or conduct denial of service attacks. Federal respondents to an industry survey agree in principle that using threat intelligence is essential to a strong security posture, but nearly a third report their organizations are not able to collect and use it effectively.[94]

To change the cost-benefit calculations of attackers, security leaders need to think like attackers in the implementation of security controls.[95] The CSCs are built on the guiding principle that "offense informs defense," which means knowledge of actual attacks provide the foundation to build practical defenses. In constructing the CSCs, top experts from many organizations pooled their firsthand knowledge of actual cyber attacks and developed a consensus list of the best defensive techniques to stop them. The CSCs are not limited to blocking compromises, but also can detect, prevent, or disrupt attacker's follow-up actions. It is no wonder the CSCs figure prominently in the NIST produced "Cybersecurity Framework." The US Chamber of Commerce believes the framework is a success. Critical infrastructure sectors and important industry elements are keenly aware of, supportive of, or using the framework or similar risk management tools.[96] The senior director for cybersecurity at the White House says that support for the framework has "exceeded expectations."[97] Still greater resources are required to grow awareness of the framework and risk-based solutions so decisions on investments are made based on risk tolerance for adversary behavior. In a survey of nearly two thousand IT security practitioners in forty-two countries, 46 percent say their budgets have increased, to on average $9.14 million annually.[98] Security spending will invariably rise as "organizations realize they need to protect against phishing, ransomware and the growing variety of threats they face."[99] However, since attackers receive "an estimated 1,425 percent return on investment for exploit kit and ransomware schemes ($84,100 net revenue for each $5,900 investment),[100] it appears they are winning the cost ratio battle.

The creating of sufficient defense capacities through implementation of security controls in an "offensive informs defense" model requires defenders to learn from each other faster than attackers learn from each other. When considered collectively, the twenty individual ISACs provide shared cyber threat information through systemic outreach and connectivity to approximately 85 percent of US critical infrastructure.[101] However, if private sector recipients find this information to be of little benefit, they are less likely to participate in sharing communities. Cyber threat information needs to be actionable in that it identifies or evokes a response aimed at mitigating risk. Shared information may be of little use if it is delayed or provided without context or in the wrong format. It needs to be relevant for use in appropriate security controls and associated security products to break the kill chain. The usefulness of shared information rests on the nature of threat itself. For example, for malware signatures to be useful, there has to be enough time for the signatures to be collected, shared, and inserted into defensive systems of potential future victims before they are attacked. This assumes an attack group will generate a consistent set of signatures that recur in multiple attacks, which likelihood is reduced by polymorphic malware, combined with shifting IP addresses. Many times attack groups evolve to use a new set of exploits and attack vectors with brand new signatures.[102]

AN INSUFFICIENT DETERRENCE OPTION

Evidence indicates deterrence by denial is not a sufficient strategy to convince malicious actors not to conduct cyber attacks. Current security mechanisms and practices are simply inadequate to achieve deterrence and likely will always be. US Deputy Secretary of Defense Robert Work told a congressional committee that "cyber intrusions and attacks have increased dramatically over the last decade, exposing sensitive personal and business information, disrupting government and business activity, and imposing significant costs to the U.S. economy."[103] Although great strides have been made in DOD cyber security through "the layering of our defenses," so that only about "0.001 percent" of millions of attacks per day are successful,[104] highly publicized data breaches at Sony Pictures, JP Morgan Chase, Anthem Health Service, and the OPM expose a failure of cyber defenses at civilian companies and government agencies of all sizes. In a 2014 survey of US companies, nearly half experienced a data breach involving the theft of more than one thousand records, up more than 10 percent from the previous year.[105] Part of the problem is the utility of protective measures, primarily security strategies, security controls, and information sharing, is diminished by sophisticated attacks that are advanced, targeted, stealthy and persistent. Cyber attacks today unfold in multiple coordinated stages across the cyber kill chain, with calculated steps to get in, establish a foothold, surveil the victim's network and steal data. Malicious actors use a variety of stealthy tactics to evade detection and maintain control of compromised systems.

In response deterrence by denial counts on a defense-in-depth strategy that proposes the layering of multiple technologies combined with best practices, where in theory each layer blocks a different aspect of multipronged cyber attacks. For example, at the delivery phase, device control blocks infected USB devices; at the exploitation phase, patch and configuration management eliminate known vulnerabilities; and at the installation phase, application control prevents unapproved executables.[106] These defenses are intended to impose cost on the attacker by shutting off their attack vectors. For instance, issue of emergency patches for zero-day vulnerabilities in Flash Player closed off exploitation by the China-based threat group APT3[107] and by a Russian APT group in Operation Pawn Storm, a spear phishing campaign against political targets in NATO and the United States.[108] Yet this threat will most likely reconstitute as APT3 has a history of introducing new browser-based, zero-day exploits, and the Pawn Storm group has been actively introducing new infrastructure and strategies for eight years.[109] Consequently, in their yearly observation of cyber attack trends, the security firm Mandiant reaffirms the need for a defense-in-depth strategy in stating that "it is more critical to focus on all aspects of your security posture (people, processes and technologies) than ever before."[110]

In the wake of the OPM hacks, in October 2015, the White House's Office of Management and Budget released their Cybersecurity Strategy and Implementation Plan (CSIP), which builds off the thirty-day Cybersecurity Sprint. The CSIP directs actions to improve capabilities for identifying and detecting vulnerabilities and threats, enhances protections of assets and information, and develops robust response and recovery capabilities. The CSIP emphasizes the need for a defense-in-depth approach that relies on the layering of people, processes, technologies, and also operations. Suggestions in CSIP include to improve security practices and controls around agency high value assets, implement tools to identify risks to systems and networks, advance information sharing on critical vulnerabilities and threats, and acquire innovative commercially available cyber security products and services.[111] As for OPM, one year later their acting director, Beth Corbet, thinks federal employees are safer now. She has outlined a number of actions taken by OPM to strengthen their cybersecurity posture, to include the:[112]

- Deployment of two-factor authentication for network users.
- Modification of the network to limit remote access only to government computers.

- Implementation of a data loss prevention system that automatically stops sensitive information, like Social Security numbers, from exiting the network unauthorized.
- Enhancement of cybersecurity awareness training, with emphasis on Phishing emails.

While these government initiatives and accomplishments are promising, Representative Jason Chaffetz reminded Federal Chief Information Officers, in a Letter from the Chairman of the House Committee investigation of the OPM data breach, that "a single vulnerability is all a sophisticated actor needs to steal information, identities, and profoundly damage our national security."[113]

Consequently it is no surprise that forensic evidence indicates malicious actors are not convinced defenses will deny their success. For instance the Fortinet Cyber Threat Assessment Program recorded over 185 million threat events in the period from April 1 to June 30, 2016, meaning many of the events succeeded in getting past traditional security defenses onto the internal network where Fortinet assessment devices were located.[114] Furthermore, Verizon reports that in 60 percent of cyber incidents, attackers are able to compromise an organization within minutes, while their detection takes months.[115] These statistics mean threat groups can bypass conventional defenses at will and wander unimpeded to obtain their objectives on the target. The hard reality that attackers can compromise an organization quickly and persist undetected for long durations indicates that the strategy of deterrence by denial will remain an insufficient strategic cyber deterrence option.

NOTES

1. John Edwards and Eve Keiser, "Raising the Cost of Cyberattacks," *C4ISR& Networks*, July/August 2015, 12.

2. Ash Carter, Secretary of Defense, "The DoD Cyber Strategy," April 17, 2015, 10–11.

3. Adam Bromwich, Symantec, "Emerging Cyber Threats to the United States," Testimony before House Committee on Homeland Security, February 25, 2016.

4. John Zarour, "How to Avoid Becoming the Next OPM," *GCN Magazine*, August 2015, 12.

5. Mandiant, "M Trends 2015, A View from the Front Lines," Threat Report, 2015, 2–3.

6. Online Trust Alliance, "OTA Determines over 90% of Data Breaches in 2014 Could Have Been Prevented," Press Releases, January 21, 2015.

7. Peter Roberts and Andrew Hardie, "The Validity of Deterrence in the Twenty-first Century," Royal United Services Institute, Occasional Paper, August 2015, 20.

8. Office of Personnel Management, "OPM to Notify Employees of Cybersecurity Incident," News Release, June 4, 2015.

9. Kirstin Finklea, "Cyber Intrusion into U.S. Office of Personnel Management: In Brief," Congressional Research Service, CRS Report R44111, July 17, 2015.

10. Committee on Oversight and Government Reform, US House of Representatives, 114th Congress, "The OPM Data Breach: How the Government Jeopardized Our National Security for More than a Generation," Timeline of Key Events, September 7, 2016, 5–13.

11. Ken Dilanian and Ted Bridis, "U.S. Officials: Second Hack Exposed Military and Intel Data," *Associated Press*, June 13, 2015.

12. Ken Dilanian, "Union Says All Federal Workers Fell Victim to Hackers," *Associated Press*, June 12, 2015.

13. Sean Gallagher, "Report: Hack of Government Employee Records Discovered by Product Demo," Arstechnica, Risk Assessment/ Security and Hacktivism Blog, June 11, 2015.

14. Charles Hall, "How OPM Could Have Avoided the Data Breach," CTOvision, CTO Blog, June 30, 2015.

15. David E. Sanger, Julie Hirschfeld Davis, and Nicole Perlroth, "U.S. Was Warned of System Open to Cyberattacks," *New York Times*, June 5, 2015.

16. The Institute for Critical Infrastructure Technology, "Handing Over the Keys to the Castle," Technical Report, July 2015.

17. Damian Paletta and Danny Yadron, "Over 21 Million Hit by Hack," *Wall Street Journal*, July 10, 2015.

18. Ellen Nakashima, "U.S. Not Naming China in Data Hack," *Washington Post*, July 22, 2015.

19. Jeff Mason and Mark Hosenball, "Obama Vows to Boost U.S. Cyber Defenses, Amid Signs of China Hacking," *Reuters*, June 8, 2015.

20. Jeffrey Carr, "Cyber Attacks: Why Retaliating against China Is the Wrong Reaction," *The Diplomat*, August 6, 2015.

21. Adam Rice, "Warnings, Neglect and a Massive Breach," *Information Security Magazine*, September 2015, 24–28.

22. Mark Hosenball and Roberta Rampton, "U.S. Personnel Agency Chief Resigns over Massive Data Breach," *Reuters*, July 10, 2015.

23. Forrester Research, Inc, "Quick Take: 12 Lessons for Security and Risk Pros from the US OPM Breach," White Paper, June 8, 2015, 1–10.

24. Eric Tucker, "Report Details Missed Opportunities to Stop OPM Cyber Breach," *Associated Press*, September 7, 2016.

25. Lumension, "Redefining Defense-in-Depth," White Paper, March 2014, 1–6.

26. FireEye, Inc. "Cybersecurity's Maginot Line: A Real World Assessment of the Defense-in-Depth Model," Report, 2014, 1–10.

27. National Institute of Standards and Technology, *Security and Privacy Controls for Federal Information Systems and Organizations*, Special Publication 800-53, Revision 4, Appendix B (Washington, DC: US Department of Commerce, April 2013), B-20.

28. McAfee, "Counter Stealth Attacks," Santa Clara, California, 2013, 1–3.

29. Tripwire, "Layered Security: Protecting Your Data in Today's Threat Landscape," White Paper, Brian Honan, 2014.

30. Kaspersky, "Future Risks: Be Prepared," Special Report, Kaspersky Lab, 2014, 1–11.

31. Vice Admiral Jan E. Tighe, USN, Commander, U.S. Fleet Cyber Command, "Cyber Operations: Improving the Military Cyber Security Posture in an Uncertain Threat Environment," Testimony before House Armed Services Committee, March 4, 2015.

32. Sydney J. Freedberg Jr. "Navy Issues New Cybersecurity Standards—With More to Come," *Breaking Defense*, February 22, 2016.

33. Crowdstrike, "Indicators of Attack versus Indicators of Compromise," White Paper, 2015, 3.

34. Nick Lewis, "How Threat Intelligence Can Give Enterprise Security the Upper Hand," E-Guide, *Tech Target*, 2015, 2–5.

35. Threat Connect, "A Financial Giant's Threat Intel Success Story," Case Study, August 2016.

36. Ponemon Institute, "2016 State of Endpoint Report," April 2016, 15.

37. IBM Corporation, "Combat the Latest Security Attacks with Global Threat Intelligence," White Paper, 2016, 1–10.

38. Nick Bradley and Michelle Alvarez, "IBM X-Force 2016 Cyber Security Intelligence Index Webcast," IBM Security, August 5, 2016.

39. IBM Corporation, "Security Network Intrusion Prevention System," Data Sheet, 2013, 1–6.

40. Dave Shackleford, "Who's Using Cyberthreat Intelligence and How?" A SANS Survey, February 2015, 10.

41. Eric M. Hutchins, Michael J. Cloppert, and Rohan M. Amin, "Intelligence-Driven Computer Network Defense Informed by Analysis of Adversary Campaigns and Intrusion Kill Chains," Lockheed Martin Corporation, March 2011, 4–5.

42. Markus Maybaum, "Technical Methods, Techniques, Tools and Effects of Cyber Operations," *Peacetime Regime for State Activities in Cyberspace* (Tallinn, Estonia: NATO Cooperative Cyber Defence Centre of Excellence, 2013), 103–31.

43. Dell SecureWorks, "Inside a Targeted Point-of-Sale Data Breach," White Paper, January 24, 2014, 1–18.

44. Palo Alto Networks, "Firewall Overview," Data Sheet, 2016: 1-6.

45. Palo Alto Networks, "WildFire," Data Sheet, 2017: 1-3.

46. Palo Alto Networks, "Breaking the Cyber Attack Lifecycle," White Paper, March 2015, 1–6.

47. Giora Engel, "Deconstructing the Cyber Kill Chain," *Dark Reading*, November 18, 2014.

48. Tim Greene, "Why the 'Cyber Kill Chain' Needs an Upgrade," *Computer World*, August 8, 2016.

49. Symantec Corporation, "Internet Security Threat Report 2014," vol. 19 (2014), 86–93.

50. Center for Internet Security, "The CIS Critical Security Controls for Effective Cyber Defense," Version 6.1, August 31, 2016.

51. Robin Regnier, "Announcing Version 6.1 of the Critical Security Controls," Center for Internet Security, CIS Controls Adopter Communications, September 23, 2016.

52. John Pescatore and Tony Sager, "Critical Security Controls Survey: Moving from Awareness to Action," A SANS Whitepaper, June 2013.

53. SANS Institute, "Critical Security Controls Solution Providers and Critical Security Controls for Effective Cyber Defense," Poster, 31st Edition, Fall 2014.

54. Tripwire, "The CIS Critical Security Controls and Tripwire Solutions," Solution Brief, 2017, 1–4; and McAfee, "Conquer the Top 20 Critical Security Controls," White Paper, 2104, 1–9.

55. SANS Analyst Program, "Reducing Risk through Prevention: Implementing Critical Security Controls 1–4," White Paper, James Tarala, June 2013, 1–12.

56. Kaspersky Global Research and Analysis Team, "The NetTraveler (aka Travnet)," 2013, 1–25.

57. Kelly Jackson Higgins, "NetTraveler Cyberespionage Campaign Uncovered," *Dark Reading*, June 4, 2013.

58. Center for Internet Security, "Practical Guidance for Implementing the CIS Critical Security Controls (V6)," Version 6.1, September 23, 2016, 1.

59. Center for Internet Security, "Practical Guidance for Implementing the CIS Critical Security Controls (V6)," 3.

60. Solutionary, "Global Threat Intelligence Report," 2016 NTT Group, 21–46.

61. James Michael Stewart, "Cybersecurity Frameworks to Consider for Organization-wide Integration, *Global Knowledge*, 2016, 1–8.

62. President Barack Obama, "Improving Critical Infrastructure Cybersecurity," Executive Order 13636, February 12, 2013.

63. National Institute of Standards and Technology, "Framework for Improving Critical Infrastructure Cybersecurity," Version 1.0, February 12, 2014.

64. Intel Corporation, "The Cybersecurity Framework in Action: An Intel Use Case," Solution Brief, 2015, 1–9.

65. Greg Otto, "U.S. Officials: World Needs to Follow Our Lead on Cyber Norms," *Fedscoop*, April 5, 2016.

66. National Institute of Standards and Technology, *Guide to Cyber Threat Information Sharing (Draft)*, Special Publication 800-150 (Draft) (Washington, DC: US Department of Commerce, October 2014), 1–26.

67. Core Security, "Attack and Intelligence: Why It Matters," White Paper, 2014, 2.

68. Cyveillance, "Intelligence for Security," White Paper, 2015, 12.

69. Dan Waddell, "Where to Find Actionable Threat Intelligence," *GCN Magazine*, April 2015, 19.

70. Bob Gourley, *The Cyber Threat* (CreateSpace, September 23, 2014), Appendix 2, 79–85.

71. FireEye, "FireEye Threat Intelligence: Get the Intelligence and Context You Need to Help Identify, Block and Respond to Advanced Attacks," Data Sheet, 2016, 1–3

72. Ed Tittel, "Five Criteria for Purchasing Threat Intelligence Services," *Tech Target*, August 7, 2015.

73. Executive Office of the President, *Presidential Policy Directive on Critical Infrastructure Protection*, PPD-63 (Washington, DC: The White House, February 12, 2013).

74. Gregory T. Garcia, Financial Services Sector Coordinating Council, Testimony before House Committee on Homeland Security, March 4, 2015.

75. Sara Sorcher, "Security Pros: Cyberthreat Info-Sharing Won't Be as Effective as Congress Thinks," *Christian Science Monitor*, June 12, 2015.

76. Eric A. Fisher and Stephanie M. Logan, "Cybersecurity and Information Sharing: Comparison of Legislative Proposals in the 114th Congress," Congressional Research Service, Report R44069, June 18, 2015.

77. Tai Kopan, "Obama to Sign Cybersecurity Bill as Privacy Advocates Fume," *CNN*, December 18, 2015; and Chris Velazco, "Budget Bill Heads to President Obama's Desk with CISA Intact," engadget.com, December 18, 2015.

78. US Congress, "Consolidated Appropriations Act, 2016," Division N-Cybersecurity Act of 2015, December 15, 2015, 1728–70.

79. Mike O. Villegas, "How Will the Cybersecurity Information Sharing Act Affect Enterprises?" *Tech Target*, October 21, 2015; and Jason Koebler, "Lawmakers Have Snuck CISA into a Bill That Is Guaranteed to Become Law," motherboard.com, December 16, 2015.

80. Mary Ellen Callahan, "Industry Perspectives on the President's Cybersecurity Information Sharing Proposal," Testimony before House Committee on Homeland Security, March 4, 2015.

81. James R. Clapper, "Worldwide Cyber Threats," Statement for the Record for the House Permanent Select Committee on Intelligence, September 10, 2015, 2.

82. National Institute of Standards and Technology, *Managing Information Security Risk*, Special Publication 800-39 (Washington, DC: US Department of Commerce, March 2011), 6–43.

83. National Institute of Standards and Technology, *Guide for Conducting Risk Assessments*, Special Publication 800-30 (Washington, DC: US Department of Commerce, September 2012), 5–13.

84. Michael Heller, "Yet another Yahoo breach compromises more than 1 billion accounts," *Tech Target*, December 15, 2016.

85. Nichole Perlroth and Vindu Goel, "Yahoo gave hacking threat low priority," *International New York Times*, September 30, 2016.

86. National Institute of Standards and Technology, *Managing Information Security Risk*, Special Publication 800-39 (Washington, DC: US Department of Commerce, March 2011), 41–43.

87. Akamai, "Cloud Security Solutions," White Paper, 2015, 1–13.

88. Akamai, "Kona Site Defender," Product Brief, 2015, 1–2.

89. Tom Ruff, "Nothing Beats Experience," Government Computer Networks, Sponsored Report, May 2016, 5.

90. Thomas Michael Finan, "The Role of Cyber Insurance in Risk Management," Statement of House Committee on Homeland Security, March 22, 2016, 1–11.

91. Bipartisan Policy Center, "Cyber Insurance: A Guide for Policymakers," Insurance Task Force, March 2016, 2.

92. Gregg Otto, "DHS Pushes on towards Cyber Risk Management, Insurance," *Fedscoop*, October 2, 2015.

93. Tony Scott, "Enhancing and Strengthening the Federal Government's Cybersecurity," Fact Sheet, The White House, June 17, 2015.

94. Billy Mitchell, "White House Renews Push to Pass CISA," *Fedscoop*, October 6, 2015.

95. Mike O. Villegas, "Can Thinking Like Cyberattackers Improve Organizations' Security?" *Tech Target*, September 10, 2015.

96. Matthew J. Eggers, US Chamber of Commerce, "Industry Perspectives on the President's Cybersecurity Information-Sharing Proposal," Testimony before the House Homeland Security Committee," March 4, 2015.

97. "At Eight-Month Mark, Industry Praises Framework and Eyes Next Steps," *Inside Cybersecurity*, October 6, 2014.

98. Ponemon Institute, "2015 Global Study on IT Security Spending and Investments," Report, May 2015, 1–10.

99. Osterman Research, "Best Practices for Dealing with Phishing and Ransomware," White Paper, September 2016: 1.

100. Osterman Research, "Best Practices for Dealing with Phishing and Ransomware," White Paper, September 2016: 2.

101. ISAC Council, "The Role of Information Sharing and Analysis Centers (ISACs) in Private/Public Sector Critical Infrastructure Protection," January 2009, 4.

102. Martin C. Libicki, "Sharing Information about Threats Is Not a Cybersecurity Panacea," Testimony before House Homeland Security Committee, RAND Corporation, March 2015, 1–6.

103. Robert O. Work, Deputy Secretary of Defense, "Cybersecurity Risks to DoD Networks and Infrastructure," Statement before the Senate Armed Services Committee, September 29, 2015.

104. Sandra I. Erwin, "Defense CIO: Cybersecurity Improving but Innovation Lags," *National Defense*, August 8, 2016.

105. Ponemon Institute, "Is Your Company Ready for a Big Data Breach?" September 2014, 1.

106. Lumension, "Preventing Weaponized Malware Payloads in Advanced Persistent Threats," Scottsdale, Arizona, February 2013, 1–4.

107. Michael Heller, "Adobe Releases Emergency Flash Zero-Day Patch," *Tech Target*, June 23, 2015.

108. Michael Heller, "Adobe Patches Flash Zero-Day Used in Foreign Ministry Attacks," *Tech Target*, October 19, 2015.

109. Trend Micro Labs Security, "Operation Pawn Storm Ramps Up It Activities: Targets NATO, White House," Trend Labs Security Intelligence Blog, April 16, 2015.

110. Mandiant, "M-Trends 2016," Special Report, February 2016, 5.

111. Shaun Donovan and Tony Scott, "Cybersecurity Strategy and Implementation Plan (CSIP) for the Federal Civilian Government, Office of Management and Budget," October 30, 2015, 1–21.

112. Joe Davidson, "One Year after OPM Cybertheft Hit 22 Million: Are You Safer Now?" *Washington Post*, June 8, 2016.

113. Committee on Oversight and Government Reform, U.S. House of Representatives, 114th Congress, "The OPM Data Breach: How the Government Jeopardized Our National Security for More than a Generation," A Letter from the Chairman, September 7, 2016: ii.

114. Fortinet, "Threat Landscape Report," October 2016, 2.

115. Verizon, "2015 Data Breach Investigations Report," June 2015, 6.

Chapter Six

Deterrence by Entanglement

The strategy of deterrence by entanglement presumes state cooperation on mutual interests encourages restraint to avoid unintended consequences and antagonizing third parties. Nations share political, economic, commercial, and strategic interdependence in cyberspace as well as some degree of vulnerability. Soft power expert Joseph Nye claims that "entanglement refers to the existence of various independencies that make a successful attack simultaneously impose serious costs on the attacker, as well as the victim."[1] Deterrence by entanglement encourages responsible state behavior by raising the perceived value of maintaining and not endangering the returns from government to government cooperation. The strategy uses a range of cooperative measures to restrain state behavior in conducting, endorsing, or allowing malicious cyber activity by itself, or its authorities, or by hacker groups, criminal organizations, and terrorist groups originating from territory under its jurisdiction. Since deterrence is partially a function of perception, the strategic option of entanglement stems from a state actor's belief that the costs outweigh the benefits of acting in an irresponsible manner. Deterrence by entanglement seeks to change the cost-benefit calculations of a state actor by communicating the ramifications of their irresponsible behavior. For a deterrence strategy to be successful, the deterrer has to maintain not just the capability, will, and knowledge to restrict behavior as necessary, but also the credible reputation to do so.[2] Therefore, effective signaling of clear expectations is fundamental to the achievement of meaningful cooperation between states. Otherwise an uncooperative state will not believe the deterrer will not tolerate infractions and therefore will not participate in cooperative measures to secure cyberspace for the good of all parties.

However, in today's global environment, a clash of competing state interests seriously challenges the strategic option of deterrence by entanglement.

For instance, the United States is a strong proponent of a free and open Internet as shown in ongoing trade negotiations and decisions on net neutrality. But some nations, such as China and Russia, are pursuing a different vision. Theirs is "predicated on absolute government control of the Internet" and anti-access policies that restrict "publishing and distributing online content."[3] In addition state-sponsored cyber theft and cyber espionage indicate differing views exist on the protection and use of intellectual property, partially based on a cultural divide. The use of state-sponsored or privately contracted APT groups allows for plausible deniability of state involvement in a cyber attack. While the state feints anonymity, the operators themselves are not put at personal risk in any way. The situation is quite simple; if states don't share and adhere to the same underlying objectives and values, then state cooperation to reduce risks and enhance security is strained. The United Nations Government Group of Experts 2013 report contends that "further progress in cooperation at the international level will require actions to promote a peaceful, secure, resilient, and open Information and Communication Technologies environment."[4]

For space deterrence, notable scholars have suggested a layered approach that considers entanglement based on interdependence and international norms as distinct elements.[5] However, in practical application, norms are a mechanism to implement the strategy of entanglement. Norms, rules, and principles of responsible state behavior, along with confidence-building and capacity-building measures form the range of cooperative measures that attempt to enhance international peace and security. However, unlike binding treaty agreements that are essential to sustaining international order, adherence to and participation in cooperative measures remains voluntary. Therefore, despite diplomatic overtures for increased involvement in cooperative measures, state cooperation for responsible behavior in cyberspace remains elusive. If countries behaved responsibly and cooperated, the magnitude of the cyber problem would diminish. Like-minded nations need to "persuade or compel those countries who take action against us in cyberspace to stop"[6] or be incentivized to rein in nonstate actors conducting proscribed activities.[7] In some cases, to elicit desired actions from uncooperative states, coercive diplomacy is necessary to evoke elements of not just deterrence but also compellence. Unlike the former that waits for the attacker to act before fulfilling a threat, the latter involves initiating an overt action that can become harmless only if the opponent complies.[8] This chapter starts with an illustrative case that depicts the use of coercive diplomacy by the US government to reach an unprecedented cyber arms agreement with China. Then after assessing legal principles for establishing responsible state behavior in cyberspace, the chapter examines the range of cooperative measures and to what level they restrain state behavior in conducting, endorsing, or allowing malicious cyber activity originating in their territory.

ILLUSTRATIVE CASE

Ahead of his first official state visit to the United States in September 2015, Chinese President Xi Jinping stated in a written transcript that "the Chinese government does not engage in theft of commercial secrets in any form, nor does it encourage or support Chinese companies to engage in such practices in any way."[9] Contrary to this pronouncement, US officials have repeatedly alleged state-sponsored Chinese hackers have stolen sensitive corporate data. For example, in May 2014, the US Attorney General accused a group of five Chinese hackers affiliated with Unit 61398 of the People's Liberation Army of carrying out a hacking campaign against American businesses to include US Steel and Westinghouse Electric. Nevertheless, nearly a year and a half after that 48-page indictment, cybersecurity experts said China has only altered the methods used by its hackers and that its campaign against US firms remains active.[10] This difference in state position prompted US officials to suggest they would use the state visit to confront China on the matter. In recognizing that the United States and China have boosted cooperation in many areas, the US National Security Advisor said President Obama "would make clear that China must change its practices in other, more sensitive areas, particularly state-sponsored, cyber-enabled economic espionage." In seeking this change, the advisor stated the United States would continue to "urge China to join us in promoting responsible norms of state behavior in cyberspace."[11]

Just a day before the arrival of President Xi in Washington, the OPM revealed hackers who stole security dossiers from the agency also got the fingerprints of 5.6 million federal employees. Although the administration has never publicly blamed China for the theft of the personnel files, American intelligence agencies have attributed the hack to China. Their concern is that China could use the fingerprints to track the true identifies of Americans entering the country, and the file data to identify, or even blackmail, intelligence agents, defense personnel, or government contractors.[12] Although stealing government records from another country is a common part of espionage, the episode intensified pressure on President Obama to act on the more serious theft of corporate data. Weeks prior to the visit, his administration developed a package of economic sanctions, "an increasingly important tool in our coercive diplomacy toolkit,"[13] against Chinese companies and individuals who have benefited from their government's cyber theft of US trade secrets.[14] The sanctions would mark the first use of an Executive Order signed by President Obama in April 2015 establishing the authority to freeze financial and property assets of individuals and entities overseas who engage in destructive attacks on critical infrastructure or commercial espionage for competitive advantage in cyberspace.[15] The intent or threat of the sanctions, along with indictments, is to impose costs for malicious cyber-enabled activities.

Nonetheless, the Obama administration held off on imposing the sanctions in hopes of resolving this issue with Mr. Xi during the state visit.[16] For weeks before the state visit the United States and China had conducted negotiations with urgency, hoping for a cyber arms agreement for the presidents to sign. A high-level Communist Party envoy came to Washington to meet with the National Security Advisor and Director of the FBI. The result of deliberations appeared initially to be a bilateral agreement that would be a generic embrace of the code of conduct adopted by the Government Group of Experts at the United Nations in July.[17] Yet on the last day of the state visit, the White House released only a Fact Sheet that stated the two presidents agreed to work together to manage differences and deepen cooperation in a number of areas, to include cybersecurity. The two countries agree that "neither country's government will conduct or knowingly support cyber-enabled theft of intellectual property, including trade secrets or other confidential business information, with the intent of providing competitive advantages to companies or commercial sectors."[18] Later President Obama said he told Mr. Xi, "The question now is . . . are words followed by actions?" and indicated the United States will apply [sanctions] and whatever tools to go after cyber-criminals either retrospectively or prospectively.[19]

US Congressional reaction to the cyber deal was guarded. "I remain skeptical that China will deliver on this promise," said Representative Adam Schiff, "but if curbing cyber theft is a journey of a thousand miles, perhaps China has taken a first step."[20] Although it was unclear how the agreement would be enforced, it could reflect an inflection point, according to Dmitri Alperovitch, cofounder of CrowdStrike, a prominent cyber security company, where the Chinese "are now obligated to respond to evidence presented by the United States."[21] Consequently only three weeks later China fulfilled that obligation with the arrest of a number of hackers at the request of the US government, showing it was serious about punishing hackers.[22] However, the unprecedented move by China could have been more a reaction to threats of economic sanctions. For despite the pledge by China's president, according to a Crowdstrike report,[23] hackers linked to the Chinese government attempted to gain access to US tech and pharmaceutical companies in the same three weeks since President Xi left Washington. One year after the deal, FireEye Chief Technology Officer Grady Summers reported the cyber firm is now conducting about ten investigations of Chinese cyber espionage a month compared to a prior average of thirty-five per month for different corporate clients.[24] Yet "absence of evidence is not the same thing as evidence of absence" as China may just be more stealthy and sophisticated in their attacks,[25] signifying a failure of the much heralded agreement to achieve deterrence by entanglement.

RESPONSIBLE STATE BEHAVIOR

A central premise for responsible state behavior in cyberspace is that global interdependence requires it. Critical components of modern life such as food, water, health, finance, energy, manufacturing, and transportation are entrenched with ICT. For society in every state, the security of the online infrastructure in these sectors is important. Yet as new cyber-related vulnerabilities are discovered, the risk of systemic disruption increases in parallel with rising connectivity. Accordingly a Chatham House report recognizes that dependencies in cyber-enabled critical infrastructure "spread across national boundaries and become global."[26] This newfound global interdependence challenges state sovereignty (defined by the Oxford dictionaries as "the authority of a state to govern itself") for maintaining security and prosperity in cyberspace. It also questions the limits of responsible state behavior in not endangering the same for other nations by conducting, endorsing, or allowing malicious cyber activity originating from their territory. Rightfully so, the US National Security Strategy eloquently states that the "increasing interdependence of the global economy and rapid pace of technological change" are linking governments in unprecedented ways, while creating "shared vulnerabilities, as interconnected systems and sectors are susceptible" to the threats of malicious cyber activities.[27] For example, in a scenario that envisages a Chinese attack on the U.S. power grid that results in costs on the U.S. economy, the economic interdependence of the two countries would mean costly damage to China as well.[28] This phenomenon should hypothetically incentivize and enable new forms of cooperation based on mutual interests.

The bilateral agreement between China and the United States represents a form of cooperation for responsible state behavior in cyberspace. Any effort to further codify norms, rules, and principles of responsible behavior by states starts with an understanding of how international law is applicable to cyberspace. International law is made by states and comes from various sources, to include treaties and conventions, that are legally binding documents among states; customary international law, which is created by consensus of states over a long period of time; general principles of law, that are recognized among civilization; and the writing and teaching of scholars.[29] In particular, general principles can be of contractual nature (in good faith) and procedural character (for advisory opinions) or of common heritage of mankind (for common spaces) or sustainable development (for the environment). In regard to international peace and security, a common core of general principles consist of: the sovereign equality of states, including the right to self-preservation, independence, jurisdiction, nonintervention, and duty not to harm the rights of other states; the maintenance of international peace and security, including the obligation to refrain from threat or use of force and peaceful settlement of disputes; and duty to international cooperation in solving international relations.[30] These principles serve as a "normative source of law, which governs situations not regulated by formulated norms." They can also serve as a "guide or framework for interpretation of conventional and customary international law." And they can serve as the "basis for the development of new rights and obligations."[31] Most importantly, the aforementioned core of principles pertaining to international peace and security applies in some manner in cyberspace.

The topic of sovereignty opens the Tallinn Manual 2.0 in Rule 1, in delineating "the principle of State sovereignty applies in cyberspace."[32] Therefore a state is "free to adopt any measure it considers necessary or appropriate with regard to cyber infrastructure, persons engaged in cyber activities, or cyber activities themselves within its territory," unless prevented by international law, such as those for international human rights.[33] At the same time, sovereignty entails "a duty to protect within the territory, the rights of other states, in particular their right to integrity and inviolability in peace and in war."[34] Based on the principle of territoriality, "states are able to legislate with regard to activities and to prosecute offences committed on their territory."[35] Typical examples of offenses that are likely to be considered a violation of state territory or integrity include cyber-enabled political influence, economic espionage, crime, terrorism, and sabotage. However, there is no clear consensus in the international community on whether acts that cause no physical damage qualify as a violation.[36] Hence it is "imperative to examine to what extent States are obliged to control and regulate cyberspace within the reach of their sovereign powers, in order to avoid being responsible"[37] for these offenses, caused by acts which originate from their territory, by the state itself, or its authorities, or by private parties under its jurisdiction.

The duty to protect the rights of other states invokes the obligation of states to take preventive measures in cases where the state has actual as well as constructive or presumptive knowledge. A state may have detected a particular cyber-enabled activity; it may be told by the Victim State; or it can be presumed to know about the activity. The prevention principle obliges states to undertake a risk assessment and notify, inform, and consult other states of risk of harm. This obligation in effect requires the state to notice malicious cyber activity, create investigative cyber capabilities to identify the source, and establish an organizational and legal framework to enable the prevention or discontinuation of such activity originating on the state's territory.[38] In addition, states are also responsible for their "internationally wrongful acts" to those whom they have injured. Such acts are composed of both a breach of an international obligation and attribution of the act to the responsible state.[39] The conduct of "state organs" of government, such as military, intelligence, and security agencies,[40] or person or group of persons "acting on the instructions of, or under the direction or control of, that state in carrying out the conduct,"[41] is attributable to the state. With regard to the wrongfulness thereof, an example is cyber operations that violate the prohibition on the use of force. Those cyber operations which cause injury or death of persons, or damage or destruction of property violate the prohibition, as resident in customary law, and codified in Article 2(4) of the UN Charter.[42] The latter was affirmed to be applicable to state conduct in cyberspace by the Group of Twenty (G-20) at their 2015 Summit in Turkey.[43]

International law principles echo the basic values of international society that are intrinsic to international order. The United States considers a rules-based international order that promotes peace, security, and opportunity to be an enduring national interest.[44] For cyberspace, one prevailing scholarly view is that international order is inevitable due to the dynamics of power and competition, particularly competition over issues of sovereignty. Inevitability is deduced from the reality that states are always negotiating over the framework of competition. Therefore this view contends as "the international system moves from a unipolar format to a multipolar one, great powers will have no choice" but to cooperate, to "soften the harsh effects of multipolarity and oligopolistic competition."[45] A counter academic view is that while correct increased competition may create incentives for cooperation on rules for cyberspace, the history of norm evolution for other emerging-technology weapons, such as chemical and biological weapons, strategic bombing platforms, and nuclear weapons, indicates otherwise. In each of these historic cases, the primary reason for developing norms was the "perception among powerful or relevant states that such norms are in their national self-interest."[46] The counterview contends that an analysis of the cyber doctrines of China, Russia, and the United States for certain categories, indicates that their calculations of self-interest might not converge in favor of robust constraining cyber norms.[47]

Formal Binding Obligations

The start point for reaching concurrence between countries on rules or norms, and also confidence-building and capacity-building measures, is the recognition that a cyber treaty for international peace and security is simply not possible and therefore other means are necessary to achieve peace and security. According to renowned expert James Lewis, there is no real alternative to using these forms of cooperative measures as "legally binding commitments have serious drawbacks."[48] Uncooperative states will most likely just ignore treaties regarding cybersecurity, as they face definitional, compatibility, compliance, and verification problems in implementation. The first issue for an arms control type treaty is what defines a cyber weapon. One cyber security industry insight into common characteristics of a cyber weapon includes both an attacker with "intimate knowledge of the workings of the targeted system" and a special "code that can bypass protective cybersecurity technology."[49] However, those characteristics are also common to penetration tests, described in the Center for Internet Security Critical Security Control 20 as to test the strength of an organization's defenses "by simulating the objectives and actions of an attacker."[50] A more explicit version of the definition is found in Rule 103 of the Tallinn Manual 2.0, where cyber weapons are considered to be "cyber means of warfare that are used, designed, or intended to be used to cause injury to, or death of, persons or, damage to or destruction of, objects."[51] Even Thomas Rid agreed that cyber weapons are "instruments of harm" where computer code causes these same effects,[52] although without pervasive consensus on the definition of a cyber weapon,[53] there is no basis for cyber arms control treaties.

Past arms control arrangements between states such as the Outer Space Treaty of 1967, the Conventional Forces in Europe Treaty of 1992, the Comprehensive Test Ban Treaty in 1996, and the Anti-Ballistic Missile Treaty of 1972 offer policy makers extensive experience in governing armaments and their deployment or use.[54] However, the technical properties of cyber weapons are incompatible with the rationale upon which these arms control treaties are based. For example, unlike nuclear weapons affordable only to states, malware is easy to use and relatively inexpensive. And unlike other kinetic weapons, malware can be reproduced and distributed at minimal cost. In addition, the rapid pace of development of malware makes any listing of prohibited weapons impossible. Even if prohibitions were possible, dual use software, like that for intelligence collection can be repurposed for malicious action.[55] The success of the aforesaid arms control treaties has been dependent on compliance and verification regimes. Yet no state would likely agree to external verification measures which would require scanning their computers and devices, including those in classified systems.[56] Therefore, rather than ban cyber weapons, some scholars contend that binding agreements should stipulate acceptable types, which adhere to attributability and reversibility. For the first quality, a responsible country would make their attacks clear in origin, by using digital signatures in attack code. And for the second, nations would use attack methods that are repairable,[57] even though this approach seems to just encourage the use of cyber arms, while under some form of control.

All complications aside, China and Russia did sign in May 2015 a bilateral agreement dubbed a "nonaggression pact" for cyberspace that demonstrated their values diverge from Western society. The treaty broadly defines cyber threats to include the transmission of information that could endanger "societal-political and social-economic systems," seemingly counter to the free flow of information, and calls for the creation of "a multilateral, democratic and transparent management system" for the Internet, implying a predominant state voice in governance versus a multi-stakeholder model. Besides detailing pledges of cooperation, such as in international legal norms and on joint scientific projects, one particular provision in the treaty pledges the parties to refrain from "computer attacks" against each other. Specifically Article 4 provides that "Each Party has an equal right to the protection of the information resources of their state against misuse and unsanctioned interference."[58] Still the language is vague and could be interpreted differently, highlighting the difficulty of implementing the precise provision, the essence of the treaty. Efforts to limit the cyber arms race are confronted by a nation's desire to maintain advantage in the domain for their own benefit. One public analysis of intrinsic challenges simply concludes that "cybersecurity treaties may be nice, but it's really every country for itself."[59] Undoubtedly any hope for that assertion to be false resides in cooperative measures found in the strategy of deterrence by entanglement.

COOPERATIVE MEASURE SELECTION

A broad range of cooperative measures contributes to the restraint of state activity, or state-sponsored or endorsed activity, of a malicious manner in cyberspace. International forum discussions indicate that cyber-related norms of behavior are the best means to guide state behavior in cyberspace. The main objectives for agreeing on norms appear to be "increased predictability, trust and stability in the use of ICTs, hopefully steering states clear of possible conflict due to misunderstandings."[60] State acceptance of a prescribed norm can constrain and regulate their behavior, under the pretense that other states will sanction violations of the norm.[61] The incentive for states to adopt norms stems from a common interest in sustaining cyberspace, in particular the Internet, for the benefit of all states. Therefore the United Nations has taken the lead on the development of norms for responsible behavior by states in cyberspace. Another cooperative measure choice resides in voluntary politically binding confidence-building measures (CBM) designed to prevent the outbreak of conflict. The Organization for Security and Cooperation in Europe (OSCE) has made progress in advancing cyber-related CBMs. Finally, the last category of cooperative measures is contained in capacity-building measures. They are intended to help secure ICTs and their use.

Norms, Rules, and Principles

A norm can be defined as a "standard of appropriate behavior for actors with a given identity."[62] Voluntary, and hence nonbinding, norms of responsible state behavior are intended to reduce risks to international peace and security. They reflect international community expectations and standards for responsible state behavior. Normative regimes are beginning to influence the development of state policy embodied in their national cyber strategies and the position on related matters of intergovernmental bodies such as the United Nations,[63] although some state views and initiatives regarding norms, rules, and principles substantially differ from international congruence based on their own interpretations of international order. For instance, from China's perspective, international order reflects the relative balance of power and resides currently in the interest of hegemons, which makes it inconsistent and unfair. China would favor an international order that contributes to the maintenance of national sovereignty and political systems. Their foundational principles for international order specify "equality of the sovereign nations, non-interference in each other's internal affairs, and peaceful coexistence of different political systems."[64]

Therefore China teamed with Russia, Tajikistan and Uzbekistan in September 2011 to submit to the United Nations their version of an international code of conduct for information security. Their letter recognizes that a "global culture of cybersecurity" needs to be implemented pursuant to a previous General Assembly resolution."[65] The letter highlights "the importance of the security, continuity and stability of the Internet" and reaffirms "that policy authority for Internet-related public issues is the sovereign right of States."[66] One purpose of the proposed code of conduct is to promote responsible behaviors of states in information space. Although adherence is voluntary, each state subscribing would pledge to comply with universal norms governing "sovereignty, territorial integrity, and political independence of all States"; not to use information and communication technologies "to carry out hostile activities or acts of aggression"; and to reaffirm the rights of "States to protect . . . their information space and critical infrastructure from threats, disturbances, attack and sabotage."[67] The draft code of conduct submission was revised in January 2015 to add that each state subscribing would also pledge not to use information and communication technologies "to interfere in the internal affairs of other States" and not to "undermine States' right to independent control of information and communication technology goods and services,"[68] in effect advocating government control of the Internet.

The code of conduct submission by China, Russia, and most of the Central Asian states is not the only regionally endorsed proposal. In June 2014, the Member States of the African Union released a Convention on Cyber Security and Personal Data Protection. It establishes a normative framework that aims to strengthen existing legislations on ICTs. The provisions of the convention are not to be interpreted in a way that is not consistent with the principles of international law, to include customary law. Actions that collect, process, transmit, store, or use personal data by the state or a person are subject to the convention.[69] Each member state is supposed to develop and adopt a national cyber security policy that acknowledges the significance of

Critical Information Infrastructure. Suggested strategies to implement this policy include international cooperation, especially on the exchange of information on cyber threats and vulnerabilities, and legislative reform. For the latter, by mandating that each state shall take legislative or regulatory measures to make attempts to gain unauthorized access, remain fraudulently, hinder functioning, enter data deceptively, or damage data in a computer system a criminal offense,[70] the convention establishes a de facto baseline for norms of expected behavior by member states, which also applies to individuals in their territory, although critics of the convention say serious concerns exist over its human rights implications, particularly provisions that restrict free speech, limit freedom of association, and broaden judicial powers.[71]

Also, eight months before the 2011 code of conduct submission, the UN General Assembly adopted a resolution, sponsored by the United States and Russia that notes "the dissemination and use of information technologies and means affect the interests of the entire international community" and expresses "concern that these technologies and means can potentially be used for purposes that are inconsistent with the objectives of maintaining international stability and security."[72] Consequently the resolution requests the Secretary-General to establish another Group of Governmental Experts, with an equitable geographical composition, to "study existing and potential threats in the sphere of information security and possible cooperative measures to address them."[73] In 2013, the subsequent group, comprised of representatives from China, Russia, the United States and twelve other nations, reached consensus on their report. They agreed that international law, and the Charter of the United Nations, is applicable and essential to promoting a peaceful ICT environment. Hence in regard to specific recommendations on norms, rules-cybe and principles of responsible state behavior, the 2013 Group of Governmental Experts concluded that:[74]

- States must meet their international obligations regarding internationally wrongful acts attributable to them.
- States must not use proxies to commit internationally wrongful acts.
- States should seek to ensure that their territories are not used by nonstate actors for unlawful use of ICTs.

These particular norms codify group determination that the principles that flow from sovereignty apply to state conduct and jurisdiction over ICT-related activities or infrastructure respectively.

While regional and organizational initiatives advance, the broader international community has not sat idle on discussing norms for responsible behavior in cyberspace. As of this writing, a total of four Global Conferences on Cyberspace have been held with representatives from governments, private sector, and civil society. The first in London in November 2011 asked this succinct question under the topic of international security: "How do we develop and apply appropriate principles of behavior?"[75] In response all delegates agreed that immediate steps should be to create shared understanding and agree on common approaches. Some delegates noted the draft Code of Conduct being circulated at the United Nations. None wanted to expend effort on legally binding international agreements. By the next iteration in Budapest in October 2012, very little progress had been made, and if anything, various actors dug in on their resistive positions. The Chinese indicated their preference for a cyberspace arms control treaty and the Russians rejected the Budapest Convention on Cybercrime,[76] although in a progressive manner, the United Kingdom asked for consensus on rules of the road and the Republic of Korea urged exploration on norms of behavior to avoid conflict between states.[77] Real progress on areas of common ground was made at the Seoul Conference in October 2013, and reflected in the *Seoul Framework for and Commitment to Open and Secure Cyberspace*. The document identified elements for an open and secure cyberspace to include under the category of international security many verbatim conclusions from the 2013 UN Group of Government Experts report.[78] The fourth Global Conference held in The Hague in April 2015, sought to build on the *Seoul Framework*. The Hague Conference "reaffirmed the applicability of existing international law to State behavior in cyberspace, as well as its commitment to exploring the development of voluntary, non-legally binding norms for responsible State behavior in cyberspace during peacetime."[79]

Three months later, in July 2015, the Group of Governmental Experts released another report that distinctly expanded the discussion of norms. In the foreword, the Secretary-General pronounced that "All States have a stake in making cyberspace more secure."[80] Thus to better represent the international community in this quest, the 2015 Group was enlarged to twenty states. Their comprehensive exchange of views on norms, rules, and principles of responsible state behavior resulted in consensus on the following additional recommendations:[81]

- A state should not conduct or knowingly support ICT activity contrary to its obligations under international law that intentionally damages critical infrastructure.
- States should take appropriate measures to protect their critical infrastructure from ICT threats.
- States should respond to appropriate requests for assistance by another state whose critical infrastructure is subject to malicious ICT acts.
- States should not conduct or knowingly support activity to harm the information systems of the authorized emergency response teams.

These particular norms could be considered a breakthrough for US diplomats pushing for an alternative to formal treaties. By delineating norms regarding critical infrastructure, the United States and other states reached "a consensus on the appropriate boundaries for state activities in cyberspace in order to avoid wide-spread, potentially devastating, damage in cyberspace,"[82] although in the spirit of concession, the United States did not reach consensus on their proposal to spell out the implications of the 2013 Group's agreement "that international law applies to cyberspace just as it does on land or at sea."[83] A bloc of nations rebuffed the proposal to prevent their interpretation of an attempt to establish US hegemony in cyberspace.

Not just states have "a stake in making cyberspace more secure," so do international corporations. More representative of the multi-stakeholder model is the Microsoft Corporation version of proposed Cyber Security Norms to limit potential conflict in cyberspace. The premise of their norms is that governments which are investing in offensive cyber capabilities have a responsibility to guide their use. Therefore, norms can better define what type of government behavior is unacceptable so that incidents do not escalate to conflict. To be effective, Microsoft believes norms also have to drive behavior change that is observable. Proposed norms are meant to reduce the possibility that states will use, abuse, or exploit ICT products and services as part of offensive operations that result in conflict. Therefore, the six norms proposed by Microsoft focus mostly on protecting global trust in technology, per the following abbreviated recommendations that states should:[84]

- Not target ICT companies to insert vulnerabilities that undermine public trust.
- Have a policy for handling product and service vulnerabilities that reflect a mandate to report them to vendors rather than to stockpile, buy, sell, or exploit them.
- Ensure that any developed cyber weapons are limited, precise and not reusable.
- Commit to nonproliferation activities that pertain to cyber weapons.
- Limit offensive cyber operations to avoid creating mass events.
- Assist the private sector to detect, contain, respond, and recover from cyber incidents.

Microsoft recognizes that norms are not an objective by themselves, but can drive demonstrable changes in state behavior if implemented, assessed for accountability, and, if appropriate, evolved. Microsoft did just that in forwarding in June 2016 a new three-part organizing model of offensive, defensive, and industry norms. Offensive norms require restraint to not choose actions that violate boundaries of responsible state behavior. Defensive norms are meant to enable risk management through improved defenses and incident response. While the first two categories are consistent with the 2014 list for states, industry norms are new in addressing their role in mitigating risks—for example, global ICT providers should not permit backdoors in their products, traffic in cyber vulnerabilities, or withhold patches from any party.[85] Scott Charney, Corporate Vice President, described the relationship among the categories in stating "as governments commit increasing resources into offensive cyber capabilities, the global ICT industry must . . . take active steps to prevent user exploitation" and "raise the bar in our defensive capabilities to deter nation-states from targeting technology users."[86]

Confidence-Building Measures

The 2015 Group of Governmental Experts proclaimed that CBMs strengthen international peace and security. In their report, they assert these types of measures "can increase interstate cooperation, transparency, predictability and stability."[87] CBMs are used as an instrument of international politics, in attempts to prevent or reduce the risk of conflict by removing sources of mistrust, misunderstanding, and miscalculation between states. They achieve this result by establishing practical means and processes for crisis management.[88] For example, CBMs have been developed and suggested for outer space activities to address state-owned threats to their sustainability and security.[89] The world's growing dependence on vulnerable space-based platforms, technologies, and information is no different than global interdependence in cyberspace. Likewise neither is the risk of conflict from the militarization of outer space and also cyberspace. The acceleration of an arms race in both domains only increases the risk of escalation and conflict. CBMs attempt to reach an adequate level of predictability of state behavior and prevent the loss of control over a perilous situation.

In 2013, the United States and the Russian Federation entered into a new field of cooperation in confidence-building. Both parties recognized not only the increasing interdependence of the world on ICTs, but also the political-military, criminal, and terrorist threats to or in the use of them. Thus in demonstrating "commitment to promoting international peace and security," they completed "landmark steps designed to strengthen relations, increase transparency, and build confidence" between their nations, to include: [90]

- A mechanism and arrangements for information sharing between computer emergency response teams to better protect critical information systems.
- Authority to use the direct communications link between Nuclear Risk Reduction Centers for this purpose.

- A link between high-level officials to manage dangerous situations related to security threats to or in the use of Information and Communication Technologies.

These CBMs are designed to "reduce the possibly that a misunderstood cyber incident could create instability or a crisis" between the two nations.[91] Although not as formal, the United States and China do pursue a model of risk reduction under the rubric of "constructive management of differences." President Xi Jinping has labeled cooperation in this manner to be "of vital importance to the global community."[92] The model applies not just to cyber security, but also to maritime disputes, as urged by the Chinese Chief of General Staff Fang Fenghui for the two sides to "manage their differences in a constructive way" in regard to South China Sea tensions.[93]

On a more global scale, the US Department of State has advanced the development of practical cyber CBMs to reduce risk.[94] This has occurred through agreement in the ASEAN Regional Forum in 2015 on a work plan for such, and in the Organization for Security and Cooperation in Europe in 2016 on implementation of an initial set of voluntary CBMs, which include:[95]

- Provide national views on threats to and in use of ICTs.
- Facilitate cooperation among national bodies and exchange information.
- Hold consultations to reduce risks of misperceptions.
- Share information on measures taken to ensure a secure and reliable Internet.
- Have in place national legislation to facilitate bilateral cooperation.
- Share information on their national organization, strategy, policies, and programs.

The development of CBMs provides tools to manage expectations of responsible state behavior in cyberspace. For example, measures for communication, exchange, and cooperation during transnational investigations facilitate norms for states to not allow malicious activity originating from their territory.[96]

Capacity-Building Measures

The 2015 Group of Governmental Experts commented that some states may lack sufficient capacity to protect ICTs and prevent a haven for malicious actors. Consequently they endorsed the 2013 Group's findings that some states may require assistance "in their efforts to improve the security of critical ICT infrastructure; develop technical skill and appropriate legislation, strategies and regulatory frameworks to fulfil their responsibilities."[97] The

2015 Global Conference on Cyberspace held in The Hague not only reached the same deduction but also took action. The founding partners of the event announced the launch of the Global Forum on Cyber Expertise, described as a global platform for cyber capacity building. The primary objectives of the Global Forum are to share expertise, experience, and best practices on thematic cyber issues; identify gaps in global cyber capacity and find solutions; and contribute to efforts to build global cyber capacity.[98] The Framework Document for the Global Forum delineates that participation is voluntary, and does not impose any legal obligation. Members are to take on new initiatives or enhance and expand existing ones to improve capacity in cyber security.[99] Today the Global Forum consists of over fifty organizations and states that are working together on a multitude of practical initiatives in the four preliminary focus areas of strengthening cybersecurity, fighting cybercrime, protecting online data, and supporting e-governance.[100]

COOPERATIVE MEASURE UTILITY

As a leader of the international community, the United States has remained eager to pursue cooperative measures to restrain state behavior based not only on mutual interests, but also on mutual trust. After success in collaboration with Russia on ICT security measures, the United States elected to pursue comparable CBMs to promote trust and assurance with China. An exchange on national policies for cyberspace was deemed the appropriate measure to head off the chance of fast escalating cyber attacks between the two nations. Therefore, prior to the US Defense Secretary visit to Beijing, in April 2014 the Obama administration quietly briefed Chinese military leadership on the Pentagon's emerging doctrine for defending against cyber attacks against the United States and for using its cyber technology against adversaries, including the Chinese. The intent was to allay Chinese concerns about plans to triple American cyber warriors in new teams for cyber operations, and the hope was to prompt the Chinese to give Washington a similar briefing about PLA units believed to be behind cyber attacks on government and corporate networks in the United States.[101] Without any guarantee of reciprocation, the briefing turned out to be a one-way exchange. Although the United States hoped for the same openness, under the guise of mutual transparency China effectively secured access to sensitive US defense information while offering little in return. The reality is that a collaborative and transparent relationship would run counter to the Chinese government priorities.[102] Ultimately the United States had no choice but to turn to other measures, in particular coercive diplomacy, to gain cooperation on mutual interests.

The result was President Xi's pledge during his state visit to Washington in September 2015 that China would not conduct cyber-enabled economic espionage. Up to that point, the Chinese government had never even acknowledged such activity. Remarkably, at the 2015 Group of Twenty Summit, President Xi repeated that commitment to the heads of state. In response, the G-20 Leaders "affirmed that international law applies to state conduct in cyberspace and committed that all states should abide by norms of responsible state behavior in cyberspace."[103] They also "affirmed that no country should conduct or support cyber-enabled theft of intellectual property with the intent of providing competitive advantages to companies or commercial sectors."[104] A month later, China announced the arrest of hackers it says breached the OPM database. However, US officials are not sure if the arrests were of the guilty parties.[105] FireEye and ISight Partners had attributed the attack to a Chinese state-sponsored APT group referred to as Deep Panda, also responsible for the Anthem breach.[106] It seems hard to believe the Chinese government would give up the Deep Panda operation that routinely steals PII from US commercial and government networks. A combination of delivered indictments and threatened sanctions may have altered malicious Chinese behavior in cyberspace shown in the OPM arrests. Yet according to Brad Bussie at the cyber security firm STEALTHbits Technologies, "nothing has changed. Attacks and the origin of the attacks have simply become harder to detect."[107]

The reality is that fundamental challenges in agreeing on and adhering to norms exist in competing views, particularly on use of the Internet. For instance, the 2015 UN Government Group of experts did not accept proposed norms related to intellectual property theft. For the Chinese, as a member of the UN Group, economic espionage in cyberspace is now part of normal business practice. China has no tradition of protecting intellectual property, evidenced by more than thirty years of licit and illicit acquisition of western technology.[108] A cultural divide exists, where the Chinese believe that intellectual property is to be rightfully copied or obtained. Confucianism holds that imitation is the greatest form of flattery and emphasizes the significance of sharing intellectual products with society, even to the extent that it would be dishonorable if a scholar makes money by selling his book to others.[109] In addition, communism discourages individual property.[110] These fundamental precepts produce the prevailing Chinese view that copying is a form of compliment rather than disrespect, and thus justly acceptable.[111] This view permeates Chinese thought to the extent that the obtainment of intellectual property for imitation is a moral duty. For illustration, after a Chinese national admitted to conspiring to hack into the computer systems of major US defense contractors to steal military hardware secrets on Beijing's behalf,[112] the state-run *Global Times* said that if he had done so, "we are willing to show our gratitude and respect for his service to our country."[113]

On the contrary, the United States recognizes acts of cyber-enabled intellectual property theft as unlawful and impermissible. Assistant Attorney

General John Carlin called the sentencing of the aforementioned Chinese national as "just punishment" for his role in a conspiracy "to illegally access and steal sensitive U.S. military information."[114] Therefore, to establish an environment of common expectations, the United States seeks to consolidate regional and international consensus on key cyberspace activities, although consensus is difficult to achieve when not just values, but basic rights diverge. For example, the US International Strategy for Cyberspace opines that "states should not have to choose between the free flow of information and the security of their networks." The reason is because the best cybersecurity solution tools secure systems "without crippling innovation, suppressing freedom of expression or association, or impeding global interoperability."[115] In contrast, some totalitarian states call for national-level filters and firewalls that increase sovereign control over Internet access and content. At the 2015 World Internet Conference, Chinese President Xi called for governments to cooperate in regulating Internet use, stepping up attempts to promote controls. The human rights group Amnesty International scorned this assault on Internet freedom to make censorship and surveillance the norm everywhere under the guise of security. For already in China, the Communist Party tries to prevent Internet users from seeing news outlets, the Google search engine, and social media such as Facebook.[116] In November 2016, China adopted a controversial cyber security law where elements, such as "criminalizing the use of the Internet to damage national unity," would further restrict online freedom.[117]

According to Christopher Painter, the US Coordinator for Cyber Issues, the area of Internet governance is where authoritarian governments are "pushing to shift from the long-standing and successful multi-stakeholder model . . . to an intergovernmental and exclusive system that could fundamentally undermine the future growth and potential of the Internet."[118] The United States counters this movement by working to support and enhance the multi-stakeholder model, as evidenced by the Commerce Department announcement in 2014 of intent to transfer its stewardship of key Internet domain name functions to the global Internet community.[119] In keeping this promise, the United States transferred the DNS to ICANN (the Internet Corporation for Assigned Names and Numbers) on October 1, 2016, even over the objectives of several US politicians that the transfer increases "the power of foreign governments over the internet."[120] In a show of contrasting views, China and Russia have advocated for a new global cybercrime treaty that controls free speech and undermines human rights, while disregarding the long-standing Budapest Convention on Cyber Crime that has already been ratified by forty-six countries.[121] From the 2015 Global Conference on Cyberspace, the chair's statement reiterates the need to ensure that fundamental human rights are protected online. The chair also notes commitment at the conference to a multi-stakeholder approach for Internet governance that includes "civil society, the technical community, business and governments across the globe."[122] While the next Global Conference in The Hague called upon all stakeholders to strengthen the evolution of the multi-stakeholder model to achieve a free and open Internet, some countries would prefer to stake out borders in cyberspace, in a form of "balkanization of the Internet."[123]

AN INSUFFICIENT DETERRENCE OPTION

Part of the problem in achieving cooperation for restraint in cyberspace is that states are not going to agree on what they don't know is acceptable; instead they will wait to see what the international community will not tolerate. For instance, China operates at a peer level and will do what it wants, inside the precise language of what is allowed, based on an assessment of its own national interests in any given situation.[124] Take for example the Chinese military buildup in the South China Sea on disputed islands. As President Obama hosted allies from Southeast Asia at a summit in California in February 2016, China stationed a modern surface-to-air weapons system, the HQ-9 on Woody Island in the Paracel chain, controlled by China but claimed by Vietnam and Taiwan.[125] Then a month later, China not only deployed anti-ship cruise missiles, the YJ-62, to the island,[126] but test fired the coastal battery.[127] The installations of these advanced weapons not only threaten US policy to sail anywhere in the world that international law allows, but also threaten to impose China's unilateral resolution on island claims that the United States has urged be settled through negotiations. Another state, namely Russia, also pushes international law and order to the edge, then recasts language to their terms. Although NATO called the Russian annexation of Crimea in March 2014 a violation of international law, Russia defended its actions as the lawful protection of the Russian-speaking minority in Crimea. However, there were really no indications that native Russians were in any danger, and even if so, that pretense could only have justified their evacuation, not the occupation of the entire peninsula. Without an invitation by the Ukrainian authorities to intervene in their country, the annexation by Russia was simply an illegal violation of the territorial integrity of Ukraine.[128]

In addition, states use proxies, groups that act as a substitute for another, to allow for "plausible deniability." By the time the Russian Parliament approved the deployment of troops into Ukraine, Russian military forces disguised as "little green men" were already present in Crimea. According to President Putin, these armed men were "members of 'self-defense groups' organized by locals who bought all their uniforms and hardware in a shop."[129] Likewise in the "Donetsk People's Republic," Russian Special Forces troops reportedly reinforced local "separatists."[130] This use of "volunteers" allowed the Russian government to deny any involvement in Ukraine for months. Even more so, Russian use of proxies in the conflict in Ukraine extended beyond the physical domain into cyberspace. Here the most prominent proxy actors have been hacktivist groups, including pro-Moscow Anonymous Ukraine and CyberBerkut. Their activities range from DDoS attacks and web defacements to the leaking of government files. While Ukrainian government officials blame the Russian government for indirectly orchestrating these operations, the latter denies accusations that it has any influence over the groups.[131] Yet the accusations are consistent with Russian government reliance on criminals and hacker groups to hide their attempts to break into American computer systems. Admiral Rogers, the head of US Cyber Command, testifies that this relationship "theoretically makes it more difficult to go to country X and say we see this activity going on, you are doing it, this is unacceptable," when they have the ability "to say it's not us, it's criminal groups."[132]

Ultimately to attribute an attack to states, or to their proxies, to hold them accountable for irresponsible behavior is a political decision, which varies depending on the target and nature of the attack. In the OPM hack, even though forensic evidence leaves little doubt that China was responsible, the Obama administration chose not to make any official assertion.[133] Likewise in hacks into unclassified networks at the State Department and White House, although investigators traced the malicious activity to hackers associated with the Russian government, US officials refrained from going public with that allegation against Moscow.[134] Like these political decisions, norms of responsible behavior are just political agreements, not binding arms control treaties, to be enforced by signature parties, or binding laws and rules that hold parties accountable. At the very best, norms can develop into shared daily practice by states and then eventually become customary international laws. Diplomatic statements, press releases, military manuals, national court decisions, legal advisor opinions, international tribunal rulings and executive orders "can all serve to develop international law."[135] Like-minded nations must actively work together to develop those customary principles if they are eventually to be seen as the law in cyberspace.

The capability to create norms of responsible behavior and other forms of cooperative measures exists, but to be credible, uncooperative nations have to believe that their interests are also at stake. Admiral Rogers has publicly communicated that point, in saying, "To my Chinese counterparts, I would remind them, increasingly you are as vulnerable as any other major industrialized nation-state. The idea that you can somehow exist outside the broader global cyber challenges I don't think is workable."[136] Nonetheless, strategic advisor Patrick Cronin pointed out that "China apparently does not want to buy in to a post–World War II international system that it did not play a role in creating."[137] Cronin believes that finding a meaningful partnership with

China will require some adjustments to the international order. Then in that new order, nations will determine through international relations what is considered to be irresponsible or unacceptable behavior. For example, espionage, by its terms, violates state sovereignty, but since states do it to each other, over time espionage has become part of customary international law established by state practice. The blurry line between cyber-enabled espionage and intellectual property theft complicates state interpretation of what are realistic and consistent norms for responsible behavior in cyberspace. For the latter activity, despite claims by the United States of massive economic damage, without actual physical damage, there is no clear consensus if cyber-enabled economic espionage even qualifies as a violation of territorial sovereignty. Until underlying state objectives and values converge to remove conflicting interests regarding cyberspace, the strategy of deterrence by entanglement will remain an insufficient strategic cyber deterrence option.

NOTES

1. Joseph S. Nye, Jr. "Deterrence and Dissuasion in Cyberspace," *International Security*, Vol. 41, No. 3 (Winter 2016/17): 58.

2. Peter Roberts and Andrew Hardie, "The Validity of Deterrence in the Twenty-first Century," Royal United Services Institute, Occasional Paper, August 2015, 8–9.

3. Ash Carter, US Secretary of Defense, "Securing the Oceans, the Internet, and Space," Speech to Commonwealth Club, Silicon Valley, March 1, 2016, 1–15.

4. United Nations General Assembly, "Group of Governmental Experts on Developments in the Field of Information and Telecommunications in the Context of International Security," A/68/98, June 24, 2013, 2.

5. Roger Harrison, Collins G. Shackelford, and Deron R. Jackson, "Space Deterrence: The Delicate Balance of Risk," *Space and Defense*, Eisenhower Center for Space and Defense Studies, 3, no. 1 (Summer 2009): 17–22.

6. James A. Lewis, "Cyber War: Definitions, Deterrence and Foreign Policy," Statement before the House Committee on Foreign Affairs, September 30, 2015.

7. Robert Litwak and Meg King, "Arms Control in Cyberspace?" Wilson Center, October 2015, 1–7.

8. Thomas Schelling, *Arms and Influence* (New Haven, CT: Yale University Press, 1966), 69–78.

9. Written Answers, "Full Transcript: Interview with Chinese President Xi Jinping," *Wall Street Journal*, September 22, 2015.

10. Elias Groll, "The U.S. Hoped Indicting 5 Chinese Hackers Would Deter Beijing's Cyberwarriors. It Hasn't Worked." *Foreign Policy*, September 2, 2015.

11. Damian Paletta, "Obama to Press Chinese President Xi Jimping on Cyberattacks, Human Rights, Advisor Says," *Wall Street Journal*, September 21, 2015.

12. David E. Sanger, "Hacker Took Fingerprints of 5.6 Million U.S. Workers, Government Says," *New York Times*, September 23, 2015.

13. William J. Burns and Jared Cohen, "The Rules of the Brave New Cyberworld," *Foreign Policy*, February 16, 2017.

14. Ellen Nakashima, "U.S. Developing Sanctions against China over Cyberthefts," *Washington Post*, August 30, 2015.

15. President Barack Obama, "Blocking the Property of Certain Persons Engaging in Significant Malicious Cyber-Enabled Activities," Executive Order, April 1, 2015.

16. Carol E. Lee and Jeremy Page, "Obama's Ties to China Leader Face Test," *Wall Street Journal*, September 21, 2015.

17. David E. Sanger, "U.S. and China Seek Arms Deal for Cyberspace," *New York Times*, September 19, 2015.

18. Office of the Press Secretary, "FACT SHEET: President Xi Jinping's State Visit to the United States," The White House, September 25, 2015.

19. Dan Roberts, "US and China Back Off Internet Arms Race but Obama Leaves Sanctions on the Table," *The Guardian*, September 25, 2015.

20. Sheera Frenkel, "Nobody Thinks the U.S. and China's New Cyber Arms Pact Will Fix Much of Anything," *BuzzFeed*, September 23, 2015.

21. Damian Paletta, "Cyberattack Deal Seen as First Step," *Wall Street Journal*, September 26, 2015.

22. Michael Heller, "Chinese Hackers Arrested at the Request of the US," *Tech Target*, October 13, 2015.

23. Ellen Nakashima, "China Still Trying to Hack U.S. Firms Despite Xi's Vow to Refrain, Analysts Say," *Washington Post*, October 19, 2015.

24. Joseph Marks, "Obama's Cyber Legacy: He Did Almost Everything Right and It Still Turned Out Wrong," *NEXTGOV*, January 17, 2017.

25. Adam Segal, "The U.S.-China Cyber Espionage Deal One Year Later," *Net Politics*, September 28, 2016.

26. Dave Clemente, "Cyber Security and Global Interdependence: What Is Critical?" Chatham House, February 2013, v–x.

27. Executive Office of the President, *National Security Strategy* (Washington, DC: The White House, February 2015), 4.

28. Joseph S. Nye, Jr. "Deterrence and Dissuasion in Cyberspace," *International Security*, Vol. 41, No. 3 (Winter 2016/17): 58.

29. Catherine Lotrionte and Eneken Tikk, rapporteurs, Summary for Panel 3, Applicability of International Law to Cyberspace and Characterization of Cyber Incidents, Cyber Norms Workshop 2.0, 2012.

30. Katharina Ziolkowski, "General Principles of International Law as Applicable in Cyberspace," *Peacetime Regime for State Activities in Cyberspace* (Tallinn, Estonia: NATO Cooperative Cyber Defence Centre of Excellence, 2013), 143–44.

31. Ziolkowski, "General Principles of International Law as Applicable in Cyberspace," 154–55.

32. Michael Schmitt, *Tallinn Manual 2.0 on the International Law Applicable to Cyber Operations,* Second Edition (Cambridge University Press, May 2017), 11.

33. Michael Schmitt, *Tallinn Manual on the International Law Applicable to Cyber Warfare,* (Cambridge University Press, 2013): 16-17.

34. Benedikt Pierker, "Territorial Sovereignty and Integrity and the Challenge of Cyberspace," *Peacetime Regime for State Activities in Cyberspace*, (Tallinn, Estonia: NATO Cooperative Cyber Defence Centre of Excellence, 2013): 191.

35. Pierker, "Territorial Sovereignty and Integrity and the Challenge of Cyberspace," 196.

36. Pierker, "Territorial Sovereignty and Integrity and the Challenge of Cyberspace," 201–3.

37. Pierker, "Territorial Sovereignty and Integrity and the Challenge of Cyberspace," 203.

38. Katharina Ziolkowski, "General Principles of International Law as Applicable in Cyberspace," *Peacetime Regime for State Activities in Cyberspace* (Tallinn, Estonia: NATO Cooperative Cyber Defence Centre of Excellence, 2013), 165–86.

39. United Nations, "Responsibility of States for Internationally Wrongful Acts," General Assembly resolution 56/83, December 12, 2001, Article 2.

40. Michael Schmitt, *Tallinn Manual 2.0 on the International Law Applicable to Cyber Operations,* 87.

41. Michael Schmitt, *Tallinn Manual 2.0 on the International Law Applicable to Cyber Operations,* 95.

42. Michael N. Schmitt and Liis Vihul, "Proxy Wars in Cyberspace: The Evolving International Law of Attribution," *Fletcher Security Review* 1, no. 2 (Spring 2014): 57–67.

43. Cody M. Poplin, "Cyber Sections of the Latest G20 Leaders' Communique," *Lawfare*, Cybersecurity: Crime and Espionage Blog, November 17, 2015.

44. Executive Office of the President, *National Security Strategy* (Washington, DC: The White House, February 2015), 2.

45. Christopher Whyte, "On the Future of Order in Cyberspace," *Strategic Studies Quarterly* (Summer 2015) 69–77.

46. Brian M. Mazanec, "Why International Order in Cyberspace Is Not Inevitable," *Strategic Studies Quarterly* (Summer 2015): 78–84.

47. Mazanec, "Why International Order in Cyberspace Is Not Inevitable," 85–95.

48. James A. Lewis, "US International Strategy for Cybersecurity," Testimony to Senate Foreign Relations Committee, March 12, 2015, 3–4.

49. Clay Wilson, "4 Defining Characteristics of Cyber Weapons," *Government Computer News*, July 2015, 15.

50. Center for Internet Security, "The CIS Critical Security Controls for Effective Cyber Defense," Version 6.0, October 15, 2015, 68–70.

51. Schmitt, *Tallinn Manual 2.0 on the International Law Applicable to Cyber Operations*, 452.

52. Thomas Rid and Peter McBurney, "Cyber-Weapons," *RUSI Journal* 157, no. 1 (February/March 2012): 6–13.

53. US Department of Defense, "Cyberspace Policy Report," November 2011, 2.

54. Paul Meyer, "Cyber-Security through Arms Control," *RUSI Journal* 156, no. 2 (April/May 2011): 22–27.

55. Louise Arimatsu, "A Treaty for Governing Cyber-Weapons: Potential Benefits and Practical Limitations," in *Proceedings 4th International Conference on Cyber Conflict* (Tallinn, Estonia: CCD COE, June 2012), 91–101.

56. Dorothy Denning, "Obstacles and Options for Cyber Arms Controls," Heinrich Boll Foundation Conference, Berlin, Germany, June 29–30, 2001, 3.

57. Neil C. Rowe, Simson L. Garfinkel, Robert Beverly, and Pannayotis Yannakogeorgos, "Challenges in Monitoring Cyberarms Compliance," *International Journal of Cyber Warfare and Terrorism* 1, no. 1 (January–March 2011): 1–14.

58. Elaine Korzak, "Russia and China Have a Cyber Nonaggression Pact," *Defense One*, August 20, 2015.

59. Robert Litwak and Meg King, "The Great Debate," *Reuters*, November 11, 2015.

60. Anna-Maria Osula and Henry Roigas, "International Norms Limiting State Activities in Cyberspace," *International Cyber Norms: Legal, Policy and Industry Perspectives* (Tallinn, Estonia: NATO Cooperative Cyber Defence Centre of Excellence, 2016), 11–22.

61. Roger Hurwitz, "A New Normal? The Cultivation of Global Norms as Part of a Cybersecurity Strategy," *Conflict and Cooperation in Cyberspace* (Boca Raton, Florida:Taylor & Francis Group, 2014), 233–64.

62. Martha Finnemore and Kathryn Sikkink, "International Norm Dynamics and Political Change," *International Organization* 52, no. 4 (Autumn 1998): 887–917.

63. Michael N. Schmitt and Liis Vihul, "The Nature of International Law Cyber Norms," *International Cyber Norms: Legal, Policy and Industry Perspectives* (Tallinn, Estonia: NATO Cooperative Cyber Defence Centre of Excellence, 2016), 23–47.

64. Shinji Yamaguchi, "China's Perspective on International Order," National Institute for Defense Studies (NIDS) Commentary, No. 46, May 15, 2015, 2.

65. United Nations General Assembly, "Creation of a Global Culture of Cybersecurity and Taking Stock of National Efforts to Protect Information Infrastructures," Resolution 64/211, December 21, 2009, 1–5.

66. United Nations General Assembly, "International Code of Conduct for Information Security," Document 66/359, September 14, 2011, 3.

67. United Nations General Assembly, "International Code of Conduct for Information Security," Document 66/359, September 14, 2011, 4.

68. United Nations General Assembly, "International Code of Conduct for Information Security," Document 69/723, January 13, 2015, 5.

69. Assembly of the Union, "African Union Convention on Cyber Security and Personal Data Protection," 23rd Ordinary Session, Malabo, June 27, 2014, 1–18.

70. Assembly of the Union, "African Union Convention on Cyber Security and Personal Data Protection," 26–30.

71. Mailyn Fidler and Fadzai Madzingira, "The African Union Cybersecurity Convention: A Missed Human Rights Opportunity," *Council on Foreign Relations*, June 22, 2015.

72. United Nations General Assembly, "Developments in the Field of Information and Telecommunications in the Context of International Security," Resolution 65/41, January 11, 2011, 1–2.

73. United Nations General Assembly, "Developments in the Field of Information and Telecommunications in the Context of International Security," Resolution 65/41, January 11, 2011, 3.

74. United Nations General Assembly, "Group of Governmental Experts on Developments in the Field of Information and Telecommunications in the Context of International Security," A/68/98, June 24, 2013, 8.

75. Foreign and Commonwealth Office, "London Conference on Cyberspace: Chair's Statement," Full Text, November 2, 2011.

76. Cherian Samuel, "Some Takeaways from the Budapest Conference on Cyberspace," Institute for Defense Studies and Analyses, October 11, 2012, 1–2.

77. Janos Martonyi, "Budapest Conference on Cyberspace: Summary by the Chairman," October 4–5, 2012.

78. H. E. Yun Byung-Se, "Seoul Conference on Cyberspace: Statement by the Conference Chair," October 17–18, 2013.

79. Bert Koenders, "Global Conference on Cyberspace 2015, Chair's Statement," The Hague, April 16–17, 2015.

80. United Nations General Assembly, "Group of Governmental Experts on Developments in the Field of Information and Telecommunications in the Context of International Security," A/70/174, July 22, 2015, 4.

81. United Nations General Assembly, "Group of Governmental Experts on Developments," 8.

82. Catherine Lotrionte, "A Better Defense: Examining the United States' New Norms-Based Approach to Cyber Deterrence," *Georgetown Journal of International Affairs*, December 23, 2013, 75.

83. Joseph Marks, "U.N. Body Agrees to U.S. Norms in Cyberspace," *Politico*, July 9, 2015.

84. Angela McKay et al., Microsoft Corporation, "International Cybersecurity Norms: Reducing Conflict in an Internet-Dependent World," December 2014.

85. Scott Charney et al., Microsoft Corporation, "From Articulation to Implementation: Enabling Progress on Cybersecurity Norms," June 2016, 1–8.

86. Scott Charney, Microsoft Corporation, "Cybersecurity Norms for Nation-States and the Global ICT Industry," Microsoft on the Issues, June 23, 2016.

87. United Nations General Assembly, "Group of Governmental Experts on Developments," 9.

88. Katharina Ziolkowski, "Confidence Building Measures for Cyberspace—Legal Implications," (Tallinn, Estonia: NATO Cooperative Cyber Defense Center of Excellence, 2013), 1–13.

89. United Nations General Assembly, "Group of Governmental Experts on Transparency and Confidence-Building Measures in Outer Space Activities," A/68/189, July 29, 2013, 1–4.

90. Executive Office of the President, "Joint Statement by the Presidents of the United States and the Russian Federation on a New Field of Cooperation in Confidence Building" (Washington, DC: The White House, June 17, 2013).

91. Executive Office of the President, "Fact Sheet: US–Russian Cooperation on Information and Communications Technology Security" (Washington, DC: The White House, June 17, 2013).

92. Lesley Wroughton and Michael Martina, "China, U.S. Say Committed to Managing Differences," *Reuters*, July 9, 2014.

93. John Ruwitch, "China, U.S. Should Manage South China Sea Differences Constructively—Chinese General," *Reuters*, May 12, 2016.

94. US Department of State, "International Cyberspace Policy Strategy," March 2016, 4.

95. Organization for Security and Co-operation in Europe, "Decision No. 1106 Initial Set of OSCE Confidence-Building Measures to Reduce the Risks of Conflict Stemming from the Use of Information and Communications Technologies," PC.DEC/1106, December 3, 2013.

96. Patryk Pawlak, "Confidence Building Measures in Cyberspace: Current Debates and Trends," *International Cyber Norms: Legal, Policy and Industry Perspectives* (Tallinn, Estonia: NATO Cooperative Cyber Defence Centre of Excellence, 2016), 129–32.

97. United Nations General Assembly, "Group of Governmental Experts on Developments in the Field of Information and Telecommunications in the Context of International Security," A/68/98, June 24, 2013, 10.

98. Launch of the Global Forum on Cyber Expertise, "The Hague Declaration on the GFCE," April 16, 2015, 1–2.

99. Launch of the Global Forum on Cyber Expertise, "Framework Document," April 16, 2015, 1–4.

100. See for example, News Item, "12–13 April: West Africa Cybersecurity Meeting," March 21, 2016, at www.thegfce.com.

101. David E. Sanger, "U.S. Tries Candor to Assure China on Cyberattacks," *New York Times*, April 6, 2014.

102. Amy Chang, "Warring State: China's Cybersecurity Strategy," Center for a New American Security, December 2014, 7–8.

103. Office of the Press Secretary, "Fact Sheet: The 2015 G-20 Summit in Antalya, Turkey," The White House, November 16, 2015.

104. Office of the Press Secretary, "Fact Sheet: The 2015 G-20 Summit in Antalya, Turkey."

105. Ellen Nakashima, "Chinese Government Has Arrested Hackers It Says Breached OPM Database," *Washington Post*, December 2, 2015.

106. The Institute for Critical Infrastructure Technology, "Handing Over the Keys to the Castle," Technical Report, July 2015, 3.

107. Doug Olenick, "U.S.-China Cyber Agreement: Flawed, but a step in the right direction," *SC Magazine*, January 24, 2017.

108. James A. Lewis, "Cyber Espionage and the Theft of U.S. Intellectual Property and Technology," Testimony to House Committee on Energy and Commerce, July 9, 2013, 1–2.

109. Guan H. Tang, *Copyright and the Public Interest in China* (Northampton, MA: Edward Elgar Publishing, 2011), 16.

110. John H. D'Antico, "A Quick Primer on Chinese Patent Law," I.P. insider, Spring 2003, 1–2.

111. Sisir Botta and Christopher Tsai, "Globalization Is a Catalyst for Change in Intellectual Property Systems: Case Studies in India and China," *i-Manager's Journal on Management* 1, no. 1 (2006): 90–96.

112. Warwick Ashford, "Chinese Man Admits Conspiring to Hack US Military Secrets," *Computer Weekly*, March 24, 2016.

113. Ben Dooley, "Chinese Media Laud Hacker for U.S. Spying," *Agence France-Presse*, March 25, 2016.

114. Robert Abel, "Chinese Businessman Sentenced for Cyberespionage Targeting U.S. Defense Contractors," *SC Magazine*, July 14, 2016.

115. Executive Office of the President, *International Strategy for Cyberspace* (Washington, DC: The White House, May 2011), 5–9.

116. Joe McDonald, "China's Xi Calls for Cooperation on Internet Regulation," *Associated Press*, December 16, 2015.

117. Sue-Lin Wong and Michael Martina, "China Adopts Cybersecurity Law in Face of Overseas Opposition," *Reuters*, November 7, 2016.

118. Christopher M. E. Painter, "Cybersecurity: Setting the Rules for Responsible Global Behavior," Testimony to Senate Foreign Relations Committee, March 12, 2015, 2.

119. INTA Bulletin, "U.S. Department of Commerce Announces Intent to Transition Key Internet Domain Name Functions," vol. 69, no. 9 (May 1, 2014).

120. Dave Lee, "US Ready to 'Hand Over' the Internet's Naming System," *BBC News*, Technology Section, August 18, 2016.

121. Greg Masters, "Global Cybercrime Treaty Rejected at U.N," *SC Magazine*, April 23, 2010.

122. Bert Koenders, "Global Conference on Cyberspace 2015, Chair's Statement," April 17, 2015, 1–8.

123. Nicholas Dynon, "The Future of Cyber Conflict: Beijing Rewrites Internet Sovereignty along Territorial Lines," Jamestown Organization, China Brief, vol. 15, no. 17 (September 4, 2015).

124. Katherine Morton, "China and the Future of International Norms," Australian Strategic Policy Institute, Strategic Policy Forum, June 22, 2011: 1–13.

125. The Editorial Board, "China's Missile Gambit," *Washington Post*, February 21, 2016.

126. Ankit Panda, "South China Sea: China Has Deployed Anti-Ship Missiles on Woody Island," *The Diplomat*, March 26, 2016.

127. Sam LaGrone, "China Defends Deployment of Anti-Ship Missiles to South China Sea Island," *U.S. Naval Institute*, News, March 30, 2016.

128. Jan Stinissen, "A Legal Framework for Cyber Operations in Ukraine," *Cyber War in Perspective: Russian Aggression against Ukraine*, Chapter 6 (Tallinn, Estonia, NATO Cooperative Cyber Defense Center of Excellence Publications, 2015), 123–27.

129. Vitaly Shevchenko, "Little Green Men or Russian Invaders?" *BBC News*, March 11, 2014.

130. Geraint Hughes, "Ukraine: Europe's New Proxy War?" *Fletcher Security Review* 1, no. 2 (Spring 2014): 106–18.

131. Tim Maurer, "Cyber Proxies and the Crisis in Ukraine," in *Cyber War in Perspective: Russian Aggression against Ukraine*, chap. 9, 79–85 (Tallinn, Estonia: NATO Cooperative Cyber Defense Center of Excellence, 2015).

132. Ian Duncan, "Cyber Command Chief: Foreign Governments Use Criminals to Hack U.S. Systems," *Baltimore Sun*, March 16, 2016.

133. Jeff Mason and Mark Hosenball, "Obama Vows to Boost U.S. Cyber Defenses, Amid Signs of China Hacking," *Reuters*, June 8, 2015.

134. Ellen Nakashima, "U.S. Not Naming China in Data Hack," *Washington Post*, July 22, 2015.

135. Catherine Lotrionte, "Cyber War: Definitions, Deterrence and Foreign Policy," Statement before the House Committee on Foreign Affairs, September 30, 2015.

136. Andrew Clevenger, "China 'Vulnerable' in Cyberspace, US Cyber Chief Warns," *Defense News*, November 21, 2015.

137. Patrick Cronin, "China's Problem with Rules: Managing a Reluctant Stakeholder," *War on the Rocks*, June 26, 2014, 3.

Part III

A Strategic Option

Chapter Seven

Active Cyber Defense

The strategy of active cyber defense is described as the real-time detection, analysis, and mitigation of network security breaches combined with the aggressive use of legal countermeasures beyond network and state territorial boundaries.[1] Active cyber defense combines internal systemic resilience to defeat malicious cyber activity after a network intrusion and tailored disruption capacities to punish the attacker. The strategy encourages adversary restraint by shaping malicious actor perceptions of the costs and benefits of any given cyber attack at a scale large enough to handle the multiplicity of malicious actors in cyberspace. Since intrusions may not always be stopped at the perimeter, active cyber defense operates at cyber relevant speed before malicious activity can affect networks and systems.[2] Active cyber defense is different from static activities, which harden networks and systems through preventive controls. Active cyber defense uses reactive activities, which stop or limit damage through detective controls and remediation actions, seamlessly automated in a common framework of integration. According to the Defense Information Systems Agency Deputy Chief Technology Officer, we need "cyber capabilities integrated with each other and automatically defending against things."[3] That means using not just a defense-in-depth strategy to layer various methods of cyber defense, but to include the tools and capabilities resident in the strategy of active cyber defense.

Admiral Michael Rogers, the head of the NSA, warned the audience at the London Stock Exchange that "it is not about if you will be penetrated, but when."[4] If true that cyber defenses cannot block an attack, then organizations have to close the time from compromise to discovery before an actor achieves their objectives. Yet in 2015, the time from evidence of compromise to discovery of compromise, or the median time that threat groups are present on a network before detection, was an astounding 146 days.[5] Active cyber defense seeks to close that gap by using synchronized, real-time capabilities not only to discover and detect the breach, but also to analyze and mitigate the threat and vulnerabilities. The difficult question to ask is whether these improved defenses are adequate enough to stop malicious actors inside the network or if an appropriate response is necessary outside the network to disrupt their activities. The use of proportionate countermeasures is allowed to some extent under international or customary law but constrained under national law, depending upon the party invoking their rights. Therefore the scope or use of active cyber defense depends on authorities to act inside or outside of the network. While the rights of an injured state to resort to countermeasures in response to an internationally wrongful act or omission are explicitly articulated by international law, an argument can be made that licensed private companies should have the right to hack back in self-defense. Hack back turns the tables on the attacker, thwarting or stopping a crime, or even stealing back what was taken.[6]

The promise of active cyber defense is to deny benefits through systemic resilience and impose costs through tailored disruption. Certain aspects of the strategy are agnostic to the origins and motivations of the malicious actor. Specifically active cyber defense capabilities deny actor objectives and raise actor costs by obstructing or interfering with their progress in the cyber kill chain inside the network. Regardless of who is the actor, their malware or techniques are detected, diverted, blocked, or terminated. Although in recognition that a perfect defense against intrusion is impossible, active cyber defense offers remedies outside the network. Either way, inside or outside the network, the strategy seeks to convince malicious actors that it is no longer worth making the attack. The strategic option of active cyber defense possesses the three necessary conditions to achieve deterrence, specifically the capability to deliver an appropriate cyber response, the communications to signal intentions, and the credibility to not tolerate malicious activity. This chapter starts with an illustrative case that depicts the virtues of active cyber defense capabilities applied across the cyber kill chain. It then examines the opportunities and issues for use of active cyber defense inside and outside the network as an alternative strategy to achieve deterrence within the cyber arena.

ILLUSTRATIVE CASE

The massive theft of data at the mega retailers Target Corporation in 2013 and Home Depot in 2014 exhibited many similarities. In both incidents attackers were able to upload malicious software to POS machines and collect unencrypted credit and debit card data for exfiltration. The Reedum malware, nearly identical to BlackPOS sold on cybercrime forums, used in the Target breach,[7] was the basis for the tool used against Home Depot.[8] The initial intrusion into the Target system was traced to network credentials stolen from a third-party refrigeration, heating and air conditioning vendor.[9] Likewise, an investigation revealed that criminals used a third-party vendor's user name and password to enter into Home Depot's network.[10] After authenticated access to the networks, attackers moved laterally to eventually compromise the point-of-sale systems at checkout counters. In both high-profile breaches, personal and financial information was exposed for millions of customers. The perplexing question of whether this exposure could have been prevented is answered in the potential of active cyber defense. That potential is based on detection, verification, and remediation of malicious behavior in the cyber kill chain, before harm or damage from the breach occurs.

Most organizations don't have reliable visibility of malicious activity in their networks. The most common approach is to look for indicators of compromise, such as virus signatures. This approach tends to produce high amounts of false positives, which can desensitize security teams to notifications. In the Target breach, the FireEye malware intrusion detection system used by the retailer actually detected the data exfiltration malware used in the attack, but supposedly the security team ignored the urgent alerts and did not allow the FireEye software to delete the malware.[11] They claimed to receive hundreds of alerts each day and had difficulty determining which were malicious.[12] This situation portrays a need for an approach that accurately prioritizes alerts. The previously described HawkEye G advanced threat detection and response platform provides that approach in using a threat feed that combines network and host sensors in order to detect and perform correlation on sophisticated and emerging threats. In addition, the platform collects a baseline of historical data across the network and hosts to determine anomalous behavior and activities. In fact, the vendor adamantly claims that "several months prior to the cyber attacks on Target and Home Depot, the Hawk-Eye G threat feed had already blacklisted the source and could have helped both retailers detect and prevent these attacks."[13] This statement supports the notion that the use of behavioral analytics with threat intelligence to detect and investigate threats in real time can optimize efforts of security teams.

In both the Target and Home Depot breaches, the start point for detection was well inside the cyber kill chain due to attacker use of valid vendor credentials. Verizon consultants hired to probe the Target networks days after the breach found "no controls limiting their access to any system."[14] Instead they discovered systems and services with either weak or default passwords and either outdated or missing security patches. These discoveries meant once inside Target's network, there was nothing to stop the attackers from moving across the cyber kill chain. The first opportunity for Target to disrupt the breach was at the delivery phase, by requiring two-factor authentication for its vendors, which means besides the stolen credentials a second step is included such as a token or phone code or security question. At the exploitation phase, Target could have paid attention to the FireEye software alerts or allowed malware deletion. At the installation phase, it is suspected that the attacker exploited a default account name in a software management system, which Target could have altered. In the command and control phase, the method used by the attackers is unclear and Target's protective options were limited to Firewalls. Finally, at the Actions on Objectives phase, Target could have whitelisted File Transfer Protocol (FTP) servers approved for uploading data, blocking transmissions to outside servers, at least one located in Russia. Outside the network, Target's FireEye software did decode the destination of the servers on which stolen credit card data was stored for days at a time,[15] opening an opportunity to disrupt the files on those servers.

Although the opportunities for breaking the kill chain appear limited in the Target breach, an analysis of the actions of the attacker and placement of resources to address capability gaps "raises the costs an adversary must expend to achieve their objectives."[16] A number of technologies and processes can be identified and applied to detect, deny, disrupt, or recover at each phase of the kill chain.[17] For example, the LightCyber Magna platform combines many of these technologies and processes across the kill chain for network and endpoint behavioral detection. Magna uses a next generation firewall at the delivery phase, an intrusion detection system at the exploitation phase, and endpoint detection and response at the installation phase. Magna embraces the industry-wide megatrend toward automated removal of advanced threats. For instance, one requirement in the trend is the ability to detect data flows, which might include outbound traffic from an internal server.[18] Magna profiles the pattern and rate/volume of data sent to outside entities by domain and destination. It detects a change or anomaly in rate/volume of data sent. In the Target breach, the malware sent stolen data to an external FTP server via another compromised Target server used to collect the credit and debit card data. Over a period of two weeks, the attackers collected and transmitted 11 GB of stolen information.[19] Not only does Magna have the capability to detect anomalously large uploads to external servers via FTP, Magna also includes a significant concentration of algorithms designed to detect the internal communications/movement of data to/from a compromised server. Magna almost certainly would have alerted on this activity (and the control of the compromised server) before the data exfiltration phase, preventing the exposure of customer financial data. Today organizations like Target do not have to rely on manual analysis and adjustments. Automated active defense solutions, inside the network, provide distinct advantages over the attacker and warrant further consideration as a way to change the cost and benefit paradigm.

INSIDE DEFENDER'S NETWORK

Although preventive controls have improved, so too have the techniques used by malicious actors to penetrate cyber defenses. They morph, encrypt, and disguise existing malware so it cannot be detected by signature-based defenses; develop custom malware for zero-day targeted attacks before signature distribution; and create evasive malware that hides from sandboxes (virtual test environments) that attempt to capture and evaluate malware intent.[20] Even if security teams can find an initial threat indicator, it often takes days or weeks to trace the attack, analyze the threat, quarantine compromised systems, and implement remediation actions. The longer that process takes, the longer the malicious actor has to achieve objectives inside the network. To break the cyber kill chain, active cyber defense synchronizes "the real-time detection, analysis, and mitigation of threats to critical networks and systems."[21] Active cyber defense creates internal systemic resilience, wherein networks and systems can withstand a potential attack. Hence, the US Defense Department has stated its intention to invest in resilient systems to continue operations in the face of disruptive or destructive cyber attacks. Documented as a form of deterrence, the US Defense Department asserts that "effective resilience measures can help convince potential adversaries of the futility of commencing cyber attacks."[22] For resilience to succeed as a factor in effective deterrence in organizations that fall outside its authority, the Defense Department counts on other government agencies to work with critical infrastructure owners and operators and the private sector to develop resilient systems in a comprehensive approach.

Typical Proactive Activities

Common active cyber defense approaches have achieved resilience by placing emphasis on proactive methods to engage or deceive the adversary before or during a cyber incident. An organization might respond to an attack using as many as three active defense concepts: detection, deception, and termination.[23] For the first concept, a variety of techniques can detect an attack, but the most prominent to attract attackers and look for their patterns of behavior are the use of honeypots and sinkholes:

- *Honeypots*: computer systems set up to act as a decoy to lure attackers away from assets of real value. They can be isolated or placed inside a production network to detect, deflect or study attempts to gain unauthorized access.[24] Honeypots elicit exploitation by attackers by the use of real or simulated vulnerabilities or by configuration weakness, like easily guessed passwords.[25] Legal issues confound the use of honeypots, in particular concerning privacy rights and entrapment accusations. Privacy concerns stem from honeypot recording and monitoring of all activity occurring on the device without consent. Entrapment concerns stem from inducement or encouragement of a person to commit a crime.[26] Yet neither privacy nor entrapment would be considered as a serious legal defense, for after all, the attacker committed the intrusion in the first place without authorization. The real issue is that organizations that deploy honeypots have to watch for their misuse, for if a malicious actor uses the honeypot as a launch point to attack other systems, then the organization could be held liable for any damages.[27]

- *Sinkholes*: a system under the control of a defender used to intercept and receive traffic redirected from infected machines, like a botnet. They can provide intelligence to craft appropriate defenses, identify infection targets or geographically locate attackers.[28] Organizations can set up an internal sinkhole where only traffic bound for an external malicious IP from victim machines in the organization is manipulated. Or they can set up an external sinkhole by registering known malicious domains as they expire or if not registered at all. Legal issues confound the use of external sinkholes in that victim machines that do not belong to your organization are now contacting a server you control, which is a criminal act in most jurisdictions. Another issue is that victims have a right to be notified if their machines are infected, which requires a reporting mechanism to do so.[29]

While honeypots and sinkholes also deceive the attacker, other methods in a deception campaign include allowing the attacker to steal documents that have false or misleading information. While this method is intended to protect intellectual property or trade secrets, there could be harm if the misleading information is accidently leaked to the public and results in damage to the organization's credibility or reputation. The final concept of termination stops the attack while it is occurring. To prevent information from leaving the network, the idea is to sever connections with the infected computer, although that might not work if the attacker has already moved laterally in the network. Each of the three options have merit but as rudimentary singular methods they have inherent limitations. Therefore, today's approach for active cyber defense focuses on the advanced automation and integration of multiple services and mechanisms to execute detection, verification, and remediation in cyber-relevant time.

New Reactive Approaches

As threat vectors grow in complexity and networks swell with connected devices, automation is emerging as a key component in network protection strategies. As stated by the Chief Technology Officer at network management and discovery tools developer Solar Winds, "automating network security can help to quickly pinpoint a breach, identify the root cause and often help to resolve the issue quicker than manually checking every endpoint and connection."[30] A corollary to automation is security event correlation, which can produce suitable remediation decisions. Those decisions can also be automated, like to revise user authorization privileges, place systems into protected zones, or redirect network flows. Once automated processes replace human operators, networks become more responsive to attacks. Humans are being overloaded with data, especially false positive alerts (errors in evaluations) from security information and event management (SIEM) systems. Automation systems can extract insights from data sets and device logs in real time. For example, Carbon Black technologies automate the continual recording of critical data before the moment of compromise, so after a breach is discovered, Carbon Black can highlight activity to better understand the cause and scope of the intrusion.[31]

The Carbon Black capability to continuously monitor connections and devices while correlating logs and data of user activity turns security automation into a reactive tool to deny malicious actors the benefit of their attack. Automation empowers security teams to act more quickly and aggressively to stop data breaches before they can threaten an organization. Today security teams lack the speed and agility to respond to a suspected data breach. Not only do teams lack the tools to identify anomalous behavior across endpoints and the network, they are not authorized to actually shut it down.[32] Given the consequences of a data breach, organizations can no longer rely on manual procedures. They have to reduce the time to query through data, detect the breach and get to the decision point on remediation. Automation enables twenty-four-hour security operations, with policy changes in remediation decisions if humans are or are not in the loop. At the same time, automation allows organizations to reduce manpower and save costs, by shifting basic and mundane tasks to machines. This benefit is important given ominous projections of shortfalls of more than 1.5 million information security professionals in the global cyber security workforce by 2019. According to Brett Helm, Chairman and CEO of DB Networks, "Intelligent IT security automation through machine learning and behavioral analysis is faster, more accurate, and frees up skilled professionals to focus on more critical issues."[33]

Besides the advantages of automation, the integration of a diverse set of capabilities improves an organization's ability to respond to a cyber attack—for example, the integration of endpoint detection and response solutions with third-party devices or services. An endpoint is an Internet-capable computer hardware device, such as a desktop computer, laptop, smartphone, printer or other specialized hardware such as a point-of-sale terminal or smart meter.[34] Endpoint detection and response solutions monitor a range of actions on these devices. For example, they track registry entries created, edited and deleted; files created, opened, modified and deleted; changes in process tables; and network connections to other systems on the network or to unknown servers on the Internet.[35] The advantage of these types of detection and response solutions is the ability to find and react to the activities of malware that may have evaded preventive controls. Yet to be effective, the endpoint detection and response solutions have to integrate easily with other devices, for example, to automatically send unknown files to a sandbox for analysis, or with other services, or to get up-to-date threat intelligence based on the actor techniques. Therefore, the actuation of active cyber defense inside the network requires combinations of capabilities to collect security data, detect advanced malware, apply threat intelligence, conduct forensic analysis, and implement remediation actions.

Single Integrated Platforms

Active cyber defense strives to provide real-time defense inside the network through automation and integration of cyber defense services and capabilities. These synchronized services and capabilities are used to discover and detect a breach, and interdict, isolate, or remove the threat. The benefits of new active defense solutions include:[36]

- Detection of known, unknown, and zero-day threats missed by most antivirus products.
- Coupling of enhanced threat intelligence and behavioral analytics on endpoint activity.
- Integration with the most effective commercial security solutions on the market.
- Threat response by policy-based automated or machine-guided remediation actions.
- Integration to SIEM systems, big data analytics, and real-time dashboards.

The need for continuous threat detection and response is becoming obvious and a number of endpoint security solutions achieve the benefits of automated investigation and removal. One such is Hexis HawkEye G, acquired by WatchGuard Technologies,[37] which provides organizations automated detection, verification, and remediation capabilities in a single integrated endpoint detection and response platform.[38]

Hexis heralded the ability of the Hawkeye G platform to remove advanced threats at machine speed before they can steal data, compromise intellectual property, or cause process disruption.[39] The platform provides visibility of threat actor activity on the endpoint through host and network sensors. The host sensor uses heuristics that analyze files, processes and registry events as they are created, modified, or executed. One hundred seventy-five different heuristics are calculated individually and then combined to give an initial threat score that is enhanced by cloud-based malware verification service. Network sensors utilize deep packet inspection technology to detect application usage by threat actors. The inspection module looks for outbound communication from infected endpoints, specifically for command and control traffic and downloading of exploits and remote access toolkits. The HawkEye G threat feed that covers malware data, phishing URLs, and controller information, is aggregated from multiple sources, to include integrated third-party devices such as Palo Alto Networks Wildfire and FireEye Network Security. After the threat is verified and assigned a unified score, a range of network and host-based countermeasures are deployed to remediate the threat. Machine-guided actions for the host include to kill an executing process, quarantine a file, remove a registry value hijacked by malware, or whitelist a process, and for the network include block access to controller URLs and divert traffic to/from an external server to a Bot Trap. Countermeasures can be executed manually or through automated policies based on multiple configurations that consider targets, scores and actions.[40] HawkEye G received a score of 4.875 out of 5 in testing of ability to identify, block, and remove threats.[41]

The other aforementioned leading platform is LightCyber Magna, acquired by Palo Alto Networks,[42] that combines automated investigation and integrated remediation to reduce attacker dwell time and minimize damage.[43] Like Hawkeye G, it was developed in response to a current lack of ability to detect active attacks. The difference is Magna detects attackers through the anomalies their activity introduces. The platform profiles normal user and device behavior and then uses attack detectors to find behavior that registers as anomalies against those profiles. Magna has hundreds of detectors across all phases of the cyber kill chain, from reconnaissance, lateral movement, command and control, and data exfiltration. Magna embraces criticism of the kill chain expressed at Black Hat 2016 that the steps to be addressed should be internal, under a presumption of breach.[44] A pertinent example is at the internal reconnaissance phase after intrusion, where the attacker is attempting to find out what servers and services are accessible or what vulnerabilities are available. Magna uses profiles of patterns of internal connections to find attack detectors, such as changes in connections, rates of connections and use of ports and protocols.[45] Magna then enhances anomalous process findings with threat intelligence and malware analysis. Upon confirmation of an active attack, Magna provides one-click remediation through integration with third-party security tools. Supported capabilities include the ability to revoke user credentials or force a password reset with Microsoft Active Directory, or quarantine breached endpoints and malicious IPs or URL domains with Palo Alto Network's next generation firewall.[46]

OUTSIDE VICTIM'S NETWORK

For the state the aggressive use of countermeasures beyond network and state territorial boundaries is governed by international law. Proportionate countermeasures are allowed in response to harm originating from a state.[47] In the cyber context, countermeasures represent disruption capacities tailored to the circumstances of the harm. For private companies, not acting on behalf of the state, a number of legal issues confront the use of these forward deployment techniques. However, US common law does admit "certain rights of self-defense and the defense of property in preventing the commission of a crime against an individual or a corporation."[48] The defense of property is more limited in range of allowable actions, roughly comparable to what is allowed for nonlethal self-defense. For private companies the relevant concept will most always be defense of property, although that right does not allow for vigilantism. An argument exists that private companies have no choice but to resort to self-help, as the government is doing too little to protect them.[49] Without policy or guidance, victims might already be taking self-help actions based on their own judgments and perceptions, which could have substantial consequences. A Black Hat survey in 2012 found that 36 percent of attendees when asked, "Have you ever engaged in retaliatory hacking?" said either "once" or "frequently."[50] The question of whether private companies should be licensed to act on the government's behalf persists in the face of debilitating cyber attacks.

Permissive Conditions

In the Tallinn Manual 2.0, Rule 20 delineates that "a State may be entitled to take countermeasures, whether cyber in nature or not, in response to a breach of an international legal obligation that is owed by another State"[51] The Rule is derived primarily from the *Draft Articles on Responsibility of States for Internationally Wrongful Acts*, developed by the International Law Commission. Although not a binding treaty, the Draft Articles are authoritative and reflect and constitute customary international law, as extensively cited by legal bodies for fifteen years and commended to governments by the UN General Assembly.[52] They define countermeasures as "measures which would otherwise be contrary to the international obligations of [an] injured state *vis-à-vis* the responsible state if they were not taken by the former in response to an internationally wrongful act by the latter in order to procure cessation and reparation."[53] Regarding what constitutes an internationally wrongful act, the responsible state would, for example, have violated a treaty or customary law obligation. Prominent among treaty obligations is the prohibition on the use of force contained in Article 2 of the Charter of the United Nations.[54] Rule 69 of the Tallinn Manual 2.0 affirms that a cyber operation "constitutes a use of force when its scale and effects are comparable to non-cyber operations rising to the level of a use of force."[55] Prominent among customary law is the principle of sovereignty, which protects cyber infrastructure located on the territory of a state. Therefore, cyber operations against that infrastructure that qualifies as a use of force would amount to a violation of that state's sovereignty. International law experts have taken the position that sovereignty can be violated even when no damage or injury results, such as in the case of the emplacement of malware or destruction of data.[56]

The sole purpose of countermeasures is to induce the responsible state to comply with its legal obligations or to remedy existing harms. They are not permissible for other purposes, such as retribution or punishment. If the target state resumes its obligations of cessation and reparation, then the injured state can no longer continue the measures.[57] Therefore, a state cannot be motivated by punitive considerations to use countermeasures, especially if the other state's violation of international law has ended. In general, countermeasures are allowed only after the injured state has asked the state in question to cease its internationally wrongful act. However, this requirement is not absolute if urgent measures without notification are deemed necessary for the injured state to preserve its rights and avoid further injury.[58] In the cyber context, countermeasures "often represent an effective means of self-help by allowing the injured state to take urgent action that would otherwise be unavailable to it, such as "hacking back," to compel the responsible state to cease its internationally wrongful cyber operations."[59] In their application, countermeasures must be "commensurate with the injury suffered, taking into account the gravity of the internationally wrongful act."[60] This can be interpreted as proportionate to the breach of obligations. This restriction is intended to avoid the risk of escalation where states respond interactively with acts of increased scope and duration. Also, countermeasures must not themselves violate the prohibition on the use of force.[61] They should to the extent feasible be taken in such a way that permits the resumption of performance of the breached obligations in question. Which means countermeasures should consist of temporary measures that produce as far as possible reversible effects.[62]

Countermeasures are allowed to be used when the breach of obligation is attributable to the responsible state.[63] The clearest case of being attributable is when acts are conducted by state organs, like military or intelligence agencies. Acts committed by persons or entities that are empowered to exercise government authority, such as by a private company under contract from the state are equally attributable.[64] Additionally, the conduct of a person or group of persons shall be considered an act of a state if "acting on the instructions of, or under the direction or control of, that State in carrying out that conduct."[65] For instance, although the Iranian activist group Cutting

Sword of Justice immediately took credit for attacking Saudi Aramco Oil Company with the Shamoon malware in 2012,[66] eventually the attack and group were attributed to the government of Iran.[67] However, incidental or peripheral association does not qualify as attribution. For instance, the patriotic hacker operations conducted against Estonia in 2007 and Georgia in 2008 were not sufficiently determined to be under the control of Russia to justify attribution, and therefore the use of countermeasures. Likewise, although the hacktivist organization calling itself the SEA has hacked and defaced over forty sites, mostly global media outlets and notable universities, to voice political sentiments in support of the Assad regime since 2011,[68] in the absence of proven instructions, direction, or control by Syria, the use of countermeasures is not an available response option for the injured state.

The limitation on use of countermeasures to acts by or attributable to states is significant since today the majority of harmful cyber operations are conducted by nonstate actors. In observation of these constraints, the plea of necessity may offer relief to states facing harmful nonstate cyber operations under certain conditions.[69] A state may invoke necessity as a ground for precluding the wrongfulness of an act if it is the "only way for the State to safeguard an essential interest against a grave and imminent peril."[70] An essential interest is "one that is of fundamental and great importance to the State concerned."[71] The peril is grave "when the threat is especially severe."[72] Examples of when essential interests are gravely and imminently threatened would be in cyber operations that debilitate the state's banking system, ground flights nationwide, halt all rail traffic, alter national health records or shut down a large electrical grid.[73] In certain cases where the exact nature or origin of a cyber attack is not clear, a state may justify cyber measures on the basis of the plea of necessity. For example, in an emergency situation, a state could decide to shut off its own cyber infrastructure, as the only way to protect itself, even if doing so affects other state's cyber systems. In this instance the state's action is directed against the danger itself, and not directed against another state or aggressor.[74] Similarly, if significant cyber operations of unknown origin target critical infrastructure, the Tallinn Manual 2.0 contends that "the plea of necessity could justify a State's resort to counter-hacking."[75] Therefore, the plea of necessity provides a failsafe for a state facing severe cyber operations when they cannot be attributed to another state. For that matter, "factual and legal attribution is not a precondition to action," only that the state "locate the technological source of the harmful operation and assess the consequences of its own response."[76] Therefore the plea can be resorted to whether the malicious actor is governmental or private.

Disruption Choices

"Only an injured state may engage in countermeasures" in response to an internationally wrongful act, or engage in counter-hacking under the plea of necessity, to disrupt a cyber operation in progress.[77] The more controversial term "hack back" usually applies when a private organization responds with a counterattack. The difference between countermeasures and hack back is accessing a computer, network or information system without authorization. An organization may be motivated to hack back against an attacker to recover or wipe stolen data or intellectual property. An organization may also be motivated to enact revenge by disrupting or damaging the malicious actor's system or degrading their capability to conduct future attacks.[78] The cyber security firm Symbiot has placed methods of hack back into three categories: (1) invasive techniques to obtain access and then pursue a "strategy of disabling, destroying, or seizing control over attacking assets," (2) symmetric counterstrikes which proportionally exploit "vulnerabilities on the attacker's system," and (3) asymmetric counterstrikes which constitute "retaliation . . . far in excess of the attack."[79]

Countermeasures and hack back are similar in that an entity, whether a state or a private company, returns fire or sends data back at the attacker in some manner to stop the attack. Thus the range of tailored disruption choices for the two is blurred by motivation and authority. The range of countermeasures represents a sliding scale of aggressive actions that may:

- Allow attackers to steal bogus files or embed beacons that reveal their location[80]
- Bait files with malware to photograph the malicious actors using their webcam[81]
- Infiltrate malicious actor networks to retrieve, alter or delete stolen data
- Implant malware to damage or ransomware to lock down actor computers[82]
- Insert logic bombs into files before stolen to damage computers when opened
- Use DDoS attacks to interfere with malicious activity

These methods are usually enabled by a combination of intrusion detection system technology to detect the intrusion and advanced traceback technology to ensure accurate targeting of the hacker.[83] Primary IP traceback schemes or techniques are link testing, packet marking, ICMP (Internet Control Message Protocol) traceback, and log-based traceback.[84] Analysis of logs (firewall, router, server and endpoint operating system) that extend from the network to the endpoint could reveal and correlate inbound and outbound attack patterns for route determination. Other methods for traceback include use of the Google Alerts function to search for stolen files, recognition of actor tactics, techniques, and procedures (TTP), and inspection of industry threat intelligence. Some form of these disruptive responses have been occurring for the past decade, by both government agencies and private companies, and software packages designed to execute them have been made commercially available to private companies.

Employment Options

Private Companies

Only an injured state may use countermeasures or counter-hacking. There is no basis under international law for a private company, such as an IT service or security firm, to act on its own initiative in response to malicious cyber activity.[85] Private companies conducting methods of hack back would be subject to national criminal law for any violations of legal statute and be held criminally liable for unintended consequences. For example, in the United States, a company that decides to hack back might face criminal and civil liability under the CFAA.[86] Specifically, the CFAA statute 1030(a)(5) prohibits and punishes the following offenses for whoever "knowingly causes the transmission of a program, information code, or command, and as a result of such conduct, intentionally causes damage without authorization, to a protected computer" and "intentionally accesses a protected computer without authorization, and as a result of such conduct, recklessly causes damage."[87] The paragraph establishes "crimes of dual intent—the intent to knowingly or intentionally intrude and intent to damage."[88] Damage is defined as "any impairment to the integrity or availability of data, a program, a system, or information."[89] Computer damage is a crime under the paragraph only if it involves a protected computer, which includes those used by the government, financial institutions, or in interstate or foreign commerce or communications.[90] Under US law, the punishment for a violation of the paragraph (summed up as knowingly causing a transmission that intentionally causes damage) depends on the severity of damage or loss, but could be imprisonment for one to twenty years, or even life, and fines up to $500,000.[91]

Arguments do exist to allow a company to exercise its rights to self-defense and defense of property. As a general principle, one has the right to defend one's self and one's property by reasonable force.[92] Hack back could be justified if traditional law enforcement schemes are inadequate in response, which are hampered by the speed by which cyber attacks create damage and the multiple jurisdictions with varying laws and procedures often used to stage the attack. Other criteria for determining if hack back is an optimal solution include whether the likelihood of striking the attacker is higher than innocent third parties and whether damage to the victim outweighs potential damage to third parties.[93] Although the CFAA appears to be clear on the matter, ambiguities do exist that could allow a company to exercise the principle of self-help. In particular, debate exists on the meaning of the term "authorization." For example even though there is no exemption in the CFAA for a private party, "does a hacker nonetheless implicitly grant authorization to a hack back when that person infiltrates a victim's systems and exfiltrates digital assets? Is authorization a binary concept, for which permission is or is not granted?"[94] If authorization is interpreted in a manner desirable to those who would engage in such activities, hack back by private companies could serve as a deterrent and supplement law enforcement. For if a malicious actor knows that a particular company will strike back, they might be inclined to not attack the company in the first place.[95]

Licensed Privateers

The Tallinn Manual 2.0 specifically states, "There is no prohibition against injured States turning to a private firm, including foreign companies, to conduct cyber countermeasures on their behalf against responsible states."[96] The injured state would be responsible for the company's actions on their behalf, although the company would be bound by all relevant restrictions and conditions on use of countermeasures.[97] For overseas firms not under the national laws of the injured state, this responsibility prevents denial of culpability by the state if undesired consequences occur. For this reason, a more viable approach to avoid liability would be for the state to deputize or license a private company under its own jurisdiction to act on its behalf. Historical precedence for the use of cyber privateers exists for centuries in the issue of letters of marque and reprisal for naval privateers, starting as early as 1205 by England and as late as 1941 by the United States, for a civilian dirigible to hunt enemy submarines.[98] Letters of marque and reprisal are basically "a license authorizing a private citizen to engage in reprisals against citizens or vessels of another nation."[99] They were originally used by governments to give private parties the authority to operate and use armed ships to attack and capture enemy merchant ships in time of war. The letters were crafted with enough specificity to ensure the private party did not exceed the intent of the government. Therefore, conceptually, the letters or licenses could be used by the government to specify the circumstances under which hack back may be performed by a private company for the defense of property.[100]

Article 1, Section 8 of the US Constitution signed in 1787 states, "the Congress shall have Power to . . . grant Letters of Marque and Reprisal." The US Congress invoked that power during the War of 1812 with Britain. Later in 1856, the Paris Declaration Respecting Maritime Law adopted a solemn Declaration that "Privateering is, and remains, abolished."[101] Notwithstanding, letters of marque have been used to counter piracy or to allow for self-defense. For instance, the British Parliament authorized private ships to attack and capture pirates after the Declaration of Paris. More recently, for all practical matters, armed private companies that protect merchant ships off Somalia from piracy serve as a form of naval privateers. Hence there is "at least a colorful argument to be made that the Paris Declaration did not render unlawful the issuance of letters of marque for purposes of self-defense in countering piracy."[102] Furthermore, one could compare cyber criminals, hackers, or hacktivists to modern-day pirates that roam not the seas, but cyberspace, threatening the activities and interests of nation-states.[103] From this point, a tentative conclusion could be reached "that letters of marque for cyber privateers might, likewise, be lawful under international law to counter cyber pirates."[104]

The United States never ratified the Paris Declaration. Whether bound by the Declaration or not, if any conclusion through broad interpretation that letters of marque are lawful holds ground, undoubtedly private companies will rise to the opportunity. This assertion is backed by the appearance in 2004 of Symbiot Security, which said its new "Intelligent Security Infrastructure Management Systems not only defends networks but lets them fight back."[105] While most of the platform consists of traditional defensive measures, like blocking or deflecting malicious traffic, it can also escalate the response and return fire. The exact extent of aggressive measures was not made clear by the company, but executives professed in a position paper that based on the lawful military doctrine of necessity and proportionality, the private sector has the right to counterstrike hostile intent with the subsequence use of force in self-defense.[106] Supposedly the controversial platform was deployed on several enterprise, government, and military networks. It is not obvious how long Symbiot maintained this stance and product, since they were acquired by Chaotic Moon Studios in 2012 for their development over the last decade of proven technologies in quantifying network risks, not for their attack response platform.[107]

Government Agencies

In the United States, the DOD, in concert with other agencies, is responsible for "defending the U.S. homeland and U.S. interests from attack, including attacks that may occur in cyberspace."[108] Therefore the DOD has been given a primary mission to "help defend the nation against cyberattacks from abroad, especially if they would cause loss of life, property destruction, or significant foreign policy and economic consequences."[109] In doing so, the department conducts DCO to preserve the ability to use friendly cyberspace capabilities and protect data, networks, and systems. DCO may be conducted in response to an attack, exploitation or intrusion on assets that the department is directed to defend. The DCO mission is accomplished using a layered, adaptive, defense-in-depth approach, with equally supporting components for digital and physical protection. A key characteristic of the DCO approach is the construct of active cyberspace defense.[110] DCO activities can occur inside the network in the form of Internal Defensive Measures (IDM) or can occur outside the network through Response Actions (RA).

The ultimate goal of DCO is to "change the current paradigm where the attacker enjoys significant advantage."[111] They strive to accomplish this goal through passive and active cyberspace defense activities that outmaneuver an attacker. DCO provides the capability to discover, detect, analyze and mitigate cyber threats. These operations taken for defensive purposes involve both DCO subcategories of IDM and RA. The primary tasks for IDM are hunting on networks for threats that evade security and directing appropriate internal responses, whereas RA are about going after the shooter with aggressive countermeasures to stop the attack, in accordance with all legal and policy guidance for operations outside the network.[112] Any cyber operation that equates to the use of force requires authority that resides at the presidential level, which would clash with a comfort level to stay inside the network.

Restriction Relief

Countermeasures provide a proportionate response for an injured state in cases where a cyber incident falls below the threshold of an armed attack. Because malicious activity in this category can still have disruptive and threatening effects, states will want to react quickly and effectively.[113] Yet there are procedural and substantive restrictions placed on the taking of countermeasures. For instance, when a state is injured by an internationally wrongful act, it may only resort to proportionate countermeasures aimed at the responsible state, or persons or entities attributable to the state, violating its legal obligations. Execution of that right can be a problem since it is difficult to attribute malicious cyber activity to a particular state or actor with unqualified certainty. Likewise, the difficulty in establishing the connection between the state and an actor is a further obstacle in the use of countermeasures. The Commentary in the Articles on State Responsibility, in the citing of the Iran–United States Claims Tribunal, affirms that "in order to attribute an act to the State, it is necessary to identify with reasonable certainty the actors and their association with the State."[114] While that association might not be possible, the determination of reasonable certainty may be possible regarding the location from where the malicious activity was launched. Under the principle of due diligence, even in situations where the state is not behind the harm to an injured state, international law does allow for countermeasures in response to harm from cyber operations originating from the state.

In essence the principle of due diligence is based on a state's legal responsibilities "when cyber infrastructure located on its territory is used by another state, or by non-state actors, such as hacker groups, individual hacktivists, organized armed groups, or terrorists, to mount the operations."[115] Rule 6 in the Tallinn Manual 2.0 provides that "a State must exercise due diligence in not allowing its territory, or territory or cyber infrastructure under its government control, to be used for cyber operations that affect the rights of, and produce serious adverse consequences for, other States."[116] This rule expresses "the obligation of states to take measures to ensure their territories are not used to the detriment of other states."[117] The UN Government Group of Experts framed the principle of due diligence in hortatory, rather than obligatory terms, in stating that "States should seek to ensure that their territories are not used by non-state actors for unlawful use of ICTs."[118] However, if a State is "unwilling to terminate harmful cyber operations encompassed by the due diligence principle as opposed to unable to do so, the injured State may be entitled to resort to countermeasures (Rule 20) based on the territorial State's failure to comply with this Rule [6]."[119] This ruling gives the injured state another option when faced with harmful cyber operations conducted by nonstate actors.

However, the obligation of due diligence only indisputably applies to a cyber operation that results in "serious adverse consequences" in another country, not one that causes inconvenience, minor disruption, or negligible expense.[120] Serious adverse consequences could involve "interference with the operation of critical infrastructure or a major impact on the economy."[121] Additionally, the obligation of due diligence attaches to a state only after the offending cyber activity comes to the attention of the state. If the state does not have the resources to investigate the cyber operations originating from its territory, the victim state may be obligated to offer assistance to the responsible state before any forcible countermeasures would be justified. If the responsible state accepts the offer of assistance, the injured state may lose the right to use countermeasures since the responsible state would have resumed its international obligation to ensure its territories are not used to the detriment of other states. If, however, the offer of assistance is rejected and the responsible state still fails to terminate an ongoing nonstate cyber operation mounted from its territory, the injured state has the right to take proportionate countermeasures against it.[122] Moreover, in response to this breach of due diligence obligation, the injured state could launch cyber operations targeting the nonstate actors. This is an important allowance given that the high thresholds in invoking the plea of necessity, namely a grave threat to an essential interest, limit its utility against nonstate actors.

In regard to thresholds, the US–China Economic and Security Review Commission asserts that international law has not kept pace with developments in cyber warfare, namely cyber espionage where stolen trade secrets are turned over to government-owned companies, clearly malicious activity not in the category of serious adverse consequences or a grave threat to an essential interest. Therefore, in June 2015 the commission held hearings on "the possibility of U.S. corporations mounting retaliatory cyber strikes against Chinese companies," although the Commission noted that today "U.S. companies cannot retaliate or 'hack back' without violating current U.S. law."[123] As a result, the commission recommended lawmakers should "look at whether U.S.-based companies be allowed to 'hack back' to recover or wipe stolen data."[124] Scholars at the Atlantic Council propose the development of a tailored deterrence approach to reduce adversarial intrusions into US private, commercial, and government networks that result in intellectual property theft or destructive effects on critical infrastructure. They assert that an important element of tailored deterrence would be "a new legal framework authorizing *certified* private sector cybersecurity providers to take limited, but meaningful steps under proper supervision."[125] The framework would describe requirements for certification and prescribe that providers register with the government. To ensure sufficient oversight, transparency, and accountability, the framework would require certified providers to articulate in advance and report on certain aggressive activities to law enforcement.

The creation of a new legal framework to use some form of cyber privateers could alleviate many of the concerns associated with private company hack back. At a Cyber Security Summit in October 2015, Admiral Rogers stated that "it's not without historical precedence that when a nation lacks capacity, it historically turned to the private sector," citing America's reliance on privateers before the navy was established. Although while not unheard of, Rogers quantified he is "very leery" of moving in that direction. "I still believe that the nation-state is best posed to apply force," Rogers said, "And I worry about what the implications are if we turn that over to the private sector."[126] Some of those implications could be the intrinsic temptation to use resident hack back capability for other than sanctioned actions. For instance, the use of hack back for revenge would turn the cyber privateers into nothing more than cyber vigilantes. Licensed privateers could prove difficult not only to trust, but also to manage without direct and persistent oversight. As Rogers opined, "It's the Wild West in some ways already—we don't need more gunslingers out in the street."[127]

AN ALTERNATIVE STRATEGY

Following his remarks that the "state of security of most companies is worse than ever," Dmitri Alperovitch, the Chief Technological Officer of the security firm CrowdStrike, asked the question "whether we should continue trying the same old tactics over and over again expecting a different result, or whether the time has come to fundamentally change our security strategy."[128]

Alperovitch noted that the US DOD has "proclaimed that it is changing its strategy to employ an active cyber defense capability" and "it is time for the private sector to adopt the same strategy which focuses on raising costs and risks to adversaries in an attempt to deter their activities."[129] Alperovitch asserted that his version of active defense is not about hack back, retaliation, or vigilantism, which could be counterproductive, or even illegal. Instead he believes an effective active defense strategy should focus on four key elements: real-time detection, attribution of threat actors, flexibility of response actions, and intelligence dissemination. This proclamation arrived with an announcement of the launch of CrowdStrike Falcon, a big data active defense platform that embodies these elements. The platform enables organizations to move beyond passive defenses by leveraging the kill chain model to obtain real time detection of what the attacker is doing and actually taking action against them.[130]

In presenting an approach that focuses more on the attacker than the exploit, the harshest critics of the company believe that "CrowdStrike will inevitably test legal and ethical boundaries in fighting hackers; the implication is that CrowdStrike offers offensive capabilities, known as hack back," which the Chief Executive Officer, Georg Kurtz emphatically denied.[131] Thus with stated, suspected, or denied capabilities, the CrowdStrike platform represents active cyber defense in the broadest sense. Inside the network, active cyber defense uses synchronized capabilities to discover the breach, isolate the threat and remediate the intrusion in real time. These capabilities operate inside the cyber kill chain to provide internal systemic resilience to withstand an attack. Outside the network, active cyber defense uses tailored disruption capacities to stop an attack. The conditions for use of countermeasures by an injured state against responsible states are well articulated by international and customary law. Delegation by the injured state to private companies to conduct cyber countermeasures on their behalf is allowed, but the private sector cannot go it alone under the concept of hack back. Besides lack of legal authority or precedence, the use of hack back brings a plethora of concerns that undermine the credibility of active defense. Foremost among them is motivation of the organization, misattribution of the attacker, third-party collateral damage, and potential escalation out of control. A new novel legal framework proposed by Anthony Glosson at the Mercatus Center that authorizes active defenses subject to third-party liability could temper excessive retribution and reduce societal risk.[132]

The imposition of any new legal framework in the United States for authorized, certified, or licensed private company response would communicate the government's willingness to increase capability to deter malicious actors. While this initiative could work well at the criminal level for theft of data, the credibility of such a move is somewhat suspect in convincing state-based or sponsored actors their attacks will not succeed. For in a direct contest, "despite the bluster of some in the high-tech community, private citizens are no match for the Russian mafia, the Russian Federal Security Service, or the People's Liberation Army in China."[133] If this contest cannot be won by American companies, then the US government has no choice but to step in and US Cyber Command is well positioned with the capability to do so. The command has designated Cyber Protection Teams to conduct the IDM mission and tasked National Mission Teams with the RA mission.[134] In testimony, the Deputy Commander of US Cyber Command, Lieutenant General James McLaughlin has avowed that the Defense Department will defend "the U.S. homeland and interests from attacks of significant consequence that may occur in cyberspace."[135] Public declarations on the use of active cyber defense by licensed private companies to defend against cyber attacks below that threshold have the potential to broaden "the range of punishments against which adversaries would have to calculate."[136] Through open communication of intentions to deliver a credible response outside the network, coupled with emergence of automated capability to stop attacks inside the network, active cyber defense is well postured to serve as an alternative strategy to achieve deterrence within the cyber arena.

NOTES

1. Robert S. Dewar, "The Triptych of Cyber Security: A Classification of Active Cyber Defense," *Proceedings 6th International Conference on Cyber Conflict* (Tallinn, Estonia: NATO Cooperative Cyber Defense Center of Excellence, June 2014), 7–21.

2. US Department of Defense, *Strategy for Operating in Cyberspace*, July 2011, 7.

3. Amber Corrin, "A Defense-in-Depth Strategy: DISA's Evolving Fight to Defend DoD Networks," *C4ISR&Networks, DISA Vision and Contract Guide 2016*, A10.

4. Danny Palmer, "It Is Not about If You Will Be Penetrated, but When, Warns NSA Chief," *Computing News*, July 16, 2015.

5. Mandiant, "M-Trends 2016," Special Report, February 2016, 4.

6. Melissa Riofrio, "Hacking Back: Digital Revenge Is Sweet but Risky," *PC World*, May 9, 2013.

7. Brian Krebs, "A First Look at the Target Intrusion, Malware," Krebs on Security, January 15, 2014.

8. Danny Yadron and Shelly Banjo, "Home Depot Upped Defenses, but Hacker Moved Faster," *Wall Street Journal*, September 12, 2014.

9. Brian Krebs, "Target Hackers Broke in Via HVAC Company," Krebs on Security, February 14, 2014.

10. Stephen Holmes and Diane Dayhoff, "The Home Depot Reports Findings in Payment Data Breach Investigation," The Home Depot, Atlanta, November 6, 2014.

11. Michael Riley, Ben Elgin, Dune Lawrence, and Carol Matlack, "Missed Alarms and 40 Million Stolen Credit Card Numbers: How Target Blew It," *Bloomberg Businessweek*, March 13, 2014.

12. Cybereason, "The Seven Struggles of Detection and Response," White Paper, 2015, 1–5.

13. Hexis Cyber Solutions, "How to Automate Cyber Threat Removal," A HawkEye G Technical White Paper, October 2015, 5.

14. Brian Krebs, "Inside Target Corp., Days after 2013 Breach," Krebs on Security, September 21, 2015.

15. Committee on Commerce, Science, and Transportation, "A 'Kill Chain' Analysis of the 2013 Target Data Breach," Majority Staff Report for Chairman Rockefeller, March 26, 2014, 7–11.

16. Eric M. Hutchins, Michael J. Cloppert, and Rohan M. Amin, "Intelligence-Driven Computer Network Defense Informed by Analysis of Adversary Campaigns and Intrusion Kill Chains," Lockheed Martin Corporation, March 2011, 3.

17. Looking Glass, "Addressing the Cyber Kill Chain: Full Gartner Research Report and Looking Glass Perspectives," Research Note, Table 1, 2016, 9.

18. Bob Gourley and Roger Hockenberry, "Automating Removal of Advanced Threats/Malware," White Paper, CTOlabs.com, June 2014, 1–7.

19. Aviv Raff, "POS Malware Targeted Target," Seculert Blog Post, January 16, 2014.

20. FireEye, "Debunking the Myth of Sandbox Security, White Paper, 2015.

21. National Security Agency Information Assurance Directorate, "Active Cyber Defense (ACD)," Fact Sheet, October 22, 2015, 1–2.

22. US Department of Defense, "The DoD Cyber Strategy," April 2015, 10–11.

23. Irving Lachow, "Active Cyber Defense: A Framework for Policy Makers," Center for a New American Security, February 2013, 1–7.

24. Margaret Rouse, "Honeypot (Honey Pot)," *Tech Target*, April 11, 2016.

25. Anand Sastry, "Honeypots for Network Security: How to Track Attackers' Activity," *Tech Target*, November 16, 2010.

26. Jerome Radcliffe, "CyberLaw 101, A Primer on US Laws Related to Honeypot Deployments," SANS Institute, 2007, 1–14.

27. Ed Skoudis, "What Security Risks Do Enterprise Honeypots Pose?" *Tech Target*, January 4, 2008.

28. David Sancho and Rainer Link, "Sinkholing Botnets," A Trend Micro Technical Paper, March 30, 2011, 1–6.

29. John Bambenek, "Principles of Malware Sinkholing," *Dark Reading*, April 6, 2015.

30. John Edwards and Eve Keiser, "Automating Security," *C4ISR& Networks,* October 2016, 14–16.

31. Carbon Black, "Disrupting the Threat: Identify, Respond, Contain and Recover in Seconds," White Paper, 2014, 1–12.

32. John Kindervag and Stephanie Balaouras, "Rules of Engagement: A Call to Action to Automate Breach Response," Forrester Research, Inc., December 2, 2014, 1–11.

33. Steve Morgan, "Cybersecurity Job Market to Suffer Severe Workforce Shortage," Cybersecurity Business Report, July 28, 2015, http://www.csoonline.com/article/2953258/it-careers/cybersecurity-job-market-figures-2015-to-2019-indicate-severe-workforce-shortage.html.

34. Margaret Rouse, "Endpoint Device," WhatIs.com, July 2013.

35. Dell SecureWorks, "Eliminating the Blind Spot: Rapidly Detect and Respond to the Advanced and Evasive Threat," White Paper, 2015, 1–6.

36. Hexis Cyber Solutions, "Active Cyber Defense: Integrated, Automated, Effective," December 11, 2015, 3.

37. Chris Warfield, "WatchGuard Acquires Hexis HawkEye G to Deliver Holistic Network Security from the Network to the Endpoint, WatchGuard Technologies, June 7, 2016.

38. Hexis Cyber Solutions, "HawkEye G: Endpoint Detection and Response," Products, August 27, 2016, https://www.hexiscyber.com/products/hawkeye-g.

39. Hexis Cyber Solutions, "How to Automate Cyber Threat Removal," A HawkEye G Technical White Paper, October 2015, 3.

40. Hexis Cyber Solutions, "HawkEye G Technical White Paper," Release 3.1, October 2015, 3.

41. John Breeden III, "Network World Gives HawkEye G 4.875 out of 5," *Network World*, December 8, 2014.

42. LightCyber, "Palo Alto Networks Completes Acquisition of LightCyber," Press Release, February 28, 2017.

43. LightCyber, "Closing the Breach Detection Gap," Data Sheet, 2015, 1–3.

44. Tim Greene, "Why the 'Cyber Kill Chain' Needs an Upgrade," *Computer World*, August 8, 2016.

45. LightCyber, "Magna Detection Technology," White Paper, November 2015, 1–6.

46. LightCyber, "The New Defense against Targeted Attacks," White Paper, March 2015, 7.

47. Catherine Lotrionte, "State Sovereignty and Self-Defense in Cyberspace: A Normative Framework for Balancing Legal Rights," *Emory International Law Review* 26 (May 28, 2013): 904.

48. William A. Owens, Kenneth W. Dam, and Herbert S. Lin, *Technology, Policy, Law and Ethics Regarding U.S. Acquisition and Use of Cyberattack Capabilities* (Washington, DC: National Academies Press, 2009), 204–5.

49. Sean L. Harrington, "Cyber Security Active Defense: Playing with Fire or Sound Risk Management," *Richmond Journal of Law and Technology* 20, no. 4 (September 17, 2014): 33.

50. Shelley Boose, "Black Hat Survey: 36% of Information Security Professionals Have Engaged in Retaliatory Hacking," *Business Wire*, July 26, 2012.

51. Michael Schmitt, *Tallinn Manual 2.0 on the International Law Applicable to Cyber Operations,* Second Edition (Cambridge: Cambridge University Press, May 2017), 111.

52. United Nations, "Responsibility of States for Internationally Wrongful Acts," General Assembly Resolution 56/83, December 12, 2001, Annex.

53. International Law Commission, *Draft Articles on Responsibility of States for Internationally Wrongful Acts, with commentaries,* fifty-third session, 2001, Chapter II, Commentary, Para. 1.

54. United Nations, Charter of the United Nations, Chapter VII, Article 2, San Francisco, CA, October 24, 1945.

55. Schmitt, *Tallinn Manual 2.0 on the International Law Applicable to Cyber Operations,* 330.

56. Michael N. Schmitt, "'Below the Threshold' Cyber Operations: The Countermeasures Response Option and International Law," *Virginia Journal of International Law* 54, no. 3 (2014): 704–5.

57. Responsibility of States, Article 49 (1 and 2).

58. Schmitt, *Tallinn Manual 2.0 on the International Law Applicable to Cyber Operations,* 120.

59. Michael N. Schmitt and Liis Vihul, "Proxy Wars in Cyberspace: The Evolving International Law of Attribution," *Fletcher Security Review* 1, no. 2 (Spring 2014): 59.

60. Responsibility of States, Article 51.

61. Responsibility of States, Article 50 (1a).

62. Schmitt, *Tallinn Manual 2.0 on the International Law Applicable to Cyber Operations,* 119.

63. Responsibility of States, Article 2 (a).

64. Schmitt, "'Below the Threshold,'" 669.

65. Responsibility of States, Article 8.

66. Kelly Jackson Higgins, "Shamoon, Saudi Aramco, and Targeted Destruction," *Dark Reading*, August 22, 2012.

67. Siobhan Gorman and Julian E. Barnes, "U.S. Says Iranian Hackers Are Behind Electronic Assaults on U.S. Banks, Foreign Energy," *Wall Street Journal*, October 12, 2012.

68. HP Security Research, "Syrian Electronic Army," HPSR Threat Intelligence Briefing Episode 3, April 2013, 22–24.

69. Michael Schmitt, "In Defense of Due Diligence in Cyberspace," *Yale Law Journal Forum*, June 22, 2015, 77.

70. Responsibility of States, Article 25 (1a and b).

71. Schmitt, *Tallinn Manual 2.0 on the International Law Applicable to Cyber Operations,* 135.

72. Schmitt, *Tallinn Manual 2.0 on the International Law Applicable to Cyber Operations,* 136.

73. Schmitt, *Tallinn Manual 2.0 on the International Law Applicable to Cyber Operations,* 136.

74. Benedikt Pierker, "Territorial Sovereignty and Integrity and the Challenge of Cyberspace," *Peacetime Regime for State Activities in Cyberspace* (Tallinn, Estonia: NATO Cooperative Cyber Defence Centre of Excellence, 2013), 189–216.

75. Schmitt, *Tallinn Manual 2.0 on the International Law Applicable to Cyber Operations*, 138.

76. Schmitt, "In Defense of Due Diligence in Cyberspace," 78.

77. Schmitt, *Tallinn Manual 2.0 on the International Law Applicable to Cyber Operations*, 130.

78. Peter Sullivan, "Hacking Back: A Viable Strategy or a Major Risk?" *Tech Target*, May 2, 2016.

79. Bruce P. Smith, "Hacking, Poaching, and Counterattacking: Digital Counterstrikes and the Contours of Self-Help," *Journal of Law, Economics and Policy* 1, no. 1.2 (2005): 177–78.

80. Sean L. Harrington, "Cyber Security Active Defense: Playing with Fire or Sound Risk Management," *Richmond Journal of Law and Technology* 20, no. 4 (September 17, 2014): 11–13.

81. Sam Cook, "Georgia Outs Russian Hacker, Takes Photo with His Own Webcam," *Geek News*, October 31, 2012; and Ministry of Justice of Georgia, "Cyber Espionage against Georgian Government, CERT-Georgia, March 2011, 22.

82. Kaspersky Lab, "Ransomware: All Locked Up and No Place to Go," White Paper, 2016, 1–16.

83. Jay P. Kesan and Carol M. Hayes, "Thinking through Active Defense in Cyberspace," *Proceedings of a Workshop on Deterring Cyberattacks* (Washington, DC: National Academies Press, 2010), 328–31.

84. Vijayalakshmi Murugesan, "A Brief Survey of IP Traceback Methodologies," *Acta Polytechnica Hungaria* 11, no. 9 (2014): 197–216.

85. Schmitt, *Tallinn Manual 2.0 on the International Law Applicable to Cyber Operations*, 130.

86. Cybersecurity Unit, "Best Practices for Victim Response and Reporting of Cyber Incidents," Computer Crime and Intellectual Property Section, US Department of Justice, Version 1.0, April 2015, 12.

87. 18 U.S.C. 1030(a)(5).

88. Charles Doyle, "Cybercrime: An Overview of the Federal Computer Fraud and Abuse Statute and Related Federal Criminal Laws," Congressional Research Service Report 97-1025, October 15, 2014, 31.

89. 18 U.S.C. 1030(e)(8).

90. 18 U.S.C. 1030(e)(2).

91. Congressional Research Service Report 97-1025, 35–37.

92. Kenneth W. Simons, "Self-Defense: Reasonable Beliefs or Reasonable Self Control," *New Criminal Law Review* 11, no. 1 (Winter 2008): 51–90.

93. Jay P. Kesan, "Optimal Hackback," *Chicago-Kent Law Review* 84, no. 3 (June 2009): 834–38.

94. Kim Peretti and Todd McClelland, "Legal Issues with Emerging Active Defense Security Technologies," Cyber Alert, Alston & Bird, LLP, January 2013, 1–4.

95. Zach West, "Young Fella, If You're Looking for Trouble I'll Accommodate You: Deputizing Private Companies for the Use of Hackback," *Syracuse Law Review* 63 (November 2012): 133.

96. Schmitt, *Tallinn Manual 2.0 on the International Law Applicable to Cyber Operations*, 131.

97. Schmitt, "'Below the Threshold,'" 727–28.

98. John Rolland, "Letters of Marque and Reprisal," Constitution Society, Blog Site, December 28, 2007.

99. *Black's Law Dictionary*, 9th ed., 2009, 910.

100. Owens et al., *Technology, Policy, Law and Ethics Regarding U.S. Acquisition and Use of Cyberattack Capabilities*, 208.

101. Paris Declaration Respecting Maritime Law, 1856.

102. Paul Rosenzweig, "International Law and Private Actor Active Cyber Defensive Measures," *Stanford Journal of International Law* (May 27, 2013): 10.

103. Joseph Roger Clark, "Arghh . . . Cyber-Pirates," Security Studies Blog Posts," May 28, 2013.

104. Rosenzweig, "International Law and Private Actor Active Cyber Defensive Measures," 10.

105. Raksha Shetty, "Networks Lash Back at Cyber Hacks," *CBS News*, June 18, 2004.

106. Dana Epps, "On the Rules of Engagement for Information Warfare," Web Blog, March 10, 2014, http://silverstr.ufies.org/blog/archives/000547.html.

107. Chaotic Moon Studios, "Chaotic Moon Acquires Symbiot Security," *PRNewswire*, April 26, 2012.

108. The DoD Cyber Strategy, 2.

109. Secretary of Defense Ash Carter, "Rewiring the Pentagon: Charting a New Path on Innovation and Cybersecurity," Drell Lecture at Stanford University, Palo Alto, CA, April 23, 2015.

110. US Department of Defense, *Cyberspace Operations,* US Joint Publication 3-12 (R) (Washington, DC: The Joint Staff, February 5, 2013), II-2.

111. Brett T. Williams, "The Joint Force Commander's Guide to Cyberspace Operations," *Joint Forces Quarterly* no. 73, 2nd Quarter (2014): 15.

112. Williams, "The Joint Force Commander's Guide to Cyberspace Operations," 16.

113. Katharine C. Hinkle, "Countermeasures in the Cyber Context: One More Thing to Worry About," *Yale Journal of International Law Online* 37 (Fall 2011): 12.

114. Responsibility of States, Chapter II.

115. Schmitt, "In Defense of Due Diligence in Cyberspace," 68.

116. Schmitt, *Tallinn Manual 2.0 on the International Law Applicable to Cyber Operations*, 30.

117. Schmitt, "In Defense of Due Diligence in Cyberspace," 69.

118. United Nations General Assembly, "Group of Governmental Experts on Developments in the Field of Information and Telecommunications in the Context of International Security," A/68/98, June 24, 2013, 23.

119. Schmitt, *Tallinn Manual 2.0 on the International Law Applicable to Cyber Operations*, 50.

120. Schmitt, *Tallinn Manual 2.0 on the International Law Applicable to Cyber Operations*, 36-37.

121. Schmitt, *Tallinn Manual 2.0 on the International Law Applicable to Cyber Operations*, 38.

122. Lotrionte, "State Sovereignty and Self-Defense in Cyberspace: A Normative Framework for Balancing Legal Rights," 904–5.

123. US-China Economic and Security Review Commission, "2015 Report to Congress," November 2015, 205–7.

124. Matthew Pennington, "U.S. Advised to Examine "Hack Back" Options against China," *Associated Press*, November 17, 2015.

125. Franklin D. Kramer and Melanie J. Teplinsky, "Cybersecurity and Tailored Deterrence," Atlantic Council, December 2013, 1–6.

126. Aaron Boyd, "Rogers: We Don't Need Cyber Privateers," *Federal Times*, October 29, 2015.

127. Boyd, "Rogers: We Don't Need Cyber Privateers."

128. Dmitri Alperovitch, "Active Defense: Time for a New Security Strategy," Crowdstrike Blog, February 26, 2013.

129. Alperovitch, "Active Defense."

130. CrowdStrike, "CrowdStrike Launches Big Data Active Defense Platform," *PRNewswire*, June 18, 2013.

131. Fritz Nelson, "Why CrowdStrike's Focus on Attackers and Active Defense Polarizes InfoSec Pros," *Pardo*, July 17, 2013.

132. Anthony D. Glosson, "Active Defense: An Overview of the Debate and a Way Forward," Mercatus Center, August 2015, 23–28.

133. James Andrew Lewis, "Private Retaliation in Cyberspace," Commentary, Center for Strategic and International Studies, May 22, 2013.

134. Brett T. Williams, "The Joint Force Commander's Guide to Cyberspace Operations," *Joint Forces Quarterly* no. 73, 2nd Quarter (2014): 16.

135. Thomas Atkin, James K. McLaughlin and Charles L. Moore, "Statement before the House Armed Services Committee," June 22, 2016.

136. Steve Weber and Betsy Cooper, "Cybersecurity Policy Ideas for a New Presidency," Center for Long-Term Cybersecurity, November 2016, 1.

Chapter Eight

Alternative Strategy Selection

For the deterrence of malicious actors in cyberspace, the strategies of retaliation, denial and entanglement have made little progress in imposing costs for, denying benefit of, and encouraging restraint in malicious activity. FBI Director James Comey said that "certain actions the federal government is taking to deter cyber threats to the country are working, at least in part."[1] He claims indictments of Chinese military and Iranian hackers "send an important and chilly wind through them," and he sees "early indications of efforts to cooperate" on norms for nation-states to not engage in theft for commercial purposes. However, his recognition that "state sponsored cyber attackers are getting more aggressive" and "criminal organizations are getting more specialized" just amplifies that current strategies are insufficient to deter the number and type of actors engaged in cyber attack campaigns. There is little doubt in the warning by Michael Daniel, the former White House cybersecurity coordinator, that "the cyber threat continues to outpace our current efforts."[2] In response, the Obama administration proposed for 2017 over \$19 billion for federal cyber security efforts, with nearly \$3.1 billion to retire, replace, and modernize legacy IT systems.[3] In addition the Justice Department asked to increase its cyber security–related funding by 23 percent to improve their capabilities to identify, disrupt, and apprehend malicious cyber actors.[4] These cost-intensive measures to improve defensive capabilities and punish actors arrive as cyber threats become more frequent and more serious, partly because of the availability of low-cost and effective hacker toolkits. Technically proficient actors are spending just over a thousand dollars on average for specialized toolkits to execute one attack.[5]

Asymmetric advantages for the malicious actor continue to shape their perceptions of the costs and benefits of a cyber attack. A reoccurring cyber security industry revelation is that "defenders must block all attacks; to win, attackers need to succeed at only one."[6] An ever expanding list of attack vectors and techniques, such as MITRE describes for lateral movement,[7] allows an actor to execute the cyber kill chain with ease, despite attempts to install security controls for denial.[8] Many tools and services are available on the open market from dark sources and overlap in their common use by nation-states, proxies, patriots, sympathizers, and criminals makes it hard to distinguish the source to impose costs. Even worse, nation-states' use of all these actors under some form of direction, control, or incitement for plausible deniability makes concentration on just the nation-state for deterrence impractical. The unrelenting motivations of the wide range of malicious actors to achieve political objectives, national pride, personal satisfaction, or monetary gain exceed international efforts to restrain behavior, especially when actors know they can operate with little risk of repercussion. Optimism for the future appears bleak, as evident in a defense report that 62 percent of respondents expected their organizations to be compromised by a cyber attack in 2016, up from only 39 percent two years ago.[9] These statistics indicate that a new way to alter malicious actor behavior in cyberspace is necessary.

This final chapter starts with how asymmetric advantages and system vulnerabilities create potential for systemic sector consequences from disruptive or destructive cyber attacks. Next, in consideration of threats that "exploit the increased complexity and connectivity of critical infrastructure systems,"[10] the chapter presents an assessment at the strategic level of the impact of traditional deterrence strategies on attacks (volume of noise across social, technical and economic systems), time (in mitigation of systemic security losses), and costs (in the order of magnitude of gross domestic products [GDP]). Given the existence of insurmountable shortfalls in traditional strategies, the chapter then examines whether the strategy of active cyber defense is technically capable and legally viable inside and outside the network for use in deterring the wide variety of malicious actors. Next an illustrative case of an alleged Russian multifaceted cyber campaign designed to interfere in the 2016 US Presidential Election process[11] depicts why active cyber defense could be a strategic option for cyber deterrence. The chapter finishes with how active cyber defense meets the conditions of capability, credibility, and communication[12] to be selected as an alternative strategy to achieve deterrence within the cyber arena.

SYSTEMIC SECTOR CONSEQUENCES

The globally unconstrained structure of cyberspace offers asymmetric advantages in the scale, proximity, and precision of malicious actor attacks. Attackers can cause a significant and disproportionate amount of damage without large resources or technical sophistication.[13] A vibrant underground hacker market provides them with tools and services to increase the scale of their cyber attacks. Countries are becoming aware of "the asymmetric offensive opportunities presented by systemic and persistent vulnerabilities in key infrastructure sectors including health care, energy, finance, telecommunications, transportation, and water."[14] Admiral Rogers, head of the NSA, said he is watching "nation states, groups within some of that infrastructure" now focused on reconnaissance.[15] An example is the Iranian hacker breach of the Bowman Avenue Dam outside of New York City in 2013. The intrusion was a test by the hackers to see what they could access. They could have controlled the flood gates if not offline for maintenance. The breach illustrates that overseas hackers can easily get into pieces of old critical infrastructure running on retro-fitted software that is connected to the Internet.[16] Likewise, attackers used remote cyber intrusions in the attack on the three power companies in Ukraine in 2015.[17] The attackers ran a phishing campaign to get into the corporate network and hijack worker credentials. Eventually they took over control center computers to open breakers and take substations offline. Then the hackers wiped files from operator stations with KillDisk malware.[18] Ukraine found evidence blaming Russian hackers for the power outage.[19] It appears the attacks were part of a multistage campaign against the Ukrainian industrial network, also targeting a major mining company and a large railway operator.[20]

While these attacks on water, energy, and transportation sector infrastructure are disconcerting, they were not necessarily destructive. Yet a few confirmed cases do exist in which a digital attack caused physical destruction. The first was a series of attacks against the Maroochy Shire Council sewerage control system in Australia in 2000 that caused raw sewage spills,[21] and the second was the 2010 Stuxnet attack on Iranian nuclear facilities. The third occurred in late 2014 at an unnamed steel mill in Germany. A malicious APT actor used a spear phishing email, one of the most common attack vectors, to gain access to the mill's corporate network and then move, most likely through trusted connections, into its production network. The final stage of the attack produced "an accumulation of breakdowns of individual components of the control system."[22] As a result, the plant was "unable to shut down a blast furnace in a regulated manner" which caused "massive damage to the system."[23] It is unclear if the attackers intended to cause the physical destruction or if that was collateral damage. The incident underscores that not all intrusions into critical infrastructure will be as careful as the Stuxnet worm that destroyed only targeted uranium enrichment centrifuges. The German steel mill attack was an isolated, not systemic attack on an industry sector, but still concern resides of the impact of destructive attacks on critical infrastructure.

In the wake of the Ukraine incident, Admiral Rogers said at the 2016 RSA Conference that he worries over an infrastructure attack in the United States that causes significant damage. He also expressed fear over attacks that would manipulate data for the purpose of crippling financial institutions. Rogers asked the audience "What are we going to do as a society when you go to your bank account, and the numbers don't match what you think they should be?" or "What do you do if your business does financial transactions, and they don't reflect what you are seeing?"[24] Those dreadful scenarios would cause systemic failure of the financial sector, and consequently cascading effects across the economy and society. Many banks have experienced denial of service attacks upon the availability of information, and intrusion attacks upon the confidentiality of information, but this new paradigm would affect the integrity of the information system. Disruption or manipulation of stock trading operations would cause a systemic global impact, as seen in January 2016 when the Chinese stock market crashed over the devaluation of its currency, driving a tumble in the Dow Jones industrial average of nearly four hundred points.[25]

The chief of strategy in the US Defense Strategic Capabilities office remarked that we see "cyber being increasingly used as a first strike weapon by peer competitors" and "non-military assets are increasingly the targets."[26] Those targets could include nuclear facilities, like in Stuxnet. A study of twenty nations with significant atomic stockpiles or nuclear power plants reveals the lesson of Stuxnet seems lost, as "too many states require virtually no effective security measures at nuclear facilities to address the threat posed by hackers."[27] A similar report affirms a paucity of regulatory standards for civil nuclear facilities, coupled with insufficient spending on cyber security.[28] Yet regardless of the catastrophic risk of a release of ionizing radiation, most of the hype over cyber intrusions has been over the relentless theft of personal, corporate or government information. For example, the German report of a destructive cyber incident got lost in the noise of the widely publicized Sony hack in late 2014. The method to deliver a hostile payload, like a social engineering attack seen in Sony, can be the same for all types of business networks, including those connected to production networks in industrial control systems.

DETERRENCE STRATEGY SHORTFALLS

Ultimately all types of critical infrastructure around the globe are at risk of cyber attack. The cost of malicious cyber activity will only rise as more business functions move online and more companies connect to the Internet. Likewise, the losses from intellectual property theft will probably increase as countries improve their ability to manufacture counterfeit goods. An Institute study found in 2015 that the average total cost of data breaches for 383 organizations in twelve countries is $4 million per year, up by 29 percent since 2013. In another institute study of IT practitioners in forty-two countries across sixteen industry sectors, 46 percent of respondents say their IT security budget increased in the past two years. While the average total revenue of the organizations in the study is $1.2 billion, on average $9.98 million is allocated to IT security activities and enabling technologies.[29] Even that might not be enough, as a study of United Kingdom organizations reveals that more than a quarter of IT decision makers admit they could do more to protect corporate data.[30] Overall, companies are generally confident about protecting networks against known threats,[31] but the landscape of unknown threats calls for definitive steps to ensure a breach does not happen, and those include the effective deterrence of malicious actor activity.

At the strategic level, the deterrence option of entanglement attempts to reduce the volume of noise across social, technical and economic systems through cooperative measures that restrain state behavior, although the impact of the primary mechanism of norms depends on "whether they are implemented faithfully and whether violators are held accountable."[32] An example is the US-China agreement not to conduct or support cyber-enabled theft of intellectual property. Here diminishment of state-sponsored attacks is a matter of trust, and for China in other domains that trust is lacking. For instance, China appears to have built "significant point-defense capabilities, in the form of anti-aircraft guns and close-in weapons systems, at each of its outposts in the Spratly Islands,[33] despite President Xi Jinping's September 2015 pledge not to militarize the islands.[34] After all, the U.S.-China cyber deal was produced through coercive diplomacy in the threat of sanctions, which came after criminal indictments.[35] Although the United States still trusts China will abide by the cyber agreement and their arrest of hackers it says were connected to the OPM breach, could mark the first measure of accountability. However, US government officials said "they suspected the involvement of the Chinese government, particularly the civilian Ministry of State Security."[36] A major challenge in attribution is that "distinguishing between the operations of official and other Chinese cyber actors is often difficult."[37] Yet the cyber agreement should work regardless of what type of actor if the state enforces it. More than a year after the agreement, Director Clapper testifies that "Beijing continues to conduct cyber espionage against the U.S. Government, our allies, and U.S. companies,[38] although at reduced levels. Regarding Iran, the 2013 New York dam cyber breach indictment brought attention to their hackers' roles in denial of service attacks on US banks starting in 2011.[39] How would the United States ever trust this belligerent actor that has conducted nearly a dozen ballistic-missile tests in the year since the nuclear deal was implemented.[40]

The deterrence option of denial attempts to lessen the time in mitigation of systemic security losses through both preventive and detective security controls that deny attack success. For instance, in the aftermath of the Ukraine power distribution attack, the US Industrial Control System–Computer Emergency Response Team (ICS–CERT) released an alert that not only depicted the attack but also listed mitigation strategies for organizations across all sectors to review and employ. It suggested asset owners take defensive measures by leveraging best practices to minimize the risk from similar malicious cyber activity. Suggested practices included use of multifactor authentication to limit remote access and Application Whitelisting to prevent attempted execution of malware.[41] ICS–CERT also recognizes that the increased integration of external, business, and control system networks to enhance productivity and reduce costs leads to vulnerabilities. The same protocols and standards that increase interoperability in the control systems community are the same technologies that have been exploited on the corporate networking domains. Open system architecture vulnerabilities that could migrate to control system domains include network reconnaissance, unauthorized intrusions and escalation of privileges. Therefore, multiple countermeasures are needed to disseminate risk over layers of protection.[42] However, as asset owners move to implement defense-in-depth frameworks, informed by cyber threat intelligence, malicious actors continue to penetrate defenses, and the proportion of breaches discovered within days still falls well below that of time to compromise, usually in minutes or less.[43]

The deterrence option of retaliation attempts to diminish the costs of systemic security losses by the threat to impose costs for hostile acts. However, the global economy is bearing the cost from cybercrime and cyberespionage, estimated to be annually around $455 billion. The estimate accounts for the loss of intellectual property and the theft of financial assets and sensitive business information, plus additional costs for securing networks and recovering from attacks, including reputational damage. For nations, those costs measured in order of magnitude of GDP are staggering. The study finds costs in high-income countries to be as much as 0.9 percent of GDP on average.[44] In the United States the loss is 0.64 percent of GDP which for a 2015 GDP figure of $18 trillion equals $115.2 billion a year. The threat of retaliation through use of all necessary means strives to shift costs to the malicious actors. For instance, Russian authorities in November 2015 raided offices used in a notorious financial hacking operation. Since the raid, a password-stealing software program known as Dyre, responsible for tens of millions of dollars in losses at financial institutions, including Bank of America and JP Morgan Chase, has not been deployed.[45] Criminal prosecutions are intended to change the calculus of costs, yet many require slowly evolving international cooperation.[46] In cases where overseas actors are unlikely to be held accountable, economic sanctions are an effort to prevent malicious actors from reaping rewards for their intrusions. However, the building of a case to use these means requires letting federal investigators examine the forensic evidence left by the intruders. That is problematic as companies are wary of cooperating in government investigations for fear of exposure to regulatory actions, privacy suits, or other civil litigation.[47]

The aim of deterrence is to "decisively influence the adversary's decision-making calculus."[48] Thus deterrence is a "state of mind brought about by an adversary's perception of three factors: being denied the expected benefits of his action; having excessive costs imposed for taking the action; and that restraint is an acceptable alternative."[49] The deterrence strategies of denial, retaliation, and entanglement seek to convince adversaries not to take malicious actions by changing their perceptions.[50] They concentrate primarily on means to deny benefits, impose costs, or encourage restraint. An adversary chooses "not to act for fear of failure, risk, or consequences."[51] These strategic options are not mutually exclusive and US doctrine, for instance, uses a mixed methodology, especially across diplomatic, legal, economic, and military dimensions. The cumulative effect of these strategies is gained from a synchronized and coordinated use of all instruments of national power in a comprehensive approach. Regrettably, evidence indicates that traditional deterrence strategies, even if applied together, are insufficient to deter the wide range of malicious actors conducting cyber attacks.[52] Critics of the US approach to "name and shame" foreign cyber threat actors believe it's just "yapping in the wind." While nation-states stand at the top of the FBI stack of threat actors, followed by criminal syndicates, hacktivists, and terrorists, Director Comey admits that "all cyber attackers are becoming more sophisticated."[53] Therefore without a doubt, an alternative strategy is necessary that encourages adversary restraint, by shaping perceptions of the costs and benefits of a cyber attack in a different way.

A SUFFICIENT ALTERNATIVE

An alternative strategy of active cyber defense would combine internal systemic resilience to halt malicious cyber activity after an intrusion with tailored disruption capacities to thwart malicious actor objectives. The question of whether a strategy of active cyber defense is *technically capable and legally viable* to deny benefits through systemic resilience and impose costs through tailored disruption was publicly examined in 2013 by the Commission on the Theft of American Intellectual Property (IP Commission). Outside the victim's network, the IP Commission noted that "while not permitted under U.S. laws, there are increasing calls for creating a more permissive environment for active network defense that allows companies not only to stabilize a situation but to take further steps . . . within an unauthorized network."[54] Inside the defender's network, the IP Commission recommended that besides vulnerability mitigation measures such as firewalls and password protection systems, companies and governments should also "install active systems that monitor activity on the network, detect anomalous behavior, and trigger intrusion alarms that initiate both network and physical actions immediately."[55] These suggestions tacitly endorse the use of automated active cyber defense type capabilities to provide internal systemic resilience through legally acceptable means as long as actions stay inside organizational boundaries.

Inside the Defender's Network

Industry solutions are actually getting better in monitoring activity and detecting malicious behavior. The security firm Mandiant reported in 2012 that the median days an organization was compromised before the breach was discovered was 416 days. That number dropped in their reports, in 2014 to 205 days and then to 146 days in 2015.[56] For companies that detected a breach on their own, which is less than 20 percent,[57] the median number was forty-six days compromised before discovery. This decline in days over the past few years most likely indicates the widespread installation of not just preventive, but also detective security controls on organizational systems. In a 2016 institute survey of IT security practitioners in the United States involved in endpoint security in a variety of organizations, 95 percent said their organizations will evolve toward a more "detect and respond" orientation from one that is focused on prevention.[58] Organizations could adopt a single integrated platform like LightCyber Magna, considered to be a single real-time detection platform,[59] or they can opt to select an endpoint detection and response solution, like one used in Magna, which comprises many active cyber defense–type capabilities, empowered by actionable cyber threat intelligence.

In cyber incidents, penetration often occurs via endpoints, for instance when malware is downloaded from a spear-phishing email to the victim's desktop or laptop, or through known vulnerabilities in older POS terminals, or by a USB stick used between the home and the office.[60] After penetrating an endpoint, the malware establishes command and control for an attacker to conduct reconnaissance and lateral movement inside the network. The identification of actions originating from the compromised endpoint provides an opportunity to break the cyber kill chain. This opportunity is the reason for a rise in commercial endpoint detection and response solutions. A worthwhile vendor solution must be able to detect, contain, investigate and remediate the incident at the endpoint. Capable solutions inventory and manage system configurations to establish a normal baseline. Then the same solution monitors configuration changes to detect unusual behavior. Such changes can be in new software or files, the registry, account information, user privileges, new processes, and open ports or communications activity.[61] The solution may contain a process or traffic then investigated through threat intelligence exchanges. Upon confirmation of malicious behavior, the solution remedies the situation through routine repairs, software de-installations, or further blocks of IP addresses.[62] Ideally to stop or limit damage, configurations will be automatically compared to indicators of compromise for quick detection, and remediation actions will be automatically run for real-time response.

To better understand possible indicators of compromise, most endpoint detection and response solutions are integrated with multiple independent threat intelligence services and feeds. They will consume these sources constantly and filter information on malware, URL domains, email sources, IP addresses, and the like, on a massive scale for organizational relevance.[63] The solutions will then compare configuration changes to relevant indicators of compromise for threat detection. As necessary a suspect change or file will be sent to a third-party threat intelligence service, like to the Palo Alto Networks cloud-based virtual malware analysis WildFire environment, "built for high fidelity hardware emulation" to analyze "suspicious samples as they execute."[64] The solution can also use a log event analysis service to identify odd behavior on systems and the time of occurrence, such as by LogRhythm labs which "collect and process all of an organization's log, flow, event and other machine data, as well as endpoint, server and network forensic data" to identify activities and automatically prioritize incidents.[65] In this fashion cyber threat intelligence "has gone from a niche product to a general-use tool."[66] Yet to be valuable for endpoint detection and response solutions, it still has to be accurate, relevant, and timely for use across each phase of the cyber kill chain.[67] That means a threat intelligence platform should also execute automated processes to provide seamless integration with endpoint detection and response solutions, such as sending a block action on an indicator.[68]

The demand for next generation endpoint security solutions is high. In a 2016 survey of enterprises across all industries, a whopping 86 percent of respondent organizations report they are not satisfied with their current endpoint protection software.[69] In response to this demand, a number of companies are well poised to grab a piece of the market, starting with Palo Alto Networks acquiring LightCyber technologies for use in their Next-Generation Security Platform and continuing with Watchguard Technologies acquiring HawkEye G capabilities for use in their Threat Detection and Response platform. WatchGuard uses a host sensor to detect security events using heuristics and behavioral analytics. Data on these events is then sent to a cloud-based threat intelligence correlation and scoring engine to generate a threat score and rank based on severity. Based on score, threats can be quickly remediated through one-click response options or through policies that enable automated responses including quarantine the file, kill the process and delete the registry value. [70]

Other notable leaders in the field include Carbon Black, Tripwire, and also CrowdStrike. Cb Response offered by Carbon Black provides real-time response and remediation. It visualizes the kill chain to find the root cause and see lateral movements to accelerate investigations. Cb Response stops attacks in progress by isolating infected systems, terminating processes and banning hashes (numerical text strings) across an enterprise. It also provides unlimited data retention for full historical review of any attack. [71] Tripwire Enterprise endpoint defense solutions are contained in an integrated suite for real-time detection, analysis and response. Tripwire monitors and compares file changes in endpoints against baseline configurations, then automatically uploads and detonates suspicious files in a sandbox provided by Lastline Enterprise, a highly rated advanced malware detection system. [72] Tripwire also monitors and correlates state changes with system events and application logs. Upon solution prediction of risk, a security analyst manually defends assets through protective controls. [73]

The CrowdStrike Falcon platform has continued to evolve with Falcon Insight serving as their endpoint detection and response solution. Falcon Insight relies on CrowdStrike's cloud-delivery architecture to collect and inspect event information on an endpoint in real time. Automatic detection of indicators of attack by Falcon Insight identifies attacker behavior and stops attacks. [74] Although white papers by notable vendors seem to just herald their capabilities, testing of endpoint security solutions shows they actually work. For example, in a test of HawkEye G for malware installed on a protected system, the solution caught the malware trying to contact its botnet handler and automatically routed traffic to a Bot Trap. HawkEye G automatically stopped the process from running on the host computer, and then encrypted and quarantined the malicious file for operator review. [75] Customers trust these solutions as evidenced by the deployment of the Tripwire endpoint defense solution in over a million business-critical systems. Given the proven qualities of endpoint security solutions available for installation today, for the category of inside the defender's network, the strategy of active cyber defense seems to be both *technically capable and legally viable* through automated and integrated capabilities that act only inside organizational boundaries.

Outside the Victim's Network

Yet even with promising advances in security solutions, the IP Commission contended that the best security systems cannot be depended upon for protection one hundred percent of the time against the most highly skilled hackers. Therefore, new ways are necessary to reverse the time, opportunity, and resource advantage of the attacker by reducing his incentives and raising his costs. The IP Commission appeared to support ways to identify and render inoperable stolen intellectual property through cyber means, such as marking electronic files with beacons and writing software that renders files inaccessible to unauthorized persons. Yet the IP Commission did not recommend specific revised laws to recover a stolen file or to degrade or damage the computer system of a hacker under present circumstances.[76] The specific reasons that the IP Commission was not ready to endorse the idea of Congress authorizing aggressive cyber actions for the purpose of self-defense, were the dangers of misuse of legal hacking authorities and the potential for collateral damage.[77]

The primary motivation for the private sector to hack back against an attacker would probably be to recover or delete stolen data, intellectual property or trade secrets on an attacker's computers or servers. Yet private organizations could be enticed to hack back for retaliatory reasons to obtain justice for any perceived harm and induced inconvenience, including to disrupt or damage the attacker's systems, and even more so, to degrade their ability to carry out future attacks.[78] Also, the choice to hack back could produce unintended collateral damage to an innocent bystander's system. Attackers often use compromised home or office computers as bots in a botnet for distributed denial of service attacks or to distribute spam in illicit schemes. They also route attack traffic through compromised computers without the owner's knowledge to hide their tracks. For the latter, just imagine, for instance, the impact of a destructive hack back on an emergency service provider, a school, or even worse, a hospital system and the associated punitive and civil damages.[79]

Despite the apparent risks of hack back, one could argue that private companies will aggressively act covertly anyway, partly due to their frustration with government inability to act in a timely and effective manner by other means, such as by legal indictments or economic sanctions. In the aforementioned 2016 institute survey of Information Technology security practitioners involved in endpoint security, 64 percent said their organizations are pursuing now or planning to pursue an offensive security capability, described as to discover who is behind an attack and then to counterattack.[80] Furthermore, the Black Hat USA 2016 conference even offered a technical course in "Active Defense, Offensive Countermeasures and Hacking Back" to learn "how to force an attacker to take more moves to attack your network . . . to detect them" and "how to gain better attribution" and "how to get access to a bad guy's system."[81] While the Black Hat site claims this could be done legally, the last objective neglects the reality that often the source of the attack is a compromised computer of an unwitting third party and any aggressive action after unauthorized access could result in undesired collateral damage.

The potential for collateral damage to an innocent third party highlights the importance of attribution. However, the determination of "absolute attribution can be difficult if not near impossible."[82] Therefore, if absolute identification is unrealistic, could a legal framework prevent mistakes and consequences from the employment of hack back in case of misattribution? One way, suggested by Anthony Glosson, to protect against the dangers of misattribution and other associated risks, would be for Congress to accommodate hack back by "adding a qualified active defense right to the CFAA. The right would balance the active defense privilege with misattribution concerns by imposing strict liability for harm caused during misdirected active defense efforts."[83] Glosson believes "firms will use active defense tactics only when they have an appropriate degree of confidence in the identity of their targets."[84] Under certain conditions, those tactics could include disruptive options to disable an attacker's system or destructive measures to destroy stolen trade secrets. Even still, a lingering concern if counterattacks were somehow made legal is that too many of the techniques would cause severe and irreparable harm to not just innocent third parties from misattribution, but also to the attacker's systems that could result in escalation. If the attacker perceives the hack back as disproportionate to the initial attack, it could invite a stronger counterattack against more valuable systems.[85]

Taking all considerations into account, the IP Commission determined that only the DHS, the DOD, and law enforcement agencies should have the legal authority to use countermeasures against targeted attackers for unauthorized intrusions into national security and critical infrastructure networks.[86] This legal authority already exists in international law for state use of countermeasures, as previously described in three distinct forms with associated conditions and restrictions:

- *Injured State*: has the right to resort to proportionate countermeasures against a responsible state for an internationally wrongful act to include a violation of a treaty or customary law obligation.
- *Plea of Necessity*: may be invoked to justify a state's resort to countermeasures when faced with a grave and imminent threat to an essential interest to include in certain cases where the exact nature or origin of a cyber attack is not clear.
- *Due Diligence*: principle allows a state to resort to countermeasures if a responsible state fails to meet its obligation to not allow cyber infrastructure located on its territory to be used to mount a cyber operation that results in serious adverse consequences in another country.

The three categories of allowable state responses represent sovereign privileges granted to nations. If the United States or its allies disrespect the law by sanctioning private hack back, others will most likely cite use as precedent.

A myriad of complications would follow that would weaken efforts to sustain customary law and create international norms. For instance, would China or Russia even know that a damaging attack by a private company is not an official cyber attack signaling state response? Also, would Iran or North Korea adopt a similar retaliatory policy through use of hacker groups not under state control or direction?[87]

The IP Commission determination on authority for only government use of countermeasures appears valid given the risks of private sector hack back. Thus the use of tailored disruption capacities is probably best left to government agencies, especially for disruptive activities outside victim's network, such as taking control of remote computers or launching denial of service attacks. However, the difficulty with this determination lies in the question of whether the government really has the capacity to defend the private sector, or even the willingness to do so, given the high thresholds for response delineated in international law and reiterated in national strategy. For instance, in the United States, the DOD mission to defend the nation and its interests applies to "cyberattacks of significant consequence" which may include "loss of life, significant damage to property, serious adverse U.S. foreign policy consequences, or serious economic impact on the United States."[88] The magnitude of these consequences would not apply to many of the cyber attacks seen today. Likewise, many of the organizations experiencing cyber attacks do not fall into the category of "national security and critical infrastructure" delineated by the IP Commission. If the government were to respond to more common incidents for more common organizations, then a new precedence would be set below the current threshold of government response.

The Department of Defense Cyber Strategy recognizes that the "private sector owns and operates over ninety percent of all the networks and infrastructures of cyberspace and is thus the first line of defense,"[89] not a surprising statement since the talent, tools, and technical capacity reside primarily in the private sector. What is surprising is that the private sector has already publicly used hack back with proven success in multiple incidents, as documented by Anthony Glosson. In his first example, Google mounted an active defense campaign in response to Chinese hacker intrusions into private Gmail accounts in 2009. Google gained access to a computer in Taiwan used by the hackers to see evidence of the attack. The evidence revealed the breaches of the so-called Operation Aurora were not only at Google, but also at thirty-three other companies, including Adobe Systems and Northrop Grumman. Google shared the evidence with American intelligence and law enforcement officials and cooperated with them to determine the origin of the attack was on the Chinese mainland.[90] In a second instance, Facebook used active defense tactics in response to the compromise of Facebook servers by the "Koobface" gang in 2011. Koobface installed a virus on user devices to draft their computer into a botnet, hijack web searches to deliver clicks to unscrupulous marketers, and trick the user into paying for fake antivirus software.[91] Facebook Security performed a technical takedown of the gang's command and control server to exfiltrate evidence and disable it. Facebook then shared its intelligence with the online security community and law enforcement agencies to rid the web of the Koobface virus.[92]

For legal use of tailored disruption capacities outside the victim's network, after taking the factors of willingness, capacity, and benefits into account, a better option than relying only on the government could be closely regulated use by licensed private companies under limited circumstances. The concept of licensed privateers to augment government capability has a strong historical basis in the maritime environment. By applying this logic to the cyber domain, a reasonable contention is that "a limited number of entities certified by the government and working with the government could add to the government's capabilities to address extensive cyber intrusions through the application of active defense."[93] To ordain this contention, revised laws might not even be necessary, as a new legal framework could capitalize on clauses in existing laws. Section 1030(f) of the CFAA's unauthorized access ban "does not prohibit any lawfully authorized investigative, protective, or intelligence activity of a law enforcement agency of the United States, a State, or a political subdivision of a State, or of an intelligence agency of the United States."[94] In essence, Section 1030(f) is "an explicit exception from the CFAA for law enforcement agencies" which allows them "to undertake normally prohibited cyberattacks."[95] Since there is "no explicit provision exempting private companies from the CFAA," an approach proposed by Zach West is to "deputize U.S. companies under Section 1030(f)."[96]

The Active Cyber Defense Task Force Project Report released in October 2016 agrees that "there is a need for government to partner with the private sector in developing and implementing a framework for active defense. Such a framework would allow forward-leaning and technologically advanced private entities to effectively defend their assets in cyberspace, while at the same time ensuring that such actions are embedded in a framework that confirms government oversight."[97] The pertinent question is what delineations or limitations should be made for the type of malicious actor and the type of disruptive action to be used against them by licensed private companies in various scenarios outside the network? In consideration of risk, a sliding scale of aggressive actions could be applied in "limited circumstances in cooperation with or under delegated authority of a national government:"[98]

- *Nation-states*: the use of countermeasures against state organs, namely military or intelligence agencies has potential to cause escalation. Therefore aggressive actions, such as denial of service or damage to their computers should only be undertaken by government agencies. Countermeasures against persons or groups acting on the instructions of, or under the direction or control of a state, could be conducted by licensed private companies but limited to embed beacons, traceback property, and delete stolen data. The Task Force Report argues that retrieval attempts are not likely to succeed because an advanced adversary would replicate, hide, or back up stolen data.[99] Thus the data should be wiped in route on a third party server before local business hours of the adversary.

- *Hacker Groups*: the use of countermeasures against loosely state-affiliated "hackers for hire" groups would be to deny their objective of stealing competitive or confidential information. For commercial victims, this activity would most likely fall below the current threshold of government response. Therefore, countermeasures could be conducted by licensed private companies but mostly limited to embed beacons, trace back property, and delete stolen data. The insertion of logic bombs into files before stolen to damage computers when opened is risky but would prevent initial access to files before replication and dispersion. The use of countermeasures against movements like Anonymous would be to halt their hacktivist campaign. The challenge is the difficulty of interfering with tens of thousands of enthused citizens using their computers for typical denial of service attacks, or worse, collateral damage to compromised computers in botnets. Countermeasures against the verified source of an intrusion, like by a skilled hacker attempting SQL injection, could be conducted by licensed private companies in order to achieve signaling, to include denial of service or implanting malware to damage the hacker's computer.
- *Criminal Organizations*: the use of countermeasures against criminal syndicates would be to halt the theft of financial assets and sensitive information. For commercial victims, this activity would most certainly fall below the current threshold of government response. Therefore, countermeasures could be conducted by licensed private companies to not just delete stolen data but bait files with malware to photograph the actor for evidence for prosecution. An alternative is to implant ransomware to lock down the computer to impose proportionate costs.
- *Terrorist Groups*: the use of countermeasures against an organized armed group like the Islamic State would fall under the category of armed conflict and is best left to the military.

Granted, the Zach West framework for use of deputized US companies adopted here is slightly different than the one suggested in the Task Force Report. Yet given the proven utility of hack back by the private sector, for the category of outside the victim's network, the strategy of active cyber defense could be *technically capable and legally viable* for use in deterring the wide variety of malicious actors—however, only by licensed private companies under the supervision and approval of proper authorities, such as by the Department of Justice under CFAA Section 1030(f) exceptions, in certain authorized scenarios.

Illustrative Case

The 2016 hack into the DNC network outlined earlier provides an illustrative case for final analysis of the sufficiency of traditional deterrence strategies or the alternative strategy of active cyber defense. The Obama administration hesitated to publicly name Russia as behind the hack into the DNC and also into other Democratic Party accounts, as the campaign was revealed to be wider than first thought.[100] Some prominent figures, such as US House Democratic Leader Nancy Pelosi, bluntly said, "It is the Russians."[101] However, US intelligence officials said, "publicly blaming Russian President Vladimir Putin's intelligence services would bring instant pressure on Washington to divulge its evidence, which relies on highly classified sources and methods."[102] Regardless, the United States issued on October 7 a statement of blame,[103] continuing their "name and shame" strategy. Russian Foreign Minister Sergei Lavrov said it was flattering but a baseless accusation, in not seeing "a single fact, a single proof."[104]

The absence of presented evidence of Russian culpability is counter to the 2015 UN Group of Governmental Experts report that accusations of "wrongful acts brought against states should be substantiated."[105] As a matter of policy, formulating the right kind of response for deterrence in this case is not straightforward. American agencies assembled a menu of options for President Obama ranging from exposing President Putin's financial ties to oligarchs to manipulating the computer code used by Russia in designing its cyberweapons.[106] Some of the options were rejected as ineffective and others as too risky. For the first, James Lewis doubted "using intelligence findings to embarrass Mr. Putin . . . would be the solution."[107] For the latter, to manipulate or even expose Russian hacking tools, which they hold dear, risks exposure of American software implants. For specific sanctions in retaliation, the impact is questionable, given the limited effect of sanctions levied on Russia for the Crimea incursion.[108] And the use of offensive cyber means to attack Russian networks would likely induce rapid escalation while the U.S. cannot ensure escalation dominance.[109] For deterrence by denial, the DNC announced the creation of a Cybersecurity Advisory Board "composed of distinguished experts in the field"[110] to prevent future attacks, and other Democratic organizations have been "shoring up their cybersecurity defenses,"[111] which might all prove to be hopeless, given the APT groups' ability to easily bypass security defenses if determined to do so. They did not try very hard in a less aggressive phishing attempt to penetrate the Republican National Committee computers at the time of the DNC hack.[112]

For the strategy of deterrence by entanglement, the question begs was the DNC intrusion really outside international norms of acceptable behavior?[113] Michael Schmitt said, "hacking the DNC's emails is an act of political espionage, which is not a breach of international law."[114] Nonetheless, Schmitt said Russia's apparent attempt to influence the outcome of the election "probably violates the international law barring intervention in a state's internal affairs."[115] Yet what proof besides circumstantial[116] exists that Russia directly gave the material to WikiLeaks or that the release was directed by Russia?[117] Even though the United States believes President Putin most likely gave broad direction to hack US political institutions, a senior administration official said, "We don't have Putin's fingerprints on anything or a piece of paper that shows he signed the order."[118] The US assessment based on analysis of intelligence, not any evidence, depicts how hard it is to achieve attribution to satisfy international law criteria for state responsibility.[119] This synopsis of deterrence strategy shortfalls is further exacerbated by FireEye saying the two APT groups "wanted experts and policy makers to know that Russia is behind it [the DNC hack]."[120] Finally, on December 29, President Obama imposed sanctions on Russian entities,[121] expelled thirty-five Russian intelligence operatives, and closed two Russian recreational compounds in the United States."[122] In addition, a Joint Analysis Report released data on malware used by Russian intelligence services.[123] President Putin said Russia wouldn't retaliate and expel US diplomats and even invited their children to a New Year's celebration at the Kremlin, in a public display of restraint aimed to embarrass the Obama administration.[124]

The reality today is advanced actors continue their operations at a high pace, adapting in the open, with little risk of real punishment. The failure of cyber deterrence strategies highlighted by the US election hacking episode, despite the past eight years of efforts by the Obama administration,[125] leaves open the question of the strategy of active cyber defense to deny benefits or impose costs. To get into the DNC network, CrowdStrike suspected the APT groups may have targeted employees with "spearphishing" emails,[126] a preferred vector used by both Cozy Bear and Fancy Bear to target their victims.[127] The use of this common attack vector which has such a high success rate meant penetration was probably inevitable.[128] After Cozy Bear installed the SeaDaddy implant and Fancy Bear installed X-Agent malware for automatic or remote execution,[129] they placed themselves already at phase five of the cyber kill chain. Although the DNC information technology team did notice some unusual network activity and reported it in late April, the files were already stolen and the damage done. Inside the network, the groups did have to move across two phases of the kill chain after installation, which opens the possibility that active cyber defense capabilities could have stopped the attack before action on objectives. FireEye has seen Cozy Bear on some systems "moving laterally within a network. They know that their tool is going to be detected by a system that they're about to move to and they'll do it anyway because they're such skilled hackers that they can compromise the system and then jump to another system and get what they need before they can be quarantined."[130] Active cyber defense operates at cyber relevant speed,[131] leveling the playing field to isolate the threat.

The president of CrowdStrike said the DNC "was not engaged in a fair fight" since "you've got ordinary citizens who are doing hand-to-hand combat with trained military officers."[132] Yet CrowdStrike, a leading private firm, are not ordinary citizens, but undoubtedly the experts in the field. They not only identified the two Russian intelligence-affiliated hacker groups in the network, but watched advanced methods to avoid detection, such as changing implants, modifying persistence methods, and moving to new command and control channels.[133] CrowdStrike considers the APT groups to be some of the best of all the numerous nation-state, criminal, hacktivist, and terrorist groups they encounter. In this incident, CrowdStrike was in the network with them and in the best position to launch countermeasures outside the network.

If the attackers were already at exfiltration, maybe CrowdStrike could have seen the files sitting on an overseas server. General Michael Hayden said he is "aware of a company that did see its data stolen, was able to track where it had gone" and "it is not yet the waking hours during the work week of the country in which they believe the source of the attack emanated . . . and so it's just sitting there on this server in a third country place waiting for the thieves to come grab it and bring it home."[134] Maybe a licensed private company, deputized under existing law, and under proper government oversight and supervision, could have traced and deleted the DNC files.

CONCLUDING CONSIDERATIONS

In the summer of 2015 eight top congressional leaders were briefed that Russian hackers were attacking the Democratic Party, but not the target because the information was so secret.[135] A year and a half later, Crowd-Strike provided proof through malware analysis that the APT group Fancy Bear that struck the DNC was a unit of the GRU, Russia's Main Intelligence Directorate.[136] The apparent motivation to affect US public opinion appears to have been greater than any perceived risk induced by current deterrence strategies. For deterrence is a matter of perception that "resides ultimately in the eye of the beholder."[137] Lieutenant General James McLaughlin has stated that the Defense Department, in a whole-of-government approach, seeks to "deny the adversary the ability to achieve the objectives of a cyber attack, so our adversary will believe any attack will be futile." Furthermore, the adversary must believe "that our ability to respond to an attack will result in unacceptable costs imposed on them" through the use of "a variety of mechanisms, including economic sanctions, diplomacy, law enforcement, and military action."[138] Cumulatively these statements describe the desired outcomes of the traditional deterrence strategies of retaliation, denial, and entanglement. The problem today is malicious actors in cyberspace do not believe that a threat of retaliation exists, the intended action cannot succeed, or the costs outweigh the benefits of acting.[139] It would be naïve and negligent to think they will not try "again and again."[140] Another strategy is necessary to induce the perception of risk and repercussion into the wide range of malicious actors engaging in cyber attacks.

An alternative strategy of active cyber defense would embrace a combination of internal systemic resilience to deny benefits and tailored disruption capacities to impose costs. Internal systemic resilience starts with closing the gap in time from compromise to discovery inside the network. Mandiant claims that its Red Team is able to obtain access to domain administrator credentials within three days of gaining initial access to a system. Once credentials are found, it is only a matter of time before the attacker is able to locate desired information. If the average time to discovery is now at 146 days, that is at least 143 days too long.[141] In response, active cyber defense can detect, verify, and remediate activity along the cyber kill chain to withstand the attack. It does not matter if attribution exists to identify exactly who is the actor, only that the attack is stopped before harm or damage from the breach occurs, to deny benefit of the attack. Outside the network, to impose costs, maybe the time has come to use tailored disruption capacities that target hackers "with some of their own weapons: government-sanctioned malware or ransomware, software that locks down a computer without a user's consent."[142]

For deterrence to be effective, the strategy must be based on capability (possess means to influence behavior), credibility (instilling believability), and communication (of right message). The level of skill seen in the DNC hacks is not limited to APT groups. As Kevin Haley, director of Symantec Security Response states, "Advanced criminal attack groups now echo the skill sets of nation-state attackers."[143] Active cyber defense has the capability to withstand an attack by any of these actors through use of numerous heuristics or attack detectors combined with automated remediation actions. Also, the DNC hack represents another use of proxy groups for plausible deniability, codified in the "inevitable Kremlin response: Prove It."[144] Inside the network, active cyber defense has the credibility to block the attack before objectives, denying the need to "prove it," or even better, outside the network, to find the files and take discrete action. Finally, the DNC hack that induced unprecedented interference in the electoral process of a nation signifies a test by Moscow of the limits of acceptable state behavior in cyberspace.[145] Signaling, a corollary to communication, is a foreign policy instrument "to change the cost-benefit calculations of states engaging in or sponsoring" malicious cyber activity.[146] Any decision to legally allow companies to engage malicious actors would communicate national resolve. Senator Whitehouse has said that "policymakers should consider allowing companies to engage in "active defense" of their networks," ranging from "tracking the flow of a company's information across networks," or to hack back where it seems "to make sense in certain, very narrow circumstances."[147] Although the parameters and limitations have yet to be fully explored, active cyber defense potentially meets the conditions of capability, credibility, and communication to be considered or selected as an alternative strategy to achieve deterrence within the cyber arena.

NOTES

1. Calvin Biesecker, "Comey Says Deterrence against Cyber Threats Showing Results," *Defense Daily*, August 30, 2016.

2. Calvin Biesecker, "White House Proposing Major Increase in Federal Cyber Security Spending," *Defense Daily*, February 9, 2016.

3. The White House, "The President's Fiscal Year 2017 Budget," Fact Sheet, February 9, 2016.

4. The White House, "Cybersecurity National Action Plan," Fact Sheet, February 9, 2016.

5. Larry Ponemon, "Flipping the Economics of Attacks," ISACA Now Blog, January 26, 2016.

6. G. Mark Hardy, "Beyond Continuous Monitoring: Threat Modeling for Real-Time Response," A SANS Whitepaper, October 2012, 1.

7. MITRE Corporation, "Adversarial Tactics, Techniques and Common Knowledge: Lateral Movement," June 27, 2016, https://attack.mitre.org/wiki/Lateral_Movement.

8. Solutionary, "Global Threat Intelligence Report: Practical Application of Security Controls to the Cyber Kill Chain," 2016 NTT Group, 21–46.

9. CyberEdge Group, "2016 Cyberthreat Defense Report," Executive Summary, 2016, 1–2.

10. National Institute of Standards and Technology, "Framework for Improving Critical Infrastructure Cybersecurity," Draft Version 1.1, January 10, 2017, 1.

11. Shane Harris and Paul Sonne, "Intelligence Chief Defends Finding Russia Meddled in Election," *Wall Street Journal*, January 6, 2017.

12. Department of Defense. *Joint Operations* . Joint Publication 3-0 (Washington, DC: Office of the Chairman, Joint Chiefs of Staff, 17 January 2017) xxii.

13. Mandiant, "M-Trends 2016," Special Report, February 2016, 9.

14. James R. Clapper, "Worldwide Threat Assessment of the US Intelligence Community," Statement for the Record for the Senate Armed Services Committee, February 9, 2016, 1–4.

15. Dennis K. Berman, "Adm. Michael Rogers on the Prospect of a Digital Pearl Harbor," *Wall Street Journal*, October 26, 2015.

16. Shimon Prokupecz, Tal Kopan, and Sonia Moghe, "Former Official: Iranians Hacked into New York Dam," *CNN Politics*, December 22, 2015.

17. Michael Assante, "Confirmation of a Coordinated Attack on the Ukrainian Power Grid," SANS Industrial Control Systems Security Blog, January 9, 2016.

18. Kim Zetter, "Inside the Cunning, Unprecedented Hack of Ukraine's Power Grid," *Wired*, March 3, 2016.

19. Pavel Polityuk, "Ukraine Sees Russian Hand in Cyber Attack on Power Grid," *Reuters*, February 12, 2016.

20. Warwick Ashford, "Ukraine Cyber Attacks Extend Beyond Power Companies, Says Trend Micro," *Computer Weekly*, February 12, 2016.

21. Marshall Abrams and Joe Weiss, "Malicious Control System Cyber Security Attack Case Study—Maroochy Water Services, Australia," The MITRE Corporation, August 2008.

22. Robert M. Lee, Michael J. Assante, and Tim Conway, "German Still Mill Cyber Attack," SANS Industrial Control Systems, December 30, 2014, 1–15.

23. Kim Zetter, "A Cyberattack Has Caused Confirmed Physical Damage for the Second Time Ever," *Wired*, January 8, 2015.

24. Greg Otto, "U.S. Power Grid Cyberattack: When, Not If, Says NSA Chief," *FedScoop*, March 1, 2016.

25. Shanghai Business and Finance, "China's Stockmarket Crashes—Again," *The Economist*, January 4, 2016; and Chris Matthews, "Why China's Stock Market Crash Could Spark a Trade War," *Fortune*, January 7, 2016; and also Corrie Driebusch and Riva Gold, "Dow Tumbles Nearly 400 Points on China Worries," *Wall Street Journal*, January 8, 2016.

26. Sean Lyngaas, "U.S. Official: Russian Cyberwarfare Getting More Sophisticated," *Federal Computer Weekly*, February 2016, 8.

27. David E. Sanger, "Nuclear Facilities in 20 Countries May Be Easy Targets for Cyberattacks," *New York Times*, January 14, 2016.

28. Caroline Baylon with Roger Brunt and David Livingstone, "Cyber Security at Civil Nuclear Facilities," Chatham House Report, September 2015, i–x.

29. Ponemon Institute, "2015 Global Study on IT Security Spending and Investments," Research Report, May 2015, 1–14.

30. Warwick Ashford, "IT Decision Makers Admit They Need to Do More to Protect Data," *Computer Weekly*, March 15, 2016.

31. Hewlett Packard Enterprise, "Companies Cautiously Optimistic about Cybersecurity," In-depth Analysis, January 2016, 1–7.

32. Scott Charney et al., Microsoft Corporation, "From Articulation to Implementation: Enabling Progress on Cybersecurity Norms," June 2016, 9.

33. Asia Maritime Transparency Initiative, "China's New Spratly Island Defenses," December 13, 2016.

34. Jeremy Page, "China's Weapons Stoke Sea Dispute," *The Wall Street Journal*, December 16, 2016.

35. US District Court, Indictment, Criminal No. 14-118, Filed May 1, 2014, 1–48.

36. Ellen Nakashima, "Chinese government has arrested hackers it says breached OPM database," *Washington Post*, December 2, 2015.

37. U.S.-China Economic and Security Review Commission, "2016 Report to Congress," November 2016: 293.

38. The Honorable James R. Clapper, et al., "Foreign Cyber Threats to the United States," Joint Statement for the Record to the Senate Armed Services Committee, 5 January 2017: 4.

39. Christopher M. Matthews, "U.S. Charges Seven Iranians in Hacking Attacks," *Wall Street Journal*, March 24, 2016.

40. Jay Solomon, "Iran Missile Launch Detected, a Possible Violation of U.N. Resolution," *The Wall Street Journal*, January 30, 2017.

41. US Industrial Control System—Computer Emergency Response Team (ICS CERT), Department of Homeland Security, "Cyber-Attack against Ukrainian Critical Infrastructure," Alert (IR-Alert-H-16-056-01), February 25, 2016.

42. National Cyber Security Division, Department of Homeland Security, "Improving Industrial Control Systems Cybersecurity with Defense-in-Depth Strategies," October 2009, 1–34.

43. Verizon, "2016 Data Breach Investigations Report," May 2016, 10.

44. McAfee, "Net Losses: Estimating the Global Cost of Cybercrime," with Center for Strategic and International Studies, June 2014, 1–23.

45. Joseph Menn, "Top Cybercrime Ring Disrupted as Authorities Raid Moscow Offices," *Reuters*, February 6, 2016.

46. Joseph Menn and Eric Beech, "U.S., China Reach Agreement on Guidelines for Requesting Assistance Fighting Cyber Crime," *Reuters*, December 3, 2015.

47. Ellen Nakashima, "Hacked U.S. Companies Have More Options, Departing Cybersecurity Official Says," *Washington Post*, March 2, 2016.

48. US Department of Defense, *Deterrence Operations Joint Operating Concept*, Version 2.0 (Washington, DC: US Strategic Command, December 2006), 23.

49. US Department of Defense, *Joint Operation Planning*, US Joint Publication 5-0 (Washington, DC: The Joint Staff, August, 11 2011), E-2.

50. US Department of Defense, *The DOD Cyber Strategy*, April 2015, 11.

51. Department of Defense, *Joint Operations.* Joint Publication 3-0 (Washington, DC: Office of the Chairman, Joint Chiefs of Staff, 17 January 2017), VI-4.

52. Joseph Marks, "Obama's Cyber Legacy: He Did Almost Everything Right and It Still Turned Out Wrong," *NEXTGOV*, January 17, 2017.

53. Calvin Biesecker, "Comey Says Deterrence against Cyber Threats Showing Results," *Defense Daily*, August 30, 2016.

54. The National Bureau of Asian Research, "The Report of the Commission on the Theft of American Intellectual Property," May 2013, 81.

55. National Bureau of Asian Research, "The Report of the Commission on the Theft of American Intellectual Property," 80.

56. M-Trends 2016, 4.

57. Verizon, "2016 Data Breach Investigations Report," May 2016, 11.

58. Ponemon Institute, "2016 State of Endpoint Report," April 2016, 16.

59. Steve Schick, "LightCyber Unveils Second Generation Magna Platform," LightCyber Press Releases, July 30, 2014, http://lightcyber.com/lightcyber-unveils-second-generation-magna-platform/.

60. Carbon Black, "Breach Detection: What You Need to Know," eBook, 2016, 1–18.

61. Ed Tittel and Gajraj Singh, *Endpoint Detection and Response for Dummies*, Tripwire Special Edition (Hoboken, NJ; Wiley, 2016), 11–16.

62. Tittel and Singh, *Endpoint Detection and Response for Dummies*, 22–24.

63. Anomali, "Operationalizing Threat Intelligence Data: The Problems of Relevance and Scale," White Paper, 2016, 1–4.

64. Palo Alto Networks, "WildFire Data Sheet," 2015, 1–4.

65. LogRhythm, "LogRhythm Threat Intelligence Ecosystem," Product Overview, 2015, 1–2.

66. Armor, "Threat Intelligence," ebook: An *SC Magazine* publication, 2016, 1–7.

67. Solutionary, "Global Threat Intelligence Report: The Role of the Cyber Kill Chain in Threat Intelligence," 2016 NTT Group, 52–55.

68. Threat Connect, "Threat Intelligence Platforms," Report, 2015, 30.

69. CyberEdge Group, "2016 Cyberthreat Defense Report," Section 4, Future Plans, 2016, 31.

70. WatchGuard, "Host Sensor," Data Sheet, 2017: 1-2.

71. Carbon Black, "Cb Response," Data Sheet, 2017, 1–2.

72. Lastline, "NSS Labs Test: Lastline Most Effective in Advanced Malware Detection," Data Sheet, 2017: 1-2.

73. TripWire, "Solutions for Endpoint Detection and Response," Solution Brief, 2015, 1–5.

74. CrowdStrike, "Falcon Insight: Endpoint Detection and Response (EDR)," Solution Brief, 2017:1-5.

75. John Breeden III, "Network World Gives HawkEye G 4.875 out of 5," *Network World*, December 8, 2014.

76. Report of the Commission, 81.

77. Report of the Commission, 83.

78. Peter Sullivan, "Hacking back: A Viable Strategy or a Major Risk?" Tech Target, June 27, 2016.

79. Sean L. Harrington, "Cyber Security Active Defense: Playing with Fire or Sound Risk Management," *Richmond Journal of Law and Technology* 20, no. 4 (September 17, 2014): 27.

80. Ponemon Institute, "2016 State of Endpoint Report," April 2016, 16.

81. Black Hat USA 2016, "Active Defense, Offensive Countermeasures and Hacking Back," SANS—John Strand, Registration Site, July 30–August 2, 2016.

82. Shane McGee, Randy V. Sabett, and Anand Shah, "Adequate Attribution: A Framework for Developing a National Policy for Private Sector Use of Active Defense," *Journal of Business and Technology Law* 8, no. 1, Article 3 (2013): 5–7.

83. Anthony D. Glosson, "Active Defense: An Overview of the Debate and a Way Forward," Mercatus Center, August 2015, 23.

84. Glosson, "Active Defense," 24–26.

85. Emilio Iasiello, "Hacking Back: Not the Right Solution," *Parameters* 44(3) (Autumn 2014): 110.

86. Report of the Commission, 80–83.

87. James Andrew Lewis, "Private Retaliation in Cyberspace," Commentary, *Center for Strategic and International Studies*, May 22, 2013.

88. US Department of Defense, "The DoD Cyber Strategy," April 2015, 4–5.

89. US Department of Defense, "The DoD Cyber Strategy," 4–5.

90. David E. Sanger and John Markoff, "After Google's Stand on China, U.S. Treads Lightly," *New York Times*, January 14, 2010.

91. Riva Richmond, "Web Gang Operating in the Open," *New York Times*, January 16, 2012.

92. Facebook Security Team, "Facebook's Continued Fight against Koobface," January 17, 2012, https://www.facebook.com/notes/facebook-security/facebooks-continued-fight-against-koobface/10150474399670766/.

93. Franklin D. Kramer and Melanie J. Teplinsky, "Cybersecurity and Tailored Deterrence," Atlantic Council, December 2013, 6.

94. 18 U.S.C. and 1030 (f).

95. Zach West, "Young Fella, If You're Looking for Trouble I'll Accommodate You: Deputizing Private Companies for the Use of Hackback," *Syracuse Law Review* 63 (2012): 139–40.

96. West, "Young Fella, If You're Looking for Trouble I'll Accommodate You," 139–40.

97. Center for Cyber and Homeland Security, "Into the Gray Zone: The Private Sector and Active Defense against Cyber Threats," Project Report, The George Washington University, October 2016, v.

98. Center for Cyber and Homeland Security, "Into the Gray Zone," 9.

99. Center for Cyber and Homeland Security, "Into the Gray Zone," 12.

100. Eric Lichtblau and Eric Schmitt, "Hack of Democrats' Accounts Was Wider Than Believed, Officials Say," *New York Times*, August 10, 2016.

101. Susan Cornwell, "U.S. House Democratic Leader Blames Russians for 'Electronic Watergate'," *Reuters*, Politics Section, August 11, 2016.

102. Warren Strobel and John Walcott, "U.S. Weighs Dangers, Benefits of Naming Russia in Cyber Hack," *Reuters*, United States Edition, August 1, 2016.

103. Director of National Intelligence, "Joint DHS and ODNI Election Security Statement," Press Release, October 7, 2016, 1.

104. Nicole Gaouette and Elise Labott, "Russia, US Move Past Cold War to Unpredictable Confrontation," *CNN News*, October 12, 2016.

105. United Nations General Assembly, "Group of Governmental Experts on Developments in the Field of Information and Telecommunications in the Context of International Security," A/70/174, July 22, 2015, 13.

106. David E. Sanger, "Obama Confronts Complexity of Using a Mighty Cyberarsenal against Russia," *New York Times*, December 17, 2016.

107. David E. Sanger and Nicole Perlroth, "What Options Does the U.S. Have after Accusing Russia of Hacks?" *New York Times*, October 8, 2016.

108. Karoun Demirjian, "Lawmakers Say Obama Should Start Thinking about Sanctioning Russia for Hacking," *Washington Post*, September 15, 2016.

109. Adam Segal, "After Attributing a Cyberattack to Russia, the Most Likely Response Is Non Cyber," *Net Politics*, Council of Foreign Relations, October 10, 2016.

110. Rich Edson, "DNC Creates 'Cybersecurity Advisory Board,' Will Notify Staff Affected by Hack," *Fox News*, August 11, 2016.

111. Eric Lichtblau and Eric Schmitt, "Hack of Democrats' Accounts Was Wider Than Believed, Officials Say," *New York Times*, August 10, 2016.

112. Shane Harris, Devlin Barrett, and Julian E. Barnes, "Republican National Committee Security Foiled Russian Hackers," *Wall Street Journal*, December 16, 2016.

113. Warren Strobel and John Walcott, "U.S. Weighs Dangers, Benefits of Naming Russia in Cyber Hack," *Reuters*, United States Edition, August 1, 2016.

114. Ellen Nakashima, "Russia's apparent meddling in U.S. election is not an act of war, cyber expert says," *The Washington Post*, February 7, 2017.

115. Ibid.

116. Threat Connect Research Team, "Guccifer 2.0: All Roads Lead to Russia," Featured Article, July 26, 2016.

117. Mark Pomerleau, "Cyber Issues from the Aspen Security Forum," *C4ISRNET*, August 4, 2016.

118. Shimon Prokupecz and Jeff Zeleny, "Intel Analysis Shows Putin Approved Election Hacking," *CNN News*, December 15, 2016.

119. International Law Commission, *Draft Articles on Responsibility of States for Internationally Wrongful Acts, with commentaries*, fifty-third session, 2001: Article 8.

120. Patrick Tucker, "Russia Wanted to Be Caught, Says Company Waging War on the DNC Hackers," *Defense One*, July 28, 2016.

121. President Barack Obama, "Taking Additional Steps to Address to Address the National Emergency with Respect to Significant Malicious Cyber-Enabled Activities," Executive Order and Annex, The White House, December 29, 2016.

122. President Barack Obama, "Statement by the President on Actions in Response to Russian Malicious Cyber Activity and Harassment," The White House, December 29, 2016.

123. Office of the Press Secretary, "Fact Sheet: Actions in Response to Russian Malicious Cyber Activity and Harassment," The White House, December 29, 2016.

124. James Marson and Anne Ferris-Rotman, "Putin Says He Won't Retaliate," *Wall Street Journal*, December 31, 2016.

125. David Fidler, "President Obama's Pursuit of Cyber Deterrence Ends in Failure," *Net Politics*, January 4, 2017.

126. Ellen Nakashima, "Russian Government Hackers Penetrated DNC, Stole Opposition Research on Trump," *Washington Post*, June 14, 2016.

127. FireEye, "APT28: At the Center of the Storm," Special Report, January 2017, 11.

128. Kaspersky, "The Dangers of Phishing: Help Employees Avoid the Lure of Cybercrime," White Paper, 2015, 1–8.

129. Dmitri Alperovitch, "Bears in the Midst: Intrusion into the Democratic National Committee," CrowdStrike Blog, June 15, 2016.

130. Patrick Tucker, "Russia Wanted to Be Caught, Says Company Waging War on the DNC Hackers," *Defense One*, July 28, 2016.

131. US Department of Defense, *Strategy for Operating in Cyberspace*, July 2011, 7.

132. Nakashima, "Russian Government Hackers Penetrated DNC."

133. Dmitri Alperovitch, "Bears in the Midst: Intrusion into the Democratic National Committee," CrowdStrike Blog, June 15, 2016.

134. General Michael V. Hayden, "HBO What to Do about Cyberattack," Council on Foreign Relations Event, October 6, 2015.

135. Mark Hosenball and John Walcott, "Exclusive: Congressional Leaders Were Briefed a Year Ago on Hacking of Democrats—Sources," *Reuters*, Politics Section, August 12, 2016.

136. Thomas Fox-Brewster, "This Android Malware Ties Russian Intelligence to the DNC Hacks," *Forbes*, December 22, 2016.

137. Michael Mandelbaum, "It's the Deterrence, Stupid," *The American Interest*, July 30, 2015.

138. Thomas Atkin, James K. McLaughlin, and Charles L. Moore, "Statement before the House Armed Services Committee," June 22, 2016.

139. Department of Defense. *Joint Operations* . Joint Publication 3-0 (Washington, DC: Office of the Chairman, Joint Chiefs of Staff, 17 January 2017), VI-4.

140. Patrick Tucker, "Russian Hackers Will Try 'Again and Again,' Warns Samantha Power," *Defense One*, January 17, 2017.

141. M-Trends 2016, 4.

142. Adrienne Lafrance, "Hacking and the Future of Warfare," *The Atlantic*, June 12, 2015.

143. "Rene Millman, "Cyber-Criminals Becoming Increasingly Professional," *SC Magazine*, April 13, 2016.

144. Andrew Roth, "How the Kremlin Is Sure to Keep Its Fingerprints Off Any Cyberattack," *Washington Post*, August 2, 2016.

145. Matthijs Veenendaal, Kadri Kaska, Henry Rõigas, and Can Kasapoglu, "DNC Hack: An Escalation That Cannot Be Ignored," Tallinn, Estonia, NATO Cooperative Cyber Defense Center of Excellence, August 5, 2016.

146. Sico van der Meer, "Signalling as a Foreign Policy Instrument to Deter Cyber Aggression by State Actors," Policy Brief, Clingendael, Netherlands Institute of International Relations, December 2015, 1–6.

147. Sean Lyngaas, "Sen. Whitehouse Proposes a Cyber IG for Civilian Agencies," *Federal Computer Weekly*, June 6, 2016.

Appendix: National Strategy Agenda

The general theory of strategy enables a nation to cope with serious challenges to national security. For the United States, the President declares that "significant malicious cyber-enabled activities originating from, or directed by persons located, in whole or in substantial part, outside the United States continue to pose an unusual and extraordinary threat to the national security, foreign policy and economy of the United States."[1] Yet this threat is not unique to the United States. In a 2016 industry survey of medium-size organizations representing ten countries across North America, Europe, Asia Pacific, and Latin America, the percentage compromised by at least one successful cyber attack in the past twelve months ranged from 63 to 89 percent, with more than half between one to five times.[2] For these countries and any other, the principles and priorities of a national security strategy can guide the use of power and influence in countering the cyber threat. The strategy can signal resolve and readiness to deter, and if necessary to defeat malicious actors that threaten the advancement or survival of national interests. A smart national security strategy relies not only on military power to protect interests but draws upon all elements of national strength as means in a comprehensive national security agenda.

For the deterrence of malicious actors in cyberspace, evidence has shown that the strategy of active cyber defense is technically capable and legally viable, at least to some extent, to enable the achievement of the central premise of deterrence; the altering of the behavior of an actor. Active cyber defense reinforces both deterrence by denial and deterrence by retaliation. A national strategy agenda for active cyber defense has promise to instill in an actor the belief that the intended action cannot succeed and that a threat of retaliation exists. According to Admiral Mike Rogers, director of the NSA, "We are in a world now where, despite your best efforts, you must prepare and assume that you will be penetrated."[3] His warning to the audience at a London Stock Exchange event came shortly after similar comments by Jonathan Kidd, the Chief Information Security Officer for the United Kingdom Met Office that "You can't assume you're not already compromised."[4] In response, Kidd contends the best course of action is to develop a strategy on how to deal with that reality. That strategy is one of active cyber defense that embraces a combination of internal systemic resilience to halt malicious cyber activity after an intrusion with tailored disruption capacities to thwart malicious actor objectives. Therefore. to implement a strategy of active cyber defense, a national strategy agenda would be based on the two pillars of resilience to withstand a cyber attack and disruption to obstruct the malicious actor.

The first pillar of resilience prepares society for surprise in cyberspace through implementation of automated and integrated capabilities that act only inside organizational boundaries. The second pillar of disruption averts malicious actor asymmetries in cyberspace through countermeasures performed either by or under the supervision and approval of proper authorities. Since resources for a national strategy agenda will never be limitless, policy tradeoffs and hard choices among many competing priorities will have to be made. To set the debate for implementation by any country, this appendix begins by delineating how the national strategy pillars of resilience and disruption, enabled through a comprehensive approach, reside currently in principle in the cyber security strategies of international organizations and multiple nations. The appendix then explores architectures and arrangements in work in the United States to strengthen the two pillars for adaptation or use as deemed fit by other nations. The appendix finishes with policy recommendations and priority suggestions to guide tradeoffs and choices in action plans that implement a national strategy agenda for active cyber defense based on the two pillars of resilience and disruption.

CYBER SECURITY STRATEGIES

A national security strategy addresses the top strategic risks to national interests. Enduring national interests typically fall into four categories, namely the security of the nation and its citizens; a strong economy that promotes prosperity; respect for universal values; and a rules-based international order. To advance these interests most effectively, leaders pursue a national security agenda that allocates resources and prioritizes efforts according to strategic risk. For the United States, standing at the top of the list of strategic risks is a catastrophic attack on the US homeland or critical infrastructure. Consequently the present US National Security Strategy stresses the importance of "fortifying our critical infrastructure against all hazards, especially cyber espionage and attack." That objective necessitates working with the owners and operators of critical cyber infrastructure across every sector to decrease vulnerabilities and increase resilience.[5] In essence, this mandate means using a comprehensive approach which brings together all elements of society to make the nation resilient in the face of diverse threats. For that reason, Presidential Policy Directive PPD-21 "advances a national unity of effort to strengthen and maintain" not just secure and functioning, but also resilient critical infrastructure.[6] The emphasis on unity of effort for the purpose of resilience is also found in other cyber security strategies of international organizations and multiple nations.

Internal Systemic Resilience

Resilience at the international level is particularly important because digitally interconnected infrastructures that span the globe create both dependencies and vulnerabilities. The potential impact on society of disruptions to this fragile equilibrium makes interaction between the private sector which owns and operates most critical infrastructure and the public sector crucial to managing risk.[7] The Cybersecurity Strategy of the EU highlights the value of this interaction in a guiding principle that all relevant actors, whether the private sector or public authorities, need to recognize shared responsibility to ensure security of information and communications technologies. Accordingly, the EU made "achieving cyber resilience" the first strategic priority for action in their Strategy.[8] To promote cyber resilience among members, the EU Strategy recognizes a substantial effort is necessary to enhance private and public capacities and processes to prevent, detect and handle cyber security incidents. Since gaps exist in national capacities, the EU suggests members adopt a national strategy and cooperation plan, with incentives for private actors to invest in security solutions and provide reliable data on cyber incidents.[9]

A central principle of the National Cyber Security Strategy of the Czech Republic is a "comprehensive approach to cyber security based on principles of subsidiarity and cooperation."[10] The nation aims for coordination of activities and enhancement of trust among all stakeholders. Main goals for protection of national critical information infrastructure include: to enhance network resistance and integrity, share information in an efficient manner, and increase capacities for active cyber defense and cyber attack countermeasures. Likewise, the Italian National Strategic Framework for Cyberspace Security recognizes that network interdependence, asymmetric threats and the pervasive nature of cyberspace calls for a holistic approach and synergistic effort of all involved stakeholders. A strategic guideline of the Italian Strategy that echoes the tenets of active defense is to "leverage the national capability to analyze, prevent, mitigate and effectively react to the multidimensional cyber threat."[11] The National Cyber Security Strategy of the United Kingdom specifically calls for Active Cyber Defense as a Defend Element in order to implement "security measures to strengthen a network or system to make it more robust against attack."[12]

The Estonian Cyber Security Strategy recognizes that civilian and military resources must be integrated into a functioning whole to ensure the ability to provide national defense in cyberspace. One of the aims of this Strategy is to "describe methods for ensuring the uninterrupted operation and resilience of vital services."[13] Therefore, the information systems that are necessary for the operation of vital services are to be managed in a way that provides the means to manage risks. Furthermore, the Estonian Strategy dictates that civil and military cooperation must "function adequately in cyberspace with regards to warning, deterrence and active defense."[14] The Cyber Security Strategy of Georgia also aims to set up a system that will "facilitate resilience of cyber infrastructure against cyber threats."[15] It calls for cooperation modalities between state agencies that extend to public-private partnerships. Like Estonia, the Georgian Strategy appeals for a new legislative framework in order to develop and implement effective security measures.

In the Pacific, Australia's Cyber Security Strategy emphasizes the need for government and business to collaborate "to strengthen our economy and national security by building greater resilience to cyber security threats."[16] To achieve the goal of strong cyber defenses, the government will "co-design national voluntary Cyber Security Guidelines with the private sector to specify good practice." Furthermore, it will "establish a layered approach for sharing real time public-private threat information."[17] Similarly, the Japanese Cybersecurity Strategy recognizes that in order to "counter diversified cyber threats appropriately; the public and private sectors must closely collaborate in sharing information on system failures possibility caused by cyber attacks."[18] Therefore, the Japanese government intends to work to build platforms for an interactive and advanced information sharing environment. The Japanese Strategy emphasizes the need to limit the information to be shared and conceal informer identities, so they will not suffer unreasonable loss or disadvantage.

Tailored Disruption Capacities

The military has a role in protecting national interests in their assigned missions in defense of the nation. For instance, in the United States, US Cyber Command teams with federal, foreign, and industry partners to help "mitigate, halt, and attribute acts of disruption and destruction and campaigns of cyber espionage; dissuade adversaries from malicious behavior; and strengthen the resilience of Department of Defense systems to withstand attacks."[19] These functions require building information sharing mechanisms to ensure regular contact with those whom Cyber Command operates and fights alongside, both inside and outside the DOD. For instance, Cyber Command teams with the NSA to leverage its proven expertise in intelligence analysis and information assurance. When necessary, the command will help other agencies defend the nation against cyber attacks from abroad, especially if they would cause loss of life, property destruction, or significant foreign policy and economic consequences.[20] And when called upon, Cyber Command will utilize appropriate authorities and policies in their role as part of the federal government's response to attacks on critical infrastructure. Besides the United States, a few other nations have developed strategies that embrace broad tenets for use of tailored disruption capacities in a comprehensive approach to cyber security.

The Dutch Defense Cyber Command, established in 2014, is a smaller equivalent of the US Cyber Command. It is the central entity in the Netherlands for the development and use of offensive capability.[21] The country's Defense Cyber Strategy delineates that offensive cyber capabilities are "aimed at influencing or disabling the actions of an opponent."[22] Since the digital systems of potential opponents are vulnerable, cyberspace can be used for operations against that opponent. The strategy recognizes that a large-scale attack against society could have enormous impact and therefore the armed forces must be capable of taking action against digital threats to society. The armed forces have a core task to make capabilities available to civil authorities on request, and with the proper legal or regulatory basis, measures can be taken to improve the security and availability of Dutch cyberspace. In organizing a comprehensive approach in response to large-scale digital disruptions, the strategy recognizes that roles, tasks, and responsibilities have to be clear.[23] Any use by the military of capabilities in cyber operations would fall under the categories of Defensive Cyber Operations for proactive detection and termination of intruders and Offensive Counter Operations for preventive attacks.[24]

In 2015, the Israeli Defense Force decided to establish in two years a Cyber Command to lead the military's operational activities, although in Israel, protection of computerized systems in the civilian sector has never been put under the protection of the Israeli Defense Force. The reason to limit the military role appears to stem from ethical, ideological, and political values. Any further analysis on reasons and roles is difficult as Israel has never published an open, formal cyber security strategy, exercising political preference to avoid formal binding declarations and even using classification to shroud the topic.[25] Yet the nation has taken public steps to review national cyber policy through commission of their National Cyber Initiative in 2010. A task force was charged with putting Israel among "the top five countries leading the cyber field."[26] Many of their recommendations centered on aspects of Research and Development infrastructure, collaboration and products. The result of subsequent efforts is impressive as "Israel is responsible for more exports of cyber-related products and services than all other nations combined apart from the United States."[27] In fact, over the past five years, the number of Israeli cyber security companies has doubled to three hundred. Given the propensity of former Israeli Defense Force members, trained to use cutting edge technologies under tight discipline, to join these companies,[28] there is no shortage of talent for tailored disruption capacities.

ARCHITECTURES AND ARRANGEMENTS

Active cyber defense focuses on "the integration and automation of many services and mechanisms to execute response actions in cyber-relevant time."[29] The term cyber-relevant time ranges from nanoseconds to minutes depending on the location of the malicious actor and activity. The elements of active cyber defense synchronize "the real-time detection, analysis, and mitigation of threats to critical networks and systems."[30] These activities strive to stop or limit damage through the integration and automation of cyber-security solutions. Sets of solutions are deployed "across the interior and at the boundary of a network enterprise."[31] They can be unique tools integrated in a single platform or individual solutions, like for endpoint detection and response. In the United States, a collaborative effort between the NSA, the DHS and the Johns Hopkins University Applied Physics Laboratory has produced the reference architecture for the fundamental concept of Integrated Adaptive Cyber Defense (IACD), supported by a cooperative arrangement for automated indicator sharing (AIS). A key principle in the design of active cyber defense is for response actions to be automatable and not inherently automatic. While the intent is for these actions to stay inside the network, there are other innovative programs in the United States that could lead to military and civilian capacity for disruptive actions outside the network.

Internal Systemic Resilience

Integrated Adaptive Cyber Defense

The goal of IACD is to "dramatically change the timeline and effectiveness of cyber defense secure integration and automation" to enable faster response times and defensive capabilities."[32] The IACD reference architecture is intended to inform and guide "cyber service providers, network owners and product vendors on the capabilities and interfaces that can enable an agile, dynamically responsive and resilient cyber infrastructure."[33] The concept starts with the premise that two key issues hamper effective cyber defense.

The first is malicious actors' ability to reuse cyber-attack tools and techniques against multiple targets because similar organizations do not share information. The second is cyber-attack response times are too slow to address alerts, primarily because existing solutions rely on humans in the loop. The latter has become even more severe because of attacker use of automated tools. IACD seeks to reverse these trends by improving cyber security automation and information sharing and encouraging interoperability between commercial tools. Accordingly the concept relies on three foundational capabilities: [34]

- Automation that enables automated sensing, sense-making, decision-making, and courses of action responses within cyber-relevant time.
- Information sharing that enables rapid sharing of indicators, analytics and effective responses among organizations.
- Interoperability that enables a variety of commercial vendor tools to function with each other without the need for custom interfaces.

The capability-based reference architecture supports a vendor-agnostic plug-and-play operating environment to enable organizations to select commercial vendor products that best suit their needs. Ultimately the fundamental objective of IACD is to reduce response time "from months to milliseconds." [35] Therefore, the reference architecture centers on the integration of solutions that provide the capabilities to accomplish goals that achieve this objective. To promote automation, IACD provides for machine implementation of capabilities to migrate people from 'in' to 'on' the loop in cyberspace operations. To promote sharing, IACD provides a robust, standards-based sharing capability. To promote interoperability, IACD enables open-standards-based capability interfaces for machine-to-machine information exchange. [36] IACD conforms to other efforts and environments, such as the NIST Cybersecurity Framework for automation of the Detect function, and to the Cyber Kill Chain for preventing any step to disable the attack. The architecture describes top-level IACD capabilities and functions, to include: [37]

- Secure orchestration, control, and management of interactions among capabilities.
- Control messaging through a standard set of messages for compliant components
- Sensor or actuator control and data normalization for secure communications of data, commands, and status of sensors and actuators.
- Sense-making that evaluates cyber events and intelligence data to determine whether an alert is necessary.
- Decision making which recommends an appropriate response based on enterprise policies and risks and impact to the enterprise.

- Response controlling that sequences workflows and coordinates responses.
- Information sharing that enables secure communications for standardized exchanges of indicators of compromise and recommended courses of action.

The IACD activity intends to increase the cost of an attack by reducing cyber incident response time and limiting actor ability to reuse tools and techniques. The concept has been proven feasible through spirals that demonstrate how the integration of commercial products can detect malware, generate indicators, and initiate and share responses between organizations.[38]

Automated Indicator Sharing

IACD conforms to the Cybersecurity Act of 2015 by enabling and promoting trusted information sharing mechanisms. The act imposed a ninety-day deadline for the DHS, in coordination with other Federal entities, to develop and implement a capability and process to commence real-time, automated sharing of cyber threat indicators and defensive measures. The department responded with deployment of the AIS system, which provides the capability for the timely exchange of relevant and actionable cyber threat indicators among federal departments and agencies and the private sector.[39] An example of an indicator is a malicious IP address. The goal of the AIS initiative is to commoditize cyber threat indicators so they are shared broadly among the public and private sector. The NCCIC manages the system to allow bidirectional sharing with participants, who will not be identified as the source of an indicator unless they grant consent. AIS takes measures to ensure appropriate privacy and civil liberties by performing automated analyses and technical mitigations to delete PII not directly related to a threat; incorporating elements of human review on select fields to ensure automated processes are functioning properly; minimizing the amount of data in an indicator to what is directly related to a cyber threat; retaining only information needed to address the threat; and ensuring any information collected is used only for network defense or limited law enforcement purposes.[40]

Also, as mandated by the Cybersecurity Act of 2015, the DHS released guidance to assist private sector and federal entities to share cyber threat indicators and defensive measures. The department published policies and procedures relating to the receipt, processing, and dissemination by all federal entities of cyber threat indicators and defensive measures submitted through real-time means and through nonautomated means,[41] along with privacy and civil liberties guidelines for such actions.[42] The act did specify that besides the creation of a real-time, automated process between information systems, other acceptable means for the sharing of cyber intelligence are through electronic mail or media and through an interactive forum on an Internet website. Therefore, the department offers electronic opportunities to share cyber threat indicators and defensive measures via web form and email. If emailed, the department requests the following fields: type (either indicator or defensive measure); valid time of incident or knowledge of topic; tactics, techniques, and procedures; and a confidence assertion for the value of the indicator (high, medium, or low).[43] Deputy Homeland Security Secretary Alejandro Mayorkas remarked at the Billington International Cybersecurity Summit, that the information-sharing legislation and platform is a collaborative effort that "protects not just various parts of the economy, but the entire online environment."[44]

The AIS capability leverages STIX (Structured Threat Information eXpression) and TAXII (Trusted Automated eXchange of Indicator Information) specifications for machine-to-machine communication. STIX is a structured language and TAXII is the preferred mechanism to exchange it. STIX describes "cyber threat information so it can be shared, stored, and [analyzed] in a consistent manner that facilitates automation."[45] The STIX framework conveys the full range of cyber threat data elements to include observables, indicators, incidents, adversary tactics, techniques and procedures, exploit targets, courses of action (contains defensive measures), campaigns, and threat actors. TAXII standardizes the automated exchange of cyber threat information. TAXII defines "a set of services and message exchanges that, when implemented, enable sharing of actionable cyber threat information across organization and product/service boundaries."[46] TAXII uses an XML data format and Hypertext Transfer Protocol (Secure) (HTTP/HTTPS) message protocols. International in scope and free for public use, STIX and TAXII are "community-driven technical specifications designed to enable automated information sharing for cybersecurity situational awareness, real-time network defense and sophisticated threat analysis."[47]

Tailored Disruption Capacities

Cyber Mission Force

In the United States the build of the Cyber Mission Force (CMF) at US Cyber Command underpins the DOD's primary missions in cyberspace.[48] The department is working to create a total of 133 CMF teams comprised of 6,200 personnel and to achieve their full operational capability by September 2018. The teams are:[49]

- Cyber National Mission Force teams to defend the nation by seeing adversary activity, blocking attacks, and maneuvering to defeat them.

- Cyber Combat Mission Force teams to conduct military cyber operations in support of combatant commands.
- Cyber Protection Force teams to defend the DOD information networks, protect priority missions and prepare cyber forces for combat.
- Cyber Support teams to provide analytic and planning support to National Mission and Combat Mission teams.

Portions of the Cyber Mission Force are honing their offensive skills in cyber operations against the self-proclaimed Islamic State. Defense Secretary Ashton Carter said "the methods we're using are new . . . and some of them applicable to the other challenges that I described other than ISIL," namely Iran, North Korea, Russia, and China.[50] The Cyber National Mission Force plans, directs, and synchronizes full-spectrum cyberspace operations to deter, disrupt, and, if necessary, defeat adversary cyber actors to defend the nation. Defending the nation missions include defending the United States and its interests against cyberattacks of "significant consequence," defense of the nation's critical infrastructure when directed by the president or secretary of defense; and alignment to the most sophisticated cyber adversaries. National Mission Force teams are tasked with the Defensive Cyber Operations RA mission to stop attacks outside the network. They are "trained to the highest technical standards" and "operate in accordance will all legal and policy guidance impacting operations outside friendly cyberspace."[51]

The obtainment of a dedicated and talented professional cyber force to conduct both offensive and defensive operations is a daunting task for the military, given national shortages in manpower with critical technical skills and competitive pay gaps with the private sector. One way to leverage the civilian workforce is through employment of cyber militias. In the United States, militias are found in the form of National Guard units. General Joseph Lengyel, Chief of the National Guard Bureau told the audience at the North American International Cyber Summit 2016 that "the civilian-acquired skills of its members enable the National Guard to make unique contributions in the cyber realm."[52] Thus the National Guard works closely with the combatant commands, especially Cyber Command, to fight off cyber incidents. Lengyel went on to say, "we practice our capabilities routinely at all levels."[53] That could include in the fight against the Islamic State, per comments on the 262nd Squadron by Defense Secretary Ashton Carter that "units like this can also participate in offensive cyber operations . . . to secure the prompt defeat of ISIL."[54] Carter says use of the National Guard "brings in the high-tech sector in a very direct way to the mission of protecting the country." The Pentagon is building new facilities while the Guard launches thirteen new cyber units across the country to have a total of thirty by 2019.[55] However, as the National Guard accelerates the fielding of cyber forces, it faces a backlog in training which includes basic skills and certifications.[56]

US Department of Defense Manual 8570.01 provides guidance for the certification of all military and civilian personnel conducting information assurance functions.[57] The certification program establishes a baseline understanding of principles and practices for each position, specialty and skill level. Approved baseline certifications and providers are published on the DISA Information Assurance Support Environment website.[58] For example, a common baseline certification is "Comp TIA Security+" for Information Assurance Technician Level I which is obtained by an examination.[59] More advanced certifications include Global Information Assurance Certification Security Essentials, Intrusion Analyst, and Enterprise Defender.[60] One certification for specialist that appears more applicable for outside the network is Certified Ethical Hacker offered by the EC-Council. A Certified Ethical Hacker is "a skilled professional who understands and knows how to look for weaknesses and vulnerabilities in target systems and uses the same knowledge and tools as a malicious hacker, but in a lawful and legitimate manner to assess the security posture of a target system(s)."[61] Courses for the range of certifications are available from a number of training providers, but the lead vendor is SANS whose website links their courses to the certifications.[62] Of note a new two-day course offered by SANS is titled "Active Defense, Offensive Countermeasures and Cyber Deception" which includes tools "to annoy attackers, determine who is attacking you, and finally, attack the attackers."[63] Since contractors supporting information assurance functions also have to comply with the certification requirements, private sector personnel could also possess necessary skills for tailored disruption.

Defense Innovation Unit Experimental

In May 2015 the Pentagon set up a new office in Silicon Valley to harness the creativity of the West Coast technology community.[64] The engineer and Navy SEAL that initially manned the Defense Innovation Unit Experimental, or DIUx, were picked for their tech sector experience and entrepreneurial mindsets. Their goal was to search out commercial dual-use technologies, to include in cyber.[65] Less than a year later the US Defense Secretary overhauled the leadership, structure, reporting, and resources of the office. It had suffered from an overly broad purpose and unrealistic demands.[66] DIUx 2.0 was launched by the secretary with new processing power in funds and a new operating system of partner-style leadership.[67] A third feature was the creation of offices in other innovation hubs, starting with Boston and Austin.[68] The result of the reboot was award of a total of $36 million in contracts for twelve projects via an acquisition technique named Commercial Solutions Opening. The largest of the awards for $12.7 went to Tanium to build a cyber situational awareness platform to monitor millions of DOD computer endpoints in real time,[69] in effect enabling timely detection that could lead to rapid response to harm.

Defense Secretary Carter highlighted in his remarks announcing DIUx 2.0 that "another way we're investing in innovation is through people," by providing "on-ramps and off-ramps for technical talent to flow between DOD and the tech sector."[70] An example of this ramp is the Defense Digital Service office that brings civilian techies into the Pentagon for a project or period of time to do something meaningful, including improving cybersecurity.[71] One of the very first initiatives of the office in May 2016 was the "Hack the Pentagon" program, the first federal "bug bounty."[72] Hackers were given legal consent to perform specific techniques against Defense Department websites and received financial awards for submitting vulnerability reports. HackerOne, a Silicon Valley firm that offers vulnerability disclosure as a service assisted in recruiting 1,410 participants that generated 1,189 vulnerability reports over three weeks.[73] The program was so successful that a second round was contracted in October 2016 with HackerOne and also Synack, but this time for more sensitive systems. A former NSA employee said these ethical hackers will "look outside the box to come up with creative attacks in the same way an attacker would."[74] A new Pentagon vulnerability disclosure policy will allow hackers to submit information with a high level of anonymity with no restrictions on citizenship.[75] The obtainment of this type of skilled talent through private sector arrangements proves that building capacity for tailored disruption is feasible and legitimate.

POLICIES AND PRIORITIES

Tony Scott, US Federal Chief Information Officer, candidly stated in late 2015, "as cyber threats become increasingly sophisticated and persistent, so must our actions to tackle them."[76] His remarks heralded the release of the CSIP for the federal government. The plan's second objective is the most pertinent to the strategy of active cyber defense, namely "Timely Detection of and Rapid Response to Cyber Incidents."[77] Accordingly CSIP directs a series of actions to "improve capabilities for identifying and detecting vulnerabilities and threats, enhance protections of assets and information, and further develop robust response and recovery capabilities to ensure readiness and resilience when incidents inevitably occur."[78] Specific improvements for objective two include examine private sector technologies for behavioral-based analytics, implement AIS, and create incident response best practices to ensure appropriate mitigation in a timely manner. Consistent with these broad themes, a national strategy agenda to implement the strategy of active cyber defense based on the pillars of resilience and disruption can be based on the following policy recommendations and priority suggestions.

Internal Systemic Resilience

Policy: Encourage the adoption of integrated and automated capability, informed by cyber threat intelligence, that can detect, verify, and remediate malicious activity in cyber-relevant time.

Priorities:

1. Design common open standards for active cyber defense inside the network that are applicable across the government as well as for critical infrastructure.

    a. Promulgate a reference architecture that centers on the automation and integration of services and mechanisms to reduce response time from months to milliseconds.
    b. Adopt, adapt, or develop common communications mediums, standard interfaces, and standard message sets to enable security tool interoperability.
    c. Demonstrate the art-of-the-possible to defenders and influence the marketplace of cyber security solutions including endpoint detection and response.

2. Create incentives to adopt common open standards for active cyber defense that can enable responsive and resilient critical infrastructure to manage the risk of cyber attack.

    a. Provide relief from regulatory requirements, certifications for government usage, or preferences for government contracts or grants.
    b. Reduce cyber insurance premiums based on positive security posture assessments of capabilities that prevent financial or data loss, service interruption, legal action, system or reputation damage.
    c. Offset worldwide shortage of cybersecurity professionals with automated intrusion responses as the number of devices, systems, and networks grow at an exponential rate. [79]

3. Develop and implement a capability and process to commence real-time, automated sharing of cyber threat indicators and defensive measures between private and public entities.

a. Grant legal protections in the form of antitrust exemptions and liability immunity to private entities that send the government indicators or measures.

b. Create a voluntary system that will encourage private and public entities to share indicators or measures while protecting classified information, intelligence sources and methods, and privacy and civil liberties.

c. Issue guidelines for the receipt, processing, and dissemination by the government of indicators and measures submitted through real-time and nonautomated means, to include guidelines concerning privacy and civil liberties.

d. Leverage proven specifications and mechanisms for machine-to-machine transmission of indicators and measures between private and public entities.

Tailored Disruption Capacities

Policy: Allow either state agencies or licensed private companies, whichever is best positioned to respond to breaches, to deploy their comparative advantage in securing victim networks.

Priorities:

1. Create a legal framework that accommodates the use of disruptive countermeasures outside the network by properly authorized entities under certain conditions.

    a. Recognize authorized circumstances for the state to employ countermeasures that are acceptable under international law, primarily for an injured state, in a plea of necessity, or in response to a lack of due diligence.

    b. Codify if a law enforcement or intelligence agency could deputize private firms to act under their authority in pursuing attackers under current provisions (such as 1030(f) in the CFAA in the United States) in limited circumstances and whether those provisions provide immunity for the firm:

    - If not, determine if a lack of explicit self-defense provisions in domestic law does not preclude the application of common law defense of property by licensed private companies.
    - Or at a minimum, add a qualified active defense right to domestic law that provides licensed private companies with

immunity from liability for third-party harm if caused during state-authorized responses.

2. Create habitual relations with cyber security industry firms and personnel to employ cutting-edge technologies in detection, verification, and remediation of malicious cyber behavior.

   a. Establish government outreach programs to find, adopt, and harness commercial dual-use high-tech solutions that enable responses in cyber-relevant time.
   b. Employ commercial and public skill sets in crowd-sourced solutions to security challenges beyond the scope and capability of government agencies such as in bug bounty programs.
   c. Engage leading cyber security vendors in the investigation of high-profile breaches to leverage and position their talent in the cyber kill chain of the most sophisticated actors.

3. Identify thresholds and circumstances for either state government or licensed private companies acting under their authority to respond outside the network to a cyber attack.

   a. Determine if the establishment of clear "red lines" for cyber attacks that warrant a response is necessary or if best left undefined to allow for some level of strategic ambiguity for political decisions. [80]
   b. Delineate what thresholds warrant a military response, such as in defense of the nation and its interests against "attacks of significant consequence" defined in the United States as loss of life, significant property damage, serious adverse foreign policy consequences, or serious economic impact. [81]
   c. Determine if responses to cyber attacks below the threshold of "significant consequences" are more suited for other agencies or licensed private companies as the military is "not involved in the majority of major cyber incidents that occur." [82]

The above policy recommendations and priority suggestions are by no means exhaustive but offer a start point for action plans. Another source to ponder is the Active Cyber Defense Task Force Project Report released in October 2016 that specifies an explicit set of relevant actions for government agencies and private sector companies to facilitate the implementation of their proposed framework for active defense. [83] Pertinent to consideration of any actions are remarks made by the Deputy Commander, US Cyber Command Lieutenant General James McLaughlin, regarding their success will be dependent on the ability to acquire "the latest, best offensive and defensive tools available" combined with the "quality" and "proficiency" of people to use them.[84] A national strategy agenda for active cyber defense based on the two pillars of resilience and disruption will bring in the best people and capabilities to achieve deterrence within the cyber arena.

NOTES

1. Aaron Boyd, "Obama: Cyberattacks Continue to Be National Emergency," *Federal Times*, March 10, 2016.

2. CyberEdge Group, "2016 Cyberthreat Defense Report," Current Security Posture, 2016, 7.

3. Privacy Section, "'It Is Not about If You Will Be Penetrated, but When,' Warns NSA chief," *Computing*, July 16, 2015.

4. Hacking Section, "'You Can't Assume You're Not Already Compromised,' Warns Met Office CISO," *Computing*, June 5, 2015.

5. Executive Office of the President, *National Security Strategy* (Washington, DC: The White House, February 2015), 1–13.

6. Executive Office of the President, *Presidential Policy Directive on Critical Infrastructure Security and Resilience*, PPD-21 (Washington, DC: The White House, February 12, 2013).

7. Dave Clemente, "Cyber Security and Global Interdependence: What Is Critical?" Chatham House, February 2013, viii–x.

8. European Commission, *Cybersecurity Strategy of the European Union: An Open, Safe and Secure Cyberspace*, Brussels, February 7, 2013, 3–4.

9. Commission, *Cybersecurity Strategy of the European Union*, 5–6.

10. National Security Authority, *National Cyber Security Strategy of the Czech Republic for the Period from 2015 to 2020*, 2015, 9.

11. Presidency of the Council of Ministers, *National Strategic Framework for Cyberspace Security*, December 2013, 6–20.

12. HM Government, *National Cyber Security Strategy 2016–2021*, 2016, 33.

13. Ministry of Economic Affairs and Communication, *Cyber Security Strategy 2014–2017*, 2014, 6–8.

14. Ministry of Economic Affairs and Communication, *Cyber Security Strategy 2014–2017*, 10.

15. The Government of Georgia, *Cyber Security Strategy of Georgia 2012–2015*, 2012, 3–5.

16. Australian Government, *Australia's Cyber Security Strategy*, 2016, 23.

17. Australian Government, *Australia's Cyber Security Strategy*, 27.

18. The Government of Japan, *Cybersecurity Strategy*, Provisional Translation, Cabinet Decision, September 4, 2015, 27.

19. Vice Admiral Michael S. Rogers, US Navy, "Beyond the Build: Delivering Outcomes through Cyberspace," The Commander's Vision and Guidance for US Cyber Command, June 3, 2015, 1–11.

20. Ash Carter, US Secretary of Defense, "Securing the Oceans, the Internet, and Space," Speech to Commonwealth Club, Silicon Valley, March 1 2016, 1–15.

21. Colonel Hans Folmer, "The Defense Cyber Command, A New Operational Capability," *Magazine Nationale*, nr. 5, October 22, 2014.

22. Hans Hillen, Minister of Defense, *The Defense Cyber Strategy*, Netherlands, June 27, 2012.

23. Hillen, *The Defense Cyber Strategy*, 4–16.

24. Brigadier General Hans Folmer, "Cyber Commander Panel Remarks," NATO Cooperative Cyber Defence Centre of Excellence, CyCon 2016 Press Release, June 1, 2016.

25. Lior Tabansky, "Israel's Cyber Security Policy: Local Response to the Global Cybersecurity Risk," in *Civil Society and National Security in the Era of Cyber Warfare*, chap. 21 (Hershey, PA: IGI Global, 2016), 481–82, 488–89.

26. James Andrew Lewis, "Advanced Experiences in Cybersecurity Policies and Practices," Discussion Paper N, IDB-DP-457, Inter-American Development Bank, July 2016, 24.

27. Lewis, "Advanced Experiences in Cybersecurity Policies and Practices," 26.

28. Tabansky, "Israel's Cyber Security Policy," 482–83.

29. M. J. Herring and K. D. Willett, "Active Cyber Defense: A Vision for Real-Time Cyber Defense," *Journal of Information Warfare* 13, no. 2 (2014): 46.

30. National Security Agency Information Assurance Directorate, "Active Cyber Defense (ACD)," Fact Sheet, October 22, 2015, 1–2.

31. National Security Agency Information Assurance Directorate, "Active Cyber Defense (ACD)," Frequently Asked Questions, October 22, 2015, 1–2.

32. IACD Community, "Integrated Adaptive Cyber Defense (IACD) Community Day: October 3th, 2016," Email Announcement, September 19, 2016.

33. K. Done et al., "Towards a Capability-Based Architecture for Cyberspace Defense," Concept Paper Approved for Public Release, US Department of Homeland Security, US National Security Agency Information Assurance Directorate, and the Johns Hopkins University Applied Physics Laboratory, AOS-16-0099; September 2016, 1.

34. Done et al., "Towards a Capability-Based Architecture for Cyberspace Defense," 2.

35. Peter Fonash and Phyllis Schneck, "Cybersecurity: From Months to Milliseconds," *Computer*, January 2015, 42–49.

36. Done et al., "Towards a Capability-Based Architecture for Cyberspace Defense," 3.

37. Done et al., "Towards a Capability-Based Architecture for Cyberspace Defense," 6–7.

38. Gregg Tally, "Proposed Capability-Based Reference Architecture for Real-Time Network Defense," Concept Briefing Approved for Public Release, the Johns Hopkins University Applied Physics Laboratory, November 16, 2015.

39. Bradley Barth, "DHS Launches Two-Way Threat Sharing System for Public-Private Collaboration," *SC Magazine*, March 18, 2016.

40. Department of Homeland Security, "Automated Indicator Sharing (AIS)," Fact Sheet, September 25, 2016.

41. Department of Homeland Security and Justice, "Final Procedures Related to the Receipt of Cyber Threat Indicators and Defensive Measures by the Federal Government," June 15, 2016, 3–10.

42. Department of Homeland Security and Justice, "Privacy and Civil Liberties Final Guidelines: Cybersecurity Information Sharing Act of 2015," June 15, 2016, 3–14.

43. US Computer Emergency Readiness Team, "Automated Indicator Sharing (AIS)," Official Website of the Department of Homeland Security, accessed on September 25, 2016.

44. Greg Otto, "U.S. Officials: World Needs to Follow Our Lead on Cyber Norms," *Fedscoop,* April 5, 2016.

45. The MITRE Corporation, "About STIX," Project Documentation, github, 2016.

46. The MITRE Corporation, "About TAXII."

47. US Computer Emergency Readiness Team, "Information Sharing Specifications for Cybersecurity," Official Website of the Department of Homeland Security, November 3, 2016.

48. Thomas Atkin, James K. McLaughlin, and Charles L. Moore, "Statement before the House Armed Services Committee," June 22, 2016.

49. Rich Abott, "U.S. Cyber Command Mission Force Teams Achieve Initial Operating Capability," *Defense Daily*, October 27, 2016.

50. Sydney J. Freedberg Jr., "Cyber War against ISIL Hones Weapons vs. Russia, China," *Breaking Defense*, February 29, 2016.

51. Brett T. Williams, "The Joint Force Commander's Guide to Cyberspace Operations," *Joint Forces Quarterly* no. 73, 2nd Quarter (2014): 16.

52. Jim Greenhill, "National Guard Uniquely Positioned to Contribute in Cyber Realm," *U.S. Air Force News*, October 19, 2016, 15.

53. Greenhill, "National Guard Uniquely Positioned to Contribute in Cyber Realm," 17.

54. Andrea Shalal, "U.S. National Guard May Join Cyber Offense against Islamic State: Carter," *Reuters*, March 6, 2016.

55. Patrick Howell O'Neil, "Pentagon Requests $12 Million for New National Guard Cyberwar Facilities in Maryland," *The Daily Dot*, March 26, 2016.

56. Scott Maucione, "As Cyber Units Expand, National Guard Has Training Backlog," *Federal News Radio*, March 15, 2016.

57. US Department of Defense, "Information Assurance Workforce Improvement Program," DoD 8570.01-M, Change 4, November 10, 2015.

58. Information Assurance Support Environment, "DoD Approved 8570 Baseline Certifications," Defense Information Systems Agency Information Assurance Support Environment Website, Accessed on October 23, 2016, http://iase.disa.mil/iawip/Pages/iabaseline.aspx.

59. CompTIA Security, "CompTIA Security+ Certification," Exam Code SYO-401, Accessed on October 23, 2016, https://certification.comptia.org/certifications/security.

60. Global Information Assurance Certification, "GIAC Security Essentials," Certifications: Accessed on October 23, 2016, http://www.giac.org/certification/security-essentials-gsec.

61. EC-Council, "Master the Core Technologies of Ethical Hacking," Programs, Accessed on October 23, 2016, https://www.eccouncil.org/programs/certified-ethical-hacker-ceh/.

62. SANS, "Information Security Training Courses," Courses, Accessed on October 23, 2016, https://www.sans.org/course.

63. SANS, "Active Defense, Offensive Countermeasures and Cyber Deception (Two-day Version)," Course, Accessed on October 23, 2016, https://www.sans.org/course/active-defense-offensive-countermeasures-and-cyber-deception-two-day-version.

64. Patrick Tucker, "Pentagon Sets Up a Silicon Valley Outpost," *Defense One*, April 23, 2015.

65. Marcus Weisgerber, "Pentagon Sends an Engineer and a Navy SEAL to Woo Silicon Valley," *Defense One*, August 5, 2015.

66. Ben FitzGerald and Loren DeJonge Schulman, "The DIUx Is Dead, Long Live the DIUx," *Defense One*, May 12, 2016.

67. US Department of Defense, "Secretary of Defense Speech, Remarks Announcing DIUx 2.0," As Delivered by Secretary of Defense Ash Carter, Mountain View, California, May 11, 2016, http://www.defense.gov/News/Speeches/Speech-View/Article/757539/remarks-announcing-diux-20.

68. Billy Mitchell, "DIUx Expands to Austin, Texas," *FedScoop*, September 14, 2016.

69. Jared Serbu, "DIU-X Touts $36 Million in Rapid Contracts, but Most Dollars Went to Established Firms," WFED AM Radio, Washington DC, October 17, 2016.

70. US Department of Defense, "Secretary of Defense Speech, Remarks Announcing DIUx 2.0."

71. Sydney J. Freedberg Jr., "SecDef Carter Wants YOU for the Defense Digital Service," *Breaking Defense*, September 14, 2016.

72. Jim Garamone, "Defense Digital Service Chief Brings Private-Sector Expertise to Job," *DoD News*, June 10, 2016.

73. US Department of Defense, "Hack the Pentagon," Fact Sheet, June 17, 2016.

74. Jared Serbu, "Pentagon Launches Next Round of 'Bug Bounties,' Including Cyber Tests of Sensitive Systems," WFED AM Radio, Washington DC, October 24, 2016.

75. Zachary Fryer-Biggs, "Pentagon Rolls Out New Policy, Rewards for Hackers," *Jane's Defence Weekly*, November 30, 2016, 11.

76. Greg Otto, "White House Cyber Plan Sets Tough Deadlines," *FedScoop*, October 30, 2015.

77. Shaun Donovan and Tony Scott, "Cybersecurity Strategy and Implementation Plan (CSIP) for the Federal Civilian Government, Office of Management and Budget, October 30, 2015, 2.

78. Donovan and Scott, "Cybersecurity Strategy and Implementation Plan," 5.

79. Peter Fanosh and Thomas Longstaff, "Narrowing Cyber Workforce Gaps with Intrusion Detection and Response Automation," *Crosstalk*, March/April 2016, 4–9.

80. Mark Pomerleau, "Cyber Red Lines: Ambiguous by Necessity?" *C4ISRNET*, September 8, 2016.

81. US Department of Defense, "The DoD Cyber Strategy," April 2015, 4–5.

82. Mark Pomerleau, "CYBERCOM Not Involved in Most Incidents," *C4ISRNET*, September 21, 2016.

83. Center for Cyber and Homeland Security, "Into the Gray Zone: The Private Sector and Active Defense against Cyber Threats," Project Report, The George Washington University, October 2016, 31–33.

84. Aaron Boyd, "Cyber Teams' First Live Campaign: Fighting ISIS," *C4ISRNET*, September 21, 2016.

Bibliography

PUBLIC DOCUMENTS

Australia. Australian Government. *Australia's Cyber Security Strategy*, 2016.

Czech Republic. National Security Authority. *National Cyber Security Strategy of the Czech Republic for the Period from 2015 to 2020*, 2015.

Estonia. Ministry of Economic Affairs and Communication. *Cyber Security Strategy 2014–2017*, 2014.

European Commission. *Cybersecurity Strategy of the European Union: An Open, Safe and Secure Cyberspace*, Brussels, February 7, 2013.

Georgia. The Government of Georgia. *Cyber Security Strategy of Georgia 2012–2015*, 2012.

Italy. Presidency of the Council of Ministers. *National Strategic Framework for Cyberspace Security*, December 2013.

Japan. The Government of Japan. *Cybersecurity Strategy*, Provisional Translation, Cabinet Decision, September 4, 2015.

North Atlantic Treaty Organization. *Assured Access to the Global Commons*. Norfolk, VA: Allied Command Transformation April 2011.

———. "The North Atlantic Treaty." April 4, 1949.

———. "Wales Summit Declaration." Wales: North Atlantic Council, September 2014.

The Netherlands. Minister of Defense. *The Defense Cyber Strategy*, June 2012.

United Kingdom. HM Government. *National Cyber Security Strategy 2016–2021*, 2016.

———. Ministry of Defence. "The Comprehensive Approach." Joint Discussion Note 4/05. Joint Doctrine and Concepts Centre, 2006.

———. Ministry of Defence. "Future Operating Environment 2035." First Edition, Joint Doctrine and Concepts Centre, December 2015.

United Nations. "Charter of the United Nations." October 24, 1945.

———. "Creation of a Global Culture of Cybersecurity and Taking Stock of National Efforts to Protect Information Infrastructures." General Assembly Resolution 64/211, December 21, 2009.

———. "Group of Governmental Experts on Developments in the Field of Information and Telecommunications in the Context of International Security." A/68/98. June 24, 2013.

———. "International Code of Conduct for Information Security." Document 69/723, January 13, 2015.

———. "Group of Governmental Experts on Developments in the Field of Information and Telecommunications in the Context of International Security." A/70/174, July 22, 2015.

————. "Responsibility of States for Internationally Wrongful Acts." General Assembly Resolution 56/83, December 12, 2001.

United States. Executive Office of the President. *The Comprehensive National Cybersecurity Initiative.* Washington, DC: The White House, March 5, 2010.

————. Executive Office of the President. *Cyberspace Policy Review, Assuring a Trusted and Resilient Information and Communication Infrastructure.* Washington, DC: The White House, May 2009.

————. Executive Office of the President. *Executive Order—Improving Critical Infrastructure Cybersecurity.* Washington, DC: The White House, February 12, 2013.

————. Executive Office of the President. *International Strategy for Cyberspace: Prosperity, Security, and Openness in a Networked World.* Washington, DC: The White House, May 2011.

————. Executive Office of the President. *National Security Strategy.* Washington, DC: The White House, February 2015.

————. Executive Office of the President. *Presidential Policy Directive—On Critical Infrastructure Protection.* PPD-63. Washington, DC: The White House, February 12, 2016.

————. Executive Office of the President. *Presidential Policy Directive—United States Cyber Incident Coordination.* PPD-41. Washington, DC: The White House, July 26, 2016.

————. Department of Defense. *Countering Air and Missile Threats .* Joint Publication 3-1. Washington, DC: Office of the Chairman, Joint Chiefs of Staff, March 23, 2012.

————. Department of Defense. *Cyberspace Operations .* Joint Publication 3-12 (R). Washington, DC: Office of the Chairman, Joint Chiefs of Staff, February 5, 2013.

————. Department of Defense. *Cyberspace Policy Report.* Washington, DC: Office of the Secretary of Defense, November 2011.

————. Department of Defense. *The DoD Cyber Strategy.* Washington, DC: Office of the Secretary of Defense, April 2015.

————. Department of Defense. *DOD Dictionary of Military and Associated Terms.* Washington, DC: Office of the Chairman, Joint Chiefs of Staff, October 15, 2016.

————. Department of Defense. *Joint Terminology for Cyberspace Operations .* Washington, DC: Office of the Vice Chairman, Joint Chiefs of Staff, November 2010.

————. Department of Defense. *Joint Operations .* Joint Publication 3-0. Washington, DC: Office of the Chairman, Joint Chiefs of Staff, August 11, 2011.

————. Department of Defense. *Joint Operation Planning .* Joint Publication 5-0. Washington, DC: Office of the Chairman, Joint Chiefs of Staff, August 11, 2011.

————. Department of Defense. *Law of War Manual .* Washington, DC: Office of General Counsel, June 2015 (Updated December 2016).

————. Department of Defense. *Military and Security Developments Involving the People's Republic of China.* Washington, DC: Office of the Secretary of Defense, April 2015.

————. Department of Defense. *The National Military Strategy.* Washington, DC: Office of the Chairman, Joint Chiefs of Staff, June 2015.

————. Department of Defense. *Quadrennial Defense Review Report.* Washington, DC: Office of the Secretary of Defense, May 2014.

————. Department of Defense. *Strategy for Operating in Cyberspace.* Washington, DC: Office of the Secretary of Defense, July 2011.

————. Department of Defense. *Unity of Effort Framework Solution Guide.* Suffolk, Virginia: Joint Staff J-7, August 2014.

————. Department of Homeland Security. *National Infrastructure Protection Plan.* Washington, DC: Department of Homeland Security, 2013.

————. National Institute of Standards and Technology, *Framework for Improving Critical Infrastructure Cybersecurity,* Version 1. 0, February 12, 2014.

————. National Institute of Standards and Technology, *Glossary of Key Information Security Terms,* NISTIR 7298 Revision 2, May 2013.

————. National Institute of Standards and Technology, *Guide to Cyber Threat Information Sharing (Draft),* NIST Special Publication 800-150, October 2014.

————. National Institute of Standards and Technology, *Managing Information Security Risk,* NIST Special Publication 800-39, March 2011.

———. National Institute of Standards and Technology, *Security and Privacy Controls for Federal Information Systems and Organizations*, NIST Special Publication 800-53, Revision 4, April 2013.

———. Strategic Command, *Deterrence Operations Joint Operating Concept*, Version 2. 0, Washington, DC: December 2006.

ACADEMIC LITERATURE

Aaronson, Michael, et al. "NATO Countering the Hybrid Threat." *PRISM* 2 no. 4 (September 2011): 111–24.

Allison, Graham, and Philip Zelikow. *Essence of Decision: Explaining the Cuban Missile Crisis.* 2nd ed. New York: Addison-Wesley Longman, 1999.

Arimatsu, Louise. "A Treaty for Governing Cyber-Weapons." *Proceedings 4th International Conference on Cyber Conflict.* Tallinn, Estonia: Cooperative Cyber Defence Centre of Excellence, 2012.

Asada, Sadao. *From Mahan to Pearl Harbor: The Imperial Japanese Navy and the United States.* Annapolis, MD: Naval Institute Press, 2006.

Barros, J. *The Corfu Incident of 1923.* Princeton, NJ: Princeton University Press, 1965.

Berkowitz, Marc J. "Shaping the Outer Space and Cyberspace Environments." In *Conflict and Cooperation in the Global Commons*, edited by Scott Jasper. Washington, DC: Georgetown University Press, 2012, 190–213.

Betz, David J., and Tim Stevens. *Cyberspace and the State: Toward a Strategy for Cyber-Power.* Oxon: Routledge, 2011.

Blaire, Dennis C., et. al. "Into the Gray Zone: The Private Sector and Active Defense against Cyber Threats." Project Report, The George Washington University, October 2016.

Bonner, E. Lincoln, III. "Cyber Power for 21st-Century Joint Warfare." *Joint Forces Quarterly* no. 74 (3rd Quarter 2014): 102–9.

Burr, William. "How to Fight a Nuclear War." *Foreign Policy*, September 14, 2012.

Cable, James. *Gunboat Diplomacy 1919–1991.* London: Palgrave Macmillan, 1994.

Coleman, Kevin G. *The Cyber Commander's eHandbook: The Strategies and Tactics of Digital Conflict.* McMurray, PA: Technolytics, 2013.

Chang, Amy. "Warring State: China's Cybersecurity Strategy." Center for a New American Security, December 2014.

Chilton, Kevin, and Greg Weaver, "Waging Deterrence in the Twenty-first Century." *Strategic Studies Quarterly* (Spring 2009): 31–42.

Clausewitz, Carl von. *On War.* Translated by Michael Howard and Peter Paret. Princeton, NJ: Princeton University Press, 1976.

Clemente, Dave. "Cyber Security and Global Interdependence: What Is Critical?" Chatham House, February 2013.

Demchak, Chris., et al. *Designing Resilience: Preparing for Extreme Events.* Pittsburgh, PA: University of Pittsburgh, September 2010.

———. *Wars of Disruption and Resilience: Cybered Conflict, Power, and National Security.* Athens: University of Georgia Press, September 2011.

———. "Cybered Conflict, Cyber Power, and Security Resilience as Strategy." In *Cyberspace and National Security.* Washington, DC: Georgetown University Press, 2012.

———. "Resilience and Cyberspace: Recognizing the Challenges of a Global Socio-Cyber Infrastructure (GSCI)." *Journal of Comparative Policy Analysis: Research and Practice* (July 12, 2012): 263–65.

———. "Economic and Political Coercion and a Rising Cyber Westphalia." In *Peacetime Regime for State Activities in Cyberspace.* Tallinn, Estonia: Cooperative Cyber Defence Centre of Excellence, 2013, 595–620.

Demchak, Chris., and Peter Dombrowski. "Cyber War, Cybered Conflict, and the Maritime Domain." *Naval War College Review* (April 1, 2014): 3.

Denning, Dorothy E. "Obstacles and Options for Cyber Arms Controls." Heinrich Boll Foundation Conference, Berlin, Germany, June 29–30, 2001.

―――. "Rethinking the Cyber Domain and Deterrence." *Joint Forces Quarterly* no. 77 (2nd Quarter 2015): 8–12.

Denning, Dorothy E., and Bradley J. Strawser. "Active Cyber Defense: Applying Air Defense to the Cyber Domain." *Cyber Analogies.* Naval Postgraduate School (2014): 64–75.

Dewar, Robert S. "The Triptych of Cyber Security: A Classification of Active Cyber Defense." *Proceedings 6th International Conference on Cyber Conflict.* Tallinn, Estonia: Cooperative Cyber Defence Centre of Excellence, June 2014.

Drezner, Daniel W. "The Hidden Hand of Economic Coercion." *International Organization* 57, no. 3 (2003).

Farwell, James P., and Rafal Rohozinski. "The New Reality of Cyber War." *Survival: Global Politics and Strategy* (August 1, 2012): 110.

Finnemore, Martha, and Kathryn Sikkink. "International Norm Dynamics and Political Change." *International Organization* 52, 4 (Autumn 1998): 887–917.

Flynn, Matthew J. *First Strike: Preemptive War in Modern History.* New York: Routledge, 2008.

Forester, Schuyler. "Strategies of Deterrence." "Theoretical Foundations: Deterrence in the Nuclear Age." *American Defense Policy.* Baltimore: Johns Hopkins University Press, September 1990, 42–51.

―――. "Strategies of Deterrence." In *Conflict and Cooperation in the Global Commons*, edited by Scott Jasper. Washington, DC: Georgetown University Press, September 2012, 55–67.

Freedman, Lawrence. "The First Two Generations of Nuclear Strategists." In *Makers of Modern Strategy.* Princeton, NJ: Princeton University Press, 1986.

Goldman, Emily O. *Power in Uncertain Times.* Stanford, CA: Stanford University Press, 2011.

Goodman, Will. "Cyber Deterrence: Tougher in Theory Than in Practice?" *Strategic Studies Quarterly* (Fall 2010): 102–35.

Graham-Yooll, Andrew. *Imperial Skirmishes: War and Gunboat Diplomacy in Latin America.* Brooklyn, NY: Olive Branch Press, 2002.

Gray, Colin S., "The Implications of Preemptive and Preventive War Doctrines: A Reconsideration." *Strategic Studies Institute* (July 2007): 1–60.

―――. *Perspectives on Strategy.* New York: Oxford University Press, 2013.

―――. *The Strategy Bridge: Theory for Practice.* New York: Oxford University Press, 2010.

―――. "Strategy in the Nuclear Age: The United States, 1945–1991." In *The Making of Strategy* (New York: Cambridge University Press, 1994).

―――. "The Whole House of Strategy." *Joint Forces Quarterly* no. 71 (4th Quarter, 2013): 58–62.

Glenn, Russell W. "Thoughts on Hybrid Conflict." *Small Wars Journal* (March 2, 2009): 1–8.

Glosson, Anthony D. "Active Defense: An Overview of the Debate and a Way Forward." *Mercatus Center* (August 2015): 3–28.

Harrington, Sean L. "Cyber Security Active Defense: Playing with Fire or Sound Risk Management." *Richmond Journal of Law and Technology* 20, no. 4 (September 17, 2014): 1–41.

Harrison, Roger, et al. "Space Deterrence: The Delicate Balance of Risk." *Space and Defense* 3 (Summer 2009).

Hart, B. H. Liddell. "The Theory of Strategy." In *Military Strategy: Theory and Application.* Carlisle, PA: US Army War College, 1983.

Herring, M. J., and K. D. Willett. "Active Cyber Defense: A Vision for Real-Time Cyber Defense." *Journal of Information Warfare* 13, no. 2 (2014).

Heuser, Beatrice. *The Evolution of Strategy: Thinking War from Antiquity to the Present.* New York: Cambridge University Press, 2010.

Hinkle, Katharine C. "Countermeasures in the Cyber Context: One More Thing to Worry About." *Yale Journal of International Law Online* 37 (Fall 2011).

Holland, John H. *Complexity: A Very Short Introduction.* New York: Oxford University Press, 2014.

Hughes, Geraint. "Ukraine: Europe's New Proxy War?" *Fletcher Security Review* 1, no. 2 (Spring 2014): 106–18.

Hutchins, Eric M., et al. "Intelligence-Driven Computer Network Defense Informed by Analysis of Adversary Campaigns and Intrusion Kill Chains." Lockheed Martin Corporation, March 2011.

Iasiello, Emilio. "Hacking Back: Not the Right Solution." *Parameters* 44, no. 3(Autumn 2014): 105–13.

Ishizu, Tomoyuki, and Raymond Callahan. "The Rising Sun Strikes: The Japanese Invasions." In *The Pacific War*. Oxford: Osprey Publishing Ltd, 2010.

Jackson, Stephen. "NATO Article 5 and Cyber Warfare: NATO's Ambiguous and Outdated Procedure for Determining When Cyber Aggression Qualifies as an Armed Attack." Center for Infrastructure Protection and Homeland Security, August 16, 2016.

Jasper, Scott. "Are US and Chinese Cyber Intrusions So Different?" *The Diplomat*, September 9, 2013.

Jasper, Scott, and Scott Moreland. "A Comprehensive Approach to Multidimensional Operations." *Journal of International Peacekeeping* 19 (2015): 191–210.

Jentleson, Bruce. "Coercive Diplomacy: Scope and Limits in the Contemporary World." Policy Analysis Brief, *The Stanley Foundation*, December 2006.

Joubert, V. "Five Years after Estonia's Cyber Attacks: Lessons Learned for NATO?" *Research Paper* 76. Rome: NATO Defense College, 2012, 5.

Jun, Jenny, et al. "What Do We Know about Past North Korean Cyber Attacks and Their Capabilities?" *Center for Strategic and International Studies*, December 12, 2014.

Kamman, W. *A Search for Stability*. Notre Dame, IN: University of Notre Dame Press, 1968.

Kesan, Jay P. "Optimal Hackback." *Chicago-Kent Law Review* 84, no. 3 (June 2009): 834–38.

Kesan, Jay P., and Carol M. Hayes. "Thinking through Active Defense in Cyberspace." *Proceedings of a Workshop on Deterring Cyberattacks*. Washington, DC: The National Academies Press, 2010.

Koval, Nikolay. "Revolution Hacking." *Cyber War in Perspective: Russian Aggression against Ukraine*. Tallinn, Estonia: Cooperative Cyber Defense Center of Excellence, 2015.

Kramer, Franklin D., and Melanie J. Teplinsky. "Cybersecurity and Tailored Deterrence." Atlantic Council, December 2013.

Lachow, Irving, et al. "Cyber War: Issues in Attack and Defense." *Joint Forces Quarterly* no. 61 (2nd Quarter 2011): 18–23.

———. "Active Cyber Defense: A Framework for Policy Makers." Center for a New American Security, February 2013, 1–10.

Laver, Harry S. "Preemption and the Evolution of America's Strategic Defense." *Parameters* (Summer 2005): 107–120.

Leed, Maren. "Offensive Cyber Capabilities at the Operational Level." Center for Strategic and International Studies, September 2013, 2–3.

Lewis, James. "Rethinking Cyber Security—A Comprehensive Approach." Sasakawa Peace Foundation, Tokyo. September 2011.

———. "Private Retaliation in Cyberspace." Center for Strategic and International Studies, May 2013.

———. "Cyber Threat and Response: Combating Advanced Attacks and Cyber Espionage." Center for Strategic and International Studies, March 2014.

———. "Economic Warfare and Cyberspace." *China's Cyberpower: International and Domestic Priorities*. Austrian Strategic Policy Institute, November 2014.

———. "The Role of Offensive Cyber Operations in NATO's Collective Defense." *Tallinn Paper* no. 8 (2015): 1–10.

———. "Advanced Experiences in Cybersecurity Policies and Practices." Discussion Paper N, IDB-DP-457, Inter-American Development Bank, July 2016.

Libicki, Martin C. *Cyberdeterrence and Cyberwar*. Santa Monica, CA: RAND Corporation, 2009.

———. "Pulling Punches in Cyberspace." *Proceedings of a Workshop on Deterring Cyberattacks*. Washington, DC: The National Academies Press, 2010.

———. "Why Cyber War Will Not and Should Not Have Its Grand Strategist." *Strategic Studies Quarterly* (Spring 2014): 23–39.

Lin, Herbert. "Escalation Dynamics and Conflict Termination in Cyberspace." *Strategic Studies Quarterly* (Fall 2012): 52–55.

Lin, Herbert, with William A. Owens and Kenneth W. Dam. *Technology, Policy, Law, and Ethics Regarding U. S. Acquisition and Use of Cyberattack Capabilities.* Washington DC: National Academies Press, 2009.

Litwak, Robert, and Meg King. "Arms Control in Cyberspace?" Wilson Center, October 2015.

Lotrionte, Catherine. "A Better Defense: Examining the United States' New Norms-Based Approach to Cyber Deterrence." *Georgetown Journal of International Affairs*" (December 23, 2013): 71–84.

———. "State Sovereignty and Self-Defense in Cyberspace: A Normative Framework for Balancing Legal Rights." *Emory International Law Review* 26 (May 28, 2013): 825–919.

Lowther, Adam. "The Evolution of Deterrence." *Thinking about Deterrence.* Maxwell Air Force Base, Alabama: Air University Press, 2014.

Luttwak, Edward N. *The Political Uses of Sea Power.* Baltimore: John Hopkins University Press, 1974.

———. *Strategy: The Logic of War and Peace.* Cambridge, MA: Belknap Press of Harvard University Press, 1987.

Lykke, Jr., Arthur F. "Toward an Understanding of Military Strategy." *Guide to Strategy,* Carlisle Barracks: US Army War College, February 2001.

Lynn, William J., III. "Defending a New Domain." *Foreign Affairs* 80 (September/October 2010): 97–108.

Maurer, Tim. "Cyber Proxies and the Crisis in Ukraine." *Cyber War in Perspective: Russian Aggression against Ukraine.* Tallinn, Estonia: Cooperative Cyber Defense Center of Excellence, 2015, 79–85.

Maybaum, Markus. "Technical Methods, Techniques, Tools and Effects of Cyber Operations." *Peacetime Regime for State Activities in Cyberspace.* Tallinn, Estonia: Cooperative Cyber Defence Centre of Excellence, 2013, 103–31.

Mazanec, Brian M. "Why International Order in Cyberspace Is Not Inevitable." *Strategic Studies Quarterly* (Summer 2015): 78–84.

McGee, Shane, et al. "Adequate Attribution: A Framework for Developing a National Policy for Private Sector Use of Active Defense." *Journal of Business and Technology Law* 8, no. 1, Article 3 (2013): 1–48.

Meyer, Paul. "Cyber-Security through Arms Control." *RUSI Journal* 156, no. 2 (April/May 2011): 22–27.

Morgan, Patrick M. "Applicability of Traditional Deterrence Concepts and Theory to the Cyber Realm." *Proceedings of a Workshop on Deterring Cyberattacks.* Washington, DC: The National Academies Press, 2010, 55–56.

Nye, Joseph S., Jr. "Cyber Power." Belfer Center for Science and International Affairs, Harvard Kennedy School, May 2010.

Osula, Anna-Maria, and Henry Roigas. "International Norms Limiting State Activities in Cyberspace." *International Cyber Norms: Legal, Policy & Industry Perspectives*, Tallinn, Estonia: Cooperative Cyber Defence Centre of Excellence, 2016, 11–22.

Owens, William A. "The Once and Future Revolution in Military Affairs." *Joint Forces Quarterly* (Summer 2002): 55–61.

Owens, William A., et al. *Technology, Policy, Law and Ethics Regarding U. S. Acquisition and Use of Cyberattack Capabilities.* Washington DC: The National Academies Press, 2009.

Pawlak, Patryk. "Confidence Building Measures in Cyberspace: Current Debates and Trends." *International Cyber Norms: Legal, Policy and Industry Perspectives*, Tallinn, Estonia: Cooperative Cyber Defence Centre of Excellence, 2016, 129–132.

Payne, Keith B., and C. Dale Walton. "Deterrence in the Post-Cold War World." *Strategy in the Contemporary World.* New York: Oxford University Press, 2002, 170–73.

Pierker, Benedikt. "Territorial Sovereignty and Integrity and the Challenge of Cyberspace." *Peacetime Regime for State Activities in Cyberspace*, Tallinn, Estonia: Cooperative Cyber Defence Centre of Excellence, 2013, 189–216.

Pihelgas, Mauno. "Back-Tracing and Anonymity in Cyberspace." *Peacetime Regime for State Activities in Cyberspace.* Tallinn, Estonia: Cooperative Cyber Defence Centre of Excellence, 2013, 31–60.

Record, Jeffrey. "Japan's Decision for War in 1941: Some Enduring Lessons." *Strategic Studies Institute* (February 2009): 1–70.

Richardson, John. "Stuxnet as Cyberwarfare: Applying the Law of War to the Virtual Battlefield." *Journal of Computer and Information Law* 29 (Fall 2011): 1–37.

Rid, Thomas and Peter McBurney. "Cyber-Weapons." *RUSI Journal* 157, no. 1 (February/March 2012): 6–13.

Rintakoski, Kristina, and Mikko Autti. *Trends, Challenges and Possibilities for Cooperation in Crisis Prevention and Management.* Helsinki, Finland: Crisis Management Initiative, June 17, 2008.

Roberts, Peter, and Andrew Hardie. "The Validity of Deterrence in the Twenty-first Century." Royal United Services Institute, Occasional Paper, August 2015.

Rosenzweig, Paul. "International Law and Private Actor Active Cyber Defensive Measures." *Stanford Journal of International Law* (May 27, 2013): 1–13.

Rowe, Neil C., et al. "Challenges in Monitoring Cyberarms Compliance." *International Journal of Cyber Warfare and Terrorism* 1, no. 1 (January–March 2011): 1–14.

Schelling, Thomas. *Arms and Influence.* New Haven, CT: Yale University Press, 1966.

———. *The Strategy of Conflict.* Cambridge, MA: Harvard University Press, 1960.

Schmitt, Michael. "Attack as a Term of Art in International Law: The Cyber Operations Context." *Proceedings 4th International Conference on Cyber Conflict.* Tallinn, Estonia: Cooperative Cyber Defence Centre of Excellence, June 2012.

———. "'Below the Threshold' Cyber Operations: The Countermeasures Response Option and International Law." *Virginia Journal of International Law* 54, no. 3 (August 2014): 697–732.

———. "In Defense of Due Diligence in Cyberspace." *Yale Law Journal Forum.* June 22, 2015.

———. "International Law and Cyber Attacks: Sony v. North Korea." *Just Security* (December 17, 2014): 1–5.

———. "The Law of Cyber Targeting." *Tallinn Paper* no. 7 (2015): 7–19.

———. *Tallinn Manual on the International Law Applicable to Cyber Warfare.* Cambridge: Cambridge University Press, May 2013.

Schmitt, Michael, and Liis Vihul. "The Nature of International Law Cyber Norms." *International Cyber Norms: Legal, Policy and Industry Perspectives.* Tallinn, Estonia: Cooperative Cyber Defence Centre of Excellence, 2016, 23–47.

Schmitt, Michael, and Liis Vihul. "Proxy Wars in Cyberspace: The Evolving International Law of Attribution. " *Fletcher Security Review.* Vol I, Issue II (Spring 2014): 57–67.

Sheldon, John B. "The Rise of Cyberpower." *Strategy in the Contemporary World.* John Baylis, James J. Wirtz, and Colin S. Gray, editors, 5th ed. New York: Oxford University Press, 2016.

Shulsky, Abram N. *Deterrence Theory and Chinese Behavior.* Santa Monica, CA: RAND Corporation, 2014.

Slocombe, Walter. "The Countervailing Strategy." *International Security* 5, no. 4 (Spring 1981): 21–22.

Smith, Bruce P. "Hacking, Poaching, and Counterattacking: Digital Counterstrikes and the Contours of Self-Help." *Journal of Law, Economics and Policy* 1, no. 1.2 (2005): 177–78.

Spector, Ronald H. *At War, At Sea: Sailors and Naval Combat in the Twentieth Century.* New York: Viking Penguin Publishers, 2001.

———. *Eagle against the Sun: The American War with Japan.* New York: The Free Press, 1985.

Stinissen, Jan. "A Legal Framework for Cyber Operations in Ukraine." In *Cyber War in Perspective: Russian Aggression against Ukraine.* Tallinn, Estonia: Cooperative Cyber Defense Center of Excellence, 2015, 123–34.

Stytz, Martin R., and Sheila B. Banks, "Toward Attaining Cyber Dominance." *Strategic Studies Quarterly* (Spring 2014): 60.

Tertrais, Bruno. "Iran: An Experiment in Strategic Risk-Taking." *Survival: Global Politics and Strategy* (October–November 2015): 67–73.

Tikk, Eneken, et al. "International Cyber Incidents: Legal Considerations." Tallinn, Estonia: Cooperative Cyber Defence Centre of Excellence, 2009.

Walt, Stephan M. "Which Works Best: Force or Diplomacy?" *Foreign Policy*, August 21, 2013.

West, Zach. "Young Fella, If You're Looking for Trouble I'll Accommodate You: Deputizing Private Companies for the Use of Hackback." *Syracuse Law Review* 63 (November 2012): 119–46.

Whyte, Christopher. "On the Future of Order in Cyberspace." *Strategic Studies Quarterly* (Summer 2015): 69–77.

Williams, Brett T. "Ten Propositions Regarding Cyberspace Operations." *Joint Forces Quarterly* no. 61 (2nd Quarter 2011): 11–16.

———. "The Joint Force Commander's Guide to Cyberspace Operations." *Joint Forces Quarterly* no. 73 (2nd Quarter 2014): 12–19.

Ziolkowski, Katharina. "Confidence Building Measures for Cyberspace—Legal Implications." Tallinn, Estonia, Cooperative Cyber Defense Center of Excellence, 2013: 1–13.

———. "General Principles of International Law as Applicable in Cyberspace." *Peacetime Regime for State Activities in Cyberspace*, Tallinn, Estonia: Cooperative Cyber Defence Centre of Excellence, 2013, 135–88.

INDUSTRY PRODUCTS

Akamai, "Cloud Security Solutions." White Paper, 2015.

———. "Kona Site Defender." Product Brief, 2015.

Armor. "Threat Intelligence." ebook, 2016.

Carbon Black. "Disrupting the Threat: Identify, Respond, Contain and Recover in Seconds." White Paper, 2014.

———. "Breach Detection: What You Need to Know." eBook, 2016.

CrowdStrike. "Global Threat Intel Report." 2015.

———. "Indicators of Attack versus Indicators of Compromise." White Paper, 2015.

CyberEdge Group. "2015 Cyberthreat Defense Report: North America and Europe." March, 2015.

———. "2016 Cyberthreat Defense Report." 2016.

Cyveillance. "Intelligence for Security." January 2015.

Dell Secure Works. "Inside a Targeted Point-of-Sale Data Breach." January 2014.

———. "Eliminating the Blind Spot: Rapidly Detect and Respond to the Advanced and Evasive Threat." White Paper, 2015.

———. "Underground Hacker Markets." Annual Report, April 2016.

FireEye. "APT28: A Window into Russia's Cyber Espionage Operations." Special Report, 2014.

———. "Cybersecurity's Maginot Line: A Real World Assessment of the Defense-in-Depth Model." 2014.

———. "FireEye Threat Intelligence: Get the Intelligence and Context You Need to Help Identify, Block and Respond to Advanced Attacks." Data Sheet, 2016

Fortinet, "Threat Landscape Report." October 2016.

Hexis Cyber Solutions. "How to Automate Cyber Threat Removal." A HawkEye G Technical White Paper, Release 3. 1, October 2015.

———. "Active Cyber Defense: Integrated, Automated, Effective." December 11, 2015.

Hewlett Packard Security Research. "Islamic Republic of Iran." Briefing Episode 11, February 2014.

———. "Profiling an Enigma: The Mystery of North Korea's Cyber Threat Landscape." Briefing Episode 16, August 2014.

———. "Syrian Electronic Army." Briefing Episode 3, April 2013.

Hewlett Packard Enterprise. "Companies Cautiously Optimistic about Cybersecurity." In-depth Analysis, January 2016.

IBM Corporation, "Combat the Latest Security Attacks with Global Threat Intelligence." 2016.

Imperva. "An Anatomy of a SQL Injection Attack." Hacker Intelligence Summary Report, Monthly Trend Report #4, September 2011.

———. "The Anatomy of an Anonymous Attack." Hacker Intelligence Summary Report, 2012.

———. "DDoS Threat Landscape Report 2015–2016." August 2016.

Intel Corporation. "The Cybersecurity Framework in Action: An Intel Use Case." 2015.

Kaspersky Global Research and Analysis Team. "The Dangers of Phishing: Help Employees Avoid the Lure of Cybercrime." 2015.

———. "Future Risks: Be Prepared." Special Report, 2014.

———. "The NetTraveler (aka Travnet)." 2013.

LightCyber. "Closing the Breach Detection Gap." Data Sheet, 2015.

———. "The New Defense against Targeted Attacks." White Paper, March 2015.

———. "Magna Detection Technology." White Paper, November 2015.

Looking Glass. "Addressing the Cyber Kill Chain." Research Note, 2016.

Lumension. "Redefining Defense-in-Depth." White Paper, March 2014.

Mandiant. "APT1: Exposing One of China's Cyber Espionage Units." February 27, 2013.

———. "M Trends 2015: A View from the Front Lines." Threat Report, 2015.

———. "M Trends 2016: Special Report." February 2016.

McAfee. "Net Losses: Estimating the Global Cost of Cybercrime." June 2014.

Neustar. "DDoS Attacks and Protection Report." Annual Report, April 2016.

Noveta. "Operation Blockbuster: Unraveling the Long Threat of the Sony Attack." February 2016.

Palo Alto Networks, "Breaking the Cyber Attack Lifecycle." March 2015.

Ponemon Institute, "The SQL Injection Threat Study." April 2014.

———. "2014 Global Report on the Cost of Cyber Crime." October 2014.

———. "2016 State of Endpoint Report." April 2016.

Securosis. "Defending against Denial of Service Attacks." October 2012.

———. "Defending against Application Denial of Service Attacks." December 2013.

Solutionary. "Global Threat Intelligence Report." NTT Group 2016.

SurfWatch Labs. "Dark Web Situational Awareness Report." 2015.

Symantec Corporation. Dragonfly: Cyberespionage Attacks against Energy Suppliers." July 7, 2014.

———. "Internet Security Threat Report." Vol. 19, April 2014.

Threat Connect, "A Financial Giant's Threat Intel Success Story." Case Study, August 2016.

Tripwire. "Conquer the Top 20 Critical Security Controls." 2104.

———. "Layered Security: Protecting Your Data in Today's Threat Landscape." 2014.

———. "Solutions for Endpoint Detection and Response." Solution Brief, 2015.

Verizon. "2016 Data Breach Investigations Report." May 2016.

Websense Security Labs. "Point-of-Sale Malware and the Seven Stages Attack Model." 2014.

———. "The Seven Stages of Advanced Threats." 2013.

———. "2015 Threat Report." 2015.

Index

About the Author

Scott Jasper, CAPT, USN (ret.) is a faculty member in the National Security Affairs department and also teaches in the Center for Civil-Military Relations and the Center for Homeland Defense and Security all at the Naval Postgraduate School in Monterey, California. He designs and delivers resident and mobile courses on Cyber Security and Defense Capability Development. He is the editor of three books: *Conflict and Cooperation in the Global Commons*, *Securing Freedom in the Global Commons*, and *Transforming Defense Capabilities: New Approaches for International Security*, with articles in such journals as *International Journal of Intelligence and CounterIntelligence*, *Strategic Studies Quarterly*, *Small Wars Journal*, *Journal of International Peacekeeping*, and the *Diplomat*.